San Francisco Bay Area Sports

SPORT, CULTURE & SOCIETY

DAVID K. WIGGINS, SERIES EDITOR

Other Titles in This Series

Separate Games: African American Sport behind the Walls of Segregation
Baltimore Sports: Stories from Charm City
Philly Sports: Teams, Games, and Athletes from Rocky's Town
DC Sports: The Nation's Capital at Play
Frank Merriwell and the Fiction of All-American Boyhood
Democratic Sports: Men's and Women's College Athletics
Sport and the Law: Historical and Cultural Intersections
Beyond C. L. R. James: Shifting Boundaries of Race and Ethnicity in Sports
A Spectacular Leap: Black Women Athletes in Twentieth-Century America
Hoop Crazy: The Lives of Clair Bee and Chip Hilton

San Francisco Bay Area Sports

Golden Gate Athletics,
Recreation, and Community

EDITED BY RITA LIBERTI AND MAUREEN M. SMITH

THE UNIVERSITY OF ARKANSAS PRESS
FAYETTEVILLE
2017

Manufactured in the United States of America
ISBN: 978-1-68226-020-3
e-ISBN: 978-1-61075-603-7
21 20 19 18 17 5 4 3 2 1

Text design by Ellen Beeler

∞The paper used in this publication meets the minimum requirements of the American National Standard for Permanence of Paper for Printed Library Materials Z39.48-1984.
Library of Congress Control Number: 2016952672

Contents

Series Editor's Preface

Sport is an extraordinarily important phenomenon that pervades the lives of many people and has enormous impact on society in an assortment of different ways. At its most fundamental level, sport has the power to bring people great joy and satisfy their competitive urges while at once allowing them to form bonds and a sense of community with others from diverse backgrounds and interests and various walks of life. Sport also makes clear, especially at the highest levels of competition, the lengths that people will go to achieve victory as well as how closely connected it is to business, education, politics, economics, religion, law, family, and other societal institutions. Sport is, moreover, partly about identity development and how individuals and groups, irrespective of race, gender, ethnicity, or socioeconomic class, have sought to elevate their status and realize material success and social mobility.

Sport, Culture, and Society seeks to promote a greater understanding of the aforementioned issues and many others. Recognizing sport's powerful influence and ability to change people's lives in significant and important ways, the series focuses on topics ranging from urbanization and community development to biographies and intercollegiate athletics. It includes both monographs and anthologies that are characterized by excellent scholarship, accessible to a wide audience, and interesting and thoughtful in design and interpretations. Singular features of the series are authors and editors representing a variety of disciplinary areas and who adopt different methodological approaches. The series also includes works by individuals at various stages of their careers, both sport studies scholars of outstanding talent just beginning to make their mark on the field and more experienced scholars of sport with established reputations.

San Francisco Bay Area Sports provides interesting stories and important insights on various aspects of the development of sport and recreation in one of America's most renowned cities. Editors Rita Liberti and Maureen M. Smith, two noted historians of sport who have published widely and often on the subject, have put together an anthology that includes fifteen chapters on topics ranging from an analysis of civic boosterism and sports venues in nineteenth-century Oakland and examination of the outstanding Santa Clara Swim Club of the 1950s and 1960s to an assessment of the influential tennis career of Rosie Casals and recounting of the efforts to create a gay Olympics. Taken as a whole, the anthology makes clear the diverse nature of sport in the city and its connection to identities based on sexuality, gender, race, and ethnicity. Just as crucial, the anthology is marked by a number of chapters that focus on, in the words of Liberti and Smith, "sport and recreation as a potentially transgressive space." This stands to reason in a city known as much for its nonconformity and radicalism as its international popularity and sheer beauty.

David K. Wiggins

Acknowledgments

Editing this collection has been a delightful project, with the quality and depth of the essays owing to our contributors and the University of Arkansas Press. We were fortunate to work with an amazing roster of contributors, many with Bay Area connections, and their essays speak to the diversity and richness of this corner of the world. Reading and editing their essays was a privilege, and we appreciate their commitment and contributions to this project. Many thanks to David Wiggins, the series editor, for his guidance and encouragement throughout the process. Thank you to Deena Owens at the University of Arkansas Press for her attention to the details of the project. Thank you to Debbie Upton, our copy editor, for her close reading of the manuscript. We are grateful to the Department of Kinesiology at Cal State East Bay for their financial support of the indexing of this collection. We also want to thank all the libraries and archives who granted permission for the use of photographs. Lastly, a good deal of thanks to our neighbors and neighborhoods in the Bay Area, whose past and present help make this such a lovely place to call home.

Introduction

On June 19, 2015, Golden State Warriors' fan Kamala Moore stood on a downtown Oakland, California, street, alongside over 500,000 others, eager to celebrate the hometown team's National Basketball Association (NBA) title, the first for the club in forty years. "It's history in the making," said Moore, presumably in reference to the Warriors' title run and the parade's large turnout.[1] While certainly not the first San Francisco Bay Area sport championship, the Warriors' title garnered massive public attention, acting as both a celebration of community and an athletic team's success. However, even as hundreds of thousands of merry-makers reveled in a sea of blue and yellow, ripples of unease were present given the Warriors' decision to move the team back across the Bay to San Francisco by the 2018 season.[2] Relocating the franchise, albeit about only ten miles away, is often a highly charged topic of discussion among Bay Area residents as it reflects tensions around brand, civic pride and engagement, public subsidy of sport structures, ecological politics, and gentrification, among others. Despite the anticipated move by the Warriors' franchise, little could dampen Kamala Moore's mood or the raucous celebration that took place last June. However, the event and the discussions stirred from it are reminders that sport, both in contemporary and historical form, is deeply connected to any number of political, economic, and social realities. The stories and issues surrounding San Francisco Bay Area sport history presented in this volume share that view.

San Francisco Bay Area sporting histories are as complex, expansive, and diverse as the region itself. The temperate climate lends itself to year-round outdoor athletic activity of all sorts. The area's physical landscape of mountains, coastal, and forested regions encourage a wide range of sport and recreational activities. Bay Area topography has long been the inspiration for observations about sport and leisure in the region. In 1891, Pierre de Coubertin, the father of the modern Olympic Games, arrived in San Francisco and soon thereafter shared his thoughts about the region's unique sense of place. The Frenchman was in the United States trying to rally interest and attendance for the upcoming International Congress of Amateur Athletic Sports in Paris in June 1894. Speaking to the Pacific Association of the Amateur Athletic Union on October 17, 1893, at the aptly named Olympic Club, de Coubertin shared his proposals with San Francisco sportsmen. He also took the time to visit two local universities, the University of California in Berkeley and the newly formed Stanford University, with both campuses leaving an impression on de Coubertin. Of his time in California, he wrote, "the very abundance of this land gives rise to a sense of unreality." De Coubertin later recalled the area's beauty, claiming, "One finds something similar in Paris, and in San Francisco, under those California skies which reminds one of the skies of Greece, at the foot of those mountains that have the pure outlines and the iridescent reflections of Hymettus."[3]

Other sporting enthusiasts, including cyclist Frank Lenz, who wrote about the beauty of the Bay Area in 1892, chronicling his cross-country bicycle trip, which ended in San Francisco after 107 days and 4,857 miles, were also in awe of the Bay Area landscape. Lenz tells readers of *Outing* that he was met in Livermore, thirty-seven miles from his destination, by George P. Wetmore, the president of the Bay Area Wheelmen, and three club members. Lenz recalled, "we rolled briskly along over splendid gravel roads to Dublin. Here is a short hill, easily surmounted. Upon reaching the top, I saw the welcome expanse of the San Francisco Bay glimmering in the bright sunlight far below and only fifteen miles in the distant. We coasted down the long hill, merrily wheeled along through Haywards [*sic*] to Fruitvale, the suburb of Oakland, and continuing down the beautifully shaded street, graced with its fine residences, we at last reached Oakland."[4] Lenz and his escorts then boarded a ferry to San Francisco. Of his arrival, Lenz shared the details of his excitement:

> It was precisely 5:45pm when the ferry-boat touched the San Francisco wharf. With a rush and a mount we rode through the building out on the busy streets, followed a short distance by some people from the boat. Turning into Market Street, we wended our way up on the cable-car slot among the din of bells, rumbling wagons, and noise and confusion from the throng of people returning home from work. At last we reached the clubhouse of the Bay Area Wheelmen.[5]

The region's natural and artificial beauty continued to be central to describing sporting experiences into the twentieth century. The *New York Times* reported in 1940, "variety" is key in describing sporting endeavors in the region. The newspaper opined on the Golden State's growth:

> Every day opens new motoring vistas, whether the car be headed northward over the Golden Gate Bridge [completed just four years earlier] and into the region of the redwoods. [Or] eastward over the eight-and-one-half-mile Bay Bridge [completed six months before the Golden Gate Bridge] across the interior valleys and into the high Sierra, or southward toward the Monterey Peninsula. In San Francisco itself, noted for its color and cosmopolitan flavor, there are sources of sights to see, places to visit, events to watch, sports to enjoy.[6]

As several essays in this volume attest, the area's distinctive setting gives rise to a rich sporting past.

This volume offers a glimpse into this history, as it explores a range of topics, issues, tensions, and personalities over a century and a half of recreation and athletics in the city and region by the Bay. For Bay Area sports fans, especially those of the San Francisco 49ers, no book of sport history is complete without including "The Catch," Joe Montana's touchdown pass to Dwight Clark to win the NFC Championship game in 1982, or for East Bay football fans, Oakland's "Raider Nation." Indeed, discussions of "The Catch" and "Raider Nation" can be found within the pages of this book (see Jeffrey Montez de Oca's "San Francisco 49ers and the Romance of Memory," and Maria J. Veri's "Sons of Oakland: The Raiders and the Raz/Rais(ing) of a City," respectively), but probably not in the way some readers assume. Montez de Oca's and Veri's contributions and the other essays in this volume move us beyond romanticized notions of sport as mere amusement, as they ask us to consider broader social, political, cultural, and economic implications of the games and activities played in the Bay Area since the mid-nineteenth century. There are any number of places in the volume where the essays challenge assumptions we tend to have of sport and leisure and in doing so inform and aid our understanding of history. We believe Bay Area sport provides an especially keen lens to explore the complex and ever-changing dynamics in the region.

The most visible sport histories within the Bay Area and, arguably, the ones most fondly recalled by local residents are of the professional teams of the second half of the twentieth century. If history were written exclusively by and for the victors the Bay Area would have much to cheer as the region's athletic teams have achieved great success over the past several decades. For example, despite the inability to get along as a team the "fightin', fussin', and feudin'" Oakland Athletics' (A's) three consecutive World Series victories, during the first half of the 1970s stand, decades later, as an incredible achievement. The feat made the East Bay city the "baseball capital of the world."[7] The San Francisco 49ers dynasty, winning five Super Bowl titles in a decade and a half throughout the 1980s and 1990s, is perhaps the most noted among local professional sport franchises.[8] In more recent years the San Francisco Giants have been busy building a dynasty of their own with three World Series titles over the last six seasons.[9]

While the cities are best known for the successes of their professional teams, area colleges and universities have a long and successful history among the nation's best in athletic competition. Currently, six Bay Area universities compete within the National Collegiate Athletic Association's highest division.[10] Perhaps most noted among them is Stanford University, considered to be one of the most successful (and one of the broadest programs with thirty-six varsity sports) overall athletic programs in the country. In each of the last thirty-nine years, the institution has earned at least one national championship.[11]

The athletic accomplishments of professional and collegiate teams around the San Francisco Bay Area, over the course of more than a century, are far too vast to do them justice in this introduction. This observation serves as a good reminder of what can and (importantly) what cannot be achieved in a volume such as this. Professional and collegiate sports are some of the most visible, but they are a mere fraction of the experiences and issues surrounding athletics and physical recreation. Similarly, a focus on athletes and coaches hailing from and/or achieving stardom in the Bay Area could fill its own volume, and indeed much attention has been given to the hometown accolades of the likes of Bill Russell, O. J. Simpson, Curt Flood, the DiMaggio brothers, Frank Robinson, and Bill Walsh, among others.[12] We offer up our own small piece of a much larger collective sport history of the San Francisco Bay Area.

The essays in this book stretch over more than 150 years beginning, roughly, with the admission of California as the nation's thirty-first state in 1850. With that said we are well aware that the region's "history" certainly did not begin at this mid-century moment, as many others including the Ohlone and other native peoples, as well as Spanish and Mexican inhabitants, lived and leisured on the land that became the San Francisco Bay Area long before much of what is detailed in the pages of this volume.[13]

In 1860 approximately 110,000 people lived within the San Francisco Bay Area. Population growth has been steady across the region, but certainly spiked at particular historical moments. By 1870 the gold rush and the completion of the transcontinental railroad pushed the region's population upward. The impact of World War II on the area's growth was enormous, particularly around the shipbuilding ports in the East Bay cities of Richmond and Oakland during the 1940s. More recently, a second "gold rush" of sorts was spurred on by the Silicon Valley's "tech boom" of the 1990s. The allure of the valley and the opportunities to be found there drew many people to the southern part of the San Francisco Bay, making them quite rich as a result. By 2015 half of the state's 131 billionaires lived in the Bay Area, many in the South Bay, altering the region's cultural, economic, and even its sporting landscape.[14] The area's population now includes nine counties and over one hundred cities, as it stretches across 7,000 square miles. At present, over seven million people inhabit the Bay Area living in urban, suburban, and rural communities. On one level the geographic boundaries of the Bay Area are expansive both in terms of its size (literally) and also the incredible array of people, making up a collage of unique places, each with their own identity. Despite its grandness of scale, the largest urban centers including San Francisco, Oakland, and San Jose anchor the region, and all sit within a fifty-mile, or less, radius of the others. This volume, with its focus on the sport histories of a region rather than a single city, attempts to capture a bit of the region's complexity and the dynamic changes brought on by such a relatively rapid population growth and subsequent demographic shifts. As the book's editors we found this both exciting and daunting.

We were eager to illustrate the Bay Area's historical diversity around gender, sexuality, race, and ethnicity in relation to how those identity markers relate to sport experiences. For the most part, we selected activities, events, or persons for whom not much has been written or critical attention paid. We even include one chapter, Louis Moore's "Boosterism, Boxing, and the Battle for the Bay: The Jeffries-Johnson Fight in the Bay Area," which examines an event that never materialized in the Bay Area, though it tells us much about the region. Several essays in the volume speak to various ways in which identity mattered in the sporting lives of Bay Area participants in terms of the way they understood themselves as well as the way they were seen by others. Important, we think as well, were the sport spaces created by marginalized individuals and communities. These spaces lent themselves to advancing notions of self-expression, self-worth, and agency among populations for whom those elements were limited by the realities of racism, homophobia, and sexism.

Sport and recreation as a potentially transgressive space is one theme that emerges in a number of the entries to this volume. Given the area's radical and antiestablishment tendencies and traditions it should be of little surprise that the reputation of the city of San Francisco and the region more broadly filters through and is reflected and reinforced within its sporting histories. Characterized as a "crucible of nonconformity,"[15] San Francisco's "sweeping bay, the discrete and sometimes colorful neighborhoods, a downtown not yet built out of existence, and image of romance and adventure, a sensation of being on the frontier—all of these things sustain San Francisco's international popularity and partly serve as a magnet drawing the disaffected or marginalized, the drop-out or dissident, the high-minded or simply those 'high' on any possible range of lifestyles, philosophies, natural substances or chemicals."[16] San Francisco's "queerness," or its brand of uniqueness, is not tangential to its identity, rather it is "sewn into the city's social fabric."[17] Judy Davidson's chapter, "The Early Gay Games: The Bay Area Years," is perhaps the most direct, of this volume's entries, in its engagement with the unique sporting spaces and personalities carved out of, and from, the region's unconventionality, with its focus on the efforts to create a gay Olympics, with its origins in San Francisco gay sport culture in the early 1980s.

Politically radical politics are not solely the province of the region's namesake city, however. Oakland's history of union activism, its strong and unapologetic links to socialist and communist labor party agendas, the city's place in relation to the rise of the Black Panther Party, and most recently the strong presence of the Occupy movement trouble any argument that San Francisco has the corner on radical progressive politics in the region. Not to be outdone in securing its place in the region as a nonconformist and antiestablishment community is Berkeley; the East Bay city just to Oakland's north positions itself as the antiwar and free speech movement center of the country.

The region's irreverent manner spills over and into the tales of the San Francisco Bay Area sporting history, adding richness and perspective to the stories. Some of the activities and individuals highlighted in this volume speak out, via athleticism, against convention and the status quo, enabling them to fit seamlessly with the region's place identity.

Some wonder, however, if the region's history of wanting to "draw outside the lines" (its subversive leanings) has reached its end, as tech industry dollars dull the edges of the area's uniqueness, resulting in a kind of corporate conformity and elitism across all aspects of life around the Bay, including sport. Income inequality and the problems associated with gentrification have long plagued urban areas. This is especially so in the Bay Area as the effects of the multi-billion-dollar tech industry, once confined to Silicon Valley, spread throughout the region. The impact on housing and commercial real estate development has been rapid, resulting in titanic shifts in population demographics as working-class families of color leave and are forced out of the region, while young and mainly white professionals move in.

The changes brought on by the tech boom reach far into the corners of peoples' lives and include conflict over sport and recreational spaces within the city. No example may be more to the point than an exchange, in August 2014 on a community soccer field in the city's Mission District. As a group of young Latinos played their usual evening 7 on 7 pick-up games, several mainly white employees of tech giant Dropbox, who lived in the neighborhood, entered the scene. Claiming to have a permit for which they paid twenty-seven dollars for an hour of field time they asked those already on the turf to leave. The ensuing debate that night and the weeks after exposes the roots of contentious relationships borne out of the privatization of public recreational spaces. For some the conflict on the field underscored a broader friction felt by many in San Francisco. Enormous sums of money from the tech-based economy are transforming a region once characterized as free-spirited, diverse, and antiestablishment to something else. As one observer noted, "The city's once-vibrant culture has been paved over to cater to the sleek, homogenized tastes (and budgets) of a single demographic."[18] A place, apparently, where money buys you access to public fields and courts. Interestingly, the Mission District dispute on/over the soccer field may be the latest, but certainly not the first Bay Area conflict surrounding the use of public space for recreational pursuits, as Linda Ivey's essay in this book, "Protecting the People's Mountain: Hiking in Marin County and the Roots of American

Environmentalism," suggests.[19] History, it seems, is as much about the patterns of continuity as change. Though the specifics of each instance are different and occurred over a century apart, public recreational space continues to be struggled over and contested.

In addition to public parks, the fields, courts, stadiums, and pools—the physical locations themselves—whether public or private, are imbued with political meaning. For example, a closer look at the three stadiums in which the San Francisco 49ers have played home contests in their seventy-year history in the city is a study in urban politics, policy, and priorities. Kezar Stadium in San Francisco, for example, was one facility among the first generation of publicly funded stadiums the United States during the 1920s.[20] The city's interest in constructing a stadium "second to none in the country" rested on the hope of maintaining San Francisco's profile in relation to other municipalities who were quickly building their own venues. "All of the leading cities in the country have their stadiums," quipped Fred Farmer of the *San Francisco Bulletin* in 1920. The "thing has started," he noted, adding, "San Francisco may soon have a stadium to rate with the best in the land."[21] The rhetoric in support of building the best and most modern publicly funded athletic structures sounds remarkably similar to more present-day justifications for such endeavors. Built for less than $500,000, Kezar hosted any number of events, including a site for reenactments of World War II battles during the 1940s.[22] The 49ers played football in the facility from the mid-1940s until the early 1970s when they moved to Candlestick Park, which had been built for the baseball Giants in the late 1950s. The $15,000,000 project met with resistance both in terms of the cost and its placement. Critics charged that the stadium was "a monument to the Mayor's [George Christopher's] poor judgment."[23] In late 2006, thirty-five years after the 49ers began playing at Candlestick team, officials announced they were moving the club to Santa Clara an hour south of San Francisco and in the heart of Silicon Valley. The highly contested move stirred much debate within the region but to no avail for those wanting to keep the 49ers in San Francisco. Former San Francisco mayor and current US senator Dianne Feinstein lamented the loss of the team, saying it was part of the city's "critical history."[24] The team began play in their new 1.3-billion-dollar South Bay stadium in August 2014.

These examples are merely a few, and far from the only, athletic spaces and places within the city's history deserving of our critical attention. Seals Stadium, the Cow Palace, Fleishhacker Pool, and even the ghostly remnants of the Sutro Baths, among others, are equally compelling in offering us insight about the cultural, social, and economic forces at play around the San Francisco Bay Area.[25]

As noted, a single book cannot adequately capture San Francisco Bay Area sport history, as there are far too many outstanding athletic dynasties, successful athletes whose home was the Bay Area, and important events, issues, and sites to be explored and examined. Furthermore, our collection makes no assertions as having the corner on exploring the area's past as other academics have published great works examining sport in the Bay Area. Kathleen S. Yep's *Outside the Paint: When Basketball Ruled at the Chinese Playground* examines the Chinese Playground in the 1930s and 1940s, the only public outdoor space in Chinatown at the time. Her book is an excellent examination of sport in Chinatown during an interesting and challenging historic period for Chinese immigrants.[26] Susan G. Zieff also looked at sport in Chinatown, beginning decades before Yep's focus and extending to the 1950s and including sports beyond basketball.[27] Noted University of California, Berkeley, professor of sport history Roberta J. Park spent much of her time as a professor examining the sporting activities of those in the Bay Area, including Chinese and German immigrants, the impact of Berkeley professors on the development of physical education, and the 1905 football crisis, a topic revisited in this collection by Brian Ingrassia's "Reforming the Big Game: The Bay Area Rugby Experiment of 1906–1919."[28] Deane Lamont continues his work on the early sporting and recreational practices of Oakland residents with his chapter in this collection, "Oakland's Nineteenth-Century Parks and Resorts: 'Lungs of the City,' Commercial Sporting Venues, and Instruments of Civic Boosterism."[29]

Our book makes no claim to be an exhaustive examination of Bay Area sport history. Rather we have chosen episodes from the region's past as a way to introduce readers to the incredible array of sporting experiences and the relationship of these issues and actors with broader themes. For every story told or issue raised in this volume there are countless others that also speak to the region's rich sport history. We selected topics and issues that represent several different geographic regions of the Bay, each shining a spotlight on a unique historical moment and setting. The essays feature at least twelve distinct sports or leisure pursuits, ranging from highly commercial professional sport to more recreational endeavors far less visible to the public but no less important to participants and spectators alike. We hope you enjoy this historical journey of sport about the Bay.

1

Oakland's Nineteenth-Century Parks and Resorts

"Lungs of the City," Commercial Sporting Venues, and Instruments of Civic Boosterism

DEANE ANDERSON LAMONT

In 1850, California became the nation's thirty-first state. Just two years later, Oakland was incorporated as a city and very soon thereafter its leaders set aside valuable downtown space for parks and declared their intention to expend considerable public funds on maintaining them. This action was motivated, in part, by many people of the time believing that urban gardens and parks could help defend and recover the physical and psychological health of city residents. Oakland's early entrepreneurs capitalized on the city's pastoral setting and the public's desire for healthy and entertaining outdoor recreation by establishing numerous for-profit parks, pleasure gardens, and resorts in and close to the city. Oakland became—for both its own residents and visitors from around the region—a well-known and much-frequented location for all manner of physical recreations and sport. After the population surge that followed the arrival of the transcontinental railroad in 1869 flattened, Oakland's civic and business leaders enthusiastically promoted their city's rustic and healthy reputation in the hope that it would entice more prospective residents to settle there instead of in other emerging West Coast cities. Now, after two world wars and a host of societal changes that its early residents probably could not have imagined, Oakland has become a modern city vastly different from its nascent form and few of its current residents would label their city the "Eden of the Pacific," but a century or so ago this was exactly how Oakland was advertised to day-trippers, vacationers, and potential residents.[1]

The Pathological City

Urbanization rapidly gathered pace in the United States after the middle of the nineteenth century and city crowding brought significant health and social problems. The increasingly populated and more densely built towns affected city folk of all socioeconomic levels, but the working classes felt urbanization's bite most deeply. Personal health was often lost as a consequence of being exposed to unguarded urban drinking water supplies, poor sewage disposal, and limited quality control of food. The human pathologies that these unsanitary conditions caused were exacerbated by having to live in close proximity to many others. The scarcity of open and green space also meant that the new urban poor were rarely able to enjoy even a brief respite from their hectic and crowded city life.

The East Coast's nineteenth-century cities were especially large and congested and their residents most severely affected. As early as 1846, Dr. Lemuel Shattuck, one of the era's public health leaders, informed the city of Boston that its core was so densely populated as to cause both "physical and moral degeneration."[2] At mid-century, he recommended that open spaces be reserved in cities so that the "artizan and the poorer classes" could be afforded the "advantages of fresh air and exercise, in their occasional hours of leisure" and that public funds should pay for parks and gardens. These and other sanitary measures were expected to lead to better physical and even moral health among urban dwellers.[3]

America's civic leaders took notice of these and other dire public health warnings and began to take steps to ameliorate squalid urban situations. More and more American towns began to reserve space for "commons" and city governments increasingly provided funds for building parks and park-like cemeteries within or near to their city limits.[4] The belief that parks served as the lungs of a city drew upon a longstanding tradition that was frequently expressed during the middle part of the century. This was fueled by environment and climate being seen as two of the primary causes of the era's greatly feared epidemics. For many, miasmas (bad air) were thought to explain the recurrent deadly curses that swept through urban America. Thus, the provision of areas where urbanites could walk, sometimes play or exercise, and take in fresh, clean air came to be seen as efficacious in the defense of the public's health.[5] A park's or public garden's "vegetation" was deemed an agent that could, as Shattuck declared in 1850, "absorb much of the carbonic acid which is produced in so great superabundance in populous places, and thus render the air more fit for respiration." Regardless of the scientific validity of this position, at mid-century many city dwellers and civic leaders found it persuasive and motivational.[6]

The cemetery and park building movement literally changed the landscape of the American city. Cemeteries with names like Mount Auburn in Cambridge, Laurel Hill in Philadelphia, and Greenwood in Brooklyn all featured landscaped gardens, tree-lined walks, and lakes. The construction of New York's Central Park during the late 1850s exemplified the belief that urban parks could benefit the health and welfare of the American urbanite. This ethos was the driving force behind the work of Central Park's designer and the nation's most famous landscape architect, Frederick Law Olmstead (1822–1903). The success of New York's Central Park provided a model for other cities to emulate. Boston, Chicago, and Philadelphia all put large parks or park systems in place during the decades following the Civil War. A city that established a park system was declaring an interest in its inhabitant's health, providing recreational alternatives to street vice, offering democratic locations where all social classes might mingle, and advertising itself as an attractive place to live. This trend would eventually reach America's Pacific shore.[7]

The Pacific Coast

Not all regions of the United States had crowded cities during the middle decades of the nineteenth century. Until the gold rush, America's West Coast had no major cities at all. In California, open space was everywhere. However, the great discovery at Sutter's Mill in 1848 brought in its wake a torrent of new people and soon San Francisco had a cramped core with all the familiar urban pathologies. Fortunately for San Franciscans, just to the east across a protected bay and by the 1850s easily accessible by ferry lay sparsely populated and semirural Oakland. Its rustic environment and various parks drew San Franciscans by the thousands—as individuals and as members of associations and clubs—during the second half of the nineteenth century. They came for healthy, and even fashionable, outdoor recreation in the unspoiled countryside and later for commercial entertainment provided in Oakland's various privately owned parks and resorts. As Oakland's population began to grow, especially after the East Bay became the terminus for the transcontinental railroad in 1869, its parks and open spaces served its own residents and clubs as well as visitors from San Francisco and other California towns and cities.

Oakland's metropolis neighbor San Francisco was the hub of the state for the entire second half of the nineteenth century. During the decade between 1860 and 1870 its population increased from 57,000 to 150,000 people. After the Civil War, San Francisco's mayor, H. P. Coon, engaged Frederick Law Olmstead to report on the subject of a possible city park for crowded San Francisco. Despite Olmstead's fame, it was William Hall's "topographical survey and park plan" that the city eventually accepted as the blueprint for Golden Gate Park with work underway at the close of the 1860s. Though Olmstead had no real role in the design and building of Golden Gate Park, his mark was left on other Bay Area locales.[8]

In 1863, Oakland's Mountain View Cemetery Association was established and land for a new cemetery, in the low hills to the northeast of the city, was obtained. When Olmstead was awarded the commission to design Mountain View Cemetery, given the famous man's past work, his retainers would have been aware that they were also securing for their city a site to be used for genteel and healthy outdoor recreation. Mountain View was dedicated in July of 1865. Olmstead was also employed to design the nearby Berkeley campus of the University of California, and later on the other side of the Bay he did preliminary work on Stanford University's grounds.[9]

America's largest cities had the most to fear from overbuilding, crowding, and health hazards, but some smaller towns also took actions designed to safeguard their current and future citizens' health against urban ills. Oakland was a quiet new city with a relatively small population at the time of Olmstead's work there, but it had the advantage of its early leaders having deliberately left parts of its built-up center in an undeveloped state. These areas not only served as "breathing spaces" and sites for outdoor recreation for the city's residents, they also helped beautify the hastily built downtown section.[10]

In his initial message to the city council in 1854, Oakland's first mayor, Horace Carpentier (1824–1918), noted that Washington Square was not only a recreation space but also a source of civic pride. By that time a "substantial and ornamental fence, affording a gratifying evidence of correct taste," had already enclosed the square. By 1869, seven blocks of the downtown area were reserved exclusively for outdoor public pleasure. These seven public squares were named Washington, Franklin, Harrison, Jefferson, Caroline, Oakland, and Lafayette. By the close of the decade, by order of Mayor Samuel Merritt, five of the seven squares had been enclosed with a "good, substantial picket fence" at a cost to the city of almost $1,000.[11]

During the 1860s, Oakland's population was still small in comparison to San Francisco's 150,000 inhabitants and New York's almost one million people, but after 1869 and the arrival of the railroad the city's population began to grow rapidly. Oakland was soon California's second-largest city and by the end of the 1870s it was home to well over 42,000 people. This growth led some of the city's leaders to express concern about the condition and use of the park squares. In his 1879 annual message to the city, Mayor W. R. Andrus addressed the issue of the central plazas. According to the mayor, though the city featured numerous public squares, the municipality had not as yet "duly considered the importance of retaining and ornamenting these grounds." Urban park areas, Andus declared, should be "held sacred for the use of the people." With an eye to the future, and no doubt aware of the role of urban parks elsewhere, he added: "As soon as the city is densely built, they will be regarded as priceless." He then announced his intent to commence the work of "beautifying" them at once, the work to be "carried on as unremittingly as the finance of the city may permit." His caveat regarding the city's finances was wise given the economic ups and downs of the century's last three decades.[12]

Despite the political rhetoric, into the late 1880s most of the city-supported parks remained largely unimproved and the two that had received significant attention had the generosity of private citizens to thank.[13] Indeed, in his 1887 message to the city, Mayor William Davis noted: "Within the city limits we have eight public plazas or little parks. The most of these breathing spaces—rest spots—are not in an attractive condition." Davis declared that he intended to improve the situation of the existing parks and build new ones. High on his list was the beautification of what he called the "water park," first known to Oakland's residents as Lake Peralta then later Lake Merritt. The little developed water park had been enjoyed by generations of Oaklanders and visitors to the area—it had been declared a wildlife sanctuary by the State of California in 1870—but Davis had grand plans for what he hoped would become a striking centerpiece of the city. In 1887, he announced that Lake Merritt was to be surrounded by a "broad and splendid driveway or boulevard."[14]

For Mayor Davis, Oakland's parks had a specific utility beyond their impact on the public's physical and psychological health. He was motivated to improve their appearance in the belief that they offered an opportunity to exhibit Oakland's attractiveness to visitors who might be persuaded to become residents. Oakland, along with other West Coast cities at the time, was involved in a campaign of self-promotion aimed at drawing new residents. In a systematic effort to attract newcomers, Oakland's boosters—its elected leaders, prominent citizens, newspaper publishers, and business and real estate associations—became hyperbolically enthusiastic about the city's healthful environment, attractive geographic location, numerous parks, fine weather, "sanitary condition," myriad sporting and out-of-doors recreational opportunities, and even its low mortality rate. During the last two decades of the nineteenth century, the city was widely and robustly advertised as the "Athens of the Pacific," the "Healthiest of Cities," and even the "Eden of the Pacific." Lake Merritt, though not as developed as Davis would have liked, was a significant city attraction in the 1880s and a place where visitors were usually taken during their stays. The water park was a critical part of the effort to promote Oakland.[15]

In early 1887, the *Oakland Daily Evening Tribune*, that seemed to share Davis's aspirations for the lake and the city, declared Oakland to be "among the handsomest cities in the U.S." Though already proud of the city's appearance, the newspaper expected that improvements to Lake Merritt would boost Oakland even further:

> when it shall have constructed her grand boulevard around the beautiful lake, which like a lovely pearl in a rich setting, occupies a romantic place in the very heart of the city, together with the contemplated park, stretching away toward Piedmont, constructed by the hand of nature itself, as the necessary lungs of a great city, with romantic glens, rolling hills, sightly and picturesque, it will then boast of a beauty and attractiveness by any city on the globe.[16]

At the end of the 1880s, though Davis could not persuade Oakland's voters to take out the necessary bonds to dramatically improve the lake, the municipality had begun to budget significantly more money for the care of its parks. In fiscal year 1890–91, over $3,000 was spent on improvements to centrally located Harrison Square alone, and throughout the 1890s the park cost the city about $1,000 per year to maintain. These outlays transformed Harrison Square into an attractive spot featuring a large expanse of well-kept lawn, walkways, and magnolia, live oak, palm, and drooping yew trees. Harrison Square and Oakland's other parks were places where citizens could take respite from their increasingly busy urban lives to enjoy fresh and healthy air and they also communicated something very important to visitors and potential residents about the quality of life that could be enjoyed in this part of the Golden State.[17]

Oakland's Commercial Parks

Though Oakland's central squares and parks, Mountain View Cemetery, and its water park were established and popular from early in the city's history they were not the only sites for outdoor recreation that visitors and the local populace utilized during the second half of the 1800s. By the mid-1870s, various resorts had been established in or on the periphery of Oakland. Rather than being controlled by the municipality, and thus reliant on tax dollars for support, these privately owned, for-profit resorts relied upon admission charges and other fees paid by users. The businessmen who ran these facilities were very aware of the public's interest in being able to escape to a pleasant and healthful outdoor setting and thus endeavored to offer this kind of environment to their paying customers. In the closing decades of the nineteenth century these businesses gave the area's citizens a place where they could enjoy the refreshing outdoors, the excitement of such entertainments as thoroughbred horse racing, and a chance to participate in or view a wide range of physical recreations and competitive sport.

The 1878 *Directory of the City of Oakland* recorded five privately owned "gardens and parks": Badger's Grand Central Park, located on the east side of Seventh Avenue between East Seventh and East Tenth streets; Humboldt Park in Temescal, at the junction of Telegraph and Humboldt; the Oakland Trotting Park, set between San Pablo Avenue and the "Berkeley Railroad," some two miles north of city hall; Shell Mound Park, adjacent to the trotting park on the same rail line; and Zimmerman's Gardens, located at the northeast corner of 2nd and Harrison.[18]

The most widely known and patronized East Bay resorts were Badger's Park, Shell Mound Park, and the Oakland Trotting Park. These establishments were significant attractions for many years. A number of the commercially run parks seem to have made their operators considerable sums of money. Others were less lucrative but provided a livelihood for those who ran them. Most of these attractions survived until the land upon which they stood became more valuable as sites for new homes or more profitable types of businesses.

Oakland's privately owned recreation and sporting ventures were viable because of the city's system of affordable public transportation and the most popular venues were located in close proximity to public transit lines. The city's first horse car line began operation in October of 1869. During the early 1870s, transit entrepreneurs opened more and more lines that ran to and from downtown and the city's main railroad and ferry stops. A number of the lines came into existence specifically to transport paying customers to sites of commercialized recreation and hotels. For example, in 1871, the San Pablo Railroad Company began a horse car service along "San Pablo Road to Shell Mound Park and the Oakland Trotting Park." That same year, Hiram Tubbs "opened the 'Tubbs Line,' to carry passengers from the train depot at Seventh and Broadway to his Tubbs Hotel" on Thirteenth Avenue. The Broadway and Piedmont Railroad invested in a well-traveled line that ran out to Mountain View Cemetery.[19]

The Oakland Trotting Park

In 1859, Edward Wiard, who was originally from Connecticut but worked as a contractor in San Francisco, purchased 115 acres of land close to the shore of the San Francisco Bay just to the north of Oakland, in what is now Emeryville. The property cost him $7,000. Included in his land acquisition were a number of large shell mounds—the shells were the remains of the principle food of the indigenous population that had considered the site of considerable cultural importance. Edward Wiard began constructing a racetrack on his new property in the late 1860s. By 1871, construction of the one-mile racetrack was complete and racing was underway. A horse car line was running to and from the facility in that first year. In 1874, the Northern Railway (later to be taken over by the Southern Pacific) connected to Wiard's property. The Northern Railway's tracks linked the ferryboat dock in Oakland (that connected directly to San Francisco) to Martinez—an important port, early gateway to the Gold Country and, in 1915, the birthplace of baseball great Joe DiMaggio—thus making access to the city's trotting park a much easier proposition for thousands more potential customers. The arrival of the steam train tracks meant increased customers for the racetrack and probably motivated Wiard to later build a pleasure park directly across from the racing facility. The railroad company also profited from the association with Wiard by way of the increased ridership it gained through pleasure seekers making their way to and from his facilities. The trains that stopped at the park every thirty minutes also contributed to the residential and commercial growth of the area surrounding the trotting park.[20]

Wiard was owner-in-residence at the trotting park and also built and managed a hotel that served the racetrack's fans. The track complex included stables, a grandstand, tack rooms, and a jockey club. Around the track emerged a significant business center featuring saloons, hotels, restaurants, and purportedly brothels. Until the end of the 1880s, harness racing or trotting was the main feature at the racetrack. However, thoroughbred horse racing also attracted considerable attention. In 1873, the first California Derby was run over a mile and one-half at the Oakland Park. This event marked the beginning of a shift that, over the next few decades, would see thoroughbred racing replace trotting as the preferred equine racing mode.[21]

Though the Oakland track was the most popular East Bay horse-racing venue during the 1870s, it was not the only facility in the area. Another track, about fifteen miles to the south, set "a mile from San Pablo Avenue in Hayward," also attracted Bay Area racing fans and further south and inland were tracks in what are now the cities of Dublin and Pleasanton. The Bay Area's sporting types could also enjoy greyhound racing at a small track located on present-day Oakland's International Boulevard (formerly East Fourteenth Street) near Elmhurst during the 1880s and 1890s. This was before the era of mechanical "rabbits" so live animals were used.[22]

During the 1870s crowds of considerable size gathered to watch the trotters run at the Oakland Trotting Park. Many at the oval had come from the "big city across the Bay."[23] The wagering that occurred was a significant part of the facility's attraction. The *Oakland Daily Transcript* of Saturday, July 10, 1875, reported on a typical weekend race. It was announced that at "Oakland park" three trotters would run for a "purse fixed at $200." There were also to be "inside stakes at $100 each." The race was to consist of mile heats with the "best three of five" declared the winner. Though wagering was a significant element in the popularity of the turf, many horse racing and trotting supporters in the East Bay did not wish to have their sport associated with the rougher pastimes of that era, like prizefighting, that also featured betting. The *Oakland Daily Transcript* seemed intent on emphasizing that the type of patron attracted to the trotting park was of a respectable class. On July 12, 1875, it reported that the attendance at Oakland

Park "consisted of men of standing and influence in the community; and quite a number of ladies graced the balcony."

Horse racing at the Trotting Park not only attracted Oakland's respectable middle class, but also a past president of the United States. In October 1879, some 3,000 people were on hand when the horse Saint Julian broke the one-mile trotting record. Former president General Ulysses S. Grant (1822–1885) observed the event that drew national attention. Other important figures were attracted by the excitement of Oakland's track. US senator and California's governor Leland Stanford (1824–1893)—famous for amassing a gold rush fortune, driving the ceremonial last spike at Promontory Point in 1869, and founding Stanford University in 1885—was a well-known Bay Area horse owner and racing enthusiast and a frequent visitor to the East Bay facility.[24]

The racetrack also attracted other sporting types. During the first few years of its existence the Trotting Park complex was from time to time the site of the Alameda County Fair. Wiard had sheds and buildings constructed in order that the prized livestock might be properly displayed during the event. During the mid-1870s, the track was also the site of live pigeon shoots. These shoots evidently also included some form of organized wagering.[25] In November of 1880, the second annual field day of the nearby University of California was held at the racetrack.[26] The students were assisted in managing the occasion by a delegation from San Francisco's Olympic Club, the nation's oldest athletic club. There were running events on the track and a one-mile bicycle race. The university's students were evidently among the best athletes in California. The school's yearbook was later able to boast that one sprinter's result was then the "fastest amateur time in the State." The press again emphasized the social rank of those present at the Trotting Park occasion by noting that the university men who took part were encouraged by "ladies" who, as the propriety of the age required, did not participate in any of the events, but "attended as spectators."[27]

After Wiard died in 1886, San Francisco's Judge James Mee assumed the Oakland Trotting Park's mortgage. Mee, born in Ireland in 1828, operated the track until his death in 1894. Immediately following Mee's demise, his estate leased the course to Thomas H. Williams Jr., president of the California Jockey Club. Williams was from a prominent Bay Area family. His father was a lawyer who had served as the state's attorney general. Born in 1859, the younger Williams attended Oakland High School, the University of California, and Santa Clara College. Under Williams's direction, the Jockey Club renovated the Trotting Park. The new grandstand, which was topped with a Japanese-style pagoda roof, was able to comfortably seat 3,000 spectators. Thousands more could stand under cover to watch the races. The newly named facility—the New California Jockey Club—was a lucrative business that flourished into the new century.

In the 1890s a number of well-known black jockeys often featured at Oakland's track. Among them were Jess "Long Shot" Conly, Felix Carr, Andrew Thomas, Willie Simms, and Alonzo "Lonnie" Clayton, who won the Kentucky Derby in 1892 when he was only fifteen years of age. During this decade the racetrack employed considerable numbers of African Americans, many of whom had migrated from Kentucky. These men, and others who worked as Pullman railroad porters, were the most visible members of Oakland's small black population. However, due to the application of powerful Jim Crow codes, the practice of allowing African American athletes to ride and earn a living at the Oakland track would not survive long into the 1900s.[28]

That the Oakland Trotting Park was situated outside Oakland's city limits was critical, in at least one regard, for its operators and patrons. During the late 1880s and early 1890s, the city of Oakland appears to have had prohibitions on gambling associated with horse racing. The racetrack, situated in an unincorporated area, was evidently not bound by Oakland's restrictive laws.[29] This advantage, though, could not shield the racetrack from an early twentieth-century political reform that swept across the United States. Progressivism was rooted in a concern with big government and business abuses, and it would eventually lead to the demise of the Oakland racetrack. Theodore Roosevelt's antitrust campaigns, which began in 1902, had ramifications for corporations across the nation. Unfortunately for the Jockey Club—that also ran the two other major tracks in the Bay Area (Ingleside and Tanforan near San Francisco)—the anti-racetrack faction of the state's Progressive reform movement considered the club's business activities to be a monopoly. In response to pressure brought to bear by progressive and anti-betting forces, the state legislature in 1910 passed the Walker-Young antigambling bill. When the law took effect in February 1911, racetrack betting became illegal in California. The last horse race took place at the former Oakland Trotting Park in that same month. Though horse racing as it had long been known at the Oakland track was outlawed, crowds would still gather at the site during the next few decades but for circuses, air shows, and motorcycle and motorcar races.[30]

Shell Mound Park

Across from his racing oval, Edward Wiard opened Shell Mound Park in 1876. The increase in customers that the railroad had provided for his racetrack in 1874 seems to have been the motivation for Wiard to open the amusement resort. Patrons could easily move between the sites by using a wooden bridge that spanned the railroad tracks. Wiard and the railroad company came to a business agreement whereby the railroad sold tickets (at a reduced rate) that included admission to the amusement park and the price of the train ride to get there.

At first, the park's main attraction was its shooting range. Various militias, some from San Francisco, made Shell Mound their headquarters. Though the site was popular with marksmen, Wiard seems to have been unable to make the kind of profit he would have liked from this enterprise. Toward the end of the 1870s, Wiard offered Captain Ludwig Siebe, who was a member of San Francisco's National Guard militia, a ten-year lease on the premises. This Siebe accepted, selling his grocery store in San Francisco and taking possession in February 1880.[31]

Siebe set about making the park more attractive to the general public, and as a result the shooting range was refurbished. The shooting booths were housed in a long pavilion that had benches for spectators, a bar, billiard tables, and a bowling alley. A number of sportsmen's clubs and veterans' organizations established permanent booths at Shell Mound.[32] To the east of the rifle range an arena was built. Footraces, tug-of-war—a popular sport that would feature in the Olympic Games during the first two decades of the next century—and public orations were held there. At other places on the grounds were Captain Siebe's home and pavilions for picnickers. At the very center of the resort stood a large dance hall with a long bar that sometimes required fifty bartenders. There was also a merry-go-round and numerous booths that offered patrons an opportunity to engage in games of skill and chance. The lone remaining shell mound also reportedly served a purpose, having had stairs attached to it and a dance pavilion placed on its crown.

The sixteen-acre park's picnic season lasted from March until November. No gas or electricity was available at the site until after 1900; before that time, Chinese lanterns illuminated the grounds during the evening. Various ethnic societies observed their national holidays at the park. Germans, Austrians, and Bohemians held their May Day celebrations at Shell Mound. Scandinavians celebrated at the East Bay resort in June. Those of French birth and descent gathered for Bastille Day in July. Ulstermen and Bay Area Scots also chose Shell Mound for their outdoor celebrations, which often involved highly competitive track and field events. On important festive days during the year it was purported that the park would accommodate 20,000 people.

The Bay Area's many ethnic associations patronized the park well into the twentieth century. In 1900, the San Francisco *Schuetzen Verein* held a ten-day shoot at Shell Mound. The $10,000 in prizes attracted some of the best pistol shots in the United States. Pistol shooting was an Olympic sport and American marksmen had been victorious in the event at the first modern games in Athens in 1896. Mass shoots continued to be a feature at the site and at other East Bay ranges. In 1909, the same German association held its "50th Anniversary Jubilee and Shooting Festival" at Shell Mound.[33]

While Siebe seems to have profited nicely from his business, neither he nor his family ever owned any part of the site. By 1886, James H. Mee was in possession of both the Trotting Park and Shell Mound. Though a new owner came on the scene, the Siebe family continued as lessee of the amusement park. However, with the arrival of the new century, Ludwig Siebe's son, William, found that as the Shell Mound property became increasingly valuable as a potential site for industrial buildings, he could only procure a month-to-month lease from the owners. By the end of World War I, the park was in serious decline. The coming of Prohibition in 1920 was the final blow. By 1924, the park's fences had been torn down to make way for conversion of the land into sites for warehouses and factories.[34]

Badger's Park

Equally as popular as the Shell Mound-Trotting Park complex was Badger's Park. In 1861, Captain Thomas W. Badger, originally of Virginia, purchased a ten-acre parcel of land in the hamlet of Brooklyn. Badger's land was bordered by the San Antonio Creek and Franklin, now Oakland's East Tenth Street. At the time of his purchase, Badger was a man of some celebrity. Born in 1828, he had gone to sea in his youth. As had many others, he came around Cape Horn to San Francisco in 1849. In 1857, Badger made a name for himself by saving the lives of hundreds of passengers aboard a stricken vessel making its way to New York City. His fame and seafaring expertise enabled him to enter the shipping business and eventually build his grand home and its surrounding resort.[35]

Badger's East Bay estate was advertised as a delightful retreat for him and later his many guests. Drives and pathways wound around the oaks, flowers, and many tropical plants with the grounds sloping gently down toward San Antonio Creek. In February 1872, Captain Badger began to transform his property into a commercial park. After the sum of $50,000 was reportedly expended on improvements, the park was ready for the public on April 14, 1872.

Of considerable importance to the success of Badger's enterprise was its proximity to public transit. The park was situated only two blocks from a railroad station. This put the resort within easy reach of visitors from neighboring East Bay towns and San Francisco. More than 4,000 paying customers turned out for the park's first day. The site was named Badger's Grand Central Park, but became known simply as Badger's Park. Easy access via mass transit combined with the fact that Oakland had no real public amusement park in the early 1870s made Badger's property very successful in attracting paying customers from all over the region.[36]

The resort incorporated several impressive buildings. The centerpiece was a pavilion for roller skating and dancing. It was said to be the largest pavilion in the state, able to accommodate 2,500 persons. Adjoining the ballroom was a large bar. Well-kept beaches lined the park's natural lagoon. Ferryboats from San Francisco, Stockton, and Sacramento docked at its pier. Within a few years the park expanded to include several dining halls (that reportedly served steam beer from the nearby hamlet of Brooklyn and oysters from San Leandro), bowling alleys, a menagerie, and various other concessions. Upon acquisition of more land to the northwest, a trotting track and amphitheater were laid out.[37]

Attractions of all types were held at the park. A tightrope walker thrilled the crowd on opening day in 1872 and, when the trotters were not running at its track, women in "skimpy outfits" titillated the crowds by recreating ancient Roman chariot races. Former US president Ulysses S. Grant gave a speech to Civil War veterans at the park in 1879 and was subsequently awarded the Freedom of Oakland by Mayor Washburne Andrus. On August 3, 1887, the *Daily Alta California* newspaper reported that a Swedish trapeze artist had tragically died from injuries sustained in a fall during a show. More traditional sporting events were also held. Regularly scheduled footraces for boys and men took place on the oval. In the late 1870s a baseball diamond was laid out on the track's infield and serious competitions began to take place.[38]

Competitive water sports also featured at Badger's Park. In 1875, the first regatta was held and it was of enough local interest that the press covered the September occasion. The race course was two miles in length. It began at the railway viaduct and continued up San Antonio Creek to the finish at Badger's Wharf. In later years, grandstands would be erected to facilitate a better view for the throngs that came for rowing events. It was reported that there was "great festivity" at the park on account of the "annual" regatta. Rowing was a popular local, national, and international sport during this time period. It became the first US intercollegiate sport in 1852 when the Harvard and Yale crews raced; in 1870 students at the nearby University of California at Berkeley formed a rowing club; and in 1900, in Paris, the American "eight" was victorious in the first modern Olympic rowing regatta.

As popular as Badger's Park had been with the area's multiple lodges, ethnic societies, and other associations during the 1870s and 1880s, various societal and economic changes led to its closure in 1893. Ethnic group gatherings had become less popular and other forms of outdoor entertainment like baseball and college football—increasingly played at stadia built specifically for them—were attracting more attention and had become serious competitors for the public's discretionary dollars. Perhaps most important, though, was that the land Badger's Park occupied had become more valuable for other uses. When it closed in the early 1890s, it was quickly sold off to railroad concerns. Soon thereafter the lagoon was filled in to handle rail traffic.[39]

Other Resorts in the Oakland Area

While Badger's Park, the Trotting Park, and Shell Mound Park competed for patrons from all over the region, they were not the only recreation and sport sites in and close to Oakland. As was the case in other American cities with significant German populations, Oakland's Germans spent considerable time together in their leisure hours. This manner of social interaction was enjoyable and also provided a forum for maintaining their homeland's culture. German immigrants in Oakland often continued the trades they'd learned and practiced in Europe. A number of Germans who lived in Oakland were trained in the science and art of brewing beer, and some of these men established breweries in their adopted hometown. Others opened saloons, hotels, and beer gardens where the results of their labors could be appreciated. The beer gardens were often affiliated with hotels, and rather than being purely drinking establishments for single men they were commonly frequented by the area's various German societies and family groups.[40]

Oakland's earliest beer garden was probably Bauhaufer's. It opened sometime before 1860 on Hopkins Street between Fruitvale and Lincoln Avenues. In the same district, the Neckhaus Gardens prospered during the 1880s. Another beer garden in operation during the last half of the century was Plittsville Park, named for Justus D. Plitt, a German immigrant who had arrived in California in 1849. Plitt's establishment was situated in the Fruitvale district on the Oakland-San Leandro County Road (later East Fourteenth Street and now International Boulevard). An astute businessman, Plitt, who owned large hotels in Oakland and San Jose, built Plittsville Park, that incorporated a hotel and beer garden, alongside the road that ran between the two cities where he operated his other businesses.[41] The most well known beer garden, in what had become Oakland's predominantly German Upper Fruitvale area by the last two decades of the nineteenth century, was Tepper's Hotel. Charles Tepper had arrived in the city in 1895. Though he had been raised in Germany, he was Dutch by birth. He settled on the corner of Hopkins Street and Dimond Avenue and opened a hotel and beer garden. Tepper's Garden became a popular picnic ground, particularly for the Bay Area's various German clubs. The establishment remained a lucrative business well into the twentieth century.[42]

In 1876, the Piedmont Springs Company purchased sixty acres of land in the hills overlooking the East Bay. A sulfur spring was "discovered" on the grounds soon thereafter. A two-story hotel was constructed and was soon attracting "City crowds." The hotel resort was another example of an entrepreneurial effort aimed at satisfying the demand for leisure time experiences away from the big city. The Piedmont Springs attempted to attract an affluent clientele from San Francisco and the well-to-do from Oakland and other parts of the East Bay. The healthy atmosphere was enhanced by the hotel kitchen's use of fresh fruit and vegetables from nearby gardens and orchards. Elaborate stables assured that the hotel was for years the resort of choice for Bay Area horse fanciers.[43] The hotel was located close to the terminus of a public transit line. On the morning of November 17, 1892, the Piedmont Springs Hotel burned to the ground.[44]

Other resort-like facilities in and near Oakland opened their doors during the 1880s. One such institution was the Fruitvale Villa. Set approximately 600 feet off the San Leandro road, the villa was owned by the "well known capitalist" John H. Church. Church took over the site in late 1886. He was reported to have spent the impressive sum of $30,000 in "adding to the already advanced beauty of the place." Its location allowed it to be easily reached from downtown Oakland either by road or the trains that ran "constantly within a few minutes walk of the Villa." The bucolic setting attracted those in search of a "pleasant place to pass a few days or weeks away from the hum of city traffic." Mr. Church's "genial hospitality," along with fine accommodations, food, wine, liquor, and care for horses, was expected to draw visitors back time and again.[45]

Outside the city limits of Oakland (on what is now International Boulevard between Forty-First and Forty-Second avenues) stood Morgan's Gardens. Opened in 1885 by Harry Morgan Jr. it hosted wrestling matches, boxing bouts, and purportedly cockfights. All these events were held in the dance pavilion. The establishment, widely known as the White House, closed its doors in 1906.[46] For at least some of its existence, however, the facility was home to more respectable athletes in training. In 1898 the University of California football team, which had been playing since 1886, utilized the White House as its training quarters.[47]

During the last two decades of the century, another business popular with sporting types was Three Mile House, also known as the Lambert House. It also stood outside Oakland's city limits. One report had it located on the Oakland-San Leandro County Road (now International Boulevard), quite close to the Morgan's Gardens site. Three Mile House reportedly served as a combination hotel and training place for boxers. During the late 1880s, it seems that a new proprietor changed the location of Three Mile House but retained the name. A newspaper report from 1887 put the establishment northwest of Oakland, one block from the San Pablo train station in the small town of Klinknerville. John Maher, a "well-known sportsman," had established an "amphitheater for athletic exhibitions" there at the "request of the California and other athletic clubs." Its proximity to the railroad line, a streetcar terminus ("within ten minutes walk"), and a main road allowed it to be advertised as particularly "accessible" and a "pleasant source of recreation" for the people of Oakland. Among the more famous who trained at Three Mile House were British-born Bob Fitzsimmons (middleweight and heavyweight world champion) and Jim Jeffries (also a world heavyweight champion and the so-called Great White Hope, who was famously defeated by Jack Johnson, the first Black world heavyweight champion). Venues like the White House could be found on the periphery of many other American cities during this era as sport entrepreneurs and their many paying customers tussled with local authorities over the morality and legality of prizefighting.[48]

City Boosting

No single event more changed the city of Oakland than the decision to make it the terminus of the transcontinental railroad. Facilitated by the completion of the railroad in 1869, the first rush of tourists and prospective new residents to California occurred in the early 1870s. In those early years the newcomers were anxiously awaited in a California that, apart from a handful of large towns and cities, was still sparsely populated. Oakland's population grew precipitously subsequent to the arrival of the Southern Pacific Railroad, but that surge of people was not sustained to the satisfaction of the city's civic and business leaders and from the mid-1870s until the early twentieth century they undertook concerted efforts to draw more new residents to the city.[49] Recognizing Oakland's long-standing popularity as a site for all types of outdoor recreation and aware that entrepreneurs had profited from providing parks and resorts to day-trippers and vacationers from all around the Bay Area for many years, the city's boosters enthusiastically promoted Oakland as an attractive city with a healthful environment to any individual or group they deemed likely to move west. Oakland's newspaper publishers, business associations, and political leadership were acutely aware that newcomers could provide an increased tax base, a rise in merchant sales, a real estate boom, and a boost to civic pride if they chose Oakland over other California and West Coast cities that were courting them.[50]

In the late 1870s, Oakland found a famous spokesperson for its recruitment strategy. Diocletian Lewis (1823–1886) was one of the leading figures in America's mid-century health reform movement. His publications on physical culture and health were widely disseminated and his exercise "system" had swept the country in the 1860s.[51] Lewis claimed to have first come to California "seeking health" in 1875. In his fifties and apparently suffering from chest ailments, Lewis chose Oakland because of its "exceptional" climate. Oakland was devoid, he said, of the "dampness which dulls" and the heat that "compromises vitality." Diocletian Lewis seemed inclined toward Oakland because its "most perfect combination of sunshine and cool breeze" offered him an alternative to the East Coast's difficult climate and a chance to recover his lost health.[52]

In March 1877, Lewis gave an address to the newly formed Oakland Real Estate and Merchants' Exchange. His national reputation made him the organization's ideal banquet speaker. As he stood before the city's business leaders, Lewis declared that he had already advised a number of East Coast consumptives that Oakland was the place to live in California. In response to the toast "Sunlight and Air," Lewis said to the real estate and other capitalists gathered, "I shall speak quite within bounds when I say that a half a million of intelligent people in the older States, who are seeking pleasant homes, are to-day turning their eyes towards this coast." Warming to his talk, he continued, "Don't be afraid, gentlemen, you who are in the real estate department; don't be afraid to run your streets far up on the foot-hills. It will all be needed. I know there is just now a pinch in money which holds everybody still, but very soon that will pass away, and then you will witness such a hegira to this coast as you have never dreamed of." Lewis seemed convinced that Oakland's healthful environment and open space would attract thousands from the East Coast, and it is evident that many in the city's real estate business took his advice to heart.[53]

During the following decades, Oakland's capitalists formed themselves into various self-promoting organizations and produced numerous pamphlets, books, and all manner of other advertising material that trumpeted Oakland's desirability as a place of residence due to its physical beauty and healthful environment. Some of this literature was distributed to visitors while they were in Oakland but much of it was aimed at external audiences and disseminated at regional and national expositions, through national magazines, in special Oakland newspaper editions, and even in advertisements placed in other cities' newspapers.

Oakland's promoters believed that in order to attract newcomers to their city it had to be an attractive, safe, and efficiently functioning place. With that end in mind, the new Real Estate and Merchants' Exchange busied itself with addressing the kinds of problems that commonly afflicted American cities. A lack of street signs was addressed—undoubtedly a concern for those in real estate development—and so too was the practice of sometimes housing smallpox patients in tents on the Bay front.[54] During the 1880s one project came to be a high priority for the Exchange: the beautification of Lake Merritt. Oakland's business leaders were well aware of the roles that urban parks were playing in other American cities, and they knew that a city seeking a positive reputation should not fall behind competitors in developing its important natural resources. In the Real Estate and Merchants' Exchange first annual report, its president stated that two years earlier he'd spent several months visiting eastern cities and was happy to declare that in none of them had he seen such "natural advantages" as were present in Oakland. Even Chicago, with its miles of grand boulevards, he said, "has not a single one that is or even can compare with, or be made equal in beauty of grandeur to what this projected boulevard around Lake Merritt might be made."[55]

Oakland was not the only California city that had grown during the 1870s, and the western flow of people continued during the 1880s. Thousands of migrants passed through Kansas City, Omaha, and El Paso on their way to the Pacific

Coast. Agents representing boards of trade in San Diego, Sacramento, San Jose, and Santa Barbara were busy distributing information favorable to their cities throughout the nation's midsection during this decade. In 1885, it was reported that 50,000 potential homeseekers visited California.[56] There were multiple reasons for the growth of cities like Los Angeles, San Diego, Sacramento, San Jose, and Stockton, but the advertising campaigns directed toward midwestern and eastern populations that were undertaken by their newspapers and boards of trade were certainly a contributing factor in attracting new residents. That Oakland had serious competition for new residents was clear. The *Oakland Morning Times* of September 2, 1886, declared, "A few months ago San Diego city could have been bought for five thousand dollars. Today ten million would not touch it. Her papers brought about the real estate boom. Oakland must be next, and the Times proposes to help the matter along."[57]

Earlier that summer, the newspaper had been pushing for Oakland to form its own board of trade in order to more aggressively compete for newcomers. On September 3, 1886, the Oakland Board of Trade was formed. With the organization only one day old, the *Morning Times* announced, "We are confident that Oakland's Board will do more for our fair city than similar associations in this state have ever done for their towns. That is saying a great deal when we remember that Los Angeles would have been a little Mexican town today, had it not been for her Board of Trade."[58]

Oakland's nascent board of trade declared that its mission was to promote Oakland in order that it might grow to be a more populated and vibrantly commercial city and within the association's first month its leaders were conferring with the railroad companies in order to obtain their cooperation in "upbuilding the city."[59] Various promotional tactics were initiated. For those visiting the city, the board's directors prepared a folder containing information about Oakland and its future promise. This was made available to the public at the board's office. By the end of its first year, the board of trade had distributed 150,000 pieces of advertising literature outside Oakland. Part of the campaign was a pamphlet titled *Oakland California* that gave particular attention to the good health and climate enjoyed by the city's residents. Public health statistics that compared Oakland's death rate with other American and some world cities allowed the publication to declare that the "mortality rate of this city is the lowest of any city in the world for its size." It also emphasized the propensity of Oaklanders to engage in outdoor recreation. The city's residents enjoyed weather that was "most favorable for human exertion" and conducive to year-round sport. Meteorological tables showed a climate that was equable throughout the year, "invigorating to the invalid," and able to render "life enjoyable to those in perfect health." In a final effort to entice the reader, Oakland's "atmosphere" was described as "pure, and at the same time mild; bracing, yet with an Italian softness."[60] Oakland's board of trade published numerous late-century promotional booklets of this type. They featured glowing descriptions of the city's parks, resorts, and other recreational facilities focusing particularly on their aesthetic appeal and the positive consequences of the ordinary Oakland resident's outdoor lifestyle.

Individual businesspersons, tourist agents, and other civic associations also were active in promoting Oakland. Real estate developers were particularly anxious that the city should continue to grow. As an example, in 1887, Oakland real estate agent William J. Dingee distributed to audiences outside northern California his *Catalogue and Price List.* Dingee focused on his city's healthful environment and recreational facilities, especially Lake Merritt and its fleet of pleasure craft in the "heart of the city" that was soon to be surrounded by a "superb park." Oakland's healthful situation was revealed in a list prepared by "Dr. E. W. Buck, health officer of the city" that showed Oakland to have the lowest urban mortality rate in the nation at 12.67 per thousand.[61]

During the nineteenth century's last two decades, Oakland's newspapers were critical instruments of civic boosterism. Real estate agents used them to advertise their property, and illustrated special editions trumpeted the city's attractions and achievements. *The Oakland Daily Evening Tribune* produced 50,000 copies of its January 20, 1887, "Special Edition." It was "Copiously Illustrated with Maps of the County and City, and Engravings of the Principle Buildings and Picturesque Scenery." The city was hailed as a "most desirable place for family residence" with "peculiar facilities for commerce" and "prospects for indefinite growth." The well-known historian Hubert Howe Bancroft declared that Oakland's "natural advantages are peculiar and unsurpassed, nowhere is air softer or sunlight sweeter" and nowhere, he said, was "health better."

A typical real estate agent's advertisement in *Oakland's Daily Evening Tribune's* 1887 special edition blared: "Are you coming to California? If so, you will, of course come to Oakland. We claim—and think we can substantiate the claim to your satisfaction—that Oakland has many advantages over any other city in the State as a place of residence." Few of Oakland's "advantages" were left unmentioned. Its climate during the "entire year" was as "desirable as any place in the State—neither too hot or too cold" and the city's "beauty of situation, elegant homes," and "beautiful flowers" seemed to make it a near perfect place to live. Perhaps as an appeal to bachelor populations, Oakland's "lovely women" were also noted. Mr. Denison, the real estate agent who'd placed the advertisement, concluded by noting that if the readers were to "come and see" Oakland, they would "exclaim: The half has never been told!" Denison would, of course, be happy to represent any party who might wish "a home in our midst."[62]

The next year's *Daily Evening Tribune* special illustrated edition used other evidence to show why Oakland was a most desirable place to locate. The city was blessed by a regular bay "breeze" that carried any and all "noxious gases away."

Oakland's much-heralded sanitary condition was due, apparently, to its nonhumid air and the good fortune of being located on a hillside and thus easily rid of sewage.[63] These factors were credited with producing its remarkably low death rate, which was again compared to other cities in the United States and even Europe, Africa, and South America.[64] These late-nineteenth-century comments reveal a continued adherence to the belief in miasmas or bad air as the cause of many sicknesses.

When the Oakland Board of Trade had been established in the fall of 1886, it took over many of the challenges that had been the domain (since the 1870s) of the city's Real Estate and Merchants' Exchange. Within a few years the older organization seems to have slipped into a dormant state. However, the Real Estate and Merchants' Exchange was reorganized on February 5, 1895, with a mission to "Promote the best interests of the city of Oakland commercially, by inducing immigration and encouraging new manufacturing industries, increased transportation facilities, and giving moral support and encouragement to the several departments of the City and County governments whereby extensions, improvements, sanitation, morality, and charity may be advanced, and our citizens mutually benefited."[65]

While the late-century focus seemed to be shifting toward attracting new businesses as well as new residents, the promotional tactics used were recognizable from earlier campaigns. One example of an "advertising medium," aimed at fulfilling the new mission was titled *Facts & Figures of Oakland, 1896*. Repeating a common theme, the pamphlet had a local doctor declare that Oakland was the "Healthiest of Cities." The city's numerous parks, sports-playing populace, effective sewers, and pure milk were all lauded and the city's climate was declared to be "conducive to longevity" and possessed of "healing qualities." The proof of Oakland's healthful environment could be seen in its low annual death rate, which was again positively compared to other US cities.[66]

In November 1896, *Oakland: Athens of the Pacific* was published. This booklet paid particular attention, yet again, to the area's aesthetic qualities, good climate, and sporting opportunities. The writers declared: "There is not a day in the year but one may indulge in outdoor sports if so desired." "Good hunting" was promised as was the opportunity to boat on Lake Merritt. The popular team and spectator sports of the day garnered special mention: "Baseball and Football can be played without fear of a storm of any kind" and "horse-racing" was noted as a "great pastime here"—the Oakland racetrack's grandstand was said to have 5,000 seats. Finally, and presumably in an effort to press home the city's salubrious climate to Midwest and East Coast readers: "if you want to skate in Oakland, you must do so on a smooth floor; for our ponds never freeze over."[67]

Newspapers continued to promote Oakland and Alameda County through the end of the century. In 1898, the *Oakland Tribune* produced *Alameda County*

Given Gillett's previous statements about the fight's legality, why did Gillett stop the battle? Gillett grounded his decision in business and boosterism, and banned boxing in a political move to win the 1915 Panama Pacific Exposition for San Francisco. San Franciscans wanted the Expo for the same reasons they wanted the fight, money. San Francisco had one competitor, New Orleans, and many believed Congress would not award San Francisco if it hosted the fight. As a *Marysville Daily Appeal* editorial reasoned, "There is one thing that New Orleans is not trying to secure and that is the Jeffries-Johnson fight. A white man who would so far disregard the color line as to enter the prize ring with a negro would be mobbed in any state south of the Mason and Dixon's line."[72] Led by the generous donations of local businessmen, residents donated nearly five million dollars to the cause of securing and hosting the Panama Exposition.

On the local and national levels, reformers successfully convinced Gillett to prevent the fight to secure the Exposition. The *San Francisco Examiner* and the *Chronicle* revealed that Congressman William S. Bennet of New York City, a Republican member of the Foreign Affairs Committee that controlled the destination of the Panama Exposition, sent a telegram to William R. Wheeler of the San Francisco Chamber of Commerce urging him to prevent the fight. Wheeler claimed that Bennet "called my attention to the fact that the church organizations and the various reform bodies throughout the East were bringing pressure to bear on Congress against the selection of San Francisco, setting forth that any city that would entertain the Jeffries-Johnson prize fight was not a fit place in which to hold an exposition of such a world-wide importance."[73] The day after Governor Gillett banned the fight Congress announced that New Orleans and San Francisco were the last two cities competing for the Exposition.[74] Coincidentally, San Francisco held the Exposition.

Aftermath

On July 4, 1910, the churches, Governor Gillett, and public opinion could not stop the fight; Jeffries and Johnson were going to battle. On this hot day in Reno, twenty thousand fans attended, while millions waited for the results by telegraph. In San Francisco, eighty thousand fans gathered outside of the *Examiner*'s building to hear round-by-round fight results and four theaters provided round-by-round reenactments of the fight.[75] Over the wires, the fans learned about Jeffries's fistic demise. Across America blacks celebrated the Johnson victory, but the celebration was short lived. To vent their anger, whites turned to violence and beat up or killed blacks that cheered too loudly.[76] If people rioted after the fight, how would they react after seeing Jeffries pummeled on film? With Jeffries losing and the riots raging, politicians across the country started to think twice about allowing the film in their city and banned the fight films.[77]

In the Bay, the battle to suppress the fight film shaped into a fight for child morality. Oddly, Mayor McCarthy, who was so adamant about having the fight in San Francisco, would not allow the pictures in his city. "The exhibition of these pictures isn't worth a single life," McCarthy argued. "The outcome of the fight caused enough deaths already, and we don't want any racial clashes here. It is up to the Board of Censorship to take the initiative." McCarthy also added, "I have no doubt that the members of this board, all of them being interested in the welfare of our youth, will proceed to bar the moving pictures of the fight without further suggestion from me."[78] Norman W. Hall, the secretary of the board of censorship, claimed, "I was approached by nearly a dozen different persons in different walks of life who almost begged me to exert whatever influence I might have on the Board of Censorship in opposition to the pictures." Hall also noted, "the negro population of San Francisco is probably not more than one thousand, and there are not more than one hundred colored children enrolled on the books of the Board of Education. The majority of people, however, appear to feel that the pictures cannot be exhibited in San Francisco without grave risks."[79] Board of censorship member Mrs. D. C. Farnham argued, "I do not approve of them. Pictures of prize-fights have a demoralizing effect on the morals of the young."[80] San Francisco's leading clubwomen also joined the anti-film fight for the children's sake. Mrs. James H. Crawford, vice president of the California Club, argued, "No good can come to any one by allowing these pictures to be shown. The fact this man Johnson is the champion fighter of this country deludes the colored race into believing that they have made great progress. It gives them a false security, sets up a degrading ideal for them, and immeasurably retards their real intelligence."[81] Henry Payot, of the board of education, argued, "I am opposed to having these moving pictures of the prizefight, or anything exhibited in San Francisco. Such an exhibition could not but be very demoralizing to the spectators, a majority of whom certainly would be boys." Payot continued, "It may have been a poor fight, but its effect, as presented to our boys in the moving pictures could not but be brutalizing."[82] On July 11, Hall and his board of censorship banned the film.[83] Political reformers had wiped San Francisco clean of the remaining fight residue.

Conclusion

The Jeffries-Johnson fight constituted the biggest fight in boxing history. Pitting two specimens of racial manhood against each other, the contest elicited racial anxieties across the country as fans waited for the outcome of the fight. The fight, however, also illuminates how Americans viewed sport during the Progressive Era, as sports represented both a successful business and a disreputable pastime. In the Bay Area, where the fight was originally supposed to be held, businessmen, boosters, and reformers fought over the right to control the Bay's future. Would the Bay stand for money and sporting mayhem or reform and purity?

Boosters and businessmen in Emeryville, Oakland, and San Francisco championed the fight for the potential economic victory it would bring their respective areas. Adventure seekers arriving to see the "Fight of the Century" would fill hotels, restaurants, and businesses. But reformers worried that these same migrants coming to view the vicious spectacle would do unimaginable damage to the reputation of the Bay. Led by church leaders, progressives took their fight to the governor to convince him to save the Bay and the state.

At first, Governor James Gillett supported the fight for the moneymaking potential, but then changed his mind. In the end, the potential lost revenue from losing the Panama Exposition, and not the reformers pleas, persuaded Gillett to ban boxing in California. Although the battle moved to Reno, Bay Area reformers continued to fight for morality and suppress the fight films. Without the ability to make money from the films, businessmen and politicians gave way to reformers. The "Battle of the Century" would not be seen in the Bay, either in person or in a theater.

3

Reforming the Big Game

The Bay Area Rugby Experiment of 1906–1919

BRIAN M. INGRASSIA

In early 1906 President Benjamin Ide Wheeler of the University of California decried the militaristic character of American intercollegiate football, complaining that the game was a dangerous and demoralizing spectacle maintained simply to make money and manufacture bogus "college spirit."[1] At the time Wheeler was writing, football was under siege. Injuries, death, and corruption had inspired reform-minded Americans to call for the game's alteration or abolition. The most famous reforms were creation of the National Collegiate Athletic Association (NCAA) and legalization of the forward pass. Yet we have to remember that other ideas about how to reform the sport were present, and some of them were also attempted. This was the Progressive Era, after all, a decades-long period when urban-industrial society was being reshaped around the globe. Although many of the era's reform movements were carried out by explicitly national groups, some also had a distinctive international flavor. Reformers even crossed the Atlantic Ocean to borrow ideas from overseas. In some cases, though, movements could be local or regional. The Midwest, for example, was one hotbed of activism, with noteworthy cadres of reformers based in Chicago and Madison, Wisconsin. Another was the West Coast, which sported its own brand of reform that was centered in California and drew upon trans-Pacific influences. Throughout America, opinions differed on the best way to make football safer and more moral. Many Californians even rejected "gridiron" football altogether and tried to replace it with rugby as played in Britain's Pacific Rim colonies. Although it did not last beyond the First World War—and it did not spread past the Rocky Mountains—the 1906 Bay Area rugby experiment illustrates both the international and regional flair of Progressive Era reforms—as well as the experimental attitude that many reformers brought to their innovations.[2]

Intercollegiate football was born on the East Coast in the 1860s before it spread to the West by the end of the century. The game took its modern form at Yale University in Connecticut in the early 1880s, when the so-called father of American football, Walter Camp (a future industrialist and clock company executive), rationalized rugby by introducing downs, timing, and yard measurements. Subsequently, Camp built Yale into one of America's strongest football powers, along with the other "Big Three" schools, Harvard and Princeton. In the early 1890s, Camp even had a direct hand in shaping Bay Area football. The first match between the University of California and the Leland Stanford Junior University was played on March 19, 1892. Stanford won by a score of 14–10, in front of an estimated 6,000 spectators at San Francisco's Haight Street Grounds. Later that year, Stanford's prominent president, David Starr Jordan, asked Camp to come out west and coach its team. The following year, California followed suit by employing one of Camp's star players, William "Pudge" Heffelfinger, to guide its team to victory. While Heffelfinger only remained at Cal for the 1893 season, Camp returned to Stanford in 1894 and 1895. By 1900, the Cal-Stanford rivalry came to be known as the "Big Game." After the 1905 contest—which Stanford won by a score of 12–5 on its new home field near Palo Alto—Stanford led the series, 7-4-4.[3]

The Big Game developed into a major rivalry at the same time football was coming under attack in the East. From the 1890s to the 1910s, middle-class reformers led crusades against corruption in politics, big business, and consumer goods such as packaged meat and pharmaceuticals. In the eyes of many Americans, intercollegiate football—which was becoming a major spectacle consumed both in stadiums and in the popular press—also needed reform. Walter Camp's innovations had seemingly turned the game into a methodical contest based on brute force rather than strategy. To make matters even worse, players wore little protective gear. Helmets were not used until the 1920s and even makeshift pads (then called "armor") were rare before World War I. College and high school football players regularly sustained serious spinal injuries at the turn of the century, and a few even died. One famous death nearly prompted the Georgia legislature to ban intercollegiate football throughout the state in 1897. Eligibility scandals, gambling, and illicit professionalism plagued the game.[4]

Although most critiques were leveled in the East, some West Coast voices contributed to the discussion. In 1903, Stanford's President Jordan told readers of the *Popular Science Monthly* that college football's value was eliminated when universities hired nonstudents to play. Jordan claimed he "would rather see football disappear and the athletic fields closed for ten years for fumigation than to see our colleges helpless in the hands of athletic professionalism."[5] This was an astounding about-face for Jordan, who had previously supported football as president of Indiana University in the 1880s before moving to Stanford in 1891.

Jordan represented a larger trend sweeping the nation, as more Americans started to clamor for football reform. Some of these turn-of-the-century voices belonged to the progressive journalists whom President Theodore Roosevelt dubbed "muckrakers" because they seemed to be just stirring up dirt with their sensational pieces. But these journalists saw it as their duty to expose the public to big problems in modern society. Henry Beach Needham and Edward S. Jordan (no apparent relation to Stanford's president) published articles in middle-class magazines like *Collier's* and *McClure's*, exposing football's problems to the progressive-minded public. Soon, even Roosevelt could not ignore the outcry. He called leaders of the "Big Three" football powers to the White House in October 1905 and ordered them to clean up football. While Roosevelt played a significant role, the real catalyst for change was the death of Union College's Harold Moore during a game against New York University (NYU) on November 25, 1905. Americans were outraged. NYU's Chancellor Henry MacCracken—one of football's most vocal opponents—convened a series of meetings in New York City in December and January 1905–1906. These meetings led to the creation of the Intercollegiate Athletic Association of the United States, which became the NCAA in 1910. One of the NCAA's key reforms, the legalized forward pass, was designed to improve football by making the style of play more "open." Proponents claimed that open play would make the game safer by spreading players out on the field, thus discouraging close formations and hard tackles. They also argued that it would make the game more moral because both spectators and officials would be better able to see the action on the field—and punish any players who broke the rules or engaged in fighting.[6]

West Coast higher education leaders agreed with their eastern brethren that something needed to be done about football. The day following Harold Moore's fatal injury, Cal's President Wheeler spoke out. Wheeler was a classics scholar and a sports enthusiast who served as a judge at the first modern Olympic Games in Athens in 1896. A vigorous administrator inspired by the era's influential German universities, Wheeler proclaimed the "addition of a few more restrictive rules is not enough." He declared that football "must be entirely made over" or else eliminated.[7] Across the Bay, David Starr Jordan echoed Wheeler. Stanford's president decreed in December 1905 that "brutality" like that which had resulted in Harold Moore's death just days earlier exposed the fact that football now placed too much importance on "muscular force" and "beefy" men. Furthermore, the game had become "dirty" and infiltrated by the "mucker," whose corruption and deceit contradicted the moral values that Progressive Era universities sought to instill in students. Such a "cad" did not belong "in the presence of gentlemen." To fix the game, said Jordan, universities needed to eradicate "dirty men" from the field.[8]

Although these university leaders were outspoken about football corruption, some people thought that the game as it was played in the West was not as bad as the violent and regimented spectacle offered in the East. In November 1905, shortly after Harold Moore's death in New York, sportswriter and former Stanford football player Waldemar Young wrote in the *San Francisco Chronicle* that the 1905 Big Game had "practically no unnecessary roughness" and absolutely "no intentional brutality." Young opined that it had been a "clean" game, and he asserted that the "Golden West" knew how to keep sport honorable. In California, said Young, sport was, "like the land . . . young and strong and not overdeveloped." Overpaid coaches did not dominate the game at Stanford or Berkeley as they did at some of the East Coast colleges, and "the spirit of 'win at any cost' ha[d] no strangle hold upon" the two major California universities. They did not favor "the delirium of winning to the satisfaction of a clear conscience." Wheeler made a similar claim, stating that Pacific Coast football had already "freed itself . . . of many of the evils" that prevailed in the East and Midwest. Such rhetoric sounded good, but historian Roberta Park has noted that such claims were overblown—California football may have appeared cleaner simply because West Coast universities played shorter schedules and so there were fewer chances for corruption.[9]

Not surprisingly, Berkeley and Stanford eventually decided to take a different course of reform than the rest of the country. On November 29, Berkeley's academic council held a secret meeting regarding the "football question." A week later, the faculty reported that they had chosen not to go along with the East Coast rules makers. They even announced that the two universities would abolish football altogether unless they could not agree on a new set of "gridiron" rules. At the meeting, Wheeler excoriated the "self-appointed" eastern rules committee, which seemed to continually refuse to make any meaningful reforms. Although easterners had "promised time and time again that the game would be reformed so as to eliminate all brutality or chance of fatal injury," each year they simply perpetuated the same rules, allowing the game to devolve even further. Wheeler said that he was tempted to follow Columbia University's lead and abolish the game, but he did not want to make a rash judgment. He would rather revise the rules. Some took Wheeler's statement to mean that the universities of Arizona, Nevada, Oregon, and Washington would soon form a "Pacific Coast League" with its own distinct set of rules.[10]

After the late-November academic council meeting at Berkeley, Wheeler and Jordan held a joint meeting of their athletic committees. Faculty members and coaches from Stanford and Cal convened at San Francisco's University Club on the afternoon of December 11, 1905. They unanimously recommended that either football be replaced with rugby, or be altered so as to "do away with existing evils." The *San Francisco Chronicle* reiterated that this decision would determine the future of Pacific Coast football, since it seemed certain that all the other colleges and high schools on the West Coast would follow in the footsteps of California's two most prominent universities.[11] The same day as the meeting, Wheeler wrote to Yale's President Arthur T. Hadley, explaining that Stanford and Cal would likely switch to rugby—probably "the Australian and New Zealand modification" of the game. He was "not at all afraid of setting up a separate Pacific Coast football game." A week later, Yale's president responded positively. Hadley even confessed that he wished the East Coast schools could "develop several separate games." Since he doubted that a single rules committee could make all institutions happy, the best outcome would be for various institutions to embrace different games so "that we might have competition between several different experiments, in order that the students and the public might see which was best."[12] Such competition, presumably, would ultimately lead to a better brand of American football—although one might reasonably wonder how much chaos Hadley's suggestion for competing varieties of football might have spawned had it ever actually been put into effect.

Over the winter, Stanford and Cal's resolve to replace football with rugby only strengthened. In March 1906 the joint athletic committee—which included Professors Frank Angell and A. B. Spaulding of Stanford, Professors G. C. Edwards and Prentiss N. Gray of Berkeley, and coaches James Lanagan of Stanford and Frank Simpson of Cal—formally recommended a switch to Canadian or Australian rugby rules. At the time, this change seemed like a temporary solution. David Starr Jordan argued that it would only last until eastern reformers made changes upon which the whole country could agree. Like others before him, Jordan claimed that nothing was wrong with California-style football.[13] Rather, he seemed to see the West Coast as a potential leader in national discussions about athletic reform.

Although several sources persisted in claiming that Californians would switch to "English" rugby, by early 1906 it was becoming clear that a colonial variety would prevail. West Coast reformers explicitly started emulating rugby as played in Britain's Pacific Basin empire. Even before the committee formally announced the switch to rugby, Stanford and Cal invited professional teams from New Zealand and Vancouver to come to San Francisco for exhibition matches and to teach students how to play the unfamiliar game. As early as Saturday, February 10, 1906, a New Zealand team defeated the British Columbia Rugby Union at Berkeley. Such exhibitions prompted Bay Area reformers to travel across the Pacific to see rugby in its native habitat. Ever the naturalist, David Starr Jordan—an ichthyologist by training, a noted Darwinian evolutionary biologist, and a pioneer conservationist—accompanied Stanford coach James Lanagan to see the game played in New Zealand and British Columbia. The New South Wales Football Club even invited Jordan to attend a match in Sydney, Australia, on June 8, 1907. It is not clear, though, whether he did attend the match. For his part, Lanagan commented that he saw Australian rugby as less warlike than American football. The coach contended that rugby taught athletes discipline, exercise, and mental self-reliance.[14]

By autumn 1906, Wheeler was explaining to high school principals in southern California why they should adopt rugby—not the "New Intercollegiate" game. Rugby was an established sport common throughout the English-speaking world: in "New Zealand, Australia, British Columbia, Canada, Scotland, Wales, England and Ireland." The reformed American game, on the contrary, was an entirely unknown quantity. Wheeler complained, "No man can as yet tell what [reformed American football] will really be. At present it is merely a body of rubs on paper." Although rugby's appeal throughout the British Empire was known, the long-term effects of new rules like the forward pass were not yet evident. Adopting rugby would allow Californians to compete with their "natural neighbors" on the Pacific Rim, including Vancouver, Australia, and New Zealand. Wheeler assured readers that even if the reformed game took hold on the East Coast—which he doubted—the West Coast would maintain rugby.[15]

Rugby's most vocal West Coast proponents argued that the game was more interesting, involved more players, and was less injurious or deadly than the old "American" game—which was dubbed "battleball" by one of the Vancouver players who visited the Bay Area. Benjamin Ide Wheeler told San Francisco readers that rugby was "more of a game and less of a spectacle, or a series of evolutions, than the American game."[16] He liked rugby because it was "freer" and "healthier" than football, and it got all players to take turns "at running, at catching, at kicking, [and] at tackling."[17] Elsewhere, Berkeley's president used quasi-imperialistic rhetoric when he called rugby "the heartiest and manliest of the Anglo-Saxon sports" and implored students to get out on the field and start playing it.[18]

David Starr Jordan had his own reasons to like rugby: the game was supposedly safer for players' vital organs, including the central nervous system. It is not surprising that Jordan took this stance. Stanford's president was a major proponent of eugenics—the early 1900s belief that the human race could be improved through selective breeding—as well as a noted pacifist who argued that wars should be ended because they killed the strongest men (and thus reduced the quality of human breeding stock). Jordan argued that rugby was better than football because it was less likely to kill players or damage their minds, bodies, and reproductive capabilities. Jordan claimed that while injuries to the extremities were bad, injuries to the brain or spinal cord could be lethal and permanently destructive. Jordan was just one of many Americans at the time who thought that the central nervous system was the location of the manly, nervous energy necessary to build a strong nation and compete in the global arena. Jordan argued that unlike American football, which was inherently warlike, rugby caused injuries that were "mainly peripheral, [and] rarely deep-seated."[19] Jordan knew that rugby injuries were common, and he even admitted to Walter Camp that "the danger to legs and arms" was at least as bad in rugby as in American football. Nevertheless, he still believed that "the danger to the nervous system and of internal injuries" was much diminished in rugby. Camp, though, did not buy this line of argument. The so-called father of American football shrewdly pointed out that the game had started out as rugby decades earlier before he guided it on its unique course.[20]

As Camp's response indicated, some Americans were not as enamored with rugby as Jordan and Wheeler. In fact, many students were downright unhappy with the change. The *San Francisco Chronicle* reported in March 1906 that Stanford's football team refused to play rugby and the student body supported their decision. The Stanford "eleven" blamed Cal for the unwanted reform, claiming that only Benjamin Ide Wheeler desired rugby. Wheeler responded by saying that the switch to rugby was a sensible solution, and it should be given a "trial" for at least the following year. He thought players would "thoroughly enjoy" rugby, and even if they did not, it would be good "to have learned another well-established form of" football.[21] Yet Wheeler was not as successful as he would have liked. He could not convince all Bay Area high schools to switch. Principal Morris C. James of Berkeley High school even scoffed, "If we are to play football . . . let's play it, and not this baby game that they have imported from over the pond." In September 1906, virtually all of southern California's high schools rejected overtures to play rugby, despite David Starr Jordan's insistence that such resistance would only make it harder for players to matriculate at Stanford or Berkeley.[22]

Although rugby initially seemed like a temporary solution, by the end of 1906 its proponents increasingly spoke of its permanence. We can speculate—based on scholarship showing that natural disasters prompt periods of rebuilding—that the massive earthquake that rocked the Bay Area in April 1906 prompted an increased acceptance of rugby reform. (This would also explain why southern California, which did not feel the quake, was less enthusiastic about rugby than northern California.) Not even four weeks after the joint committee decided on rugby, an estimated 7.8-magnitude tremor rocked San Francisco, sparking fires that destroyed the city and killed as many as several thousand residents. To the south, the Santa Clara Valley was hit especially hard, and many of Stanford's magnificent

Mission-style buildings were ruined. Some people in Palo Alto immediately cast the future as a time for rebuilding. Harvard's influential philosopher-psychologist William James was then teaching temporarily at Stanford, and he considered the disaster "a *perfectly* 'god-given' opportunity to re-launch Stanford." Jordan agreed. Just hours after the earthquake, he told students that the university would "build itself again."[23] As rebuilding progressed, rugby started to seem like part of the new order—one that was here to stay.

By September, both universities prepared for the upcoming rugby season. At one Stanford rally, a crowd of five hundred students heard from Coach Lanagan, trainer "Dad" Moulton, and team captain E. P. Scott. Moulton said that rugby was a totally new game, unfamiliar even to him, yet he was sure that the team would be successful if they could just capture the "same old spirit" that had animated them in the past. Lanagan echoed Moulton, saying that it would take some time to learn the new game. While summering in Canada, he had discovered that rugby could not be mastered in three to four weeks; it might take two to three seasons to learn the sport fully. Athletes could not commit only halfway. To win at the new game, they would have to be as determined and play as hard as they had at football. At Berkeley, students got acquainted with the new game quickly as the university spent $8,000 to enlarge its fields to accommodate rugby.[24]

The first rugby Big Game was held at Berkeley on Saturday, November 10, 1906. Students from both universities gathered on opposite ends of the grandstands to root on their respective squads in the latest installment of the storied rivalry. The *San Francisco Chronicle* wrote that "[t]he big bell in the tower of the library up on the campus was still pealing the noon hour when the first ribboned Californians appeared at the gate and demanded admission." Hal Bingham and Sam Hume, the Cal yell leaders, were there, along with the band and the "Noise Boys" rooting section, with their blue and gold megaphones. On the other side of the field, Stanford yellers Kellogg and Hatzell led the estimated 750 cardinal-clad students in cheers and songs. Nearly 16,000 spectators filled the stands, reportedly the second-largest sporting crowd ever west of the Mississippi (the largest had been at the 1904 match at Berkeley). Stanford won their third series match in a row by a score of 6–3.[25] After the game, Jordan proclaimed, "Rugby is all right and it has come to stay."[26]

After that first rugby Big Game, some observers reflected on the big changes that had swept the Bay Area that year. One San Francisco sportswriter thought about rugby as he wandered the Phoenix-like post-quake city "on swarming ferry-boats, on big, dust-covered trolley cars, in the desolate-looking burned district, where the clank of steel sounds a day-long anvil chorus chanting of the city that is to be, and out beyond Van Ness [A]venue, where sprinkling wagons suppress the dust." If he could have his way, he would go further and fashion a new game altogether. Rugby was a fine sport, but it seemed that the players could not quite get the old one out of their system. They had even imported tackling into rugby—apparently "infus[ing] something of their characteristic strenuous life and unrestrained enthusiasm" into the new game. The sportswriter, though, meant this observation less as critique and more as a jumping-off point for his own suggestion. Since California had a mild and scenic climate that might allow it become the athletic leader of the Americas, its residents should experiment even further by trying out association football (soccer) and lacrosse. Californians could then devise a new game that combined the elements of those sports with those of gridiron football and rugby. After all, unlike Great Britain and the East Coast, the West was "not tied to traditions." It could freely choose the best that the various games had to offer and then create something even better: "Why may not California produce the type of game that will best express the spirit of her people, the open fearlessness, the zest, [and] the dogged . . . determination that makes the rebuilding of San Francisco absolutely certain?"[27]

Despite such optimistic projections, rugby appears to have been becoming somewhat entrenched in the Bay Area (at least at Stanford) by the end of 1906. In December, a professional rugby player from New Zealand wrote a long, rambling letter to David Starr Jordan. The author, A. H. Baskerville, was a prominent professional rugby player in New Zealand. Baskerville hoped to talk Jordan into hiring him as Stanford's coach at a $5,000 annual salary. He promised that with his guidance, a team could beat any team from the East Coast or even the British universities. The existing record of correspondence indicates that Jordan considered Baskerville's offer at length.[28] By January 1907, Jordan told Stanford students that rugby was there to stay. The following year, all games would "either be Rugby, with a slight modification in the scrum, or an extremely modified form of American football."[29]

Jordan, with Wheeler's help, waged a campaign to convert colleges and high schools throughout the Pacific Slope to rugby, in part to open up a path to international competition. By December 1907, Jordan sang rugby's praises as he toured southern California. Although he may have convinced the faculty of Los Angeles High School that rugby was a better game, most of the players there were "violently opposed" to replacing football. Jordan met a similar reaction at Occidental College in Los Angeles, where he criticized American football as "unethical, un-Christian, and unsportsmanlike," lambasting the eastern rules committee for corrupting the game in order to give itself more power over college sports. The *Los Angeles Times* reported that even though Jordan's audience was initially receptive to his comments, by the end they sat silently in shock. One Occidental professor disagreed with Jordan's harangue: there was little "roughness" in the game as played in Los Angeles, and East Coast reformers had made significant improvements to the game. He saw no need to give up and switch to rugby.[30]

Jordan attempted to spread rugby beyond California. In February 1908 he sent a letter to President Charles Van Hise of the University of Wisconsin, and then forwarded copies of that letter to hundreds of other administrators throughout the nation. Jordan made two major recommendations in his missive. First, he insisted upon implementing rugby nationally. Second, he proposed eliminating professional coaches. By switching to rugby, he claimed, universities could virtually eliminate dangerous injuries to college men and inspire more students to get involved in a simpler, less regimented sport. Meanwhile, banning professional coaches would presumably rid football of the disdainful influence of money and a victory-at-all-costs mentality. Dozens of administrators replied to Jordan's circular letter. Many encouraged his efforts or even expressed an interest in learning more about rugby. A few respondents, though, were skeptical. Unless all major universities banded together and forced change, individual colleges could merely alleviate problems within their own institutions. Like many other respondents, Van Hise sympathized with Jordan, but he also resisted his overtures. It seemed more prudent to stick with the recent moderate reforms, such as the forward pass.[31]

Jordan was not Stanford's only rugby missionary. After four years of West Coast rugby, psychology professor Frank Angell wrote a piece for the magazine *The Independent* that reported on the experiment's progress. An expert on the nervous system, Angell had trained with pioneer experimental psychologist Wilhelm Wundt in Germany, helped edit the *American Journal of Psychology*, and published articles on physical and mental reaction time. He also served on Stanford's athletic committee starting in the 1890s, was the official timer at many Stanford track meets, and was a member of the joint committee that recommended switching to rugby in 1906. Angell recalled that football had once been a "manly" sport avidly followed by professors. Over time, though, Camp and Heffelfinger had turned it into a precise yet unhealthy contest of "exhausting mass and momentum play." Rugby was better collegiate sport, he said, because it got more men on the field and inspired them to keep playing later into the academic year. Rugby provided "exhilarating exercise without any harmful results," and its players developed skills that players of the old game never had to learn. Angell even argued that rugby helped develop players' minds and made them into quick thinkers. Rather than drilling monotonous plays into players' heads, rugby included "rapid changes of play where quick thinking and ready agility had to play their part." Many old football stars, it seemed, were "too slow in the head" for rugby. Like Jordan, Angell was more concerned about protecting nerves than he was about making the game exciting for spectators. He and the committee were aiming to support a game "which if rough did not have formations which invited broken necks and

Stanford and Cal square off against each other in a rugby match, circa 1908. *Courtesy of Stanford University Archives.*

concussion of the brain." Elsewhere, Angell recorded his disdain for professional coaches, whom he argued were merely good at drilling players in specialized routines.[32]

Had the West Coast really purified intercollegiate athletics by embracing Pacific Rim-style rugby, as Angell and others claimed? Of this, we cannot be sure. But we do know that Stanford and Cal played the Big Game under rugby rules from 1907 to 1914. During this period, Stanford won four matches (1907, 1908, 1913, and 1914), while Cal won three (1909–1911), with a tie in 1912. Eventually, a number of other colleges adopted rugby, including the University of Southern California, University of Nevada, Santa Clara University, and Saint Mary's College. Many (certainly not all) high schools in California also adopted rugby. Some sports enthusiasts, though, did not want to see rugby take too great a hold on the West Coast. In March 1909, the *New York Times* reported that an "American Football Association" had met in San Francisco recently and planned to bring in a coach from one of the major East Coast universities in order to teach high school athletes in California "the revised American game of football." This plan was part of a larger campaign carried out by Harvard's former coach William T. Reid Jr. (son of a former University of California president), who hoped to prevent rugby from taking root in West Coast high schools.[33]

Despite such attempts to stem the tide, trans-Pacific connections were giving rugby a more solid hold on the West Coast. In December 1909, the University of California rugby team traveled to Vancouver to play three games held between Christmas and New Year's Day. The winner received the Cooper-Keith trophy. On May 17, 1910, an "all-American" team with players from Stanford, Cal, and Nevada left San Francisco for a three-month tour of New Zealand and Australia, where they were scheduled to "play all the representative rugby fifteens of the Antipodes." In June 1910, an All-American Rugby Football Team—comprised of students from Stanford, Cal, and Nevada—lost to the University of Sydney by a score of 17–6.[34]

An increased number of American players were heading to British Columbia or Australia to play rugby, but athletes also continued to head in the other direction. Stanford's Frank Angell even acknowledged the impact the "British colonial teams" had in popularizing rugby on the Pacific Coast. Teams made up of "firemen, college students, and small farmers" from British Columbia and New Zealand had demonstrated "sportsmanship" and shown Californians "football played for the love of the game."[35] In 1910, an Australian team visited California and played a team made up of star players from the various rugby-playing universities. Later that summer, the New South Wales Rugby Union invited the Americans to visit Australia. The following year, Victoria's team traveled to California, and in 1912 Australia's team played a series against the California Rugby Union. In December 1912, the Oxford University Athletic Club invited Oxford and Cambridge rugby players to form a combined team that would travel to the Pacific Coast the following fall. There, they would play eight games against a team made up of players from Stanford, Cal, and various athletic clubs.[36]

The switch to rugby was facilitated by these Pacific crossings, but it was still not easy. In addition, the reform did not eliminate competitive tension and hard feelings between Cal and Stanford. In November 1912, Stanford officials sent Cal a warning that they would not tolerate poor sportsmanship in the upcoming Big Game on November 9. Heavy rains turned Berkeley's California Field into a muddy quagmire, and 23,000 spectators witnessed a boring, sloppy match that ended in a 3–3 tie.[37] Indeed, Bay Area rugby was not always the most artful—especially considering that West Coast players were still learning the game years after the reform was inaugurated. In 1913, J. D. Gulney of New Zealand's all-star rugby team bluntly told Stanford's players, "You don't know how to play the game." Not surprisingly, his "frank criticism" depressed many of the athletes who had been playing rugby for years.[38]

By the spring of 1914—just months before the outbreak of the First World War—the rugby experiment was falling apart. On April 8 the University of Southern California (USC) announced that after three years of rugby, it would revert to the American game. Since none of the other colleges in the Los Angeles area had switched to rugby, this move made sense to the faculty athletic committee, which voted unanimously to return to football. Although USC did not totally cut off athletic relations with Stanford and Cal, it did prioritize local colleges in scheduling. Warren F. Bovard, USC's athletic director, gave his reasons for abandoning rugby. He said that with more players, it was harder to control a rugby match than an American football game. In addition, there were fewer officials to regulate the game, which made rugby "much rougher." Bovard also preferred the American game's more interesting variety of scoring: "Kicking from touch makes Rugby a comparatively monotonous game."[39]

Rugby also suffered as Americans were cut off from international competition by World War I. Athletes from Vancouver were scheduled to compete against Stanford in rugby and crew in autumn 1914, but they were unable to travel to the Bay Area. In September, Stanford psychology professor Frank Angell received a letter from Vancouver informing him that the rowing club's quarters now served as a barracks and the athletic field was now a drill grounds. Indeed, so many footballers were serving in the army that they were arranging no matches.[40]

The last Stanford-Cal Big Game played under rugby rules was in November 1914, when the two undefeated teams matched up at California Field and Stanford won, 26–8. The following spring, the University of California returned to American football and severed athletic connections with Stanford. Although the split was ostensibly about freshman athletic eligibility, Roberta Park argues that the "hidden reason was Berkeley's desire to return to American football." Cal was inspired to return to the old game, in part, by the 1915 Panama-Pacific International Exposition held in San Francisco. This world's fair demonstrated that the Bay Area had finally bounced back from the 1906 earthquake and had become reintegrated into national and international life. Initially, its organizers sought to entice major eastern football powers—including Harvard, Yale, Syracuse, Penn, and Michigan—to play football exhibitions at the exposition's stadium. Since rugby had become the California game, though, it appeared that the easterners would have to compete against one another, unless Oregon or Washington would agree to play. Yet other arrangements were considered, too. Perhaps the team from the Carlisle Indian School in Pennsylvania would play one of the West Coast schools, or maybe Stanford and Cal would play their Big Game at the exposition. By September 1915, the fair's organizers were still trying to persuade Stanford and Cal to reconcile so the Big Game could be played there. Ultimately, though, they were not successful.[41]

Cal eventually decided to play its 1915 Big Game against the University of Washington; the Huskies won handily, 72–0, but the gate receipts were not insignificant and a closer rematch between the two schools gave Cal some hope.

Meanwhile, Stanford kept playing rugby and routed Santa Clara University 30–0 in the closest thing it had to a Big Game that year. Once Cal abandoned rugby, though, the well-intentioned reform was all but over. Many California high schools followed Berkeley's lead by going back to gridiron football. In October 1915 the *New York Times* proclaimed from afar that West Coast rugby was "Doomed." Stanford remained the last rugby stalwart, its faculty proclaiming that the university would never return to the American game. Nevertheless, East Coast observers noted that the general return to football would "bind the East and West more closely." Eventually, they thought, California teams would be good enough to play eastern schools again.[42]

In May 1916, Stanford students just barely chose to keep rugby, voting 441 to 392 against returning to American football. Even though the tide had nearly turned in Palo Alto, the Stanford administration was still not really willing to admit it. President Ray Lyman Wilbur carried on his predecessor's tradition (Jordan had retired in 1913) by calling American football a "menace." Wilbur asserted that the old game was run by coaches, not players. Coaches harbored a win-at-all-costs mentality and held secret practices, which made football "a power for harm."[43]

The United States entered World War I in April 1917, and the rugby experiment continued to unravel. It started with teams fielded by the Student Army Training Corps (SATC). The SATC was an organization—similar to today's Reserve Officer Training Corps, or ROTC—that used college and university campuses to train men for military leadership positions. The SATC was founded in 1917 and had 525 chapters throughout the United States, including both Stanford and Cal. By fall 1918, the "pigskin warriors" of Stanford's SATC played Cal's regular team in an American-style Big Game. The game was unofficial, since Stanford's team technically consisted of military personnel, not regular students. Students at Stanford even saw this match as an adjunct to military training.[44] Nevertheless, the SATC match did pave the way for football's return. By August 1919 Santa Clara dropped rugby and Stanford officially returned to gridiron football, playing the annual Big Game with California on November 22, 1919—one year and eleven days following the armistice that ended World War I.[45] The decision to return to American football was even supported by Stanford trustee Herbert Hoover, a noted engineer and wartime humanitarian who later served as US president from 1929 to 1933.[46]

The West Coast rugby experiment was a progressive reform with both regional and international roots. But by the late 1910s, international combat inspired nationalist sentiments in the United States, just like in many other nations around the globe. As many resources as possible—including cultural ones—had to be harnessed to strengthen national solidarity and identity. Indeed, it appears that Stanford's return to American football soon after the war's end was a way for the university to show that it was located firmly in the national mainstream. Many Americans did not like the idea that some universities were playing a "foreign" variety of football, rather than a home-grown variety. Football was deemed a sport that could prepare young men's bodies for the military service that would help the United States maintain international superiority. In the years following the war, many American universities even constructed massive, reinforced-concrete football stadiums that were either implicitly or explicitly designed as World War I memorials. Stanford and Cal were no exception.[47]

In the twenty-first century, Bay Area universities still enjoy tremendous success in intercollegiate rugby, a long-term result of their roughly decade-long abandonment of American football. It is important, though, to realize that the 1906–1919 rugby experiment was not just an aberration, a blip in an otherwise unbroken rivalry series. It was a result of the West Coast's contribution to a national discussion about football reform and progressive politics. Although this Pacific Rim-inspired reform did not supplant East Coast innovations like the NCAA and the forward pass, it does illustrate an important Bay Area episode in American sport history.

4

Bay to Breakers

The Original Fun Run

CLAIRE M. WILLIAMS

In a 1984 interview published in *Runner's World*, the race director of the Bay to Breakers is asked a seemingly simple question: "Why is this race different?" Terri Robbins's answer, in part, is as follows: "What makes the race unique to San Francisco is our leniency and our willingness to let runners express themselves on the course. We're not trying to run a heavily-guarded 'police state' race. We think there are many reasons people run in the *Examiner* Bay to Breakers: one is to win, one is to feel a great excitement in competing against others, and a lot of people run for the joy of being out in the open air."[1] Although accurate, this description of the uniqueness of the Bay to Breakers is as understated as the costumed participants are not. For example, one writer provides this warning to potential participants: "If you are claustrophobic or have a fear of large toothbrushes, the Bay to Breakers is not your race. But if it is companionship you desire or people with antennae that excite you—have we got a race for you!"[2] Along similar lines, in his seminal history of the Bay to Breakers, Leonard Wallach described the 1975 race as having a carnival atmosphere: "There were runners dressed as clowns, horses, cowboys, riverboat gamblers. There were women in long dresses and parasols, gays in drag, gentlemen in tuxedos, band masters in uniform."[3] In more recent races, many participants continue to dress in similarly colorful ways, or participate not dressed at all. Yet, the zaniness that we have come to expect at the annual Bay to Breakers footrace is only part of an athletic and social tradition that dates back more than a century.

The inaugural Bay to Breakers was run in 1912, making it the longest continuously run footrace in the United States.[4] While much has changed since the initial contest, some aspects have remained largely the same. The race's course continues to start on the Bay side of San Francisco near the Embarcadero and end on the Great Highway at the Pacific Ocean, winding its way from the "bay" to the "breakers." The distance, too, has remained mostly the same, though it was not until 1983 that the course was fixed at 12 kilometers (7.46 miles).[5]

In terms of change, two events stand out as perhaps most notable. The first is that until 1964, the event's moniker was the Cross City Race. While significant, the name change in and of itself is not necessarily noteworthy. The *reason* for the name change is of note: 1963's event had only fifteen participants, symptomatic of two decades of poor management and a historical low from which it was not clear that the race would survive. The second is a series of related events, in that race participation grew exponentially after the name changed to the Bay to Breakers and the *San Francisco Examiner* took over its sponsorship in 1966. In 1971, an official women's division was finally added to the race, and at the race's seventy-fifth anniversary in 1986, 110,000 participants set a Guinness World Record for the "largest footrace."[6] During this time the race's reputation for "belonging to the bacchants" as well as "belonging to the serious runners" was solidified, as was its alignment with San Francisco's broader reputation for being an "open, progressive, tolerant, and liberal city."[7]

In the twenty-first century, road races of various distances happen every weekend (and sometimes on weekdays) of the year throughout the United States. Participation in these events has skyrocketed, and women now outnumber men at every distance except the marathon.[8] Many of these races seek differentiation from one another through promises of unique finishing medals, continuous on-course entertainment, and/or distinctive themes. Yet, it is easy to forget that the ordinariness of running and jogging, as well as participation in road races themselves, is a relatively new phenomenon. As was the case with the Cross City Race, participation in such events has been both formally limited (e.g., through rules and regulations related to amateurism and sex) and informally limited (e.g., social norms), attracting only serious runners with intentions of racing to win. The Bay to Breakers helped democratize and make accessible what was once the purview of few, and sets the gold standard for market differentiation to which other races aspire. Most other races, however, lack the history and panache of San Francisco itself, such that the Bay to Breakers' "masquerade and costume ball is as much a part of the race as are the piers, pavement, and beach."[9]

This chapter will trace the history of the event, situating it within the context of its host city, San Francisco, as well as highlight the people, traditions, and moments of change that shape our present understanding of the Bay to Breakers.

The Cross City Race Gets Its Start (1912–1936)

According to Francis J. Mannix, when Hillard L. Baggerly, the sports editor for the *San Francisco Bulletin*, proposed the idea for the race his suggestion was met with universal support.[10] Baggerly's motivation to start the race was likely multi-faceted. By all accounts, the Cross City Race was a tool to foster civic pride as part of San Francisco's recovery from the great 1906 earthquake and resultant fires that devastated the city (nearly 500 city blocks were destroyed, approximately 3,000 residents died, and 200,000 were left homeless), as was San Francisco's 1915 Panama Pacific International Exposition, honoring the opening of the Panama Canal, of which the race was to be part.[11] The involvement of the *Bulletin* in its founding, however, is not surprising as newspapers during the early twentieth century played a vital role in the promotion and institutionalization of organized sports in the United States as a way to boost circulation.[12] Finally, Baggerly was no doubt familiar with the Dispea Race, first run in 1905. The Dispea started in Mill Valley in Marin County, just north of San Francisco, and ended at Stinson Beach, approximately seven hilly miles later. A subset of the Olympic Club, the oldest athletic club in the United States, sought to capitalize on a rising interest at the turn of the twentieth century for hiking, pedestrianism, and distance running. The Dipsea continues to be run annually.[13]

Mannix described the Cross City Race as a distance that "won't be too long or too short . . . [but is] long enough to be exciting."[14] Throughout the announcement for the first race, Mannix went to great lengths to champion the race's advantages, likely to attract area runners and to ensure success in its inaugural year: the six-mile course (the specific course had not yet been decided upon) "isn't much compared to some of the cross-country runs that have been held about here and it will be a great deal easier than some of them," "the easiest road will be taken," and "there will be trophies for club runners, university runners, school runners and unattached runners. This method is absolutely fair for every one and although the starting time will be the same, it is easy to see where the respective chances lie."[15] From its beginning, although even more true today, "everybody is welcomed."[16]

The Pacific Athletic Association (PAA) set the rules and regulations of the race. Participant entry forms were printed in the *Bulletin* and required race "applicants" to send in their completed entry form, including name, address, club affiliation, and PAA registration number, prior to the date of the race.[17] Early races were limited to men over eighteen who had lived in California for at least three months prior to the date of the race.[18] A prerace, on-site physical exam had to be passed, a requirement until the late 1960s when the number of participants made the practice prohibitive.[19] While entry to the race itself was free, participants had to be registered as amateur athletes with the PAA. Through the requirement of amateurism, race organizers adopted "a cardinal principle of American upper-class sporting ideology," such that the pastimes of ordinary people (who may wish or need to participate in athletics for pay) should be separate and distinct from the upper class (those who could afford to remain amateurs). At the time, the upper class looked down upon athletes who received payment for playing sports as they believed they did so with impure motivations (pay, not fair play); professional athletes were completely banned from participation.[20] When an entry fee to the race was added in 1978, it cost one dollar and registration with the Amateur Athletic Union (AAU) cost four dollars.[21]

The course for the race has remained largely unchanged since its inaugural running, although adjustments throughout its history (seven total) have been due to such factors as road construction.[22] Participants start on the Bay side of San Francisco near the Embarcadero, originally outside the Ferry Building, and now under the Bay Bridge. They start at the intersection of Howard and Main Street, take a right on Ninth Street, take a left up and over the challenging Hayes Street Hill with an 11 percent grade at its steepest point and past the iconic "Painted Ladies" of Alamo square (a row of Victorian homes built between 1892 and 1896), continue along Fell Street and the Golden Gate Panhandle, enter Golden Gate Park and run past the indifferent American bison who reside there (and have since 1890), and end on the Great Highway at Ocean Beach. A postrace dip in the Pacific Ocean is an unofficial race tradition for many.[23]

New Year's Day 1912 marked the first running of the Cross City Race and was slated to include 175 "fully trained athletes," although only 140 started the race and 120 finished. The *San Francisco Call* proclaimed that "most of the best known distance and cross country runners of this vicinity have entered,"[24] and the *Sausalito News* predicted that "a race to the Cliff House on New Year's day, when all the east is blanketed with snow, will be another boost for the land of sunshine, fruits, and flowers."[25] Although this type of race was common on the East Coast, this was the first of its kind in the West.[26] Thousands of spectators were expected at the finish line.[27]

Saint Mary's College of California (then located in Oakland and now located due east in Moraga) student Robert (Bobbie) Vlught won the inaugural Cross City Race in a time of 44:10, finishing only seconds before the second- (Oliver J. Millard) and third- (Edgar Stout) place finishers.[28] In addition to the close finish and significantly quicker finishing times than were first expected, at least three runners were disqualified from the race after allegations that they rode to the finish via machines proved true. Each received a six-month ban from racing to "think over [their] foolishness."[29] The following year, 126 participants finished the race. Vlught won in a time of 40:59, again beating Millard by mere seconds.[30] In 1914, Vlught purportedly slowed down just before finishing, allowing Millard to finish first. Vlught is alleged to have said: "I won it twice and it's time for someone

Saint Mary's College student Robert "Bobbie" Vlught wins the inaugural Cross City Race, January 1, 1912. *Courtesy Saint Mary's College of California.*

else to win."[31] Vlught graduated from Saint Mary's in 1913, in conjunction with the college's golden jubilee celebrations, and was granted a gold medal for "rapid calculation and speed and accuracy in manipulating the adding machine."[32]

In addition to individuals contending for awards, the Cross City Race included club competitions as well. The first five runners' finishing times for each club were added together and the lowest combined time took home the prize for the top club. The Olympic Club of San Francisco was a perennial favorite at the Cross City Race finishing as the top club in twenty of the first twenty-five races.[33] Throughout the years, a number of different clubs entered the competition (e.g., Italia Virtus, Unione Sportiva, Young Men's Hebrew Association [YMHA], Humboldt Club, Young Men's Christian Association [YMCA], Petaluma Spartans, Hawaiian Athletic Club, Berkeley Cal Club, Stockton Flying "A" Club, Santa Clara Valley Youth Village, West Valley Track Club, Mail Carriers Club).[34] In 1929, five member of the Japanese Showa Club entered the race, including V. Yamakawa, who had previously run the Cross City Race for the Humboldt Club in 1922.[35] In the early 1930s, members of the "Four Seasons Club, Showa Club, Catholic Filipino Club, Russian Club, Japanese Athletic Club, Druid Club, D'Artanga Club, and the Chinese Club" ran in the Cross City Race.[36] The variety of athletic clubs with entrants to the Cross City Race reflects the racial and ethnic diversity in California at the time and should come as no surprise as "sporting communities based on class, race, and ethnicity . . . helped to preserve traditional cultural patterns as well as serve as agencies for the formation of larger ethnic communities."[37] Furthermore, "sports could both ease the transition of ethnic groups into American society and aid them in protecting and even enhancing their distinctive identities."[38]

Just as Mannix promised in his article promoting the first event, the Cross City Race has included categories of competition. Such categories included high school (added in 1912), Army-Navy (1914), an A. G. Spaulding Company–sponsored Veteran's Cup for runners over forty years old (1914), and a Catholic Cup for the first student of a Catholic college to cross the line (1915). Other trophies were offered by the YMCA and the YMHA, to runners from out-of-town, and to unattached runners. In 1928, an award was added for the thirteenth-place runner, and a sweater was given to the eleventh-place finisher as well as to the fourteenth-place finisher.[39] In 1924, two new trophies were added to the race: the A. G. Spaulding Company, ubiquitous at the time and instrumental to the institutionalization of rules and equipment for a variety of sports, sponsored a trophy for the first person to reach the intersection of Fillmore and Golden Gate Avenue and Judge Matthew Brady sponsored a trophy for the first runner to enter Golden Gate Park.[40] Today, prizes are awarded in three divisions to both men and women: elite, Bay Area, and masters. A bonus is given to the fastest male and fastest female finisher to run from the base to the peak of Hayes (Street) Hill.[41]

For winning the Cross City Race, Vlught earned a trophy and the top twenty-five finishers "were awarded gold buttons to commemorate their great run."[42] In 1922, all who crossed the finish line in less than seventy-five minutes were awarded silver bars, and the top ten finishers were given free tickets to the circus.[43] In 1925, silver bars were replaced with silver medals.[44] Certificates were given to all participants, regardless of finishing time, starting in 1930.[45]

In the first twenty-five years of the race, the number of race finishers varied between a high of 126 in 1913 to a low of thirty-five in 1919 and 1927. The average number of finishers was sixty. The time between when the first racer crossed the finish line and when the last finisher crossed the finish line was quite small in comparison to today, reinforcing that in its early years, Cross City participants raced with the intent to move quickly and perhaps win in contrast to today. For example, in 1919 the difference between the first and last finishers was just under twenty-three minutes while in 2015, the difference was more than four hours.[46] Runners Oliver J. Millard (1914, 1915, and 1917) and William Churchill (1920, 1922, 1923, and 1924) were the most notable of the winners during this era with their many victories, and Fred McWilliams, in 1922, was the first African American participant.[47] In 1928, the first of many race date changes moved the event from New Year's Day to Sunday, January 29, to accommodate the growing interest in football, and in 1930 the race had its first sponsorship change from the *San Francisco Bulletin* to the *San Francisco News*.[48] Both changes foreshadowed the ways that the race dropped in importance to those organizing it, resulting in a stagnation of interest over the next quarter century of iterations. At its twenty-fifth anniversary in 1936, however, fifty-six finishers enjoyed the largest crowd of spectators in the event's history at 25,000.[49]

Era of Decline (1937–1961)

From 1937 until 1963, the average number of Cross City Race finishers per race was just thirty-five, with a high in 1940 at sixty-five participants and a low in 1963 at fifteen participants. Sponsorship changed several times from the *San Francisco News* (1930–1943), to the San Francisco Junior Chamber of Commerce (1944–1951), to the Twin Peaks Parlor (1952–1963). The San Francisco Junior Chamber of Commerce was a local organization dedicated to civic improvement, and the Twin Peaks Parlor was a chapter of the Native Sons of the Golden West, a historical and charitable organization comprised of Californians born in the state.[50] Notably, neither were newspapers. While the *San Francisco News* in later years also failed to cover and promote the Cross City Race adequately, during this era, newspapers were a primary forum for the promotion of sporting events. Without a newspaper inherently invested in its success, the Cross City Race faltered. Additionally, the decline in the number of participants can perhaps be attributed to attention paid to more pressing needs in relation to World War II followed by the reemergence in the 1950s of San Francisco's long-standing history of bohemianism. Thanks to the literary efforts of Lawrence Ferlinghetti, Allen Ginsberg, and Jack Kerouac, among many others, and the community radio station KPFA, which supported a "diversity of artistic and political expression,"[51] San Francisco became a countercultural mecca.

Furthermore, contributing to the decline in participation was the lack of apparent promotion of the race by its sponsors. In 1934, for example, aside from the occasional entry form printed in the paper, there was no mention in local papers until ten days beforehand, and in 1941, the entry form was not published until eleven days before the event and prerace publicity was almost completely absent.[52] In 1947, Prescott Sullivan of the *San Francisco Examiner* commented on this trend: "In late years [the Cross City Race] has sort of gone to pot, although never in the past was its decline so great as it has been this year: Credit for that must go to the Junior Chamber: When the young men of the Junior Chamber of Commerce took over; they talked big of what they were going to do. Then without turning a wheel, they promptly forgot the whole business. As a result the Cross City Race will start tomorrow at 9:30 a.m. with barely a line of advance notice unless you count this slight mention."[53] This lack of attention would continue in the years to come, and as a result of this inattention, the date of the Cross City Race became unpredictable. After the change in 1928 from New Year's Day to the end of January, the race was run in the months of February and March, and in 1943 the race was not run until October. In 1949, the race was run in May for the first time and, in 1962, the date was firmly set (and remains) as the third Sunday in May, although the AAU tried to move it around to accommodate their scheduling needs.[54]

Despite the fluctuation of race date and lack of attention, this era featured a number of repeat winners. Ed Preston (1938, 1939, and 1940), Fred Klein (1944, 1945, 1946, 1948), and Jesse Van Zant (1953, 1954, 1955, 1957) all proved their prowess with three or more wins each. If Van Zant had not forgotten to reset his clock in accordance with Daylight Savings Time in 1956 resulting in a missed race, he may have been able to add one more win to his name.[55] In 1950, Elywn Stribling of San Francisco, the first African American to win the race, did so in 42:57.[56] At the fiftieth anniversary of the race in 1961, thirty-one runners finished and Jack Marden of San José won with a time of 41:30. Coverage of the golden anniversary was neither celebrated nor properly acknowledged.

The Bay to Breakers Takes the Lead (1962–1986)

Although Herman Gene Gurule set a course record in 1963 finishing in a time of 40:15:07, that year's race was most notable for its historically low number of participants as well as being the last year of the Twin Peaks Parlor sponsorship.[57] After surviving its near collapse in 1963, the Bay to Breakers' current popularity, reputation, and embodiment of San Francisco's cultural liberalness was solidified in the two decades leading to its seventy-fifth anniversary in 1986. It was during this time that "groupies" began participating in the race, women were granted official entry, the word "centipede" took on new meaning, and a Guinness World Record was set in 1986 for the largest number of participants in a single footrace.[58]

New Sponsorships, Walter Daly, and the First Running Boom

In 1964, sponsorship of the Cross City Race returned to a newspaper, this time the *News Call-Bulletin*, a consolidation of previous San Francisco papers, two of which had been the race's founding sponsors. As part of the race's rebirth, the paper renamed the Cross City Race the Bay to Breakers, and a reporter from the paper named Walter Leslie Daley Jr. (or simply Walt Daley) began covering the race as part of his regular assignment.[59] In 1966, the *San Francisco Examiner* took over the *News-Call Bulletin* as well as sponsorship of the Bay to Breakers. Daley's continued and prolific coverage of the race, in combination with the first running boom in the United States, led to its rapid growth. For example, in 1966 Daley wrote of the race: "Eager-beaver runners—all sizes and ages—were mixed in with more experienced long-distance athletes today and posited for the starters gun . . . at last count it looked as though well over 200 runners would accept the challenge the race offered."[60] In fact, 277 racers would accept and finish the challenge, a nine-fold increase from its low only three years earlier. Also in 1966, "groupies," or groups of people who entered the race together and had office, neighborhood, or familial affiliations, began entering the race, frequently donning similar T-shirts, which should be considered the precursor to the costumed running that later became ever-present.[61]

Renewed attention to the race from its sponsor coincided with the first running boom in the United States, which occurred in the 1970s and early 1980s. Pamela Cooper argues in *The American Marathon* that part of the rise in popularity of long-distance running during this time can be attributed to the Cold War: Competition between the West and communist Eastern Bloc countries included success in athletics, and in this case, the realm of long-distance races.[62] International success by American runners such as Frank Shorter, winner of the 1972 Olympic marathon, Steve Prefontaine, antiestablishment cult hero, and Mary Decker (Slaney), owner of multiple world records, contributed to the popularity of the sport.[63] Six-time winner of the Bay to Breakers (1968–1973), Kenneth C. Moore, should also be named as one of these athletes.

Fitness rose in importance for nonelite and nonmilitary civilians as well. According to Darcy Plymire, "concerns about production and consumption patterns were at the heart of the dis-ease that fueled the running boom."[64] Running provided a vehicle through which white-collar workers could gain control over their lives. NASA scientist Kenneth Cooper's *Aerobics* (1968), Jim Fixx's *The Complete Book of Running* (1977), and George Sheehan's *Running and Being: The Total Experience* (1978) became wildly popular texts that provided information and motivation for individuals to improve themselves, a departure from previous health-related movements that focused on societal improvement.[65] Importantly, women joined the quest for self-sufficiency, and the assertion of physical prowess became part of the larger women's liberation movement.[66]

For the Bay to Breakers, new sponsorship and the running boom led to race sizes that expanded dramatically in a short amount of time. After record low participation in 1963, participation increased from 128 in 1964 to 804 in 1969. In 1971, the first year women were officially allowed to enter the race, there were 1,900 participants, and just five years later in 1976, the race was called "The Great Stampede" and had an estimated 8,000 finishers.[67] In 1981, 27,000 participated in the race,[68] and in 1986, at its diamond jubilee, the 110,000 total participants (only 78,769 registered) set a Guinness World Records for the World's Largest Footrace.[69]

Leonard Wallach was one of the people ushering the Bay to Breakers through this incredible growth, and resultant challenges such as a city council resolution in 1977 by then city supervisor Dianne Feinstein to ban it completely due to a perceived "lack of planning, including traffic control, street closures, emergency vehicles, police, fire, and ambulances."[70] Wallach ran his first Bay to Breakers in the late 1960s after retiring from a four-decades-long career with the US armed forces, during which time he served in three wars and received numerous awards for his service.[71] Then living in a San Francisco YMCA, a co-resident persuaded Wallach to run the race with him. Wallach recalls: "I ran it, and to say the least it was a profound experience. At the finish line, people—complete strangers—were embracing. These were the days when I didn't know anybody. I mean, I used to go to confession just to have somebody to talk to. This Bay to Breakers phenomenon fascinated me."[72] Although a distinct event from the 1967 Summer of Love, which brought thousands of people to San Francisco and "gave birth to, or helped solidify, several key movements—including the Free Speech, Gay Rights and Civil Rights movements," the Bay to Breakers began to reflect the free-spirited nature of San Francisco and its inhabitants during this time.[73]

Wallach began researching the historical origins of the race and eventually turned his feature story into a full-length book.[74] *The Human Race: Bay to Breakers, Largest Run for Fun in the World* was published in 1978 and chronicles, year by year, the first sixty-six years of the race. *The Human Race* also includes introductory chapters related to the race course and strategies for running a successful race, including the following related to sportswear: "You needn't spend a lot of money outfitting yourself to run. Buy the most economical sweat clothes, inexpensive running shorts and T-shirts . . . , and take your time before putting out too much money for shoes. In short, don't get caught up in running fashions," and the following in relation to the hazards of running: "A liberal application of petroleum jelly between the thighs and buttocks goes a long way to prevent chafing caused by heat or distance."[75] Wallach's "how-to" sections found within a historical text remind us, again, of how new running was to a wider population than it had been otherwise.

Now with a vested interest in the race and wealth of experience managing people, Wallach volunteered to take charge of the safety of the participants. In 1979, Wallach began his tenure as race director and became a recognized expert in "megarace" management, which included helping to direct the men's and women's marathons at the 1984 Olympic Games in Los Angeles.[76] Before Wallach took over the Bay to Breakers, there had been numerous instances of runners starting early and everyone else following, leading to a chaotic and unsafe start for those at the front.[77] In a particular effort to protect the elite athletes at the start of the Bay to Breakers from the masses, Wallach created a "Human Wall," which consisted of volunteers linking arms in an effort to separate the latter group from harming the former.[78]

One of the Bay to Breakers most directly inspired descendants is Sydney, Australia's City to Surf event. The 14km race started in 1971 after the editor of the *Sydney Sun* newspaper learned about the Bay to Breakers from one of the paper's correspondents, who was working in New York at the time, and decided to start its own "fun run" similarly encouraging costumed runners.[79] The first race featured just over 1,500 participants while recent races have impressively grown to 85,000.[80] The winner of the Bay to Breakers in 1971, Kenny Moore, was invited to Australia to compete in the City to Surf (he won), and the first Australian to cross the finish line was invited to San Francisco to compete in the Bay to Breakers in the following year.[81] This international runner exchange of the first American and Australian female and male finishers of each race continued until the mid-1990s.[82]

Women Participate Unofficially Then Officially

Historically, women and girls have been excluded from participation in sports and physical activity, and prohibition from competition in the Bay to Breakers is no exception.[83] Due to societal expectations of middle- and upper-class women, as well as the scientific belief of the harming effects of athletic participation on women's bodies, women's track and field events were not added to the Olympic Games until 1928.[84] At the conclusion of the 800-meter race, which was the longest women's running event contested, several women competitors fell to the ground after its conclusion, likely due to physical and emotional exhaustion.[85] Although common after men's races, as a result of misconceptions of women's physical capabilities, the 800-meter race, and any event longer, remained absent from the Olympic Games program until 1960. Furthermore, the AAU, which governed track and field events as well as other amateur sports for much of the twentieth century, "prohibited women from competing in any distance over 2.5 miles" prior to 1971.[86] Women's participation in road races in the 1960s and 1970s grew more quickly than in track and field because road races fell outside the purview of the AAU.[87] However by 1974, the AAU had changed its rules and hosted its own marathon championship race for select women runners. Finally, in 1984, the women's marathon was added to the Olympic Games program.[88]

Because the AAU sanctioned the Bay to Breakers, these prohibitions and misguided beliefs meant that women were excluded from the event completely for much of its existence. However, the first documented instance of a woman's participation in the event was Barbara (Bobbie) Jane Preston (née Burke), in 1940. Her soon to be husband, Edward C. Preston, won the race in 1938, 1939, and 1940.[89] Some consider Burke the first costumed participant as she dressed as a man in order to participate.[90] Others, however, consider the runner dressed as Captain Kidd in the same 1940 race as the first costumed participant. Either way, both the tradition of the costumed runner as well as women's official entry into the race took decades to take hold.

Under increased pressure to allow women entry into the race and changing attitudes toward women's participation in rigorous sport and physical activity, but still heeding the AAU's strict limits on distances sanctioned for women's participation, the Bay to Breakers added a mile and a half race for women in 1965 and 1966.[91] After the AAU increased the distance limit for women to ten miles, the Bay to Breakers added an official women's division in 1971, before which time unofficial women runners had already become commonplace.[92] Dr. Frances K. Conley won with a time of 50:45. As related in *Off Our Backs,* a news journal for, by, and about women: "After she won the 17.3 [*sic*] mile 'Bay to Breakers' footrace in San Francisco, the reporters asked Fran Conley two questions: was she married? and where was she from? Then they described her as a 'Palo Alto housewife.' She is Dr. Conley, a brain surgeon at Stanford University Hospital."[93] The youngest winner, male or female, was Mary Etta Boitano, who won in 1974, 1975, and 1976 at the ages of eleven, twelve, and thirteen, respectively, as well as in 1969 at the age of six before the official addition of a women's field.[94] In 1997, for the first time, the number of female participants was more than the number of male participants, a trend that continues today (e.g., in 2014, approximately 54 percent of runners were women).[95]

Centipedes

In the late 1970s, another group of runners were starting their own tradition, which would in 1986 (for men) and 1987 (for women) become officially sanctioned divisions for competition in the Bay to Breakers. In an interview with *California Track & Running News*, Dwayne "Peanut" Harms explained the origin of the "centipede," a group of thirteen runners tethered together, five feet apart from one another: "It was a group decision that we came up with at one of the Aggie Running Club meetings. The Aggie RC was an official university club at UC-Davis made up of competitive runners, faculty members, and community people. We ran every day, raced every weekend, and we were looking for something a little different to do. In 1978, we chartered a bus to go to the Breakers and we wanted to do something crazy, fun, and different. My next recollection is in the auxiliary gym at Davis, ripping up garbage bags, cutting holes in them, and attaching them together with tape." The name "centipede," the number of runners, and the distance apart from one another were completely arbitrary.[96]

In 1979, the *Nor-Cal Running Review* included the following centipede-related announcement: "The Aggie RC has announced the 1st Annual National Club Centipede Championships in conjunction with this year's Bay to Breakers. Teams must consist of thirteen runners with a 'floater' and must keep strictly to the rules set forth by the I.C.C.R. (International Council on Centipede Racing)." Interestingly, this notice is posted just above information related to the 1980 Olympic Marathon Trials with no hint of irony. After only a year's time, the centipede had gone from fun-loving shenanigans to serious business. Since its inaugural running, the Aggies Running Club has dominated both the men's and the women's centipede divisions, each winning the vast majority of races, although neither holds the record for the fastest course time. Participation on the Aggie Running Club centipedes is dependent upon membership in the club, unlike on some of the other teams who actively recruit fast participants.[97]

Today's centipedes have the option of running in either the "Fun Runner" (i.e., Velocipede: Men only; Speedypede: Women only; Splitpede: Coed. No more than 7 of one gender; Minipede: Youth, 9th grade or below, with 3 boys and 3 girls) or "Seeded" categories, each of which has its own set of rules "adopted by the International Centipede Congress long, long ago." In the "fun runner" categories, Twinkie feelers are required on each segment of the centipede and the final runner must wear a stinger. A 360-degree "Lenichi" turn, in which the entire group runs in a complete circle, is required. If a segment of the centipede cannot continue, "the replacement must give the centipede's official password to exclude unauthorized participants." For the "seeded" centipedes, these requirements are optional, but highly encouraged. Seeded centipede participants must meet strict qualifying standards in order to participate (i.e., Men: 42:30 12K; Women: 48:30 12K).[98] A notable moment in Bay to Breakers history is when, in 1981, "cupcake-cute" Janet Oehm beat the leading (men's) centipede marking the first time an elite female runner had done so.[99] The next woman to beat the first (men's) centipede, although many credit her with being the first woman to do so, was Joan Benoit Samuelson in 1985, winner of the first Women's Olympic Marathon. True to the spirit of the race and in honor of her home state of Maine, Samuelson wore lobster claw oven mitts on her hands as she "clawed her way to a course record."[100] The seriousness with which some people take the centipede division and the rules involved, coupled with its inherent silliness, capture the spirit of the Bay to Breakers well.

The Largest Footrace (Seventy-Fifth Anniversary)

The seventy-fifth running of the Bay to Breakers occurred on May 18, 1986. To commemorate the event, as well as its own twentieth year of race sponsorship, the *Examiner* published a guide to the anniversary titled *Breakers: The Magazine of the Examiner Bay to Breakers* and the CBS affiliate KPIX Channel 5 broadcast live from the event and then compiled a special highlight show hosted by Wayne Walker and Diana Nyad, noted marathon swimmer. *Breakers* captured the unique aspects of the Bay to Breakers, its celebrity status, as well as its inclusion of elite athletes. For example, it featured a welcome note from the *Examiner*'s editor and publisher, William R. Hearst, a brief history of the race, an introduction to the oldest participant (Ivor Welsh, age ninety-one, running his eighth straight), strategies for the top racers, San Francisco-based celebrities' commentary on the Bay to Breakers and on running in general (e.g., Robin Williams, Whoopi Goldberg, Huey Lewis, and Barbara Boxer), a feature on Ibrahim Hussein, who was vying for his third victory in a row, and advice for last-minute race preparation. KPIX Channel 5 posted reporters at the start and finish of the race as well as covered two spots within the course. Reporters also stayed with the lead male and female runners, one reporter was dedicated to interviewing the centipedes, and one followed runners in an electric truck searching for wacky costumes. Three helicopters also helped provide well-rounded coverage to the event in its largest year ever.[101]

In a 1983 interview, Len Wallach expressed his goal for the Bay to Breakers to have 100,000 officially registered participants at its seventy-fifth anniversary.[102]

Instead, the race reached 110,000 total participants with 78,769 officially registered and the reminder running as bandits (aka unregistered participants, an annual tradition at the Bay to Breakers).[103] *Breakers* projected that runners in 1986 would be 61 percent male and 39 percent female, over two-thirds of participants would be between the ages of twenty-one and forty, 42 percent would have a college-level education and 27 percent would have postgraduate education, and 42 percent ran only zero to ten miles per week with 35 percent running eleven to twenty miles per week. In brief, the vast majority of participants were young, well educated, and ran recreationally.[104] Costumes popular in 1986 followed recent topical, newsworthy events of the year, such as the centennial anniversary of the dedication of the Statue of Liberty, the sighting of Halley's Comet (visible from earth only every seventy-five years or so), and the Chernobyl nuclear disaster in the Ukraine.[105]

In addition to the record being broken for the most participants in a footrace, course finishing records were broken as well. Olympian Ed Eyestone won the men's race in a time of 34 minutes and 38.5 seconds, breaking Ibrahim Hussein's 1985 course record by just over 20 seconds. Olympian Grete Waitz won the women's race in a time of 38 minutes and 46 seconds, breaking Joan Benoit Samuelson's 1985 course record by 68.8 seconds. The Cal Aggies centipede team won, again, breaking their own record with a time of 38 minutes and 51.5 seconds, and for at least the second year in a row lost to the top female finisher, much to their chagrin. For winning the race, both Eyestone and Waitz won round-trip tickets to Paris as well as the use of a 1986 BMW for the year.[106]

The unprecedented growth of the Bay to Breakers (the race went from 27,000 participants in 1981 to 110,000 in 1986) did not come without its challenges, such as managing the sometimes conflicting needs of the elite athletes and the recreational runners. For example, in the mid-1970s, the elite athletes, who were invited to the race and started at the front, feared entering the race because it was "too dangerous" and "too disorganized" because there had been a stampede at the start and one year the field started seven or eight minutes early, catching many at the front off-guard.[107] In 1986, some top competitors from the Bay Area felt slighted and out-right ignored by the Bay to Breakers' recruitment of top international competitors. As quoted in an article by Caroline Scarborough, local runner Brad Hawthorne stated: "it's just as well, because to tell you the truth, the Bay to Breakers is getting a reputation around the United States as the all-star wrestling of running."[108] Some may argue that the roughness around the edges of the race has been part of its personality and charm from the beginning. While some of this remains, the subsequent three decades can best be characterized by the tension between the free spirit of the race and the competing desire by corporate sponsors and many San Franciscans for a more orderly event.

From Organized Chaos to Corporate Management (1987–2015)

The second running boom started in the 1990s and since then, the total number of road race finishers in the United States has increased 300 percent with women increasing their participation in events from 25 percent of finishers in 1990 to 57 percent in 2013.[109] In terms of actual number of participants in 2013, over 10.8 million women and over 8.1 million men finished road races and more women than men participated in all road race distances except the marathon.[110] With the increased level of participation has come the need for the professionalization of race management to ensure participant enjoyment as well as safety, especially in light of the bombings at the 2013 Boston Marathon. The Bay to Breakers has been no different. In the final decade of the twentieth century, the Bay to Breakers maintained its status quo by welcoming new, unique traditions as well as catering to increasingly elite participants. In the first part of the twenty-first century, however, the race has faced a number of challenges including a rotating door of race owners and title sponsors and a growing impatience for public intoxication and resultant poor behavior on race day. Efforts to manage complaints about the event led one group to accuse race organizers of attempting to "sanitize San Francisco 'culture' from the event" in the name of profit maximization.[111] This particular allegation should be considered alongside mounting fears that San Francisco may be "losing its soul," due to its proximity to Silicon Valley's technology industry and the influx of mostly young, white, and wealthy tech workers contributing to its gentrification by electing to live in San Francisco rather than in the valley.[112] What remains to be seen is how and in what ways the Bay to Breakers will continue to reflect the historical free spirit of San Francisco in the face of these challenges.

Twentieth Century Ends in Status Quo

From 1987 until 1999, participation in the Bay to Breakers remained consistently strong, with the *San Francisco Chronicle* reporting anywhere between 61,000 and 100,000 participants, including both those who had registered and those who had not, annually. The *San Francisco Examiner* remained the owner and title sponsor of the race, and themed costumes reflecting popular culture also thrived. In 1990, for example, disaster themed costumes were expected in observance of the October 1989 Loma Prieta earthquake that devastated the Bay Area, a fitting observance in light of the race's historical origins.[113] Although already almost one hundred years old, a number of notable race traditions got their start during this same time period.

First, in 1990, the Bay to Breakers began offering prize money (in addition to in-kind gifts) to its elite-level competitors as a way to attract high-performing athletes.[114] Although modest in relation to other professional sports (male and female winners in 2015 earned $3,000, and the largest single prize of $40,000 was awarded in 2009 to Kenyan Sammy Kirop Kitwara for winning the Battle to the Breakers, coming in first overall, being the fastest person to summit Hayes Street Hill, and for setting a course record), the prize money has served its purpose by inducing more road runners of a high caliber to participate.[115] Along these lines, the last time an American won the men's race was 1986 and the last time an American won the women's race was 1993.[116] From 1993 to 1996, the Bay to Breakers hosted the US 12-kilometer national championship road race as a way to attract top American talent; however, the Bay to Breakers no longer wanted to host this championship when, in 1997, USA Track and Field decided to host a men's 10-mile championship on the same day in New Jersey. Bay to Breakers organizers argued this move would dilute the men's field at their race and thus decided to take a stand against this decision by declining to host the 12k championship, which they have not done since.[117]

Second, in 1993, Ed Van Sicklin founded the Bare-2-Breakers, "a notoriously dysfunctional group of fun loving demonstrators who peaceably assemble only once per year as a 'political affiliation' of individuals to exercise their Civil and First Amendment rights of Free Speech."[118] While there had been nude runners before the founding of the Bare-2-Breakers, including Van Sicklin himself, this is the first known formal organization of nude runners. The group wears matching Bare-2-Breakers hats during the race in order to indicate their participation in a legally sanctioned expression of free speech. In their first year participating together, six of the naked runners were arrested, but not charged, as the arrests were later deemed illegal. In the early 2000s, race organizers tried to prohibit naked runners, however, restrictions seem always to have left loop-holes exempting the Bare-2-Breakers from their rules (e.g., naked running was prohibited, but Bare-2-Breakers members walk). As of February 1, 2013, nudity has been banned in San Francisco except for children under five years old and at city permitted events like the Bay to Breakers.[119] The judge in the case ruled that while "nudity is not inherently expressive," and thus protected speech, people have become accustomed to seeing naked people at events like the Bay to Breakers and, consequently, "are not 'unwillingly or unexpectedly exposed' to sights they'd rather not see."[120] It seems that for now naked runners, whether formally part of the Bare-2-Breakers group or not, may continue to practice their self-expression, although the ban on nudity for some has been considered antithetical to San Francisco's reputation for openness and yet another sign of San Francisco's changing culture.[121]

Third, in addition to the wacky costumed participants who run with the tide, the Bay to Breakers also features the "Salmon Run": a group of participants donning giant salmon costumes who run the race in reverse, from the breakers to the Bay, symbolically "spawning" at various points along the route. The San Francisco Cacophony Society, whose members were "in pursuit of shared experiences beyond the pale of mainstream society," started this tradition in 1994.[122]

Finally, the Bay to Breakers features a tradition in which participants toss tortillas in the air at the start of the race. The first known print reference to this tradition was in 1995 and the official origin of the tradition seems unknown to race officials.[123] One author opined that the start of the race resembled a concert and the soft shell tortillas replaced what otherwise would have been Frisbees accompanying the beach balls and balloons being hit back and forth by competitors.[124] Race officials have started to discourage the tossing of tortillas because they prove incredibly difficult to clean up after thousands of people have run and walked over them on their way to the starting line.[125]

Bay to Breakers in the Twenty-First Century

After more than thirty years with the same owner and title sponsor, since 2000, the Bay to Breakers has had three different owners and six title sponsors. In 2000, the Hearst Company sold the *San Francisco Examiner* to the Fang Family, owners and publishers of the *San Francisco Independent*, a free paper. Included in the sale was the Bay to Breakers trademark.[126] In 2004, Philip Anschutz bought the *San Francisco Examiner*, including the Bay to Breakers, which his company, the Anschutz Entertainment Group (AEG), then operated until 2013.[127] In October of 2013, the Wasserman Media Group bought the Bay to Breakers race from AEG.[128] After the *Examiner* was dropped from the title of the race in 2002, Albertsons (2003–2005), ING (2006–2010), Zazzle (2011–2012), Zozi (2014), and Zappos (2015) have all been title sponsors of the race. In 2013, the event lacked a title sponsor, although Craigslist signed on in the months leading up to the race as a presenting sponsor (i.e., Bay to Breakers presented by Craigslist).[129] These shifts in ownership and sponsorship are likely due more generally to the increasing sophistication of sport sponsorship (i.e., sponsors now more than ever want to see measurable returns on their investments) and more specifically due to the fear of harm to sponsors' brands from the ongoing challenges of organizing "the world's longest party."[130] For example, unofficially, ING decided not to renew its five-year sponsorship due to the bad publicity the race had garnered in relation to "revelers and runners urinating, defecating and generally behaving rudely."[131] Furthermore, in 2013, a man attending a Bay to Breakers party fell from the roof of a four-story building to his death.[132]

According to at least one participant, the 2008 race was the "booziest" he had seen in his nine years of participation contributing to San Francisco residents' increased weariness of Bay to Breakers participants and spectators making ready use of lawns and flowerbeds to relieve themselves.[133] In response to these concerns, in 2009, race organizers tried to ban all alcohol, nudity, and floats (somewhat commonly configured to transport kegs filled with beer). After public outcry at these restrictions, a compromise was achieved in that only glass bottles and floats with kegs were banned and floats had to be officially registered.[134] In 2010, the same bans existed and a $250 entry fee for each float was added to help defray race-related expenses.[135] For the one hundredth anniversary of the event in 2011, there was widespread concern that the race had run its course as it took organizers months to find a title sponsor after ING decided not to renew its contract. Instead, the race garnered more participants than it had in recent years with 43,945 registered finishers and continued its trend toward restrictiveness by banning all alcohol and floats, moving the race start time to 7 a.m., and adding additional fencing, particularly along the Golden Gate Panhandle, to discourage participants from leaving the course to urinate or otherwise.[136]

The aforementioned efforts seem to have addressed some of the complaints related with the event, but certainly not all, and not everyone agrees with the changes. In 2009, San Franciscans concerned with the bans founded the grassroots organization Citizens for the Preservation of the Bay2Breakers to "preserve the fun" that they saw being taken out of the race by its corporate sponsors.[137] One seemingly simple solution for which the group has advocated is an increase in the number of portable toilets on the race course in order to decrease the occurrence of public urination. At the 2015 event, 1,100 portable toilets were made available, a notable increase from 2008 when there were only 537 (equal to one toilet for every 111 of the estimated participants that year).[138] While recreational racers debated various restrictions, elite runners were busy setting course records. In 2009, Kenyan Sammy Kitwara Kirop finished the men's race in 33:31, and in 2010, Kenyan Lineth Chepkurui finished the women's race in 38:07.[139]

A significant turning point for the Bay to Breakers, as well as mega races worldwide, in relation to race management, was the bombings at the 2013 Boston Marathon which killed three people and injured more than 260.[140] Occurring just over a month before the Bay to Breakers that year, race organizers had to quickly decide how to proceed. Several security measures were put in place, including an increased police presence at the race, replacement of trash cans with clear receptacles, and temporary surveillance cameras. Additionally, opaque bags larger than 8.5" x 11" x 4" were banned, allowing only for smaller transparent bags. Unregistered runners were also banned from the race, although some undoubtedly made their way from start to finish without being removed from the course.[141] Perhaps unsurprisingly, 2013 was deemed the cleanest in years as participants were not able to carry as much with them.

Conclusion

In recent years, the Bay to Breakers can be characterized by its tension between the desire to maintain its reputation for the eccentric and its need for greater risk management strategies in light of real or perceived terrorist threats. Additionally, it has yet to be seen how a changing and gentrifying San Francisco in which "the median monthly rent is already the highest in the country and is still increasing at a rate three times the national average"[142] will affect the event. As San Francisco works to (re)define itself in relation to its newest residents, the Bay to Breakers provides a connection to the city's past that should provide a reminder of the many ways that the city has changed over time for better and for worse. While the future of both San Francisco and the Bay to Breakers is unclear, what is clear is that even after more than one hundred races it has not lost its celebratory nature, and as the longest continually run footrace in the United States there are many notable winners yet to cross the finish line and traditions yet to be established.

Notable Course Records (through 2015)

Fastest Woman	Lineth Chepkurui, Kenya	38:07 (2010)
Fastest Man	Sammy Kitwara, Kenya	33:31 (2009)
Most Wins (Women)	Laurie Binder, USA (4)	1979–1980, 1982–1983
Most Wins (Men)	Kenneth Moore, USA (6)	1968–1973
Fastest Centipede (Women)	Impala Racing Team	46:37 (2012)
Fastest Centipede (Men)	Team LinkedIn	36:44 (2012)
Most Wins (Centipede, Women)	Aggie Running Club	24 (of 29 total)
Most Wins (Centipede, Men)	Aggie Running Club	30 (of 38 total)
Largest Footrace (Guinness World Record)	110,000	1986

5

Protecting the People's Mountain

Hiking in Marin County and the Roots of American Environmentalism

LINDA L. IVEY

In 1920, a core of the civic leadership in Mill Valley, California, was up in arms. There was a scourge facing their pristine town, a haven of natural beauty within mere miles of the city of San Francisco. They were organizing local voices, determined to see that "something may be done to rid the county of this evil of which we complain." In front of the Marin County Board of Supervisors, representatives of thirty-six different organizations spoke out against and asked for assistance to get rid of "a certain kind of hiker," whose conduct could only be described as "reprehensible."[1]

Local newspapers at the time had been reporting on what had been tagged "the hiking problem." There were dozens of eyewitness accounts of "unseemly" behavior by "unchaperoned parties of youngsters who spent the night on the trail."[2] Further, flowers "gathered ruthlessly by picnickers,"[3] and "lunch remnants, tin cans, cartons, and newspapers (left) as evidence that (picnickers) enjoyed a good lunch"[4] were increasingly seen as disrespectful and destructive behavior on the part of weekend *tourist-hikers*.[5] Although in retrospect concerns about aggressive flower picking may seem silly, the more serious issues emerged over time, with concerns about trail safety, protection of plant life, and fire suppression. Dedicated members of local hiking clubs, a different group of hikers who ostensibly had fostered a deeper affection and appreciation for the wilderness in Marin, made it their mission to educate the tourist-hiker, and by extension, protect their natural environment.

Around the turn of the twentieth century, Mill Valley was host to a number of such hiking clubs. For the most part, these clubs began as basic activity-oriented social groups, but in the face of the evolving "hiker problem" grew into a highly organized base of environmentalism in northern California. This chapter suggests that the intimacy of hiking bonded these regular hikers in a specific way to their local surroundings, inspiring a protectionist impulse. Club membership developed an identity as "stewards of the land"; their role in protecting the local environment began with concerns about littering and trespassing, and was transformed into one of teacher and promoter of environmental awareness, appreciation and guardianship of wild spaces, and a sustainability ethic within the environmental tourist industry. Perhaps unexpectedly in this history of hiking in Marin, we find the seeds of environmentalism in the United States.[6]

Hiking in Marin

Hiking has a fairly deep history in Marin County. "Hiking"—as a conscientious activity defined somewhat in correlation with being in the wilderness, but particularly in opposition to a sedentary, urban lifestyle—first appears as a distinctive leisure time activity in Marin County near the end of the nineteenth century. Residents of Mill Valley in the southern part of Marin structured their leisure time around hiking up the majestic 2,500-foot Mount Tamalpais looming over their town, as well as on local trails into nearby redwood forests and down to Pacific coast beaches. But a key part of understanding the story of hiking in Marin is that residents also built their businesses around these natural attractions. Just a short ferry ride north across the San Francisco Bay, Marin's natural environment enticed city dwellers who wanted a getaway from the urban pace of San Francisco. Outdoor pursuits such as hiking underlined the early economy of this area, supported by visitors that reportedly came by the thousands on weekends during the summer months.

Hiking, or walking—terms sometimes differentiated on the basis of rigor, or time spent, or the wildness of the setting—can arguably be distinguished from other forms of outdoor recreation by its slowness, its meditative quality, its intimacy with place. The focus is on the personal, and while certainly on more treacherous trails athletic skills may be vital, most anyone can hike to some degree, at any moment, and commune with the outdoors according to their personal desire. In her 2001 book *Wanderlust: A History of Walking*, environmental writer Rebecca Solnit writes:

> [T]he subject of walking is, in some sense, about how we invest universal acts with particular meanings. Like eating or breathing, it can be invested with wildly

> different cultural meanings, from the erotic to the spiritual, from the revolutionary to the artistic. . . . (The history of hiking) begins to become a part of the history of the imagination and the culture, of what kind of pleasure, freedom, and meaning are pursued at different times by different kinds of walkers. That imagination has both shaped and been shaped by the spaces it passes through on two feet.[7]

In essence, this chapter investigates the meaning that devoted hikers have found in the act of hiking in Marin County, and considers the impact that hiking has had on the local imagination. Solnit begins this particular book wandering through the Marin Coast of the late twentieth century, appreciating the protected open space, and pondering its meaning to "people like me who are heirs to the cultural tradition of walking in the landscape for pleasure."[8] This was likely written in a universal sense, but specifically, she could not have been more on point. The intimacy of this local relationship with Mount Tam, the trails to the coast, and the redwoods surrounding Mill Valley laid the foundation for hiking to become something more than a casual walk in a pretty setting.

In fact, hiking in Marin has long been embedded with deeper meanings. Hiking has been a pastime. It has been a means of locomotion, of getting from one place to another in the days before prolific autos, and where kids traipsed to Stinson Beach or up Mount Tam as a way to spend their summer day. It has been an economy, bringing in city dollars. It has been a cause for concern, when these tourists brought suspect behavior and attire, and left visible and unwanted evidence of their sojourns.

In Marin, hiking has also been an identity. Initially, to be the "right kind" of hiker one was a local, who knew the complex geography of trails big and tiny, up the mountain and down, between houses and back and forth to beaches and hidden lagoons. But the identity of hiker—like most identities—was not static. San Francisco day hikers may have been seen initially by locals as a group apart, but so many returned frequently, regularly, and became as attached to the mountain as anyone. In the intimacy of hiking, these weekend regulars developed an attachment to this place as deep as those who called it home. As such, locals and weekenders co-developed a most notable identity of hikers in Marin—that of protectors.

By the 1920s, the "hikers of Marin" were a mixture of locals, transplants, and regular city sojourners, bonded by a love for Mount Tam and its surroundings, and by a mission to protect what they called "the People's Mountain." They were impassioned, on a self-proclaimed duty to "save the mountain." From what or whom were they saving it? The short answer is: those *other* hikers previously mentioned—those *tourist-hikers* who ostensibly did not share the deep love and concern for the health and vibrancy of this natural region. The long answer speaks to a growing sense in the United States of protecting and respecting the wild spaces we had previously sought to tame and develop. In this odd little story about hiking, nature, economy, and identity, we can see how and why some people come to fight for their local environment (and the environment in general), and find a bit of what spurs the green within us all.

A Sense of Place

The San Francisco Bay Area holds bragging rights to some of the most stunning natural scenery in the United States. Marin County in particular boasts scenic overlooks of the Bay, the city, and the rugged Pacific coast. Over five hundred miles of spectacularly vistaed trails are a hiker's paradise. Perhaps most striking today is the amount of anomalous protected space in the high stakes real estate market of the San Francisco Bay Area. The Golden Gate National Recreation Area covers over 75,000 acres of open space, much of it in Marin County. This is no coincidence.

At the heart of this conservation, and this tale of hiking, is the town of Mill Valley. Officially established in 1890 with land designated by the Tamalpais Land and Water Company, Mill Valley's beginnings were largely inspired by a railroad spur that had been built out from functioning line in Marin County.[9] By many accounts, the town was founded with tourism in mind, and with the hope of building a local economy around visitors to Mount Tam.[10] In 1896, local developers built the Mill Valley and Mount Tamalpais Scenic Railway, a spur from Mill Valley to the peak of Mount Tam, specifically catering to the tourist clientele. It was dubbed "the Crookedest Railroad in the World," and by 1902 featured the "gravity car" as a thrilling if not seemingly risky way down from the peak (locals recall the frequency with which the gravity car jumped the tracks).[11] Just as the name describes, tourists flew down from the peak by sheer gravity, with only a brake to navigate the car down the curving tracks. If nothing else, it was a tourist attraction to be sure. In 1907, after the establishment of Muir Woods National Monument, an additional railroad spur was built to Muir Woods, and the railway was renamed the Mount Tamalpais and Muir Woods Railway.[12] Between these attractions and the physical beauty to which they afforded access, a day trip to Mill Valley for visitors to San Francisco was promoted as an excursion not to be missed.

But Mill Valley was not a tourist stop alone. It was a small town at heart, defined by its local families and a seemingly romantic attachment to their place at the foot of the mountain. The sense of tight-knit community can be gleaned from oral histories conducted with longtime residents of Mill Valley, a community that was intertwined with its local environment. The "outdoor spirit" seemed to

Residents of Mill Valley, California, at once treasured and profited from the beauty of their natural surroundings. The Gravity Train down Mount Tam symbolized the extraordinary local tourist industry that flourished around the love of hiking. *Courtesy of the Lucretia Little Room, Mill Valley Public Library.*

weave throughout childhood memories, and included skinny-dipping, baseball, boy scouts, and to be certain, hiking.[13] As local resident Shayer Robinson recalled:

> Kids in the early days—our fun was to do what we called hiking. We didn't hike because we liked to walk but because we *had* to hike if we wanted to go somewhere . . . It wasn't unusual for kids to leave Friday afternoon and not get back till late Sunday night. We'd go over (to Stinson) with a blanket and some food and just fiddle around the beach, with big bonfires. Muir Woods . . . was a popular place to go. Not that kids had any particular interest in seeing the big trees, after they'd seen them once! But in the absence of modern forms of entertainment . . . it was entertaining just to be going somewhere.[14]

Historically, local residents visited the now well-trod destinations as much as any weekender—Redwood Canyon (Muir Woods before it was a National Monument); the "Big Lagoon" or "Bellow Beach" (Muir Beach); Willow Camp (Stinson Beach). These magnets for tourists were spots to which kids would hike on any given weekday—then run naked, play ball, camp out. They would think nothing of an evening hike up Mount Tam "just for the exercise."[15] These places were their backyard. Local George Pimlott recollected that he "used to do a lot of hiking . . . I'd hike bare foot over to Muir Woods, sometimes to show people the way."[16] And while generally speaking it seems the tourist "traps" were not of interest to locals (who easily climbed Mount Tam and would never bother to take a train) sometimes the temptation was too much. Pimlott recalled climbing aboard the gravity cars if there were no other passengers and ringing the bell down the whole mountain. High school students would sometimes charter a train car to take friends to the top of the mountain for a dance in the Tavern on top, dance until midnight in the moonlight and take the gravity cars home.[17]

Recollections about the early days of hiking also reveal among community members an almost encyclopedic knowledge of the trails in and around the town and the mountain. They recall short cuts, side trails to good water sources, innumerable little trails through and around the town, and the paths to take to avoid the tourists. They knew the trickiest trails to avoid and the most beautiful paths to seek out. They had an intricate sense of place. Recalling music, family hikes and donkey rides, horseback riding and the like, local Karen Connelly recalled, "we just had good, simple times."[18] Local resident Shayer Robinson similarly mused:

> It was a simple life, and families all joined in. There were lots of picnics and Sunday gatherings of families and that type of thing. It seemed a much closer knit community. . . . [T]here seemed to be a kind of community spirit, a general community getting-together. Everybody seemed to trust his neighbor to do the things that needed to be done. Most of these things weren't formalized until later, and then they became committees and agencies and other things.[19]

The caring for the local place, at least in local memory, was rooted in this sense of a tight-knit community and a shared space. These efforts had to become "formalized" as Mill Valley hosted more and more crowds on the weekends, those visitors that locals perceived as less invested and less respectful.

The residents' sense of community entangled in the landscape of Mill Valley was also affected by the local economy—one based largely on a tourist industry that brought thousands into this small town to enjoy the beauty of the place. Local businesses grew up alongside the scenic railway and the tourist industry, including mountain top inns and taverns and other amenities designed for the hiking set. Even the train schedule catered to the regular visitors from San Francisco, with the last gravity car left the mountaintop about 4 p.m., meeting up with the train arriving from Muir Woods (after 1907), so the weekend visitors could begin their trek back to the city via rail and ferry. Weekends were certainly the busiest times for Mill Valley, whether hikers stayed overnight or came just for the day on Sunday.[20]

There were community-oriented businesses—drugstores, groceries, barbershops—that were supported by full-time residents.[21] But the preponderance of local entrepreneurs targeted the weekend surge of visitors. Tourist businesses ran the gamut from well-established restaurants and hotels—some seasonal, some year-round—to camping sites and rented cottages. Smaller businesses, including ice cream stands and little concessions, were strategically located: kids would sell chocolate bars and lemonade along the trails, and knowing that "city slickers" would head to Muir Woods via the Cascade Trails and the big steps, the Grethel family had a little soft-drink stand at the end of the trip.[22] Another local institution, a Mr. Agezelow, sold peanuts and ice cream in Old Mill Park, and also had little businesses throughout the region—his older son would even meet the trains with a bag around his neck to sell peanuts.[23] More sizable businesses came in varied forms beyond the tavern or inn. The Dowd's rented donkeys for 25 cents an hour; the donkeys would hike along with visitors, and carry their packs (and locals, for that matter).[24] One notable business was Barth's Retreat—also known as the Hikers' Retreat—run by the Odlin family. It housed a couple dozen lockers and showers for day hikers to use when they arrived in Mill Valley and before heading back to the city.[25]

Mill Valley was a quiet hometown, about five days a week. But to sustain its economy, the town endured—and aggressively invited—a massive transition nearly every weekend of the year.

No Tourist Should Fail to Visit

Advertisements deeming the necessity of visiting the beauty of Mount Tam, or the World's Crookedest Railroad, filled local publications and drew thousands of visitors during the weekend into Mill Valley's restaurants, hotels, and campgrounds, and boosted local economies ranging from roadside stands to donkey rides to the railroad itself. Full-page ads promoted the Mount Tam–Muir Woods excursion from San Francisco as one "no tourist should fail to visit." With round-trip rail starting at $1.90, magazine readers were encouraged to inquire about the "indescribable and ever-changing kaleidoscope of enthralling scenic effect" at their hotels.[26] Local business marketed tie-ins: Mario Hardware Co., for one example, promoted specials on certain items, "just the things you need for those week-end hiking and auto trips."[27]

The promotion of Marin hiking did not stop with physical attractions. Hikers also widely and proudly extolled their recreation as healthful to body and soul. At base, hiking was promoted for exercise, but also as a healthful way of "giving to the mind change of thought," simply by getting into a new environment.[28] The endorsement spoke to more than a promotion of their hobby or their local industries. It reflects a philosophical, turn-of-the-century concern of what was happening to the American as the country quickly industrialized and urbanized. In the context of the emergence of a "modern" San Francisco, hiking clubs in Marin published newsletters and promotional tracts to encourage public participation in the "out of doors." As one editor wrote, "the song of the open road, the lore of the wild, the cry of out of doors has been the sanest, most hopeful, most reassuring, amid all the notes of the feverish latter day of city herding and scrambling for gold in the crowded market places."[29] These voices joined back-to-the-land advocates and writers in espousing a reconnection with the tradition of a rugged American frontiersman, eschewing a lesser-American coddled by the conveniences of modern urban living. Hiking advocates claimed, "Substantial gains come from an enjoyment of the beauty of nature," and suggests, "If, then, we would have a sane and hardy manhood in our civilization, let us preach the gospel of the simple life, the joy of the hills, the power of nature."[30]

Indeed for urbanites, hiking was presented as a direct path back to the healthfulness of a life before civility softened us, and as a way to "put more 'God' into these man-made mechanisms" found in developed metropolitan life and solve "part of the larger problem of conservation—the conservation of human values."[31] Local hiking clubs encouraged urban visitors to engage, with headlines in hiking newsletters proclaiming, for example, "Saturday Hikes Good for Business Men." The benefits were promoted as good for body and mind and inevitably individual success, as "walking in the country enables a man to put aside his business troubles, and thus it acts as a quieting influence on the nerves. The man returns from the walk with a broader view and a calmer understanding of life's problems."[32] Advocates argued for the mental health of an outdoors experience:

> The discovery, or shall we say the rediscovery, of out-of-doors is an exploit of men and women immured with the walls of city life. The vision comes clearest to those withdrawn from continuous touch with the natural elements and to such the revelation has all the charm and zest of original adventure, of discovery that can be made for one's self alone. . . . One of the results of modern urban life is a new way of looking at nature. From the strains and stresses of a concerted mental and nervous existence we turn with relief to the green trees, the rolling hillsides, the rushing streams, the wildwood pathways.[33]

The promotion of hiking and outdoor activity in Marin brought the locals woes as well. Mill Valley increasingly faced the issues arising from "the hiking problem"—that incoming day folk who did not invest in the spiritual nature of the hike, or develop the attachment that regulars club members did, brought trouble for the environment. There was, in effect, a community-wide love/hate relationship with the tourist-hiker who kept the economy afloat but kept the folks aflutter. For Mill Valley residents, there were clearly two kinds of hikers.

The Root of the "Problem"

The weekend overcrowding of Mill Valley was the tip of the iceberg, but a significant issue nonetheless. Mill Valley residents remember "the early days" as a time where their small town swelled to hold a zoo of outsiders on the weekends. The numbers locals recall vary, but nonetheless give you a sense of the scene, and of how that tourist influx was perceived. One local recalled, "In the early days as many as eight and ten train cars would come into Mill Valley on a Sunday. There might be five or six thousand people. They'd take off and go hiking all over the place."[34] Another remembered that "they came by the thousands. You could hardly walk through the streets for the people starting for hikes on the mountain."[35] Local resident Keith McLellan remembered specifically how this prompted local vigilance in containing the impact: "the hikers became so numerous on Sundays that a Mr. Davis, who lived near Kenilworth, became sort of self-appointed deputy and wore a badge and turned back hikers so they could no longer go up Throckmorton Avenue. They had to go back to the Old Mill Trail, which is now the Dipsea Trail, in order to do their hiking."[36]

The "us vs. them" dichotomy between locals and tourist-hikers existed, but was not dye-cast. Many visitors were such regulars they came to adopt Mill Valley as their place. Some of the perceived divisions were lighthearted—children watching the hikers come in and giggling at the funny ways they dressed. Virginia George remembers the "costumes" that visiting hikers felt the need to don—short pants and knapsacks, which at the time, and for locals who hiked regularly as a nonevent, seemed a bit over the top.[37] As another example, when women began wearing pants and boots to hike (rather than long skirts and heels), the stares and the critiques spiked. One letter writer to a San Francisco newspaper "advocated the employment of chaperones to patrol the trails for the purpose of protecting young men from women who wear knickerbockers."[38] Locals also revealed a degree of disdain in letting tourists suffer the consequences of their inexperience. George recalled seeing hikers return from the mountain on their way to catch the train to the city "carrying these big bouquets of what they thought was a beautiful red plant. Well, it was poison oak. We were so stinking as kids, we wouldn't let them know what they were carrying."[39]

Rash-inducing or not, the sampling of local flora actually grew to be quite a point of contention. The sense was that visitors would pick local flowers and greenery as part of their "nature getaway"—and the reality was that they would often discard them on the side of the road before getting home. The "littering" aspect of this was an early irritant among Mill Valley locals, but so was the concern that "natural beauty was being destroyed."[40] The concern was described in terms of preserving a pretty landscape—with clear dismay directed at the person, the infringer, who did not respect the land and landscape the way a local or regular hiker did.

Locals also targeted weekenders with a running commentary on morality and the *behavior* residents hoped to keep out. One element of the "problem hiker" had to do with the frivolity or friskiness of youth. Local papers reported break-ins along the trail, but more often there was concern about simply being rude. In 1920, the *Marin Journal* reported on boys from San Rafael spending the night in the local jail on a charge of disturbing the peace. The boys' testimony revealed that they "had conducted themselves in a more or less boisterous manner . . . also that some of them had 'tasted' the contents of two bottles which they carried on their hiking trip. The contents proved to be wine."[41] The following year the *Sausalito News* reported on "young rowdies of San Francisco" who had boarded the Sunday ferry "under the impression that they could be rough and vulgar on the Mill Valley train," and were "deported" back to the city.[42] These behavioral complaints were the early stages of the problems associated with disinvested visitors. But they were enough to begin the movement to organize local groups to protect their natural surroundings. Local newspapers alerted the community of the growing problem at hand, and the move to address it:

> CONDUCT OF HIKERS UNDER DISCUSSION
>
> The "mountain week ender" problem has become a serious one to the welfare organizations of Marin county and San Francisco, who have to do with the task of directing the conduct of children, young men and the young women. A large meeting was held Tuesday afternoon in San Francisco and attended by several Mill Valley people, at which plans for curbing the tendencies to misbehave of young hikers, were discussed. At the conclusion of the meeting it was decided to hold another gathering . . . at which concrete measures for coping with the evil will be settled upon.[43]

Although weekend tourism was problematic and concerning to locals, the story of Mill Valley and the burgeoning Mount Tam protectorate should not be read as a simple story of a beautiful town in a fight against being overrun by tourists. The development of the hiking industry and the concomitant growth of environmental concern in Marin were not separate phenomena from urban development in San Francisco, at least not in a cultural sense. As geographer Richard Walker argued in his historical geography of the San Francisco Bay Area, "the city and the country co-evolve."[44] Marin became an escape *as* the city grew and this identity of place and the identity of the local culture were formed in tandem with San Francisco's urban development after the gold rush. The hiking culture was at once pulling crowds in and developing a mindset that was wary of those crowds and their impact on the landscape.

It is also important to consider the historical context of San Francisco's development, just a few miles away. By the end of the nineteenth century, the city had pulled out of its gold rush growth frenzy and become a prominent and increasingly sophisticated urban center of the West Coast. Walker describes the approximately 250,000 strong population of San Francisco at that point as "settled, wealthy and bourgeois," and "nurturing a new found love for travel, outdoor recreation and natural scenery."[45] Historian Marguerite Shaffer elaborates on this idea, arguing that by the turn of the twentieth century, tourist industries had "manufactured and marketed America as 'nature's nation,' defining a history and tradition that manifested an indigenous national identity sanctioned by God and inscribed across the natural landscape."[46] As this fascination with the landscape as vacation destination took hold, the natural environment was seen by many Americans as a "public birthright," and the fight against privatization took on a tone that was pro-open space, pro-public access, and in support of the right of the people to play in the land.[47]

Mill Valley hikers supported the call for open space and for public access. They did not want to limit access to the natural landscape of Marin. They did, however, express a desire to educate those who came to the open space that constituted their hometown, their back yards.

Protecting the People's Mountain

In 1916, an article on the nearby sheltered beach town of Bolinas extolled the town as "the ideal spot for rest: there are no crowds, no 'attractions'" and further notes that "there are rumors of trolley lines and railroads that shall sometime reach Bolinas, but the lovers of the little haven of rest shrink from the possibility of the crowds and rush."[48] Contemporary culture in Bolinas remains notoriously similar, with stories of confiscated directional road signs and other efforts to keep out the crowds. Why would there be such hostility toward the outsiders wanting to see the beauty of your fortunately located hometown?

The hiking enthusiasts and nature protectors throughout Marin faced the dilemma that was wrestled with by naturalists from John Muir to Aldo Leopold, from the turn of the twentieth century on. The natural beauty of the United States had come to be seen as a birthright for Americans, and much of the rhetoric surrounding early twentieth-century environmentalism was about the right of the public to enjoy the natural scenery of the country and not have it locked up by private ownership. But early nature tourism economies such as we find in Mill Valley quickly felt the tension between opening up the beauty of natural destinations for all Americans, and the impact of the tourists on the fragile ecology of these places. In Mill Valley, a movement led by local hiking clubs promoted both the public right to the open spaces in Marin, but also the duty of those visitors to take care of the places they visited. Up through the 1910s, these clubs led to work in making Mount Tam a fully public space. When this battle was successfully engineered, their mission shifted to protecting this commons and teaching the gospel of wildlife and wilderness protection to the visitor tourists of Marin County.

The complaints about the tourist-hikers had become familiar by the turn of the twentieth century: the crowds, the trash, the ruthless flower picking . . . by 1902, the fight on the part of Mill Valley residents to protect their home turf from the carelessness of visitors began to take formal shape. Local resident Kathleen Connelly remembered when the visible impact prompted a call to action: "A group of women got quite concerned over the condition in which the visitors left the valley after their day's outing. The women felt something must be done about so much of the natural beauty being destroyed."[49] A headline in the local paper signaled the call: "Outdoor Art Club Formed in Indignation Over Destruction of Plant Life." The new mission was shaped by a singular question: "How can we protect this great beauty which is truly an inheritance?"[50]

The Outdoor Art Club was one example of the early phase of a growing vigilance on the part of local residents concerned with protecting the environment. And while the record of their actions reads as a group of concerned citizens picking up trash, there was something bigger beginning here. A concern about the wildflowers, for one example, developed into a formal campaign aimed at educating visitors and serious hikers about the variety of flora in the region and developing a respect for the natural terrain. These were predecessors of outdoor education in terms of biodiversity and the local ecosystem.

The concern for the environs of Mill Valley continued to grow over the first decades of the twentieth century. While the Outdoor Art Club exemplified local civic voices that fought to protect their town from careless hikers, the baton was firmly grabbed by the "devotees of the out-door life" who were bonded to the mountain as regular and invested hikers.[51] Many of these hikers were locals, but the group was actually more diverse. As historian Barry Spitz noted: "The explosion of tourism (late 19th to early 20th centuries) had an impact on the fragile ecology of the mountain, and increasingly worried private landowners, some of who tolerated hikers. But it also introduced visitors, many from San Francisco, who became involved in the effort to preserve Mt. Tamalpais."[52] San Franciscans initially visited the outpost of rural beauty as a weekend escape. But many came to visit regularly, with beach spots and campgrounds becoming their places, as legally owned land and as cultural property. One hiker wrote fondly of an "initiation" from a "tenderfoot" to a true lover of Tamalpais, and developed into a "long and intimate acquaintance."[53] In some cases, they relocated permanently to their adopted primordial home—many in the aftermath of the 1906 earthquake as a matter of necessity, some as their attachment became stronger, and the commute became easier. By 1912, local hiking clubs—composed of both locals and city-visitors—were categorizing hikers not by their permanent address, but by their behavior in the land. The clubs saw their membership as a class apart, describing themselves as the "type of hiker (who) was careful of fire and always left a clean camp." In contrast they described the day-trippers who would "make so much noise and (leave) so much rubbish, " the "unorganized hikers" who "became a problem about this time all around the camp spots; they were a fire menace and left the camps littered with all kinds of rubbish."[54]

The efforts to protect Mount Tam and its environs formalized and diversified by the beginning of the 1910s. The Tamalpais Conservation Club organized on February 27, 1912, with the purposes of "generally, the conservation of things animate and inanimate in Marin County, California, and particularly the preservation of the scenic bounties and fauna of Mt. Tamalpais and its spurs and slopes, and its ultimate acquisition as a public park."[55] The TCC formed in 1912 as an umbrella organization for the many hiking clubs who enjoyed the environs of Mill Valley.[56] The leadership, the membership, and the publications of this organization were prolific in their exertions to help keep guard, and to "keep this wonderful playground clean, orderly, and free of rowdyism and vandalism . . . (and) protect the privilege of the hikers on Tamalpais by educating the public to observe all protective rules on the mountain."[57] By 1925, the TCC had approximately 1,200 members; the TCC's president commented at the time that the growth of the TCC "has been a steady, healthy growth—one that makes for permanence."[58]

The first "phase" of protecting Mount Tam and the open space in the region came with the support and promotion of keeping the landscape open to the public and not subject to private development. The mountain, after all, was "too sacred for private ownership and greed."[59] Working with local civic leadership and wealthy, like-minded benefactors, the TCC assisted in the campaign. In April 1912, voters in Marin County began the process to establish the Marin Municipal Water District and subsequently bought out through bond measures the private water companies in the area.[60] Among the most influential of the voices in this battle was William Kent, US representative, wealthy landowner in Marin, and most famously, donator of the land tract that became Muir Woods. Kent's role as public benefactor is historically interesting, given he went on to become a leading voice in fighting John Muir's campaign to protect the Hetch Hetchy Valley in Yosemite National Park from development for hydroelectric power in 1913.[61] But in the same era, the hikers of Mill Valley lauded him as an environmental hero, and his rhetoric portrays as a fervent promoter of saving "the people's mountain." Kent himself promoted this image: "I have thrown open all the land which I own, with the exception of a very small area immediate to my home, to all people who desire to tramp over it, and who are willing to respect the rights of others by not destroying wild life or committing other acts of depredation."[62] Kent's campaign for public access won out, and as a result, the TCC heralded in 1917: "a great mountain of such bewildering beauty and such affluence in wild life as to afford personal enjoyment in its pursuit and of such residential value by reason of its scenic charm and its contiguity to the greatest city of the West as to become prized by private ownership, is about to become the estate of the people."[63]

With the passage of the Water District, the duties of the TCC were hardly over; in fact, in addition to trail maintenance "perhaps even more important is the abiding value of the Club as a rallying center of the moral forces seeking to promote the highest use of the mountain."[64] The president of the Tamalpais Conservation Club made it clear in his speech at the 1918 annual meeting that now members could "enjoy the privilege which we sought in the beginning—freedom of the mountain and its slopes," that each member should also "*feel that he is a 'Guardian' of the mountain*."[65] Indeed, the TCC fully embraced the claim that they were saving the mountain for "all, regardless of race, creed, or language to follow the trails for health, pleasure and recreation." One-time TCC president M. F. O'Brien confirmed that this inclusivity came with a responsibility of those who accessed the prize mountain:

> The aim and objects of the TCC are unselfish for we have been working all these years to protect and keep open the mountain and its slopes to all those who like to roam in the open, all those who, like ourselves, enjoy hiking and appreciate the benefits that they get from this exercise. Hiking brings health and friends, the kind that last. So let us do something for the mountain that does so much for us: let us try to repay by some small act that debt we owe the mountain, satisfied in the knowledge that every act of service, every hour of labor that we give is rendered to the honor and glory of the mountain.[66]

By 1919, the TCC was officially steering in a different direction, the next phase of protecting the mountain, claiming that it "interests itself no longer in (the area's) acquisition as a public park but rather in their policing, in order that the springs, streams and reservoirs remain unpolluted."[67] This new function of the

TCC was clarified and heavily promoted for the next several years. The TCC's newsletter reiterated in dozens of issues the new calling for members after having secured public access. Specific concerns and campaigns were used to rally the troops and strengthen the commitment to protecting this open space.

Once again the guardians' eyes turned toward the "newcomers"—those tourist-hikers who had long given local Mill Valley residents headaches. The fear of fires due to inexperienced visitors sloppiness or carelessness dominated much of the concern. TCC club members were voluntarily building rock fireplaces at campsites to reduce the hazard, and the club took a firm "no fires except in the built fireplaces" stance in their self-appointed roles as guardians.[68] Indeed, fire prevention was at the core of the club's concerns. Or, at least it was the concrete access path toward a justified organizational push toward environmental stewardship.

The TCC published and pushed rules for hikers. In earlier years, rules focused on respecting private property and the "wasteful plucking of wild plants."[69] As the years progressed and the land became public, fire prevention seemed to lend a more urgent and concrete issue to buoy the authority of hiking club-generated guidelines. Regulations that were designed for preventing fire were inclusive of warning against littering and loitering in nonapproved places. The TCC cited the Municipal Water District's regulations on sanitation as a basis for their posted rules.[70] As such, the TCC incorporated an agenda above and beyond fire prevention, promoting a basic respect for the outdoors they had long espoused. And, within the language of the rules, lay the groundwork for public education in terms of conservation of open spaces.

The education of others became the central calling of the TCC, in effect preaching the gospel of respectful interaction with nature and mindful use of the landscape. In some instances, this meant direct contact on the trails. Hiking club members were urged to "teach thoughtless young walkers" about the risk of fires and the senselessness of littering.[71] But largely they set examples, cared for the trails, recruited new converts, and advertised the work they accomplished. To this educational end, the TCC posted notices throughout the recreational region. On the notices, the language was placed in the context of legal ramifications. Visitors were warned that it was *unlawful* to harm trees and foliage (without the consent of the owner); to have picnics in the middle of roads on private property (without the consent of the owner); to have bonfires, carry fire arms (presumably for hunting); or to "make use of vulgar, obscene, profane or offensive language, gestures or epithets, or to indulge in indecent or disorderly conduct."[72] The language within newsletters had a persuasive tone, asking for help in the cause of keeping Mount Tam safe, and letting readers know that the members of the TCC were counting on their support.

The membership itself was also constantly appraised of their mission, to "save" the mountain, "care" for the mountain, "conserve" the mountain. The TCC employed a rhetoric that held the membership responsible for the landscape after the mountain had been protected against private development. The TCC regularly reminded their membership that "the Mountain is yours . . . guard and care for it," and that "the word 'guardian' on your TCC badge means what it says."[73] The TCC also consistently recruited for active, engaged membership. Indeed, the TCC expressed hope that all hikers would become members of a hiking club, as the clubs were conceived of in order to "educate their members, tell them how to conserve the beauty of the out-of-doors,"[74] and the TCC considered it their "duty" to "(bring) into our ranks all those who are interested in the work that we are carrying on."[75] Recruitment via newsletters and hiking club literature was at times emphatic: as one newsletter author communicated in capital letters: "IF YOU HAVE A HIKING FRIEND WHO IS NOT A MEMBER OF THE TCC TELL HIM THE TCC MAKES THE TRAILS AND THE MOUNTAIN POSSIBLE TO HIM."[76]

While the TCC heralded the slogan "Keep the Mountain Clean," the nature of the education started to evolve through the 1910s and 1920s. A respectful relationship to the landscape and the mountain came to mean a deeper understanding of the landscape through which one was wandering. A message tinged with ecological significance began to weave throughout the club's literature. Nearly fifty years before an understanding of ecosystems began to permeate the environmentalist movement, hikers in Marin were seeing beyond the beauty right in front of them. Admonishments regarding vandalism changed from concerns about a well-kempt area to concern about extermination of local flora. The club urged visitors to "make friends with nature," to understand the species they regularly enjoyed, and to "study botany, forestry and geology (to) add to your love of the out-of-doors."[77] Alice Eastwood, a longtime TCC supporter and curator of the herbarium at the California Academy of Sciences, published a "plea for the protection of the wild flowers," warning about endangered species of flowers in the region, and imploring visitors to exercise caution, if not restraint, when coming across the beauty of these flowers on a hike. Specific directions were included as to how to pick flowers sustainably, cutting stems and leaving enough to produce a flowering stalk for the next year, but that "wild flowers are loveliest in their native homes."[78] While this evokes the earlier concerns of the Outdoor Art Club in protecting local flowers, the languages shifted from protecting the beauty of the landscape to protecting the species that made their home there. Arguably, hikers and the outdoor enthusiasts of the Mill Valley area were bringing their efforts forward into more broadly conceived ecological thinking. Arguably, in this sense, they could be cited as forebears to the modern environmentalist movement of the 1970s, taking root in local environments.

This big claim needs to be only tempered a bit with a quick reminder of the context in which the TCC was taking shape. As the TCC was celebrating the success in keeping Mount Tam public and setting about protecting her, the infamous battle over the Hetch Hetchy Valley was culminating in 1913. The very public fight between John Muir and the Sierra Club on the side of protecting untrammeled wild space, and US chief forester Gifford Pinchot, who championed a wise-use doctrine when utilizing our natural resources, had garnered quite a bit of national attention. So Mill Valley hikers who indeed may have included Sierra Club members in their ranks were no doubt acutely aware of the growing urgency of this conversation on a national scale—if for no other reason than their intimate relationship with one of the key players, Rep. William Kent. They were directly exposed to this "first wave" of environmental action, and indeed could be considered a part of this movement.

In this "first wave" story, hikers play a special role. High school students may learn about this battle as a way to access the tension between preservationists and conservationists, a questionable dichotomy that nonetheless prompts in-class debates over how we should live within our land. Where should these hikers—a cohort to Muir's Sierra Club, but products and perpetuators of a viable tourist industry—land in this dichotomy? Perhaps they float in the continuum: protectionist, but fighting for public access; defenders of wilderness untrammeled but using the language of sustainable tourism and development. They are perpetrators of a civic environmentalism, one that grew from a local identity cocreated by love of their land and local economic development based on tourism. These protective hikers took an intense pride in their home, in their mountain, and they developed into an organized army of guardians and educators driven to protect their local wild spaces. They did not want to shut out tourists—they simply wanted the right kind of hiker.

At the turn of the twentieth century, environmental tourism—what historian Paul Sutter called a "dysfunctional, leisure-based relationship with nature"—was beginning to boom. Sutter's descriptive was in reference to the ideology of naturalist Aldo Leopold, who bemoaned among other things the implication of automobile access and tourism development for its potential impact on what he called the American "wilderness." Alternatively, others have recently argued that recreation and tourism can be the key to ethical development in people of respect for the natural environment.[79] Certainly the story of Mill Valley and Mount Tam show that care for the land and tourism can have a tricky, tangled relationship. The same tourism also created environmentalists, those hikers who returned repeatedly and became instrumental in the work of the TCC. They too worried about the impact of tourism, and yet used that tourism to spread the gospel of a sustainable land ethic.

Through the actions and publications of the TCC we can bear witness to the development of the activist hiker. We see how these guardians of the mountain fought to keep the space open to the public. We also witness the uneasy relationship between public access, the tourist industry, and environmental protectionism. We see an early struggle to develop a sustainable environmental tourist industry. The members of the TCC and other devoted hikers in Marin became not only protectors of their landscape, but also proselytizers of a sustainable ethic when it came to enjoying the beauty of America's public open spaces. Their particular and intimate attachment to the landscape—both as local residents and regular, intrepid hikers of the mountain and its environs—arguably formed the basis for an active environmentalist tradition in the northern San Francisco Bay Area, offering an example of how environmentalism has deep roots in smaller communities, such as Mill Valley, that loved, respected, and became stewards of their local landscapes.

Epilogue

Perhaps the roots of environmentalism in Marin that sprung from locals and hikers was in some sense a reaction to the "bulldozers in the countryside," at least in a metaphorical sense vis-à-vis the imprint of those crowds on the Marin "countryside."[80] Here is where *local* environmentalism begins—not in a top-down process, not in the words of Muir filtering down to locals, but rather germinated in the heart of this cocreated urban/rural space. This story is not simply about a reaction to the advance of the bulldozers, be they machines or weekend hikers, but the development of a conservation ethic, concerned about sustainability within their functioning economy rather than protecting a pristine place.

In the aftermath of a devastating fire in 1929 that destroyed, among other things, the historic railroad up Mount Tam, the people of Mill Valley rebounded in time to face the national economic depression. Significant changes awaited the hikers and the locals in the 1930s, and the trajectory of their role of environmental protectors. By the early 1930s, the programs of the New Deal would bring in workers from the Civilian Conservation Corps to open space around the country, the Bay Area and Marin included, and took up the calling of, among other things, trail maintenance. In 1934 locals founded the Marin Conservation League—primarily in anticipation of environmental issues arising from the completion of the impending construction of the Golden Gate Bridge—and further coalesced the community watchdog element in protecting the natural environment of Marin. The formation of this organization, as it turned out, did bode well for the future strength of environmentalism in Marin. At the same time, the establishment of the state parks that continue to provide built-in protection from overdevelopment began, starting with the establishment of Stinson Beach State Park in 1939. The Golden Gate Bridge was completed in 1937, and it would forever change the patterns of traffic and settlement in Marin County. While this construction led to the development of expanded freeway systems through Marin especially in the years following WW II, the story that ensues is far more complex than more traffic leading to more population and more environmental damage.

With the completion of the Richmond/San Rafael Bridge in 1958, and the development of the freeway system through Marin County in the Cold War development boom, the number of homes in Marin increased, as did the population and the need for water. In 1964, the West Marin Development Plan seemed to spell doom in terms of promoting unfettered development along the coast north of the city. But throughout the 1960s, the tide shifted as environmentalism seemed to take on a new life. In 1968, the pro-growth voices on Marin County's board of supervisors lost their majority, and by 1973 a new, relatively simple general plan appeared to shore up the protective impulse embodied by the TCC decades earlier. Urban development would be restricted to the eastern part of the county, with the middle and north reserved for agriculture and the west for open space and recreational use. The population stabilized at about 250,000 (and remains stable to the date of this writing). By 1972, legislation ensured the establishment of the Golden Gate National Recreation Area, a protected space of over 75,000 square miles.[81]

The activism and successes of environmentalist voices in Marin County in the 1970s were strengthened by their context as well, one of vibrant social revolution in the Bay Area. The concomitant resurgence of Bay Area environmentalism, boosted by Hippie culture, the Old Left in Berkeley, and the long-term local influence of the Sierra Club, led to vocal groups around the Bay, and ultimately the first Earth Day in 1970.

Throughout these times the roots of protecting Mount Tam and the surrounding Marin open space ran deep; they were locally ingrained, and they were personal. They were embedded in the words of the TCC:

> The mountain is "ours" in many different ways, according to the points of view which suggest to us individually a sense of possession: it is ours as a constant and characterful distant vision; ours as a high eminence affording a splendid panorama ocean, bay and rugged hills; ours as a restful challenge to set our powers of physique and endurance against the resistances of the upleading trails; ours as a treasure house of wonderful growing things; ours as a fountainhead of refreshing life-giving streams; ours as a great wildwood playground with its peace balm of the lonesome trail, its music and ringing laughter of careful companionship, and its quiet communion of kindred spirits; and ours as a shrine to which to lift our eyes for that benediction which is the strength of the hills and of the beauty of the feat of those who climb the mountain. To many of us "our" mountain means of all these things.[82]

6

All in the Same Boat

Ky Ebright, Masculinity, and Cal Crew in the 1920s

ADAM FITCH

"Ready to Row!" "Power twenty!" "Stroke Higher!" Commands yelled from a leather megaphone to coxswain Don Blessing found their intended target, the eight oarsmen of the University of California, Berkeley, crew team representing the United States in the Olympic Games. From the stern of the crew's shell, Blessing watched the effects his shouts had on the men, as the blue-tipped oars raised and lowered at a furious clip on the narrow Sloten Canal in Amsterdam on August 10, 1928. Blessing's handling of his team that day on the water was, in the words of a *New York Times* correspondent who was reporting, "One of the greatest performances of demonic howling ever heard on the terrestrial planet . . . He gave the impression of a terrier gone suddenly mad. But such language and what a vocabulary! One closed his eyes and waited for the crack of a cruel whip across the backs of the galley slaves."[1]

Unlike the other crew teams competing that August, the coxswain of the American team sat in a raised seat. From this vantage point, Blessing did everything he could to annoy the other crews during the races; bashing the sides of the boat with his tiller handles, shouting abuse, and waving a white towel above his head. The Sloten Canal was not wide enough to accommodate more than two boats at a time, so teams had to complete many heats and semifinals before the ultimate race for Olympic Gold. The final competition between the two remaining teams consisted of the Americans and their chief rival, Great Britain. The American team took the lead, and won with half a length for victory. Winning the gold meant everything to Don Blessing and the eight men rowing for the American team, representing both Berkeley and the nation. No one was prouder or felt his contribution worth every sacrifice more than the man who yelled those commands through the megaphone that day, the team coach, Carroll "Ky" Ebright.

Ebright dedicated most of the 1920s cultivating and training his teams at Cal, creating increasingly better crew members and superior groupings of men, simultaneously allowing him to better understand and improve his own coaching skills. The team that won victory that day in Amsterdam was the result of years of training men, and would be just one of many future glories for Ebright. In the days when Olympic teams were chosen, not from a collection of outstanding men, but whole teams, Ebright was a star. As a coach, Ebright learned to perfect the molding of a team into a competitive organism moved by a desire to achieve victories. He was among the greatest coaches Berkeley ever had. "For most of his coaching career, his focus was to win," remembered Blessing, "He used to say to us, 'Get ahead and stay ahead,' and we did."[2]

America in the 1920s was well suited for the kind of competitive coach Ebright became, and in many ways America embodied his philosophy. Fresh from the victory of the First World War, the United States was getting ahead and taking the lead—in economic expansion, in American cultural influence and, as was the case of the Cal crew team in the 1928 Olympic Games, in sport. America's chief rival, Britain, was being eclipsed in the world by the rising American power of capital and the seemingly boundless opportunity afforded men who could compete to become the business leaders driving the new economics of the postwar twentieth century. The men who trained under Ebright went on from Berkeley to become the type of business executives and leaders who helped propel American growth and influence. America was shaping a type of masculine ideal in the 1920s, namely the corporate man. How could a sport like men's crew help us understand America in the 1920s? What were the qualities that these men had that made them attractive to crew and American business? What did the men in the crew team at Berkeley take with them into corporate America, and how were they able to fit in so easily within American business? This story looks at how men's sport and Cal crew became emblematic of the 1920s, and how competitive masculinity was part of the early twentieth-century experience in America.[3]

Established in the United States in the mid-nineteenth century at Harvard and Yale, men's collegiate crew had been an exclusively East Coast tradition. Only in the early twentieth century did rowing make any significant appearance in the American West. Mirroring a growing shift in population and power to the West Coast, the University of California Boating Association, representing UC Berkeley rowers, was founded in 1868. It was the first for the Bay Area, and allowed young men to compete in a sport seen as a masculine rite, popular with the athletes and students. Another California school, Stanford University, formed a team in 1902; however, that team was disbanded by 1920. The University of Washington established a team in 1903, and with Stanford out of the picture, Washington had a vested interest to keeping rowing alive at its only other significant rival, Cal Berkeley, in the 1920s. Keeping a competitor on the West Coast meant that Washington could keep racing to create the possibility of a chance at the Olympics. A consequence of this decision was a rivalry between Washington and Berkeley that is still palpable today.[4]

Collegiate crew in the 1920s was immensely popular. It was a part of mainstream American culture, equal in popularity to baseball and football. Sports competitions, broadcast by the new medium of radio, let Americans from all walks of life share in the excitement of the sport. American spectators listening in could revel in the glory of the wins and share in the commiseration of the losses. Radio brought more people together in the 1920s sharing in the cultural experience of sports than at any other time in American history. In an era before television, radio provided a means of sharing the American practice of sports enthusiasm. Crew was so popular that the majority of mainstream newspapers had a rowing correspondent to report on races similar to the reporter at the Olympic Games. The newspaper, like the radio, also reported details of the races and team specifics. Sporting magazines debated crew members' diets and clothing. Crew coaches were often surrounded by fans during victories, signing autographs and taking interviews. As in a stock corporation, everyone seemed to have something invested in the team. People with stakes in the success of crew teams; the athletes, the friends and families rooting for them, the trainers that trained them, the fans and the alumni of the school, the bookies and people with bets on the races, the promoters, the ticket-holders were all invested in seeing a crew team succeed. The general public who furiously read up on races in the newspapers and listened in on radios also felt like they had a stake in the sport. In accordance with this level of public involvement and popularity, the crew coach was also supremely invested, and coaches like Ebright were well compensated to keep up that enthusiasm.[5]

Berkeley's crew team was made up of white males who competed in a sport that required strength, dexterity, and structure as they worked together as a team. Along with competitive sport like crew, men had specific roles in the early twentieth century. Men were expected to fight in combat, as they had in the Great War, and they were responsible for breadwinning and providing for a family. Women were largely confined to the home, were not encouraged to compete in sport, were largely kept from the public sphere (for example, they were forbidden the right to vote), and were expected to commiserate with members of their own sex. Men were highly visible in competitive sport, allowing them to join in an activity that could give them an appealing air of masculinity and an important social camaraderie with other men as well as connections with their tribe. The men in the crew team at Cal were expected to train hard and win; the boys that entered the university were in turn expected to go on to be the masculine ideal in American life. Cal required teachers to mold men in the classrooms, and coaches were responsible to guide the best men in the competitive rituals of sports. In 1924, the Cal crew committee, in charge of selecting coaches for the Berkeley team and headed by the stockbroker Dean Witter, hired Ky Ebright from the University of Washington to provide his get-ahead philosophy and his new brand of winner-takes-all leadership.

Ebright was an only child and grew up in Seattle, Washington, with a father in the steel business. Seattle was a booming area of the country during the Great War, as Boeing Airplane Company took advantage of the local Spruce wood to supply the burgeoning United States Navy with a source of material for the construction of airplanes. Ebright attended the University of Washington and finished with a business degree, with plans to follow in his father's footsteps in the steel industry. While at the University of Washington, he coxswained for the Washington crew team, and was briefly a pilot in the Army Signal Corp during the Great War. After he graduated, however, he was drawn to the competitive nature of crew, and by the early 1920s he was hanging out in the boathouse helping train the Washington team. In 1923, at the suggestion of boatbuilder George Pocock, Ebright took the job offer at Berkeley to coach just when the team was looking for someone to keep it competitive. It was Don Blessing, the future coxswain for the Amsterdam team, who picked Ebright and his wife up at the train station. Ebright, according to his protege and successor as crew coach, Jim Lemmon, had an arrangement with the University of Washington that if things didn't work out at Cal he could have his old job back. Ebright, enthusiastically, went to work at Cal.[6]

"The Little Admiral," Ebright's nickname the boys on the Cal team gave him, developed strategies for becoming the best at picking eligible men and at training them. He would begin to sift for gems on the first day the boys were dropped on campus. Ebright sent his new freshman coach, Russ Nagler, and a group of seasoned older crewmen off to the registration lines. As incoming freshmen had to enlist with the ROTC, each male had to pass beneath a yellow ribbon set at six feet off the ground. Every male that could not pass under or had to duck below the ribbon was approached by Nagler and the varsity crew members. The initial questions were designed to sound innocuous to the young men who were approached; "How tall are you?" "How much do you weigh?" "Are you going out for another sport?" "If not, why not choose crew?" At first Ebright insisted on a soft sell for fear that the students would be encouraged to go for basketball or football. Nagler was instructed to get the phone numbers and addresses of eligible crew members. Once Ebright had weeded through the eligible men, then the hard-sell approach was administered to those who seemed like good fits for the Cal team. Crew meetings on campus were set up and phone calls to the potential rower's dormitory were made to tell him about the times and dates that the crew would be expecting them.[7]

Once Ebright had accumulated the raw material necessary for his team, he set about training the men on how to excel as individuals so that they could bring his team victory. Men's crew requires both intense physical and mental stamina. Individual strength and dexterity are required by rowers who must meet physically demanding athletic training. The recruits for Berkeley crew had no previous experience, as there were no prep schools or high schools with crew teams in the United States at the time. Ebright had to physically train these men in the methods and stamina of rowing, and they had to learn from scratch. This had benefits as the boys could be molded early and had not developed habits detrimental to any rower that could not be unlearned, but it also meant that they came in with no idea of how a team worked. He made sure that each member of the team was on the water every day and that they rowed only after a full day of classes. Ebright often had them on the Oakland Estuary well into the evenings, doing what it took to keep them motivated. He insisted that everyone on his crew excel in their studies as well. As Buzz Schulte, one of his oarsmen, recalled, "He yelled, goaded, teased, whatever it took to motivate his boys."[8]

The crew members had to be back on campus by the last dinner service at seven or they did not eat. This often meant that the boys did not make it or were the last few people in line for cold dinners. Although the 1920s were known as a time when colleges threw parties and all-night drinking sessions with underclassmen, Ebright forbade smoking or drinking; he particularly did not want any athlete to consume any alcohol. In all kinds of weather, windy or cold, crew members were training for at least three hours a day. Running alongside the crew boat, Ebright pounded the sides of his coaching launch with his megaphone. He developed a style of coaching that was just what he felt the men in his crew needed, encouragement and demanding leadership. Ebright was aware that the physiology of rowing requires dedication, but crew members also had to maintain mental stamina. The individual rower must have a working intelligence of how the boat operates as a whole. Rowing with all its complexities in precision required knowledge of how to best benefit speed on the water and on how to accelerate the entire team. The team strength depended on each member and what side of the crew shell that boy was responsible for. Ebright knew what to look for in the able-bodied men he had gathered, but he also needed to win their respect and have them understand his position. Ebright instilled a dedication in his team and in a faith in his own ability. "He was God to me," Don Blessing recalled.[9]

Part of organizing a successful team, from Ebright's perspective, was in fostering relationships needed to make the team work. Men of the same height, weight, age, and economic and social backgrounds often bonded naturally. Even as they may have been given over to their natural inclination to become beholden to their peers, it was the dedication to their new sport and to their coach that Ebright wanted to impress upon them. He was making men that could compete and men who could win Olympic championships. Once Ebright identified the individual crew member's capacity for both the physical and psychological challenges of crew, once he instilled in them a respect for his abilities, and when he had fostered bonds among the men, he then taught them teamwork. One of the most difficult aspects of this training is the obstacle of having to convince eight men to take orders from the coxswain. Any group of men over the height of six feet must have felt insecure taking orders from a single coxswain who was shorter in stature, but it was crucial. Eight men, with seemingly limitless physical endurance, would have to give their all to one individual often half their size who was taking direct orders from Ebright. Management of crew at Cal was organized with the coach in the lead position followed by the coxswain for the varsity team. The freshman coach looked after training of potential freshmen and sophomores. There were also varsity players vying for a leadership position in the organization of command. For these team members, management was organized like a pyramid, selected from upperclassmen. These men were allowed to wear a large letter "C" on their jackets, and their primary duty was to relieve the coaching staff of administrative tasks. They also worked with the coach in training the senior crew members. The senior manager worked out of the boathouse and played a vital role when organizing trips to events, booking rooms, keeping track of train timetables, and making arrangements for the transportation of boats and equipment.[10]

Ebright understood the importance of rewarding those who learned the rules and were the most single of mind in making the whole team great. There were no scholarships to attract potential prospects to Berkeley, and no rewards to offer the individual players who went out for crew. In the mid-1920s Ebright approached the man who had gotten him his job, Dean Witter, a former Cal crew member and by then the most successful stockbroker on the West Coast, to provide a trophy cup to the "most valuable player" on the Cal crew team. As Cal went on to win victories under Ebright's leadership, the team itself was attracting men who were eager to align themselves with the masculine ideal of competitor. A varsity man on the Cal crew team wore a letter jacket, had a toned physique, and with Ebright's increasing victorious mantra, they were becoming

Berkeley's Olympic Team of 1928. Ky Ebright, *far right. Courtesy University of California Berkeley Athletics.*

more popular than the football or baseball players on campus. Ebright made all this happen for potential males by imparting knowledge of the sport but also through toughness. "Everyone respected what he said even if it made them mad," Don Blessing recalled, "He was it—we learned to win from him and not lose."[11] His get ahead philosophy was communicated with the toughness and aggressiveness of a boardroom CEO. That toughness made the men angry and resent him as much as it made them regard their newfound status well worth the effort. "He was tough, there was no doubt about it. I remember one time a former student of Ky's said he never would have won the Olympics if he hadn't been so mad at Ky," said Ebright's wife Kathryn.[12] Ebright's toughness and ability to garner the respect, as well as the ire, of his team members is was what made the team successful.[13]

Validation of Ebright's coaching tactics paid handsome dividends throughout the 1920s. When Ebright took over the racing program in 1924 the team lost to the University of Washington by ten boat lengths. In 1925 Cal lost to Washington by eight boat lengths, and in 1926 they lost by five. In 1927, Ebright's team won over Washington, beating their team by four lengths. Cal won very big in 1928. Ebright had his sites on Olympic Gold throughout the 1920s and that year the Cal team won not only against Washington but took the lead over Harvard and Yale to become the team to compete in the Olympic Games. Berkeley won against every school at the Poughkeepsie races to be the representative school for the United States in the Olympic Games. It was in Amsterdam that Ebright would compete on behalf of the United States, just as the United States was competing economically and politically with the other nations of the world. Ebright took his American team to Amsterdam to take on the world.[14]

General Douglas MacArthur, who later famously ushered in another era of American economic expansion with the surrender of Japan following the Second World War, was recruited to be president of the American Olympic Committee at Amsterdam following the sudden death of the previous president the year before. MacArthur oversaw the preparation of the American team for their competition, marching in front of them during the opening ceremonies like a commander leading his troops into battle. He told the American competitors that they were to win medals: "We did not come three-thousand miles just to lose gracefully,"[15] he said. One journalist wrote that MacArthur's meetings with the coaches and managers "had about the same chilling spiritual temperature as a bank director's meeting."[16] During the games, when a boxing team manager threatened to withdraw his fighters over a bad call, MacArthur responded, "American's don't quit!"[17] Following the victory of the Cal crew for the United States, MacArthur asked Don Blessing to meet his son. "MacArthur took me out to dinner with him because I was a fiery, outgoing young guy. He wanted some of me to rub off on his son, who was my same age, but very awkward and shy."[18] The team was also asked by the Queen of Holland to meet with her at the royal palace, and was given a victory wreath as the "Star Spangled Banner" was played in their honor. Overall America won fifty-four medals, the most medals won by any country that year.

Unlike today, the Olympic crew team in 1928 was chosen from one school and was not made up of all the top athletes in the nation. That fact made the team's reception back home at Berkeley electric. Ebright and the whole crew went up Telegraph Avenue, entering through the Sather Gate surrounded by a cheering crowd. A ceremony with an overflowing crowd at the Greek Theater was held in their honor; the men had come home victorious. More than ten-thousand people showed up for the return of the team from Amsterdam in what was considered "the greatest homecoming celebration in the history of Berkeley."[19] Although this 1928 team would be graduating in two years, Ebright had his sites on future Olympic glories, and he began to spread a new slogan for Cal crew: "California's crew in California's Olympics."[20]

Ebright's coaching left a lasting imprint on his team. As he oversaw the development of the skills that he helped hone and bring to their fullest potential, certain characteristics, very desirable to corporate business in America, revealed themselves. Like sport, American business had fascinated and was a large part of American life in the 1920s. In 1925, President Calvin Coolidge famously said to a group of newspapermen, "After all, the chief business of American people is business."[21] Coolidge's statement encapsulated the importance business had on the American character. The two were intertwined. In the 1920s, American capitalism produced goods and marketed these goods to a consuming public, and the public in turn credited business with their new ways of life. Ebright had been molding men in ways that were being implemented by corporations eager to have what Cal and Ebright were producing. The cream of masculine power and authority were picked up by corporate America seeking to better the business of managing profit and equity.

America took the lead in economic expansion in the 1920s. Mainly as a result of the First World War, the United States became the world's largest creditor with over 15 billion dollars invested in overseas markets, surpassing by many lengths the previous chief economic power, Great Britain. Consumer goods such as cars and radios were purchased by American and foreign consumers, who were being targeted by the newly created mass-marketing firms. These new items revolutionized how Americans lived. The radio, remember, had brought together its sporting audience. All these amenities could be purchased on credit. Stocks in the companies that produced this new life could also be purchased on credit. The manufacturing and marketing of products and equities required executive leadership. Just as Ebright had promised his most valuable crew member a coveted silver cup, business executives were paid bonuses and incentives to perform. The firms hiring men were skeleton-like organizations very similar to the ways that the Cal crew team was organized. These business organizations were looking for men with the particular qualities Ebright was honing to fill both the upper-level management and boardrooms of corporations. Although the wealthiest Americans were the true beneficiaries of most of the economic growth in the United States, a man had the opportunity to compete to get into top executive positions. This gave an enterprising young man the chance at the ultimate goal of becoming part of the business success permeating American culture.[22]

Ebright stressed physical fitness and discipline with his team; he emphasized organization in his crew training; and each team had a managerial component that crew men strove toward. Men Ebright coached worked to be the most valuable player, and yet each man knew how important it was to choreograph movements of the oar requiring a dedication to the other men in the boat. Ebright's toughness made for winners, winners who competed on the water and could compete in the boardrooms of America. As one of Ebright's later crewmen, the actor Gregory Peck put it, "The agony of the last mile or half mile and the knowledge that you can't quit even if you die. That has to have some effect on character."[23]

Ebright's type of masculine ideal, one who would get ahead and stay ahead, was embraced by corporate America. It was a type of masculinity that American business wanted. As Percival White, a proponent of business marketing, said in 1922, "Business is not a part of American life; it *is* American life. The American businessman . . . has no friends but business friends, no interests but business interests . . . From this tremendous acceleration of life, the American has no escape."[24] Cal crew was the life of the men Ebright had every day for hours of training and competition; crew *was* their life. Men that Ebright coached learned skills catering to business careers stressing individual initiative that kept in mind the ultimate goal of producing profits for their corporations. From the Oakland estuary to Dean Witter's Wall Street was a natural course, and men who had the ability to create ties and bonds to a CEO had learned it first from their coach. This was where competitive crew and competitive business intersected for the American male living in the 1920s.[25]

Ebright coached many men that ended up in successful careers. There were strong connections the boys he mentored had between success in America and Cal crew. Certainly being tall was a criterion, as was being Caucasian. So too was having an education and family that stressed education as a means to further advantage success in life. But it was Ebright's coaching philosophy that really made successful men. It even gave potential to the coxswains coached by Ebright. Don Blessing, unsurprisingly, became a stockbroker. He worked in the Bay Area for fifty years and retired in 1959, but not before becoming part owner of the Oakland Raiders football team. All of Ebright's rowers in the Olympic Games went on to receive University of California degrees, and with some notable exceptions, went into successful executive and professional positions in American business. Whichever business or profession the crew members took up, they took with them the skills and philosophy taught to them from Berkeley and Ky Ebright. It meant being successful in a market economy derived from competition and being the right kind of man for the right time.[26]

As long as business was good in America, it was a kind of hubris that was not only tolerated by Americans but embraced by an active audience. In the decade of the 1920s everything seemed to be going up; hemlines, stock prices, and airplanes. Competitive sports in the 1920s like crew spawned fiercer and more incredible competitions, daredevil exercises with individuals playing tennis on the wings of planes or balancing themselves high up on skyscrapers. Outside the boathouse and out of the waters of the Oakland estuary where the Cal crew team practiced, Americans were enjoying their new modes of living, even if that life, in the end, was beyond their means. Credit allowed Americans the ability to purchase the cars, refrigerators, radios, even stocks and bonds that concealed real problems in the American economy. As the divide between rich and poor became starker in the late 1920s, real problems revealed themselves. Americans increasingly became incapable of buying, even on credit, the very goods businesses were trying to sell. Overproduction in agriculture was only the first to become apparent, and while the stock-market crash in 1929 did not start the Great Depression, it signaled its beginning. As the economist John Kenneth Galbraith put it, "In the autumn of 1929 the mightiest of Americans were, for a brief time, revealed as human beings."[27]

The Great Depression that followed the 1920s at Berkeley greatly affected college life and Cal crew. Funds dried up for equipment; men had to find work and could not be so easily seduced for sports in their spare time; and money for the program questioned even the viability of crew as a sport at Cal. The Depression affected all American Collegiate crew departments. Yet Ky Ebright proved he could be great and championed the program while trying to keep costs at bay. George Pocock, the man responsible for recommending Ebright to Cal in the first place, produced boats for both the Washington and Berkeley crew teams throughout the 1920s. He was the boatbuilder for the shell that won the 1928 victory for Cal. Ebright now began to demand Pocock change the designs of the boats he constructed for Berkeley and asked for price reductions. "You will not be able to get your old prices much longer, it will just be impossible to pay them," Ebright wrote Pocock, "the goose that laid the golden egg is gone."[28]

If America had grown weary of business and business leaders, Ky Ebright was still coaching to produce the same kind of champions he had always coached. The training never slackened even in the lean years, and Ebright still insisted on the same proven philosophy of getting ahead, even if the motivations Ebright used did change. Gone were the days when the men would be contented with a silver cup. In the 1930s, when times were at their hardest, Ebright managed to secure funding for a training table so that the boys that he mentored could get a meal and not have to rush back to campus in time for dinner. Motivated by the promise of a plate of hot food to any two boys who could work their way into the varsity boats, Ebright created a possibility for freshman crew members to at least have the hope for a hot meal with varsity members that he might not have otherwise gotten. During the depression years, the two boys who won were always grateful to have the food.[29]

In all, Ky Ebright won three Olympic gold medals for Berkeley and the United States, seven national varsity championships, and two junior varsity championships, and his record has not and will never be beaten. Ebright set the standard for Berkeley as the leader in West Coast rowing, coaching his teams for over thirty-five years. Ebright, never satisfied with maintaining a monopoly on the sport or his place in it, sought to spread the sport widely, while also retaining the loyalty of those who went before. He looked to set up a potential ready flow of money when it was needed, learning a lesson from the lean times of the Depression. The Cal Crew Alumni Association, set up by Ebright, secured the potential source of needed funds for expenses that might arise in the future for Cal's continuing strive for success. At the time of Ebright's retirement he had amassed a list of a thousand former crew members that could be relied on for donations.

Ebright invested in rowing by encouraging crew outside of the collegiate experience in an effort to improve the prospects for the survival of the sport. At the junior colleges, he encouraged providing competition and competitors that sent freshmen to Berkeley. With Ebright's assistance, training at Sacramento Junior College provided a good source of this competition for the Cal team freshmen. At the high school level, Ebright sought to get more young Californian men interested in the sport to better the prospects of freshmen rowers who had advantages over their untrained predecessors. He encouraged the growth of the sport so that the rowing experience could produce greater champions. His successor as coach of the Cal team, Jim Lemmon, summed up Ebright's career best: "Thus ended the Ebright story with the establishment of California rowing at a national and international level by a coach respected by all who row. No man had ever had such an impact upon the sport and no man ever will. Not the least of his accomplishments was the effect he had on the hundreds of young men who were so fortunate to have him as a coach."[30] Ebright's greatest contribution to American rowing was in the effect he had on the men he coached, and the preparation he gave them to enter into American life had different effects on how men understood themselves.

America continued the tradition of the 1920s, encouraging global consumerism and neoliberal capitalism, influencing other nations to adopt a get-ahead philosophy in the pursuit of bigger profits, and projecting America's image and status in the world. American business today is still producing the greatest amount of wealth, as well as experiencing the divide between wealth and income that has not been seen in America since the 1920s. Business has not, however, held the same status in American culture as it did in the 1920s. The business of the American people, in the words of President Coolidge, has not continued to be business. The two do not enjoy the same close relationship as we have most recently seen in the 2008 subprime mortgage crisis and the subsequent Occupy movement. Competitive sports in America still produces leadership positions, but America's love affair with business has changed.[31]

Although it seems comical to a modern reader, there was a religious component to the business environment of the 1920s. American business had for some

American's become at that time a religion.[32] At his retirement ceremony, after thirty-five years of coaching Cal crew, the president of the university, Clark Kerr, stated that after "really getting to know Ky Ebright and crew," he was convinced that "crew was fraternal by nature," but was also convinced, as he became more familiar with the sport, that "rowing must [also] be a religion."[33] If American business had taken on the same religious aspects as crew competition in the 1920s, exemplified by the coaching style of Ky Ebright, it is not one shared in a sport that has become increasingly egalitarian and diverse over time.

Women today make up the largest portion of collegiate rowers in the United States, far out-populating the men. Some 6,500 women competed in college rowing in 2012 according to the NCAA, compared to just over 1,500 men.[34] Initially not taken seriously, or considered a stunt, when it was first attempted at Yale in 1970 following the passage of Title IX, it is now the fastest-growing women's sport.[35] Women can, because of NCAA guidelines, also be coxswains on men's teams. Men also no longer define their masculinity in the same way as they did in the 1920s, relying on competition as something exclusively male. A diverse collection of competitors in collegiate crew, a sport that was once only populated by men, has emerged. In the Bay Area and across America, collegiate sports have undergone changes where women, as well as other groups, participate in greater numbers than ever before. Lesbians, gay men, and transgender athletes are becoming more visible in sporting culture in general, for example, and perhaps there will be a larger presence of racial and ethnic groups visible on Cal crew teams and college crew teams in the United States.

Crew and American ideals have changed since the days of Ky Ebright, but there is continuity. At Berkeley, crew remains very popular; the sport has endured and is now a tradition on par with the races at Harvard and Yale. In a shell named after and christened by Don Blessing, the Cal crew coach Stephen Gladstone led his team to a victory in 1999 for a 5-minute, 23.6-second finale that has not been beaten. The boys that pass through the Ebright Boathouse on their way to practice pass by the memorabilia of the tradition that made Berkeley and American history in the sport that created men and leaders in the American way of life. Hidden in the rhythm of the strokes of the Berkeley team are the machines of American individuality and the win-at-all-costs philosophy of Berkeley crew's greatest coach, as part of the twentieth-century experience, and testament to the presence of sport in the Bay Area.

7

Off the Bench

Asian Americans and Sport in the Santa Clara Valley during the Mid-Twentieth Century

JOEL S. FRANKS

In December 1949, the *San Jose Mercury*'s sports pages focused largely on Bay Area football. A few teams in the region were headed to postseason bowl games. The then-famous East-West Shrine game was scheduled for kickoff up at San Francisco's Kezar Stadium, and the youthful San Francisco 49ers appeared set to join the National Football League in 1950 after four years in the soon-to-be-defunct All-American Football Conference. Interestingly, featured among the many articles about football were stories about the third annual National Oriental Basketball Tournament.

After two years in Seattle, the choice of San Jose made sense as the tournament's site for a host of reasons. Unlike Seattle, the little city of about 95,000, fifty miles south of San Francisco, was relatively accessible to the many Asian American basketball teams in the Bay Area and Central Valley. Moreover, it was but an eight-hour drive from Los Angeles, which housed an abundant number of Japanese American teams. Finally, it was home to perhaps the finest Japanese American team in the United States—the San Jose Zebras.[1] It was not just local and California as Asian American squads from throughout the United States showed up in San Jose. Early in December, the *Mercury* alerted readers to expect the all-Japanese American Chicago Huskies to compete in the tournament, claiming the "Oriental" team was the first "simon-pure non-college team from East of the Mississippi to play in San Jose."[2] The local press continued its enthusiastic run up to the tournament announcing that San Francisco teams, including the Filipino American Mangoes' five and the Chinese Saints, defending tournament champions, were scheduled to play, as well as a combined Chinese and Japanese American five from Seattle. Other teams garnered attention from local dignitaries as the Japanese American all-stars from Hawai'i were feted by San Jose's mayor upon their arrival. As elite athletes from around the nation converged on the South Bay city, the *Mercury* promised readers "some of the most colorful basketball games of the season," marking the tournament as "one of the most outstanding sports events in the history of San Jose."[3] Sadly for the locals, the Zebras were upset by the "Seattle All-Stars" in an early round. A few days later, the Zebras avenged their loss to the Pacific Northwesterners, but it was too late for the Zebras to advance to the championship rounds. A capacity crowd of 2,500 then jammed into San Jose State's cozy basketball gym to see the Hawaii All-Stars upend the defending champs. The *Mercury* claimed the exciting game manifested plenty of "fast action." And as solace to locals, the Zebras beat the Huskies for the consolation championship.[4]

The 1949 Oriental Basketball Tournament tells noteworthy stories about mid-twentieth-century Asian Americans in the Santa Clara Valley and elsewhere. Of course, Asian Americans today and many of the rest of us reject the term of Oriental as a means of pigeonholing the experiences of people possessing Asian and Middle Eastern descent. However antiquated the term might seem today, its use spoke to the hopes of at least some post–World War II Asian Americans that they could transcend the ethnic distinctions dividing them in the United States. After all, Asian American ethnic groups suffered from intense forms of personal and institutional nativism and racism in the United States by mid-twentieth century. At the same time, the tournament respected ethnic distinctions, understanding that, while Asian American ethnic groups possessed nativism and racism in common, Chinese American experiences differed from Japanese American or Filipino American experiences even if non-Asians could not always grasp the character of those differences.[5]

Since nativism and racism substantially isolated Asian from other non-Asian communities for many years in the United States, Asian American communities forged ethnic-based organizations such as the San Jose Zebras. In doing so, these communities used sport to unite members across generational and other social distinctions. Moreover, community leaders hoped sport would encourage ethnic pride and steer participants away from unsavory behavior that might embarrass the community. Finally, sport offered participants an opportunity to do something they enjoyed but were often not able to do at school because of family and work responsibilities on the one hand, and the bigotry of the outside world on the other.[6]

Accordingly, sport became a way for Asian Americans to express their ethnic identity. Ethnicity, conceived as a social construct, is learned. It is an intersection of local and national cultures nurtured in the original homes of immigrants and the local and national cultures prevailing in their new homes. Ethnicity, moreover, is performed in a myriad of ways depending upon a variety of factors such as origins and timing of immigration, as well as where immigrants and their offspring lived. Additionally, age, class, gender, and the kind of political-legal institutions and practices immigrants encountered influenced not only how the dominant society engaged them but how they understood themselves. By competing in the Oriental Basketball Tournament, the Zebras and other teams were performing ethnicity—that they viewed themselves as Japanese, Chinese, or Filipino but also as Americans. Moreover, the tournament was an intercultural event and as such provided a space in which Asian Americans, while sharing common circumstances related to racism and nativism, could negotiate the interethnic distinctions and tensions as Chinese, Japanese, and Filipino Americans.[7]

This chapter examines Asian American sport in San Jose and surrounding municipalities located in Santa Clara Valley and, in doing so, offers an interesting lens to explore two related issues.[8] It will explore the role of community sport among Asian American ethnic groups in Santa Clara Valley, and it will focus on how sport served to push Asian Americans in Santa Clara Valley across often treacherous cultural borderlands to compete with and against people representing other racial and ethnic groups. Asian Americans in the Santa Clara Valley probed the democratic possibilities of sport by using it to develop and maintain durable ethnic communities that helped them endure nativism and racism, while claiming access to what key Latino/a scholars have called "cultural citizenship"; that is, in the case of the United States, the right to assert ethnic distinctiveness while accessing a full measure of political and legal rights in a society that claims to value democracy.[9]

Asian American Community Building in the "Garden of the World"

Exploring the histories of Asian Americans in Santa Clara Valley throws into sharp relief both the racism they faced and the ways they resisted oppressive practices and policies. Chinese immigrants forged the earliest Asian American presence in Santa Clara Valley. Lured by the California gold rush, Chinese immigrants journeyed across the Pacific in the 1840s and early 1850s to America. Most hoped to find enough gold to get their families out of debt—a debt exacerbated by natural catastrophes, overpopulation, and China's desperate war with Britain over its right to refuse the opium pedaled by the English.[10]

Disappointed in their efforts to find enough gold and fearing the racist and nativist violence of the gold fields, Chinese people, many of whom possessed agrarian backgrounds, sought income in the agricultural economy developing in

Santa Clara Valley. Furthermore, white landowners, anticipating cashing in on the valley's climate and soil, sought a controllable labor force to work their fields and orchards. Initiating a pattern, which historian and journalist Carey McWilliams recognized as characteristic of California's "Factories in the Field," white landowners employed Chinese first and then other Asian immigrants to perform the kind of labor that native-born European Americans usually refused to do. While Chinese immigrants were, therefore, hired as agricultural workers, some were able to rent farmland or at least engage in sharecropping, with the hope, if not the promise, of a profitable outcome.[11]

Yet California's anti-Chinese fervor rendered life in Santa Clara Valley precarious for the Chinese. Arson destroyed San Jose's Chinatown twice—in 1870 and then again in 1887. White landowners grew leery of hiring Chinese. In part, landowners feared the fact that the Chinese were far from passive, despite or because of their marginalized position. For example, Chinese immigrants forged partnerships with others of their ethnicity in an effort to gain landownership, thus threatening white hegemony. Despite these acts of resistance, the ability of Chinese immigrants to own land was curtailed by a state constitution revised largely by the anti-Chinese Workingmen's Party of California in 1879. This and rural violence helped push Chinese immigrants out of agricultural areas like Santa Clara Valley and the congressional passage of the Chinese Exclusion Law (1882) further persuaded agribusiness in the South Bay to turn from Chinese to Japanese labor in the late 1800s and early 1900s. Yet like the Chinese, Japanese immigrants were expected to quietly fill the region's agricultural needs. Like the Chinese, they encountered racial nativism and relatively efficient efforts on the part of the US government to curb Japanese immigration to America. They too preferred to own land rather than work for European Americans.[12]

Filipino immigrants faced many of the same problems as other Asian immigrants to the South Bay and California. While Chinese and Japanese immigrants engaged in labor disputes, Filipinos proved more adamant about it, thus exacerbating an ardent anti-Filipino movement. Writer and Filipino immigrant Carlos Bulosan remembered suffering a physical assault by white vigilantes in San Jose while participating in a farm labor strike in the 1930s. Yet perhaps more troubling to European Americans in California than Filipino labor militancy, *Pinoys*[13] believed they had the right to court white women. When things got particularly nasty in late 1929 and early 1930, a leader of San Jose's Filipino community urged that local *Pinoys* steer clear of white males in public, but especially refrain from appearing on city streets with white women. Largely provoked by anti-Filipino racism, the Tydings-McDuffie Act in 1934 substantially limited Filipino immigration, while denying Filipino immigrants in the United States access to federal services in the midst of the Great Depression.[14]

The result of racial nativism and restrictive immigration legislation was relatively small Asian ethnic communities in Santa Clara Valley. This population pattern remained well after World War II in this part of the Bay Area. While the Japanese American population grew to three thousand by 1960, Filipino and Chinese Americans remained under one thousand in the same period.[15]

Community Sport

As the largest Asian ethnic group in the mid-twentieth-century Santa Clara Valley, Japanese Americans forged a vigorous *Nihonmachi* near San Jose's old Chinatown north of downtown, and sport continued to be an important hinge upon which the community was formed. There, they built homes and small businesses, the latter aimed in the early twentieth century at servicing Japanese immigrants and their offspring living throughout Santa Clara Valley. Despite the vibrant communities in which Japanese Americans lived they could not significantly alter the racism that pervaded the world beyond their neighborhoods. As a result, life was uncertain for Japanese immigrants and their offspring in and around San Jose. Their labor might be welcomed by some whites in the region, but an intense anti-Japanese movement engulfed California and was clearly in evidence within Santa Clara Valley by the early 1900s. Many Japanese immigrants came to the United States to labor in agriculture, and as a result the vast majority were men. These young men, believed by progressive reformers and even those within the Japanese American community to be involved in vice and other illegal activities, were thus the focus of corrective action. Community leader Mas Akizuki lamented, "Most of [our] men were single and they played around whenever they had some money. The main entertainment was billiards and *hana fuba* (Japanese cards). There were seven or eight boarding houses and the first floor of each house had a billiard parlor." Akizuki and other community leaders hoped competitive athletics would divert young men from vice. In this way sport became a site for expressive agency among young male Japanese Americans, as well as a form of social control. Soon sumo wrestling leagues, basketball competitions, baseball games, among other physical activities were central elements in the lives of Japanese American men in Santa Clara Valley.[16]

Across the expanse of great teams and athletes, the San Jose baseball team, the Asahi, very clearly illustrates the power and potential of sport within a marginalized community. The Asahi's popularity within the community grew rapidly in the years just after the team was organized in 1913, according to historian Ralph Pearce. The *San Jose Mercury* claimed that "practically the entire Japanese colony" watched as just a few years later, this nine was victimized by a no-hit shutout by a "Los Angeles High School Japanese team" pitcher. By the 1920s the Asahi were drawing thousands to a Japantown ballpark. They played the best semipro teams in the Bay Area, in addition to other Japanese American nines in northern California. Moreover, teams from Japan visited San Jose to oppose the Asahi and the Asahi, in turn, journeyed across the Pacific to play in Japan.[17]

The Asahi not only offered San Jose's Nikkei a source of ethnic pride until World War II, they also managed to erect a cultural bridge to European Americans. The *San Jose Mercury*'s Jack Graham often praised the Asahi in the 1920s. In 1922, Graham extolled just about everything about the Asahi and their "Jap diamond." While many Californians demanded greater restriction of Japanese immigrants, Graham contended that the team "has the biggest bunch of rooters behind them of any team in the city, their diamond is probably the best in town and fast games are the rule." Graham continued, "The writer wishes to state that anyone wishing to see enthusiasm should witness the Japanese team play."[18]

Baseball teams were not the only athletic squads to foster community cohesion and pride. In the 1930s, San Jose's Japanese American community was represented by a male basketball team known as the Zebras. Sponsored by the city's lone Buddhist Church, erected in the midst of San Jose's Japantown, the Zebras were considered one of the best Japanese Americans squads on the West Coast and one of the best independent fives in the region. In 1934, the *San Jose Mercury* called the Zebras "a high powered Japanese basketball team" after they downed a Santa Clara High School squad, 32–28. Reporting that the Zebras had

Japanese American baseball players at San Jose's Japantown ball park in the 1920s. *Courtesy John C. Gordon Photographic Collection, San José State University Library Special Collections & Archives.*

entered a Northern California Young Men's Buddhist Association Tournament in January 1934, the *Mercury* described the squad of San Jose High School stars and neighborhood talents as "the mighty mites, lightweight in proportion, but experts in ability," and quite capable of using teamwork to overcome often taller opposition.[19]

World War II brought with it an intense racist backlash against Japanese Americans, and sport provided an avenue to help negotiate these difficult times. Indeed, Japanese Americans used sport as a tool to build and strengthen community amid the harsh realities of the internment camps into which they were forced by the US government in early 1942. The injustices of internment, however, failed to dim enthusiasm for basketball among the Zebras and many other Pacific Coast Japanese Americans. Japanese Americans from San Jose were generally interned at the Heart Mountain camp in Wyoming. In January 1943 a columnist for the camp newspaper, the *Heart Mountain Sentinel*, lamented that a gym had not yet been built for internees. Underscoring a dogged spirit and its place in the Japanese American community, the writer continues, "This means you'll have to don your pea coats, invest in some earmuffs, scarves, snowshoes, and some cough drops, before going out and cavorting on the courts." Clearly, internees were intent to play plenty of hoops despite the many obstacles before them. The Heart Mountain community responded with public support of the Zebras. The *Sentinel*, for example, lauded Zebra star Chi Akizuki as a "demon ball handler [who] stole the show." The team's success, winning the camp championship in 1943, was cause for recognition, and the *Sentinel* honored the Zebras for their "team coordination and fighting spirit."[20]

Before and after internment, Japanese American communities supported the idea of young females playing basketball and other community sports. Accordingly, young women from San Jose demonstrated their prowess at camp basketball and received recognition for their achievements. Basketball talent was a family affair as Akizuki's sister, Agnes Akizuki, starred when the Heart Mountain High School girls' team defeated Powell High, 27–19. Bernice Hinaga's athletic proficiency garnered headlines as well; she played for the camp's best girls' squad, the L'il Yokums, along with top scorer Jane Nakamoto.[21] Sport was not solely the province of boys and men. Communities took pride in young female participants' involvement in basketball, as these press report examples attest.

Racist realities persisted after the war ended, as did Japanese Americans' steadfast determination to continue their participation in athletics. World War II meant that Japanese American ballplayers in places like San Jose could no longer identify themselves as members of an Asahi nine given the association of Asahi with Japan. Amid these constraints Japanese American ballplayers and the community from which they came maintained a love affair with America's national pastime through the internment period and long after. Baseball-loving Japanese Americans from Santa Clara Valley rallied around the familiar name of Zebras at Heart Mountain, and the team continued to play under the same moniker upon their return to the valley after the war. Two years after V-J Day, the *San Jose Mercury* sports pages promoted a game between the Zebras and an all-Japanese American nine from Santa Barbara. At the same time, the Zebras competed in the Northern California Nisei Baseball League with nines from Monterey, Lodi, Richmond, Suisun, Florin, and Stockton. The Zebras' success was not only won within their own community but also extended to competition against non-Japanese American nines. Unfortunately, a Humboldt County nine called the Crabs canceled a visit of the Zebras when they learned that they would be hosting Japanese Americans. Frank Shimada told historian Ralph Pearce, "That was probably the lowest point we ever had."[22]

Similar to their baseball counterparts, the basketball Zebras hit the ground running after World War II, forming one of the better Asian American fives on the Pacific Coast. Like their baseball peers, these hoopsters competed against Japanese American and non-Japanese American squads. Late in 1949, the Zebras won the 1949 San Francisco Nisei Invitational Tournament thanks largely to the play of Chi Akizuki, Hide Kashima, and Eichi Adachi. Calling the Zebras a "classy local Nisei team," the *Mercury* reported the next week that they had garnered first place at a Buddhist Church–sponsored tournament in San Mateo with Akizuki and Kashima leading the way. In this mid-century moment, just months after the war and their confinement in the camps ended, the Zebras vied against predominately white opponents in the San Jose City League. Early in 1946, the Zebras downed hoopsters sponsored by a local auto sales company, 40–33. In December 1949 the Zebras decisively won a San Jose Winter League game, 50–25, sparked, once again, by Chi Akizuki's sixteen points.[23]

Throughout the 1930s and 1940s Chinese American and Filipino American athletes joined with the Japanese American athletes in a wide variety of sports laying claim to both athletic space *and,* as a result, civic participation in the nation's democracy. Led by brothers Harry and Jimmy Lee, the San Francisco–based *Chinese Digest* informed readers, in early 1936, that the San Jose Chinese hoopsters traveled down to Watsonville to defeat the local Chinese American five. Around the same time, the San Jose Chinese hosted a barnstorming five from Missouri. Harry Lee sparkled, leading his team to a 24–20 victory and notching fourteen points in the process. A few days later, the San Jose Chinese greeted the Young Chinese Club five from Oakland and lost, 27–23. The next month, Harry Lee poured in thirty-four points, but his team still fell to the Trojans Athletic Club, 71–61. These newspaper accounts provided the community with descriptive details of athletic contests, while simultaneously serving as a point of pride. While relatively small in number, Filipino Americans in Santa Clara Valley took up community hoops after World War II as well. Notable among them was the San Jose Agenda team, founded by Albert Bueno and Leo Escalante. In the spring of 1950, San Jose hosted a Filipino American basketball tournament at the city's Civic Auditorium. A five from San Jose, presumably the Agenda, participated as well as teams from Oakland, Vallejo, San Francisco, Livingston, Stockton, and Livermore. As author and activist Peter Jamero points out, such tournaments provided a strong sense of community among West Coast Filipino Americans.[24]

Asian Americans in the Santa Clara Valley participated in other athletic activities beyond basketball and baseball, though much of it remained segregated. Tennis, for example, attracted Chinese Americans in prewar Santa Clara Valley. In the late 1930s, the *Chinese Digest* identified Esther Chow, the daughter of a Chinese immigrant father who operated a grocery store in San Jose, as one of the top Chinese American tennis players in the area. The Chinese American publication also mentioned that San Jose resident William Wong participated in a tennis tournament sponsored by the Chinese American Citizens' Alliance and Chinese Tennis Club. Chow and Wong, moreover, combined as a doubles' team in the Chinese Pacific Coast Tennis Championship of 1936. The mere fact that the Chinese American community hosted a regional tennis championship is a testament to the value and importance placed on the activity.[25]

The same can be said for the sport of bowling, where Japanese Americans enthusiastically took to the activity, while being marginalized by the sport's governing bodies. After World War II, bowling enticed many Santa Clara Valley Japanese Americans despite the fact that, until 1950, the sport's dominant organizations, the

America Bowling Congress and the Women's International Bowling Congress, discriminated against nonwhites. In 1947, the *Mercury* announced an impending San Jose Nisei Invitational Handicap Bowling Tournament at the Valley Bowl. Men's and women's teams from all over California were expected to participate. During the early 1950s, the *San Jose Mercury* informed readers that a Nisei Bowling League operated in San Jose. Moreover, Japanese American women earned some publicity for their bowling skills. When the *Mercury* told readers about the Nisei Women's League in 1951, it identified Alice Ichishita as a top performer. In 1960, the *San Jose Mercury* published a photograph of Lucy Minamishi, described in the caption as "Petite . . . [and] well known in Nisei kegling circles." The thirty-five-year-old bowler, according to the *Mercury*, had just rolled a very impressive 665 series at Cherry Bowl in Sunnyvale. Sayo Tagame was another top female bowler in the valley, according to the *Mercury*. Among males, one of the great bowlers to emerge from the valley was Santa Clara's Frank "Fuzzy" Shimada, a magnificent all-around athlete who wound up bowling professionally.[26]

Sport reminded Asian Americans in Santa Clara Valley that they belonged to transnational, diasporic communities. Such is the case, for example, with boxing among Filipinos as the emotion and tenacity with which they fought was, at least in part, a response to their marginalized status. Whether living in Santa Clara Valley or elsewhere in the US Empire, Filipinos embraced prizefighting and, in particular, Pinoy prizefighters. Historian Linda España-Maran writes that the passion working-class Filipino immigrants summoned for their boxing heroes largely reflected their "conflict with the dominant society." She adds, "Regarded as no more than cheap 'stoop' labor and meek service workers by an insensitive host society, Filipinos engaged in strategies that offered the possibility of dignity and self-definition." Boxing provided one strategy. *San Jose News* columnist Buddy Leitch remarked in 1936 that Filipino "brown skin boxers have a big following among their countrymen who travel miles to support their favorites." Over a decade later, columnist Alex Fabros of the *Philippine Mail* declared, "The San Jose Civic Auditorium has always been the scene of fistic victories for Filipino boxers in the past," adding that Pinoys in San Jose "always flocked to witness" top Filipino boxers. Across Santa Clara Valley sport was far more than an athletic contest among Asian Americans. The games and events fostered avenues of self-expression and agency.[27]

Crossing Cultural Borders

Sport provided opportunities to create community within Asian American populations during the early to mid-twentieth century. Though most of these activities were carried out in segregated settings, this was not always the case. It is in those spaces, where Asian Americans crossed cultural and ethnic boundaries to participate in sport that we are afforded a valuable lens to better understand the dynamics of racism. Asian American females in Santa Clara Valley ventured across gender and class as well as racial and ethnic boundaries to play with and against non-Asian Americans in a variety of sports. Yet this movement, across borders, was not without issue, as athletically ambitious females faced institutional impediments. Historian Valerie Matsumoto reminds us how gendered and classed arrangements in rural settings limited Asian American female efforts to extend themselves beyond the home to participate in athletics. Matsumoto writes that many of the rural Japanese American parents living in California in the middle of the twentieth century felt they needed their daughters at home to help not only with work around the house but tending younger children. At the same time, Asian American communities in more urban settings such as San Francisco proved perhaps surprisingly amenable to females participating in community and school sports.[28]

Between the world wars, Santa Clara Valley offered a home for many recreational but competitive teams and leagues in baseball, softball, and basketball. In general, these teams and leagues reproduced the racial and gender hierarchy pervading American society. Alice Hinaga grew up in an athletically inclined Japanese American farm family. In the 1930s, night ball, mingling elements of baseball and softball and, of course, played under the lights, engaged Hinaga's considerable talents as a pitcher and hitter for a number of teams in San Jose. The athlete's dominance was reported, in 1933, for example, when Hinaga struck out fourteen batters as her Red and Whites squad shut down the Pacific Telephone Girls. For Hinaga and her female contemporaries, athletics provided a rare path down which young women could transgress cultural and ethnic boundaries. Even so, female participation was largely confined to limited interscholastic competition under the auspices of organizations such as the Girls' Athletic Association (GAA).[29] Hinaga and other Japanese American young women such as her sister, Beatrice, Mitsui Muyata, Helen Tokunaga, Leah Tokunaga, Tatsuye Suyeishi, Mitsuye Suyeishi, and Ellen Okagaki took part in GAA sports at San Jose High School in the 1930s.[30] Despite their commitment to, and enthusiasm for, sporting participation, young females' activities remained at the margins of broader athletic activity for Asian Americans in this mid-century moment.

Despite the difficulties facing would-be Japanese American female athletes in agricultural settings, some were able to take part in high school sports in the more rural areas of Santa Clara Valley prior to World War II. Tayeko Kiyomura played on Mountain View High's senior class basketball team as early as 1919. In the mid-1930s, Alice Higuchi and Sadako Oyama captained basketball squads at Santa Clara High, and classmate Sumiko Takedo captained a volleyball contingent. And at Campbell High School during the 1939–1940 academic year, Lily Takimoto, Mary Nakagawa, and Evelyn Yoshida played basketball.[31] While not always welcomed, Japanese Americans resettled in San Jose and the suburbanizing areas of Santa Clara Valley after World War II, and girls soon carried on sporting traditions within area high schools.[32] For example, the 1950–1951 yearbook for San Jose High reveals that Betty Inouye and Lillie Ishizaki took up basketball during the fall semester. Indeed, the yearbook shows a photograph of Inouye displaying her shooting form. Several Japanese American female residents of east San Jose participated in James Lick's GAA during the 1953–1954 academic year. Young women did not simply participate but took on leadership roles as Kay Nomi served as the organization's president. She was joined by the daughter of a prewar farm laborer, Betty Okayama, as well as Janet Sasaki, Violet Kawamoto, Nancy Ishizaka, Ikako Tsukuda, Keiko Tsukuda, Joyce Oyama, and Midori Uchiyama, whose father was a farmer before World War II. Ten years later, Bernice Yonekawa, Karen Komachi, and Hideka Oda were female athletes at James Lick High.[33]

Young men in high school during this period enjoyed many more competitive interscholastic opportunities than their female peers. This, in part, explains why Asian American males were decidedly more likely to engage in cross-cultural athletic competition. San Jose High School suited up several Asian American boys before and after World War II. In 1925, Russ Hinaga starred on San Jose High's baseball team. Joe Jio shot and dribbled for the 110-pound basketball five during the 1927–1928 academic year. Dubbed the "Japanese boy" by the *Mercury*, Frank Ichishita was a regular for San Jose High's unlimited five during the 1929–1930 season. Ichishita, moreover, was considered a valuable member of San Jose's grid team as a fullback, while pitching for the school's nine. In lightweight basketball, San Jose could boast of several Asian Americans in the early to mid-1930s. Vic Hirose captained the D basketball team in 1934, while Chinese American Harry Lee captained the C team on which Mitsu Ishikawa and George Hinaga also starred. The next year Sal Jio captained a San Jose High lightweight hoops team. Five years later, Chi Akizuki excelled on the 120-pound team. And in the weeks before the Pearl Harbor attack, Frank Yoshioka and Yoshi Minato sparked the 120-pound hoopsters at San Jose High.[34]

Beyond the schoolyards, Asian American males competed in recreational, but still highly competitive leagues. In adult basketball Frank Ichishita suited up for a five sponsored by Gibino Meats. In baseball, Russ Hinaga stood out for the Milpitas nine. Indeed, Hinaga captained the multiethnic Milpitas aggregation. In February 1930, the *Mercury* reported that Hinaga, "the doughty little Milpitas man," struck out eleven batters in a game against Lake Almaden.[35]

After World War II, Japanese American boys returned to San Jose High's courts and fields. In the late 1940s, Ray Matsunaga stood out as a hoopster for

San Jose High, and Ben Yoshihara was one of his teammates. Hash Taketa earned a spot as a guard on the second team all-county football squad after the 1950 campaign, while also catching on the school's baseball team. As a lightweight hoopster, Tom Sakamoto was an all-leaguer in the early 1950s. In the fall of 1952, Mits Fukumura proved an accurate passer for the varsity eleven. And Terry Maruyama's "floor game and peerless scoring" earned praise from the *Mercury* in January 1960.[36]

After World War II, a handful of Asian American males crossed racial frontiers to play with and against non-Asian Americans. Athletically skilled second- and even third-generation Asian Americans were reaching or had reached young adulthood. Moreover, World War II created an America, at least in the early postwar years, which was more receptive to racial frontier crossing if, for no other reason, than to distance itself from Nazi Germany and vex communist propaganda that American capitalism stymied true democracy. In 1946, the *San Jose News* told readers that the S.P. Stores nine fielded "Frank Wong, speedy long hitting Chinese outfielder." In the late summer of 1947, two Zebra stars, George Hinaga and Babe Nomura, took the diamond with whites on the Southside Market nine. And an independent team from Sunnyvale suited up, according to the *Mercury*, "Sam Sugimoto, a classy young shortstop from Mountain View" in 1950.[37] Mention of Asian American success in the local press can be critically read in a number of ways, including as a dominant narrative suggesting that only in a democracy could opportunities for racial and ethnic minorities be fostered, respected, and encouraged.

College Athletes

College athletics provided another location in which Asian Americans resisted the contours of racism and marginalization. Several Asian Americans competed for the region's three primary four-year schools—Stanford, Santa Clara, and especially San Jose State. Many of these athletes were more than just "benchwarmers." While the United States prepared to intern West Coast Japanese Americans in the spring of 1942, Hawaiian Japanese Dick Miyagawa boxed his way to a national championship for San Jose State. Miyagawa's reward for crossing the Pacific to enroll at San Jose State was incarceration in a concentration camp before the government allowed him to move on to the University of Wisconsin, for which he won a national championship as well.[38]

Following the war, southern Californian Babe Nomura created excitement for San Jose State College's football team. The *San Francisco Chronicle* pronounced Nomura a "very fast and shifty runner, and a good passer." The press periodically lauded Nomura, though identity markers remained in place. The *San Diego Union* printed the contention that "San Jose's Japanese-American halfback" could star on any eleven on the West Coast. The praise was seemingly deserved as Nomura made the all-conference team in 1946.[39]

As a public institution and thus relatively accessible to first-generation college students, San Jose State offered something of a welcome mat for some Asian American athletes before and after World War II. As one example, Sal Jio played well for San Jose State's freshman hoops team during the 1935–1936 season. In the late 1930s, the wrestling squad included George Takayanagi. A few years later, George Konoshima joined Dick Miyagawa on the boxing team in 1940. Jake Kikuchi a "190 pound Japanese American guard from Los Angeles" was Babe Nomura's teammate after the war, and Jim Kajioka was a 250-pound tackle for the Spartans in the early 1950s. The 1953 Stanford vs. San Jose State football programs reveals a Spartan roster that included Tom Yagi, a fine center and linebacker from Livingston, as well as that Lincoln Kimura served as team trainer and Larry Shishido as team manager. Ken Matsuda joined the Spartan's backfield in the mid- to late 1950s, and halfback Tommy Uyeda was one of his teammates. Also on the team in the mid-1950s was talented running back Mel Soong, recruited from Hawaii. And Herb Yamasaki performed well as lineman for San Jose State in the late 1950s and early 1960s. In baseball, Tom Okagaki was a fine second baseman for the Spartans before Japanese American relocation, while returning to the Spartans' nine after the war. Wrestling at San Jose State after World War II were Ben Ichikawa, George Uchida, Robert Fukunaga, and Kiyoshi Oshiba. In the late 1950s and early 1960s, T. C. Chung excelled as a boxer. Meanwhile, Yosh Uchida became what sports columnist Mark Purdy has called "one of San Jose's human treasures." After World War II, the San Jose–raised Uchida started as a judo instructor and coach at San Jose State. In the next thirty-five years, his teams won thirty-two national championships.[40] Importantly, these varied athletic experiences and opportunities took place at San Jose State, the oldest public institution in the state of California.

The region's major private colleges, Stanford and Santa Clara, occasionally offered opportunities as well for Asian American athletes. Described as a "diminutive forward" in the *Daily Palo Alto*, a Japanese American from San Francisco, Fred Koba, played varsity hoops for Stanford in the early 1920s. During the next decade, Mark Kai-Kee and Yuji Imai boxed for Stanford. After World War II, a Japanese American from Placer County, George Goto, played basketball briefly for Stanford before transferring to Sacramento State. The *Pacific Citizen* asserted that Goto's career at Stanford had been limited by an injury. Nevertheless, it did report that he did well against Santa Clara, notching eight points off the bench and shining as a stingy defender.[41]

Santa Clara University is not known as a NCAA powerhouse, but it has been represented by talented athletes and well-respected teams. For example, Santa

Clara's eleven made its way to the prestigious Orange Bowl on January 1, 1950. There they downed a Kentucky eleven coached by the renowned Paul "Bear" Bryant. One of the stars of the game for Santa Clara was Chinese Hawaiian Abe Dung, a versatile backfield performer who shined both on offense and defense, as well as a punter.[42] Attending Santa Clara at about the same time was Filipino American Eddie Chavez, who played both varsity basketball and baseball for the Broncos. After starring on the freshman hoops' squad, Chavez did not play much in the way of varsity basketball for the Broncos. In baseball, however, Chavez emerged as a "brilliant right hander," according to the *Mercury*. When Santa Clara beat the College of the Pacific in early March 1950, the *Mercury* maintained the "5-7 pepper pot . . . stole the show" by striking out five after taking over the mound in the fifth inning and hitting a double to boot. According to the Santa Clara University 1950 Yearbook, he achieved a parsimonious 1.88 ERA in league action.[43]

The ability of individual Asian Americans to make college athletic teams in the middle decades of the twentieth century suggests the democratic possibilities of sport. But it is important to remain mindful of sport's limitations. Dick Miyagawa, after all, still wound up in a concentration camp despite winning a NCAA boxing championship for San Jose State. Moreover, it is vital to remind ourselves of the historical context for post–World War II Asian American participation in college sport at San Jose State and elsewhere. Post–World War II America in general witnessed a substantial breaking down of racial barriers in amateur and professional athletics. Beyond Jackie Robinson, Asian Americans such as divers Sammy Lee and Vicki Manalo, basketball player Wat Misaka, football and baseball player Wally Yonamine, and swimmer Ford Konno were crossing cultural borderlands to participate as champion Olympians or professional football, basketball, and baseball players in the late 1940s and early 1950s. As mentioned earlier in this piece, the integration of Asian American athletics may have been encouraged by World War II idealism and Cold War pragmatism. Moreover, as historians Ellen Wu and Cindy I-Fen Cheng point out, the latter helped in reproducing Asian Americans as a distorted symbol of American racial progress to combat communist propaganda and still the militancy of the burgeoning civil rights movement.[44] The impetus for positive social change did not simply rest with the dominant group's actions and motivations, however. Asian American athletes resisted dominant understandings of who and what they were expected to be. Sport settings across the mid-twentieth century were an important vehicle for that change.

Conclusion

Today, Santa Clara Valley is no longer the "garden of the world." Silicon Valley's tech industry and institutions of higher education, eager to train prospective employees for Apple, Google, EBay, and Hewlett-Packard, among others, have lured Asian immigrants very different from those who migrated to San Jose and surrounding largely agricultural communities one hundred years ago. That is, the valley's diverse Asian American population is significantly Chinese, Filipino, Vietnamese, Indian, and Pakistani descent. Moreover, the region has proven somewhat hospitable for Asian immigrants and their children who have developed meaningful community institutions in and around San Jose. However, the other side of Silicon Valley has remained on the lookout for inexpensive and exploitable Asian labor. But in more recent years the need is not for Asian farmworkers but Asians to labor in restaurants, hotels, day care centers, hospitals, convalescent homes, and semiconductor companies. Meanwhile, Asians and Asian Americans possessing excellent education and experience in technology, science, and business encounter the Silicon Valley's version of the glass ceiling.[45] Racism remains, though it takes on different forms within particular historical moments.

While Santa Clara Valley's Asian Americans differ from the region's mid-twentieth-century counterparts in terms of nationality and occupation, they too have embraced sport. Asian American athletes of all ages and skill levels pervade the valley's basketball courts and golf courses, swinging baseball and cricket bats, tackling ball carriers, and nurturing their backhands. Asian Americans, such as Stanford's Lindsey Yamasaki, as one example, have starred in Division 1 athletic programs in the Santa Clara Valley. Elite Asian American athletes earn the attention of the valley region and the world, as well. Perhaps this is embodied most keenly and recently by the "mania" invoked by a Taiwanese American from Palo Alto—Jeremy Lin.

Still, long before Jeremy Lin handled a basketball for the first time, Asian Americans athletes in the Santa Clara Valley represented their ethnic communities and school fives. Some gained a modicum of fame by way of local ethnic or mainstream newspapers. Nearly all played in comparative anonymity. Yet, however obscured by racial nativism, Asian Americans in mid-twentieth-century Santa Clara Valley demonstrated the possibilities and limitations of sport as a democratic undertaking.

8

San Francisco 49ers

The Romance of Memory

JEFFREY MONTEZ DE OCA

There is a moment frozen in the minds of San Francisco Forty Niners' fans known as "The Catch." It occurred on January 10, 1982, with fifty-eight seconds left in the NFC Championship Game against the Niners' nemesis, the Dallas Cowboys. Famously, Joe Montana rolled right under pressure from Dallas's vaunted "Doomsday Defense." With fractions of a second left before he was either sacked or run out of bounds, Montana threw the ball high to the back of the end zone where a leaping Dwight Clark caught the ball for a touchdown. The frozen image of Clark snatching the game-winning touchdown symbolizes a threshold moment in the history of the franchise and the psyche of its fans: a shift from humiliation to dominance befitting a global city.

Prior to the 1981 season, the Forty Niners had been a perennial disappointment to the city and its fans. During their thirty-one years in the NFL before 1981, the 49ers had only four strong seasons (1957, 1970, 1971, and 1972), and each of those ended bitterly. In 1957, the 49ers (8-4) hosted the Detroit Lions for the Western Division playoff. Leading 27–7 in the third quarter, the Forty Niners lost 31–27 to a team led by its backup quarterback. After winning the Western Divisional title in 1970 and 1971, the Forty Niners lost each time to the Cowboys in the NFC Championship. The Niners won their third consecutive Western Divisional title in 1972 and again faced the Dallas Cowboys in the divisional playoffs. As in 1957, San Francisco jumped out to an early lead (21–6) in the second quarter and led 28–16 in the fourth quarter before backup quarterback Roger Staubach led the Cowboys to a 30–28 victory. After three exciting but disappointing seasons, the 49ers became one of the weakest NFL teams in the 1970s. The Niners were 2-14 in Bill Walsh's first year as head coach and general manager (1979), and their 6-10 record in 1980 included an eight-game losing streak.

As a Forty Niners' fan growing up in Berkeley, California, in the 1970s, a time and place whose sports world was dominated by the Raiders, I still remember the exuberance and redemption that Niners' fans felt when Montana and Clark made The Catch. The Niners had seemed unable to win big games, as a 1971 *Sports Illustrated* article stated, "In the saloons and salons of Baghdad-by-the-Bay, the faithless winced and waited for 'El Foldo,' which blows into town as regularly as the Pacific fog."[1] As my family jumped and screamed for joy in our basement, my next-door neighbor ran up and down our block screaming out of control, and nobody thought worse of him. Not only had the Niners broken a thirty-five-year big game jinx, they did it against "America's Team," whose success in the 1970s mocked their own bitter disappointment.

In 1981 fans began calling themselves the "49ers Faithful" to suggest loyalty to a historically unsuccessful yet popular team. And while the Faithful were confident approaching the 1982 Super Bowl, little did anyone know that the 49ers were at the beginning of the Bill Walsh–Joe Montana "Dynasty." Between 1981 and 1989, the Forty Niners won four Super Bowls, seven divisional titles, and made the playoffs eight times. Further, Bill Walsh's vaunted "West Coast" offense changed the game of football. At the same time, the 49ers' success also triggered critical reactions. Critics who preferred run-oriented offenses complained that the West Coast offense was based on "finesse" and trickery rather than taking on opponents directly. So despite achieving success equal to the Green Bay Packers of the 1960s and the Pittsburgh Steelers of the 1970s, critics disparaged the Forty Niners as a finesse team that was boring and predictable. Detractors also called the 49ers Faithful "Brie cheese and chardonnay" fans to project a Yuppie character onto the city. While criticism can be understood simply as personal preference for styles of play, sociologists argue that taste and preference are actually patterned choices rooted in the institutional organization of society.[2]

In this chapter, I focus on aspects of the Forty Niners and San Francisco's history typically obscured in public memory. More specifically I focus on how frozen moments such as The Catch and the Dynasty obscure what came before those moments and how those moments are perceived through broader social forces. Since frozen moments encourage us to focus on a part of the picture, for example, Clark hanging in the air or a smiling Joe Montana holding his arms above his head to signal a(nother) game-winning touchdown, they also discourage us from looking outside of the frame. To excavate what is typically overlooked, I first sketch a history of San Francisco to highlight aspects of the city that get obscured by its romantic image, then I focus on the 49ers in the 1950s and 1960s to remember what the Niners' fans were like in the "bad old days," and finally I focus on the class and gendered construction of the team during the Dynasty. My point is not to reify the "we were so bad and then we were so good" narrative typical in Forty Niners' history telling. Instead, I want to first argue that the contemporary focus on the Dynasty obscures the early history of the 49ers, particularly the class character of San Francisco. Second, I argue criticism of the 49ers during the Dynasty was as responsive to changes in global capitalism as it was to either the team or its fans. In other words, our perceptions of teams and fans are refracted through broader institutional relations and social forces.

Empire by the Bay

When people think of San Francisco a number of romantic images likely come to mind. Foggy hills climbed by quaint cable cars might be the place where they left their heart. Perhaps it is Chinatown's mysterious streets or Fisherman's Wharf seafaring and whaling past that come to mind. Others might think of the bawdy days of the Barbary Coast and the prospecting argonauts of the gold rush. Others still might think of Beats sipping espresso, young women provocatively dancing during the Summer of Love, or Harvey Milk breathlessly leading a political rally in front of beautiful (and expensive) Victorian houses. Images of San Francisco as an exciting, progressive, and romantic city are a part of its mythology. Lurking beneath the postcard images is a voracious urban growth machine that draws in people and resource to produce tremendous wealth.

Gray Brechin argues that the history of San Francisco is inseparable from capitalist development and the imperial ambitions of the United States.[3] After the small Mexico village of Yerba Buena became a part of the United States, renamed San Francisco in 1847, and gold was discovered in 1848, the city began to draw "everything from the Rockies to China, and from Alaska to Chile, into its growing maw. Far more than whales and bears were pulled towards extinction as the city's transformative powers grew. Forests were leveled on all Pacific shores, rivers and lakes vanished, and the bay from which the city took its name was filled, poisoned, and plundered, while wildlife and natives within the vortex were speedily exterminated."[4] In other words, San Francisco's growth was tied to the global economic expansion of the United States and that growth exerted tremendous violence on the people and the land captured in its markets. Centrally located on the Pacific Coast at the mouth of the San Francisco Bay, the city served as a conduit between western and eastern economic interests in the United States as well as being a gateway for US imperial ambitions throughout the Pacific, including Hawaii, the Philippines, Japan, and China.[5] While the gold rush was central to San Francisco's initial growth and built the economic infrastructure, especially metallurgy, necessary for further growth,[6] it was ongoing wars in the Pacific and urban-industrial growth in the region that continued to drive its growth after the boom years of the gold rush.[7] In short, an urban economic elite used a combination of environmental and commercial forces to transform San Francisco from a camp (Yerba Buena) into a global city in about thirty-five years.[8]

When viewed through the fog of its romantic imagery, it might be surprising to think that San Francisco was the transportation and manufacturing center of the West Coast. As recently as 1938, the San Francisco port was second in value only to New York.[9] And it remained a leading port city on the Pacific Coast until the 1950s when cargo containers moved shipping to the ports of Long Beach-Los Angeles, Oakland-Alameda, and Seattle.[10] In 1860, SF produced 60 percent of the West Coast's manufactured goods.[11] The dominant industries were lumber and woodworking, metallurgy and machining, food processing, and animal processing.[12] The smelters and foundries as well as its Pacific location made San Francisco an ideal location for naval and weapons manufacturing that were used in expansionist wars in the Pacific. So just as the military was necessary to protect San Francisco's mining interests, it also fostered its economic growth.[13]

The importance of industry and shipping to the political economy of San Francisco gave the city a strong working-class identity and made it a leading site of militant labor activism.[14] The work that longshoremen did was dangerous, physically challenging, and took a good deal of knowledge to move enough cargo to fill a five-mile freight train in two days and a night.[15] The labor conditions as well as the corruption of city and union officials led San Francisco's workers to organize and strive for progressive change.[16] Perhaps the most famous labor action was "Bloody Thursday" on July 5, 1934, when a battle between police and strikers left two dead and hundreds injured.[17] In 1936 the Maritime Federation of the Pacific called a strike that stopped all shipping on the Pacific Coast. The strike cost shipping-related industries "$700 million—up to that time the most costly strike ever in U.S. maritime history."[18] Although the major industrial actions did not always net workers' desired gains, they radicalized and trained labor to fight for workplace justice and broader political issues for decades. Bruce Nelson calls the mid-twentieth-century labor activism in San Francisco a "syndicalist renaissance" when longshoremen and seamen were able to "take control of hiring, improve wages and conditions, and agitate around a host of political issues, from police brutality in San Pedro to the civil war in Spain."[19]

Manufacturing in San Francisco plateaued between 1890 and 1930 when it began moving to other parts of the Bay Area.[20] The movement of industry into South San Francisco, Oakland, and Richmond was driven by San Francisco's economic elites, and it effectively made the entire Bay Area a single economic unit supplied by vast regions of western North America and the Pacific.[21] Despite the loss of manufacturing, San Francisco remained the banking center of the western United States.[22] San Francisco's leading capitalist class factions began a strategy of economic redevelopment in the 1950s that ultimately transformed the city's skyline and political economy. As manufacturing and wholesale jobs dropped substantially and total population fell 10 percent, total employment rose in the 1960s and 1970s, especially, in the finance, insurance, and real estate (FIRE) sector. By the mid-1990s, only 15 percent of jobs remained blue collar and San Francisco was second only to New York City in international commerce and banking.[23] Redevelopment begun in the 1950s transformed the city's landscape by the 1980s, most famously symbolized by the TransAmerica Building and the Moscone Convention Center.[24] As part of the redevelopment process, San Francisco financed Candlestick Park, the eventual home of the 49ers, to attract the New York Giants baseball team and to make San Francisco a big league city.[25]

Less visible than the monuments of capitalist development is the violence that economic redevelopment inflicted on working-class and poor communities

Aerial view of Candlestick Park. *Courtesy Photographs in the Carol M. Highsmith Archive, Library of Congress, Prints and Photographs Division.*

of color in the guise of "urban renewal." Racialized urban-economic strategies have long been a part of San Francisco's history. Japanese students were segregated in schools when San Francisco-based industries experienced economic and territorial competition in the Pacific with imperial Japan in the early 1900s.[26] Without the political backing of Japan, the Chinese endured even worse conditions over a longer time.[27] In the mid-1960s, under labor mayor John Shelley, low-income African American and Japanese homes were destroyed to make space for the Geary Street expansion and high-rise buildings.[28] While economic development was orchestrated by economic elites to speed the movement of capital and enrich themselves,[29] it destroyed working-class neighborhoods, such as South of Market, and exasperated poverty and segregation in communities of color.[30] Historical memory of economic violence led African American residents of Bayview-Hunters Point to oppose investment in Candlestick Park in the 1990s since they felt that increasing real estate value harmed them. Or as residents stated, they learned in the 1960s that "urban renewal" was a euphemism for "negro removal."[31]

The history of San Francisco is tied to capitalist development that privileges some by dispossessing others. The gold rush of 1849 infused the city with the capital that began its inexorable growth. Mining wealth funded the economic infrastructure that made San Francisco the transportation and manufacturing center of the Pacific Coast. Its location and the economic ambitions of leading capitalist class factions made it a global city that was further fueled by US imperialist wars in the Pacific throughout the nineteenth and twentieth centuries. Transformations in capital moved manufacturing and transportation out of the city. As skyscrapers were built in the 1960s and 1970s, the FIRE sector expanded and the labor force became increasingly white collar, the class character of the city changed. Economic redevelopment also attacked the city's working-class and poor communities, who, like manufacturing, were segregated and pushed out of the city limits. With the growth of new technologies (computers in Silicon Valley and biotechnologies in Berkeley-Emeryville) as well as the growing prestige of Napa Valley and Sonoma wine production, San Francisco was a leading global city in the late twentieth century and a key node in the global flows of capital.[32]

Professional Football on the Barbary Coast

In 1946, amid economic redevelopment, professional football came to the Pacific Coast when the Forty Niners were founded as an original member of the All-American Football Conference (AAFC).[33] The AAFC was a professional football league from 1946 to 1949 when the National Football League (NFL) absorbed it. San Francisco was an excellent post–World War II location for a professional team since many soldiers who had passed through it during the war wanted to return to settle or visit as tourists.[34] Although the Niners ran second only to the Cleveland Browns in the AAFC,[35] which is one of the reasons they survived the merger, they struggled upon entering the NFL. For instance, on September 24, 1950, the 49ers went into halftime with a lead but "were rudely tumbled into the cold world of reality by the beefy, hard smashing Chicago Bears" in the second half.[36] Sports writers in 1950 explained that the franchise had moved into a real professional football league, and it would take time to catch up with established NFL teams.[37] Despite their poor performance, commentators argued the NFL made San Francisco a major league city by bringing the best football teams to town[38] and that fans needed to support the team until they eventually became champions since that is how to keep a NFL franchise.[39]

The 49ers performed even worse in the 1960s than the 1950s. Popular history books from the time, such as *San Francisco 49ers* (1974), struggled to construct a glorious past. They could focus on the hard running of Hugh McElhenny, the speed of Gene Washington, the "Million Dollar backfield," R. C. Owens inventing the "Alley-Oop" in 1957, or coach Red Hickey innovating the shotgun formation in 1960.[40] But the team did not have a single championship and rarely made the playoffs. In the 1960s, the local press tended to explain the 49ers poor performance by describing their seemingly endless stream of injuries. One article stated, "When the 49ers boarded the plane in San Francisco [for Philadelphia] some were limping, some sniffing and some nursing broken bones."[41] Another article used pictures of post-op scars on the knees of different 49ers players to illustrate football's danger to the human knee.[42] Still another article joked that the Niners' woes were a boon to a local hospital, "St. Mary's Hospital has a first class pro backfield but the San Francisco 49ers are in a lot of trouble."[43] Although the team did not win many games, the fans were exciting.

Just as San Francisco workers on the waterfront in the mid-twentieth century shaped the color and character of the city so too the 49ers' fans shaped the color and character of Kezar Stadium. The 49ers' fans of the 1950s and 1960s have been referred to as "obstreperous,"[44] "rumbustious disciples,"[45] and "among the most bibulous and truculent in the league."[46] Fan violence was noted as early as 1953 as Ron Fimrite commented, "Philadelphia [Eagles] players were shocked to find that among their opponents were bottle-wielding fans and even belligerent members of the pep band."[47] In 1964, fans reportedly got out of control when a St. Louis Cardinals' fullback dove for a one-yard touchdown on fourth down but fans thought he had been stopped.[48] An article titled "Kezar No Place for Babies" explained, "it was a day in which bitter meanness flowed into the stands, and San Francisco fans stopped the game for several minutes with the wildest outburst of booing which we've ever heard at Kezar."[49] The 49ers' fans, also called

"Kezar's Cruelty Brigade" for their treatment of Niners' quarterbacks,[50] were so violent that team officials contemplated building a moat around the field but instead settled for a wire fence to protect the Niners' players from flying objects when leaving the field.[51] Fan violence hit its zenith following the 49ers last game in Kezar, a 17–14 loss to Dallas in the 1970 NFC Championship, when fans began tearing the stadium apart and rioting. "A group of more than 20 young men went on a postgame rampage near the west end zone, throwing bottles and cans and attacking spectators. Thirteen people were treated for cuts and bruises, and 22 arrests were made."[52]

Ron Fimrite's profile of James S. Todt, a San Francisco bartender, avid 49ers fan, and president of the John Brodie Fan Club, showed that alcohol was a major part of fan behavior. Game days for Todt and his gang typically began in a bar before they took a chartered bus to the "dilapidated" stadium. Sardined onto splintered wood bleachers in Kezar, Fimrite wrote, "Contiguity can breed contempt, and Todt and his seatmates were soon involved in a surprisingly hostile debate on the relative merits of [quarterback John] Brodie and his rookie heir apparent, Steve Spurrier." The debate escalated and Todt's wife sprayed champagne into her neighbor's face, which triggered a typical Kezar melee where there "were no arrests and only a few minor injuries." When Todt met his hero John Brodie in a sauna, he claims Brodie was surprised by his appearance since he expected Todt to be covered in bruises.[53] Indeed, my father went to see the Niners twice in the 1960s and says the only things he really remembers about the games was getting splinters from the rotting wood bleachers and walking past the first aid station where two or three guys "had blood just flowing from their heads."[54]

Fan violence belies San Francisco's Brie cheese and chardonnay image. In fact, fan violence was not limited to Kezar or 49ers' fans. In a 1964 game between Lincoln and Balboa High, "there was a full-scale riot involving rooters outside Lincoln's stadium shortly after the game."[55] That game could partially be explained by Lincoln's 51–3 rout of Balboa.[56] However, that was not the only example of fan violence at a high school game in the mid-1960s. The previous year fans of a San Francisco high school team had blocked another team's bus and poked knives through its open windows.[57]

Media coverage of fan violence in San Francisco supports what an older 49ers fan told me when I interviewed him in 2001 about football in the 1950s and 1960s. "Frank" was a lifelong football fan who grew up in San Francisco in the 1930s and 1940s. He attended Niners' games regularly but often found Kezar unsettling. He explained that most Niners' fans, at that time, were longshoremen who liked to drink and fight. When we reflect back on the history of San Francisco this is not surprising. Up to the 1970s, San Francisco had a strong working-class core with a history of militant labor activism, especially in the 1930s. By the 1950s and 1960s labor was declining with the collapse of shipping and manufacturing, and working-class neighborhoods were under attack by urban renewal. I am not trying to equate labor activism with football hooliganism. Instead, I am arguing that San Francisco still had a working-class milieu, albeit shrinking and under attack, wherein expressive forms of fanship would be more culturally consistent than a restrained style of middle-class fanship.[58] The media explained fan violence as resulting from the 49ers poor performance, the discomfort of an outdated, dilapidated stadium, and alcohol consumption.[59] While those were all likely contributing factors and triggers of fan violence, they do not explain violence at San Francisco high schools in the 1960s. Underlying factors were likely an expressive working-class culture experiencing the economic violence of redevelopment. Transformations in capital enriched economic elites but dispossessed the working class, which no doubt created frustration expressed as fan violence, among other ways.

Brie Cheese, Chardonnay, and a Dynasty on the Dock of the Bay

In San Francisco, the Dynasty past is always present. Every current team, coach, and quarterback needs to wrestle with the image of the Dynasty. Gwen Knapp of the *SF Chronicle* made this clear in Jim Harbaugh's first season coaching the 49ers when she wrote, "With Sunday's win in Detroit, Jim Harbaugh probably proved that the 49ers have found the head coach to return them to greatness. He definitely established that, on his watch, the *Chardonnay and Brie image from their first dynasty* won't be making a comeback."[60] In Harbaugh, Knapp sees continuity of success on the field and difference in terms of manliness. "If Bill Walsh once untucked his shirt, briefly flashed some abdomen, and if he chest-bumped an offensive lineman as he raced across a field after a big victory, YouTube doesn't have the clip. He definitely didn't offer up a handshake that turned the losing coach into a special-teams gunner and drew most of the players from both teams into a skirmish."[61] Knapp contrasts an effusive and physical Jim Harbaugh to the memory of a restrained and cerebral Bill Walsh.

While obviously playful, Knapp's humor rests on a Cartesian dualism that animated perceptions of the Forty Niners throughout the Dynasty era. Cartesian dualism sees mind and body in binary opposition so that the mind develops in opposition to the body.[62] From this perspective the body is base and driven by impulses and sensations whereas the mind symbolizes transcendence and the higher orders of society. Applied to the Niners, Walsh's cerebral style was linked to high culture. Writing in *Sports Illustrated*, Rick Telander described Walsh as "the silver-haired gent who turns out signal callers the way Stradivarius turned out violins"[63] and Jim Murray of the *LA Times* claimed, "You half expect [Walsh's] headset is playing Mozart."[64] These writers use *classical* music (i.e., high culture) as a metaphor for Walsh's scholarly approach to football.

Walsh's scholarly (i.e., mindful) approach to the game appeared deviant in the 1980s. As one writer stated: "The result in San Francisco has been a quirky, iconoclastic, emphatically unpredictable sort of football. It is true California football, never quite grasped before it changes, irreverent toward tradition, pressing at imagined limits and upsetting the doctrinaire to the point of causing moral disapproval."[65] Walsh himself contrasted his pass-oriented approach to the "traditional" football of the Midwest and figures like Woody Hayes and Bo Schembechler who coached Harbaugh at Michigan. Walsh saw traditional football as predictable and reliant upon perfect execution of superior players,[66] which is great for top teams but disadvantages poorer teams, for example, Indiana compared to Michigan in the Big Ten.[67] Whereas running plays like Vince Lombardi's famed power sweep requires perfect execution of all eleven players to succeed,[68] a quick pass play requires perfect execution by only two players (quarterback and receiver) and adequate performance by the rest of the team.[69]

In 1979 the Niners had a dearth of superior players relative to top teams such as the Steelers and the Cowboys. By taking advantage of the 1977 rules changes that opened up the pass, Walsh's team could compete with better staffed teams by throwing short, quick passes and not trying to out muscle them.[70] But this less muscular approach led Walsh's West Coast offense to be framed in effeminizing language, "In Walsh's first two years in San Francisco the 49ers would win with finesse, with silk handkerchiefs in the air and rabbits popping out of a hat."[71] As the years passed and the 49ers' talent pool increased through clever draft choices and trades, Walsh's approach born of poverty (in Cincinnati actually) made the 49ers the dominant team of the 1980s.[72] The West Coast offense was so effective even Big Ten colleges adopted more sophisticated offensive strategies as a 1982 *Sports Illustrated* article stated, "You'll see right there in cold squared-off digits what Bill Walsh, new blocking rules, California and colored gloves—among other things—have done to college football: Passing isn't just up, it's way up."[73] Walsh's success allowed many of his assistants, such as Mike Holmgren, Andy Reid, Sam Wyche, Jon Gruden, Mike Shanahan, Denny Green, and Ray Rhodes, to spread the West Coast offense throughout the NFL over succeeding years.

The effectiveness of the West Coast offense obscured the fact that the 49ers' success was equally built on aggressive defenses. For instance, after Dwight Clark made The Catch and while my neighbor was screaming in front of our houses, it was a sack of Danny White and a forced fumble that stopped the Cowboys from reaching field goal range and stealing back the victory. Throughout the 1980s the Niners probably won more close games on defense than by Joe "Cool's"

(Montana) last-minute touchdowns. Walsh, for his own part, began his career coaching and designing defenses.[74] Regardless, the image of Walsh as cerebral kept the 49ers labeled a "finesse" team, which in the hypermasculine world of football is a euphemism for unmanly.

In addition to a sophisticated offense, the 49ers were also known for a precise, machine-like system that generated yards, scores, and quarterbacks.[75] An offense based on short, quick passes "felt *engineered*. The virtues it exalted above all other were precision, consistency, and predictability. . . . [Walsh] had infused the passing game with two new qualities: dullness and safety."[76] The fact that Walsh scripted the initial plays of every game added to the image of the 49ers as a machine that robbed individuals of spontaneity and agency: "Neat, clean, everything was accounted for but the score. You could almost hear the click of tumblers as the intricate mechanism was set into motion.... It was all down there on Walsh's little sheet of paper. Click went the tumblers. A sweep for seven more yards, a quick pitch to Cooper for 21. First down on the Oilers' four. Click."[77] It did not matter in Walsh's system, critics argued, if Kenny Anderson, Dan Fouts, Steve DeBerg, Joe Montana, Steve Young, or Jeff Garcia were running the offense since anyone, it seemed, could be effective in his system. "The system was the star. Walsh had imported into pro football the spirit of a Japanese auto plant—Total Quality Management."[78]

Like the Japanese auto industry in the 1980s, Walsh's system had its detractors. A nostalgic reaction to the 49ers' success crystalized after the New York Giants won the Super Bowl in 1991 as "smash mouth football," Don Pierson wrote in the *Chicago Tribune*, "A tremendous sigh of relief was heard throughout the National Football League Monday . . . Conventional football reigned."[79] New York Giants tackle Lomas Brown described smash mouth football in 2001 as "trying to pound it [run the ball] and eventually if we pound it enough and pound it right, something will give."[80] Smash mouth football harkens to Woody Hayes's "three yards and a cloud of dust" philosophy since it relies on a run-oriented, "ball control" offense and strong defense. Smash mouth teams typically run out of the I-formation to exert extra muscle from a fullback and tight end at the point of attack. Pierson cheerfully exclaimed, "Not every Super Bowl champion needs Joe Montana, or even the better quarterback on the field. . . . *There is hope for backup quarterbacks everywhere.* There is glory in handing off, in hitting the hole, in having bigger guys in a big man's game."[81] By accentuating large bodies over clever minds and simplicity of design over sophisticated engineering, smash mouth football harkens to a time before either Walsh or Total Quality Management. Smash mouth football suggested that average guys could win at a time when manufacturing capital was moving off-shore and average (white) guys were getting downsized all over the country.

The blue-collar image of smash mouth football also contrasted with the Brie cheese and chardonnay image of San Francisco's (Yuppie) Faithful.[82] In conservative circles of the 1980s, "wine and cheese" had become a negative term for so-called liberal elites.[83] As recently as 2008, Pat Buchanan used "Chablis and Brie cheese" as an epithet to label San Franciscans as wealthy liberals indifferent to the struggles of real, working-class Americans.[84] Even though Gwen Knapp (cited above) hoped that Jim Harbaugh's Big Ten masculinity would shield the current 49ers from the Brie cheese and chardonnay moniker, the characterization of San Franciscans as wealthier, softer, and less manly than blue-collar fans in other cities persists. Filip Bondy wrote in New York's *Daily News* that because San Franciscans are wealthy and highly educated, "All the real [Bay Area sports] fanatics live in working-class Oakland and cheer for the Raiders."[85]

While Bondy's class comparison to Oakland in 2012 is based more on stereotypes than fact, he does speak to the Bay Area's actual history. Manufacturing moved from San Francisco to Oakland in the mid-twentieth century and economic redevelopment made San Francisco a leading city of the new economy in the late twentieth century. The term *new economy* refers to transformations in capital, primarily, between 1970 and the 1990s that was characterized by a shift from a manufacturing to an informational economy.[86] While college-educated professionals that worked in the FIRE sector (i.e., yuppies) were beneficiaries, the transformation was highly traumatic in regions dependent on manufacturing such as the upper Midwest (i.e., the "rust belt") since seemingly overnight families and entire communities lost their livelihood. The result of the transformation was a new economy that is highly technological, globally integrated, and where inequalities are exasperated especially along the lines of education and wealth distribution.[87]

Transformations in capital that offshored manufacturing jobs in the 1980s had a profound impact on working-class men's ability to enact the manhood of their fathers and grandfathers.[88] As working-class white men became economically unable to support a family solely on their wages, images of hard-bodied men that harkened to industrial era masculinity became increasingly popular and politically powerful.[89] Political leaders at this time used symbols of change such as the rising Japanese auto industry, immigrants, intellectuals, and women in the workplace as scapegoats for the complex economic changes that actually hurt industrial workers.[90] So while these symbols provided a materialization of white working-class pain, they also obscured the abstract economic processes that dispossessed the white working class. A clear expression of the pain and nostalgia experienced in the 1980s is *Field of Dreams* (1989).[91]

At a time nostalgic for hard white male bodies in control, the popularity of smash mouth football makes sense. It especially makes sense as an alternative to San Francisco's West Coast offense that was perceived as intellectual, effeminate, and that robbed strong men of spontaneity and agency. Moreover, San Francisco's yuppie fans were the beneficiaries of not only a new offense but also the new economy. This is not to say that football fans watched the 49ers win a Super Bowl and then agitated against unfair labor conditions as the Longshoremen did in the 1930s. In fact, I am arguing the opposite. It is far more likely that workers found pleasure and redemption in watching Jim Burt knock Joe Montana unconscious in the 1986 NFC Divisional Playoffs. At a time when workers were moving away from collective action, suffering from stagflation, and voting for the Republican Party, cheering for smash mouth football teams could be as cathartic as cheering for Sylvester Stallone in *Rocky* (1976) and *Rambo* (1985) who represented strong even if average white guys fighting back against diabolical forces beyond their control.[92]

When the Lights Go Down in the City

Within the world of sport, history is very important. But the typical sport history is a history of great moments like The Catch; great players like Joe Montana; great coaches like Bill Walsh; and of course great teams like the 49ers' "Dynasty." This history becomes moments frozen in our minds like a postcard picture of Lombard Street shrouded in a fog of emotions. These images become powerful when linked to the time, place, and circumstances of their occurrence. The Catch evokes such a powerful memory for Niners' fans like me since it was a "historical moment" that I shared with my family and friends. Similarly, Dallas fans rue that moment since it not only stopped the Cowboys from making a fifth Super Bowl appearance, it also symbolizes the decline of America's Team in the 1980s. That loss to the Niners also made Dallas's victory over them in the 1993 NFC championship similarly momentous. These memories can be dear to us when reminiscing with family or bragging to friends about "our" success. But they also narrow our field of vision and can limit how we understand sport in our everyday lives.

Professional sport teams are always linked to the economic development of a city and region.[93] That means they not only have personal value, they also have economic value. The establishment of a professional football team on the West Coast of the United States in the postwar was part of attracting capital to a city going through a process of economic transformation. Building Candlestick Park to attract the Giants was also a feature of economic redevelopment that transformed the city's skyline. The behaviors and image of the fans we can also see as linked to economic development, such as when the Forty Niners' fans who went from being "among the most bibulous and truculent in the league"[94] (i.e., hard drinking and combative) in the 1950s and 1960s to being Brie cheese and chardonnay snobs in the 1980s.

Sport history is typically a romantic history. It is emotive. It helps us build emotional bonds with other people and things. Since sport's romantic history has personal value to fans in their everyday lives, it also has economic value to the media and the sport franchises. Not only do fans bond over collective memories, they also create powerful emotional attachments to their favorite franchises, misrecognized as "their" team. Many of the 49ers' Faithful felt betrayed when Bill Walsh benched Montana and then traded him to Kansas City. Raider fans felt even more betrayed when Al Davis moved the Raiders to Los Angeles in 1982. As teams, players, and games become an integral part of fans' everyday lives, fans feel ownership over the franchises. But fans' ownership is emotional not legal or economic. Fans profit from their emotions and memories they own but franchise owners profit from the fans. So when the ever-present economic realities of professional sport tear through the romantic veneer, fans feel cheated and betrayed since it is not what they had bought into. But in fact it is the owners that have bought them. This chapter has tried to understand sport not simply as the heroic efforts of great athletes and brilliant coaches but also as institutions woven into the fabric of society. This means that people draw on the economic realities of everyday life to interpret and understand sport even if all they see is a romantic image and not the economic forces that structure their lives. It is my hope that fans can enjoy the sports they watch but also remain conscious of the economic realities that structure their lives.

9

Pioneers in the Pool

The Santa Clara Swim Club Mermaids of the 1950s and 1960s

MAUREEN M. SMITH AND MATTHEW R. HODLER

At the 2012 Olympic Games, two American teens burst onto the international swim scene with gold medal performances. Seventeen-year-old Missy Franklin won five medals, four of them gold, while teammate Katie Ledecky, the youngest member of Team USA's swimming roster at only fifteen, won a surprise gold in the 800m freestyle. These two teen phenoms harkened back to a time of American women's swimming dominance of the 1950s and 1960s, an era when age group swimming provided America's Olympic swim teams with its teenage-laden lineup of medalists.[1] During this time period, the Santa Clara Swim Club, located in the San Francisco Bay Area, was instrumental in developing world-class female swimmers.

Swimming in the Bay Area has a long rich history that begins decades prior to World War II, with a number of iconic swimming pools constructed around San Francisco, including Fleishhacker Pool, the Crystal Plunge, and the Fairmont Plunge.[2] Women's swimming in the United States experienced tremendous success in the limited number of events available to them in the Summer Olympic Games, though West Coast swimmers were not among the nation's top swimmers. San Francisco's place in American swimming was realized during World War II. The premier female swimmer in the 1940s was Ann Curtis, born in San Francisco and swimming for the San Francisco Crystal Plunge team. Curtis won the coveted James E. Sullivan Award in 1944, given to the country's top amateur athlete, and after missing out on the canceled 1944 Olympic Games, Curtis swam to two gold medals in the London Games in 1948.[3]

Swimming in the Bay Area experienced tremendous growth post–World War II, with the creation and development of club teams, reorganized by the Amateur Athletic Union, in the 1950s as a means to promote water safety, sporting activity, and eventually sporting excellence and national pride.[4] With its temperate climate and post–WWII boom in the construction of swimming pools, California and the San Francisco Bay Area were at the forefront of the youth swimming boom that fueled America's Olympic aquatic teams in the 1960s.[5] In an era when girls' sport opportunities were limited, with few high school competitive teams, swim clubs served as an alternate site for girls sport development, skill acquisition, and competition.[6] The Berkeley YMCA and the Santa Clara Swim Club were among many Bay Area swim clubs, hosting boys and girls in their year-round efforts. Youth swim meets were routinely reported in several Bay Area newspapers, such as Hayward's *Daily Review*, the *Oakland Tribune*, and the *San Mateo Times*. Teams from Oakland, San Rafael, San Leandro, Hayward, Berkeley, and Santa Clara competed for Pacific Association titles, and contended for national AAU titles. With few high school or college teams to speak of, age group swim clubs were the primary training site for girls in the sport of swimming in the pre–Title IX era. Women's swimming, once it moved away from the teen pixies of youth swim clubs and aged into the college level, seemed to mature overnight, with the majority of America's Olympic swimmers coming out of college programs rather than swim clubs, swimmers in their twenties instead of their teens. While Santa Clara Swim Club continued to attract top youth swimmers, local college teams at University of California, Berkeley, and Stanford University were created in the 1970s and have continued the Bay Area's dominance in aquatic competition.

This chapter examines the dominance of the Santa Clara Swim Club (SCSC) mermaids beginning in the 1950s and their role in women's Olympic swimming before the implementation of Title IX and the subsequent emergence of high school and college swim teams for women. The SCSC girls swim team is an example of specialization in youth sport as early as the 1950s. The team's achievements were celebrated during an era of few opportunities for girls and women in sports, in part because of the SCSC contributions to Olympic success. Moreover, the SCSC epitomized the growing role of youth swimming as one avenue in America's efforts to develop fitness among young people. Emphasis, in this chapter, will be given to a number of young female stars, including Chris von Saltza, Donna de Varona, Claudia Kolb, and Pokey Watson, as well as coach George Haines, as the SCSC established itself as one of the nation's greatest sporting dynasties, winning consecutive Amateur Athletic Union national titles in the 1960s and playing important roles in international competitions, including the Olympic Games.

The American Swim Scene in the 1950s

AAU age group swimming started in 1951 and served as a "proving ground" for America's best swimmers and potential Olympic team members. Carl O. Bauer and Beth Kaufman are considered the father and mother of the national youth swimming program, which replaced various organizations and groups around the United States that had previously served a small number of young swimmers. AAU championship meets began a year later, in addition to the local meets offered by regional districts.[7] The number of young swimmers steadily increased, beginning with fewer than 50,000 swimmers and growing to over 800,000 in 1961.[8] President Dwight D. Eisenhower, in 1956, signed Executive Order 10673, establishing the President's Council on Youth Fitness as one means to address the concerning lack of fitness among American youth. The AAU Age Group swimming program fit nicely within this fitness movement, and the organization made efforts to tie their mission to the efforts of Eisenhower and his successor, John F. Kennedy. Swimming, by the early 1960s, was an essential part of America's development of young people. Thought to not only benefit physical fitness among youth, swimming also served to foster social and emotional gains for participants.[9]

The growth of age group swimming's effect was felt almost immediately in international competitions, including the Pan Am Games and the Olympic Games. Still, the breakout performance of America's female swimmers in 1956, despite winning the most medals, was "overshadowed in some ways by the swimming brilliance" of their Australian competitors.[10] By 1958, Kaufman predicted that "future national champions and members of U.S. teams" would come from age group swim programs. The performances of 1958 led Kaufman to claim the results were "conclusive proof" of the value of AAU swim programs.[11] Later that year, Rose Mary Dawson, coach of a girls' swim team and mother of three girls in age group swimming, claimed, "the AAU has a unique and exclusive license in developing women's competitive swimming" in the United States, noting that high schools and colleges were of little help. Dawson shared her philosophy, noting that the AAU swim programs were not focused on "producing 10 year old or 12 year old champions," but rather teaching the fundamentals of swimming in such a way to "maintain their interest and happiness" in the sport so as thirteen- or sixteen-year-olds, the swimmers would have their "best chance of making the Olympic team."[12] While she urged moderation for young swimmers, Dawson viewed the "ultimate" objective of AAU swimming as reaching the Olympic Games, not country club championships.[13] In another sign of the sport's growth, by 1961, there were close to 600 swimming events held annually, up from 114 in 1953.[14] Swimming had become a year-round sport across the nation, most notably in California.

Jack Clowser, writing in *Amateur Athlete*, wondered why boys were permitted to participate in athletic competitions in high school, but not girls, and suggested that other countries were ahead of the United States in the promotion of physical fitness for all. Seeing the limited intermural offerings for girls as boring, Clowser saw the need for greater "encouragement" at the high school and college levels, noting the success of the few interscholastic swim programs in parts of the country.[15] By the late 1950s, the performances of America's female swim talent were being favorably compared with male performances of thirty years prior (even revealing that the girls outperformed these previous male performances). Such data comparisons were meant to serve as evidence that these girls were, in fact, talented and athletes worthy of appreciation, even if they were not perceived as equal to their contemporary male teammates.[16] The AAU touted their celebration of girls' involvement in sport, specifically in swimming, marking the organization as a bit more progressive for the time period. Harold Zimman, the publisher of *Amateur Athlete*, suggested America was having a difficult time ridding itself ofVictorian restrictions when it came to girls being physically active and swimming was seen as one of the few sports, the AAU proffered, that "affords our girls a chance to develop their full potential."[17]

Santa Clara Swim Club

George Haines graduated from San Jose State College in 1950 and was hired to teach physical education and coach boys swimming at Santa Clara High School. In 1951, Haines founded the Santa Clara Swim Club, with the team first training at the Stevens Creek Dam and a local naval base, along with the Santa Clara High School pool, until the construction of the official Santa Clara Swim Team pool, now called the George Haines International Swim Center, in the mid-1960s.[18] Haines coached boys and girls at the SCSC and from the start, the girls' team was competitive in national swim competitions. At the second AAU National meet in 1953, Haines's SCSC girls team finished in third place. Over the course of the next two decades, Haines and the SCSC mermaids won twenty-nine national indoor and outdoor titles, winning their first title in 1957, and establishing themselves firmly on the national and international swim scene. Haines's arrival to Santa Clara, "a burgeoning community where the prune-plum orchards were fast giving way to subdivisions," was perfect timing.[19]

The first half of the 1950s represents SCSC's early phase in age group swimming, with some individual successes and noteworthy team performances. SCSC competitions were covered in the local newspapers, including a 1952 swim meet hosted by the Mill Valley Tennis Club that attracted over two hundred swimmers from several local teams, including the San Francisco Olympic Club, Oakland YMCA, San Rafael Elks, Berkeley City Club, Lafayette Swim Club, San Jose YMCA, along with teams that had traveled a bit farther for competition, such as the Multnomah Athletic Club from Portland, Oregon. Sisters Patricia and Sylvia Ruuska are identified as girls to watch on the Berkeley YMCA team.[20] At the 1952 National Junior Olympic Championships, swimmers from northern California amassed enough victories to lead the Pacific Association to the team title. Among the winners were ten-year-old Kathleen Thompson of the Berkeley City Club with five national titles and triple title winner Carol Tait of the Santa Clara Swim Club.[21]

Hayward's *Daily Review* sponsored their second annual Hayward Championships in 1953 and notified readers with an across-the-top headline announcing the event hosted at the Hayward Plunge. Local teams included the Berkeley City Club, led by 1952 Olympian Barbara Stark, Berkeley YMCA, led by "little" Sylvia Ruuska (who the previous year set the 25-meter freestyle record for girls ten and under), the Livermore Aquacowboys, the Santa Clara Swim Club with "bonafide junior record-holder" Carol Tait and twenty-five teammates, and San Leandro Beavers with the biggest roster at thirty-four swimmers. The newspaper proclaimed the 238 "aqua stars" as northern California's "finest swimmers" and predicted national record performances.[22] At the Metropolitan Swimming Championships held in Albany, Stark was upset by Nancy Simons of Kentfield, making ten-year-old Sylvia Ruuska of the Berkeley YMCA the outstanding performer of the meet, winning three events, two in national record-setting times, and tying for second in two other events.[23] At the Far Western Swimming and Diving Championships hosted at Fleishhacker Pool in San Francisco, Stark won the 100-meter backstroke event in the junior and senior divisions, though her Berkeley City Club team finished in fifth place behind Portland's Multnomah Athletic Club, Los Angeles Athletic Club, SCSC, and San Francisco's Crystal Plunge Swim Club. SCSC was led by Ann Howry and Carol Tait.[24] The next year, Stark successfully won her third consecutive 200-yard backstroke title swimming unattached from the Crystal Plunge Swim Club in San Francisco at the AAU indoor national championships in Daytona Beach, Florida.[25]

Tait was consistently among the nation's best in her events. At the AAU senior national championships in 1954, Tait won two titles.[26] That same spring, Tait continued her dominance against local competition, winning two events and leading the SCSC to the team title at the third annual East Bay Metropolitan Swim championships hosted in Albany. Contributing to the coed title were teammates Ann Howry, Susan Doll, Pat Kearns, Julie Tait, Barbara Bertholf, Sandra

Balch, and Pat Mahaney.[27] Three weeks later, in the same pool, fourteen-year-old Susan Doll set two records at the Berkeley YMCA swimming championships.[28] At the sixth annual Berkeley Women's City Club meet, Tait established a new national record in the 200-meter freestyle for fifteen- and sixteen-year-olds.[29] Tait's success did not go unnoticed in the local press. In a feature on Tait, the *San Mateo Times* anticipated the young swimmer's chances of qualifying for the 1956 Olympic team. Tait had her sights set on breaking Ann Curtis's world record in the 440-yard freestyle. The Menlo-Atherton High School student was described as "supremely confident in her ability but not to the point of being snippy about it." The article notes that Tait learned to swim as a seven-year-old in Clear Lake on a family vacation. Swimming six days a week for SCSC, Tait's coach, George Haines, reported that she would reach her peak in the next two years and would be hard to beat. To close the feature on the teen swimmer, Tait responded to a question about the style of swimming, telling the reporter, "I don't mind racing suits. I'm swimming to win, not to look pretty."[30] At the Pacific Coast swimming championships in Livermore, Tait set a new national record in the 200-meter freestyle for fifteen- and sixteen-year-olds.[31] Tait's commitment to swimming, her practice schedule and dedication, were signs of the shift in girls swimming and the seriousness with which it was approached by swimmers, coaches, and the American news media. The success of girls and women in swimming strengthened America's Cold War arsenal in their rivalry with the Soviet Union that played out in a number of sports between the countries' best athletes.

Tait, along with El Cerrito's Mary Lou Elsenius, were the only two Bay Area girls to represent the United States at the 1955 Pan-American Games in Mexico City.[32] The 1955 Far Western AAU Swimming and Diving Championships attracted over 600 entrants from more than fifty cities in the western United States, including Tait, who earlier that year defended her AAU titles in the 200-yard and 500-yard freestyle events. The drumbeat for Tait's membership on the upcoming 1956 Olympic team continued.[33] That spring, Tait's SCSC team finished fifth at the indoor swimming championships in Daytona Beach, Florida.[34] At the Los Altos AAU swimming meet, national AAU age group records were set by SCSC swimmers Chris von Saltza and Jane Wilson, with SCSC soundly beating their opponents.[35] By the summer of 1956, the SCSC was on the national radar. In coverage of the upcoming San Leandro Relays, the *Daily Review* cited Haines and his girls team as "one of the nation's best teams for years," noting the "almost uncountable" number of national records set by the team. Swimmers of note, as identified by the newspaper, included fourteen-year-old butterfly swimmer Jane Wilson and twelve-year-old Chris von Saltza, an all-around star, along with Mary Mahaney, Doxey Ransom, Roz Skold, and Susan Doll.[36] Two weeks later, at the Santa Clara Valley Swimming Championships, von Saltza, at age twelve, established a new women's world record in the 500-yard freestyle in five minutes and 52.5 seconds.[37]

Despite their individual successes and rise as a team, the SCSC did not send any female swimmers as part of the women's swimming delegation to the 1956 Olympic Games in Melbourne, Australia. In a surprising disappointment, Tait failed to earn a spot on the Olympic team. Sylvia Ruuska, of the Berkeley YMCA, at thirteen years old, was the youngest member of the delegation at the Games.[38] The US women won the most medals in the swimming events, with three golds, five silvers, and three bronze medals, including Ruuska's silver medal in the 4x100-meter freestyle relay and her bronze in the 400-meter freestyle. The young Bay Area native appeared to be a lock for the 1960 Games, while her Bay Area rivals were also on the rise.[39]

In April 1957, the AAU Senior National Women's Swimming and Diving Championships were held in Beverly Hills, California. At these championships, Ruuska set a world record and von Saltza, as a thirteen-year-old, set an American record, marking the two Bay Area swimmers as the nation's top aquatic phenoms. Von Saltza led the SCSC to their first team title, "dethroning" the Walter Reed Swim Club, and Ruuska's Berkeley YMCA team finished in fourth place.[40] According to Baldwin, the meet "gave everyone a look at the younger set of swimmers that are dominating the record sheets," and revealed the growth of women's competitive swimming over the last five years. Three world records, six American records, and eight championship records were established in the Beverly Hills pool.[41] It was the April 1957 meet that put SCSC on the national and international stage, indicating who to watch in the lead up to the much-anticipated 1960 Rome Olympic Games. Chris von Saltza emerged as a favorite and for the next three years leading up to the Rome Games, von Saltza and Ruuska developed a rivalry that showcased their youth, talent, and the growth of women's swimming.[42] This first team title initiates the next phase of the SCSC's history, the start of their championship run, and the rising star of Chris von Saltza.

In anticipation of the outdoor national swimming and diving championships, *Amateur Athlete*, the voice of the AAU, published a feature on Ruuska in August 1957. Ruuska began swimming at the age of nine, and was coached by her father, Meikko, an electrician and coach at the Berkeley YMCA since 1945.[43] At the meet, which featured Australian Olympic swimming sensations Dawn Fraser and Lorraine Crapp, von Saltza finished second to Crapp in the 440-yard freestyle, setting an American record. SCSC teammate Jane Wilson upset Ruuska in the 220-yard butterfly event.[44] SCSC defended their indoor title, winning their first outdoor title, with the top five teams coming from California.[45] Ruuska, Berkeley YMCA teammate Mary Lou Elsenius, and von Saltza and her SCSC teammate Wilson, were honored with certificates of merit from the Doten Sport

Institute's weekly radio show on KLX.[46] *Amateur Athlete* put von Saltza and diver Paula Myers, who tied for high points of the meet, on the September cover. That fall, Ruuska was awarded the outstanding athlete in the Pacific Association and was the organization's nominee for the Sullivan Award.[47] To close the year, at the San Francisco Park and Recreation Department's second annual age group and senior swim meet, Ruuska won four events and finished second in another, with von Saltza winning one event in her age group, in a time faster than Ruuska.[48]

The two young teens continued their cross bay rivalry in the new year. In February 1958, von Saltza bettered three American freestyle records in a dual meet against the Los Angeles Athletic Club.[49] A week later, Ruuska signaled her intent to stay in top form, setting a world record in the women's senior one-mile swim, beating von Saltza by sixty yards at the Alameda Naval Air Station Invitational Swim Meet.[50] In April 1958, the newly constructed Joe Perkins Natatorium in Dallas hosted the AAU Senior Women's Indoor Swimming and Diving Championships, the first held in the Southwest.[51] Haines and the SCSC won their third consecutive AAU title with fifty-nine points, edging the Berkeley YMCA in the championship's final event, the relay, where "Chris brought down the house with her brilliant backstroke leg."[52] Von Saltza's American record performance in the 100-meter freestyle on the meet's opening day earned her front-page accolades from the *San Mateo Times*.[53] Two days later, the local newspaper hailed von Saltza for breaking her own record in the 250-yard freestyle.[54] Berkeley YMCA tied with the Kris Kristensen Swim School for second with fifty-three points each. Von Saltza finished the meet with twenty-three points to Ruuska's twenty-one points. Only two weeks later, von Saltza bested Ruuska's American record in the 400-yard individual medley.[55]

At the outdoor championships in August hosted in Topeka, Kansas, SCSC won their fourth straight AAU title, with 65 points over the Los Angeles Athletic Club and Berkeley YMCA. Ruuska won four events and finished with the high points award (with 28) of the championship, with von Saltza finishing second (with 23). Von Saltza won the 100-meter freestyle and set a new world record in the 200-meter backstroke. Ruuska set a world record in the 400-meter individual medley. In the most exciting event of the meet, Ruuska and von Saltza went head to head, trading leads in the 400-meter freestyle, with Ruuska pulling away for the win. The championships drew record crowds to the meet.[56] In thirteen events, new records were established in twelve, including four new world records. Ruuska's four wins at a national championship were the most by a female swimmer since Ann Curtis in the 1940s. The performance of the women heightened expectations that the United States would do well at the 1960 Olympic Games.[57] It was noted that the average age of the swimmers entered in the national meet, and the most likely Olympic hopefuls, was between fifteen and sixteen years old, with some not looking "old enough to go into the deep end without a counselor."[58] Two young Olympic hopefuls, Ruuska (age sixteen) and von Saltza (age fourteen), starred in the "Parade of Champions," hosted by the Berkeley City Club in November.[59] To celebrate the SCSC victory, *Amateur Athlete* feted the team's championship (indoor and outdoor) 4 x 100-meter freestyle relay of Jane Wilson, Doxey Ransom, Susan Honig, and Chris von Saltza, on their December cover.

Von Saltza began the 1959 season by breaking five of her own records in a meet at San Jose State College.[60] The next month, the two teen rivals, von Saltza and Ruuska, traveled to Australia for several weeks competing in a series of swim meets and exhibitions, including the Australian national championships.[61] In the first competition, held in Brisbane, Australia, von Saltza set a new Australian record in the 200-meter backstroke, winning the event. Ruuska finished second in the 400-meter freestyle to Australia's Ilsa Konrads. Both swimmers' families were excited to hear of their daughters' results.[62] Ruuska and von Saltza continued their winning ways down under when each earned titles at the Australian swimming championships.[63] SCSC's title reign was snapped at the indoor senior championships in April 1959. Illness forced von Saltza out of the national meet, and, in her absence, Ruuska won high point honors, with the most first-place finishes, and led her Berkeley YMCA team to the national title.[64]

SCSC hoped to win back the title at the outdoor meet in the summer to be held in Redding, California, with von Saltza back in the pool.[65] Ruuska was in fine form all summer leading up to the championships. In a feature on the athlete, Hank Solomon considered her the "most versatile woman afloat."[66] Ruuska led a five-girl team to Redding, which included her sister Patricia, and teammates Anne Bancroft, Carolyn Schuler, and Donna de Varona. Ruuska and the Berkeley YMCA bested their Bay Area rivals for the second time that year, winning their second AAU title by a one-point margin, 76–75, won in the final event of the meet, the 440-yard medley relay. The SCSC A team relay won the event, but their B team missed fifth place by eight-tenths of a second, missing out on the needed points to win the meet. In what may have seemed like a consolation prize, Chris von Saltza bested Ruuska for the high point award with 26 to 24. Von Saltza and her relay teammates, Anne Warner, Kathie Simicek, and Doxey Ransom, set a new American record in the 440-yard medley relay.[67] In her first appearance in a national meet, twelve-year-old Donna de Varona did not score a point, "but provided a lot of encouragement to her four teammates."[68] As a collective, the talented "girl" swimmers "served notice to the rest of the world that they will present a great challenge at the Rome Olympics," as evidenced by the four world records, eleven American records, and fourteen meet records established at the championship event.[69] In September, von Saltza led the "all-conquering" American team in the Pan Am Games, winning an unprecedented five gold medals in the week-long event held in Chicago, another sign of things to come in the upcoming Olympics.[70]

The Olympics in Rome loomed over every meet in 1960.[71] It was anticipated that the nation's top swimmers would compete in the Senior Women's Championship Meet because of the Olympics, but the performances would also indicate how the "women will fare in Rome."[72] In the lead-up to those championships, von Saltza was featured in *Amateur Athlete*, with details of her start in swimming as an eleven-year-old with coach George Haines, and her record-setting performances since. It was noted that she trained before and after school and on weekends, while a student at Los Gatos High School.Von Saltza also stated she would retire from swimming when she started college in the fall of 1961, as she did not believe college courses would allow for training and she wanted to focus on school.[73] At the AAU indoor championships in Bartlesville, Oklahoma, von Saltza did not disappoint, winning four events for a total of 28 points, and leading SCSC to 83 points and the title. Berkeley YMCA tied with LAAC for second place with 40 points each. The *Oakland Tribune* informed its reader of the Bay Area residents in competition, such as twelve-year-old Donna de Varona, a student at Stanley Intermediate School in Lafayette, and her teammates who attended area high schools.[74] Von Saltza, the "brilliant blonde" and "best prospect" for the Olympics, was joined on the podium by new teammate Lynn Burke, who moved from Flushing, New York, to train with Haines and SCSC.[75] Burke moved in with the von Saltza family to accommodate her westward move to the SCSC, and soon after Anne Warner from nearby Menlo Park joined the SCSC.[76] With Burke and von Saltza at the helm, the SCSC team added another national title to their impressive collection. At the conclusion of the meet, it was announced that Haines would be the head coach of the women's Olympic swimming team later that year.[77]

In the summer months leading up to the Games, the preview of the women's team was hopeful and celebratory about the role of age group swimming. Baldwin turned her attention "to the newcomers to Olympic competition" and voiced the sentiment shared by many in swimming that the 1960 team was "made up 10 or 12 years ago" in the "magnificent" age group swimming program.[78] At the top of Baldwin's list of swimmers was von Saltza, whose "fantastic record . . . is known everywhere." "If American swimmers have created a 'scare' throughout the world," Baldwin claimed, "this blonde mermaid is largely responsible for it."[79] The team would be determined at the Olympic Trials in Detroit, less than three weeks after the outdoor national championship meet in Indianapolis.

At the outdoor championships, the outcome seemed hardly in doubt as von Saltza and Burke, called "two big, handsome look-alike blondes" by the *Los*

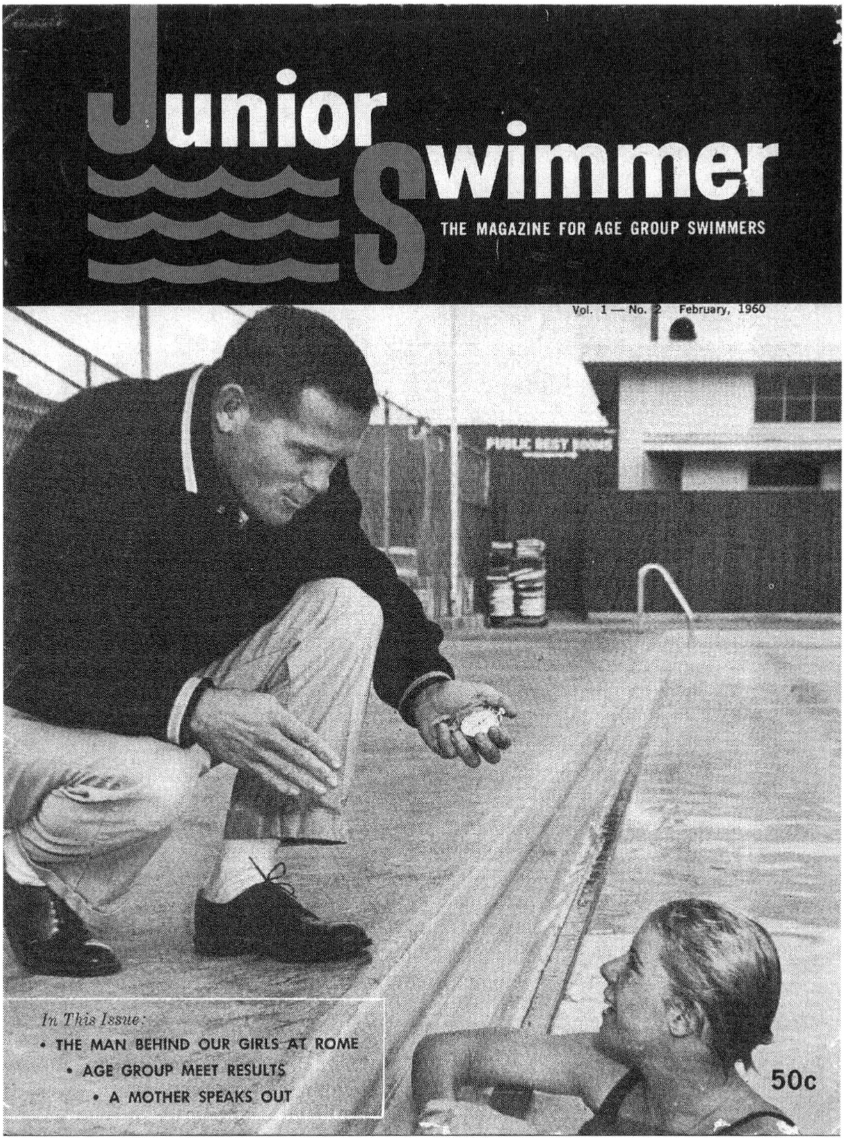

George Haines coaching Chris von Saltza, cover of *Junior Swimmer,* February 1960. *Courtesy International Swimming Hall of Fame.*

Angeles Times, led their SCSC team to another title.[80] Three world records were set, one by Burke in the 100-meter backstroke, and another by Berkeley YMCA swimmer, "tiny, 13-year-old" Donna de Varona, who beat her teammate Sylvia Ruuska for the record time win in the 400-meter individual medley. SCSC swimmer Ann Warner won titles in the 100-meter and 200-meter breaststroke events. Eight American records and eleven meet records were also broken in pursuit of Olympic dreams.[81]

In Detroit, von Saltza, Burke, and Warner won their respective events, qualifying them for the Olympic squad. Haines, in assessing his 1960 Olympic team, thought it was the "best-balanced one to ever represent" the country in the Olympic Games, and saw Australia as "the team to beat."[82] Ruuska, like Tait four years prior, failed to earn a place on what would have been her second Olympic Games team. The changing of the guards in American women's swimming had occurred.

The American women did not disappoint. At those 1960 Olympic Games in Rome, sixteen-year-old von Saltza was the winningest female athlete among the entire US delegation, winning three gold medals and one silver medal.[83] Lynn Burke added two gold medals, and the SCSC duo (and their American relay teammates) accounted for the US women's team's five gold medals (out of eight events). The youth of the team, even with von Saltza's pending retirement, bode well for the next Olympiad in four years.[84] When the 1960 AAU All-American Team was named at the start of 1961, women's swimming was dominated by SCSC and other swimmers from the Bay Area.[85]

At the National AAU Indoor Swimming Championships held at the newly constructed half-million-dollar outdoor pool at the Hialeh Municipal Pool in Miami in April 1961, the American swimming establishment was already looking ahead to Tokyo 1964. The average age of the entrants was fifteen and a half years old. Haines claimed the women "will be harder to beat than ever," and Ben York, chairman of the US Olympic Women's Swim Committee, suggested the "group of youngsters we have now is better, comparatively speaking, than the prospects we had four years ago."[86] Von Saltza, who won four events at the meet (100-yd freestyle, 250-yd freestyle, 500-yd freestyle, 200-yd backstroke), was absent from these Olympic predictions. The thirteen-year-old Donna de Varona, though, was believed to be a sure thing, winning the 200-yard individual medley and finishing second in two other events. Despite von Saltza's four golds, SCSC was unable to defend their team title and finished third at the meet to the Multnomah Athletic Club.[87]

There was some concern related to the youth movement in swimming, which had been hailed as the force behind the nation's aquatic success at the 1960 Olympic Games. Dawson, both a coach and swim parent, stated that "age group swimming has become so dominant that it threatens to take over senior swimming." This fear was actually realized in California, according to Dawson, where "age group swimming in the past has turned out the greatest number of senior champions." Haines was interviewed for his perspective and suggested that while he believed children should learn to swim at five or six, they should not "go into serious competition and heavy training until they are 11 or 12 years old." Burnout was a concern among many who saw the dangers of ten-year-olds winning national titles.[88]

Despite these concerns, young female swimmers continued to set the standard. At the 1961 National AAU Senior Women's Swimming and Diving Championships in Philadelphia, fifteen-year-old Carolyn House was the most recent teen to turn the sport on its head with three titles. De Varona, swimming unattached and often referred to as "the baby" of the 1960 Olympic squad, won the 400-yard individual medley in world record time and the 200-meter individual medley in an American record, but lost the high point award by two points to House. The Vesper Boat Club dethroned SCSC for the title, with LAAC coming in second and SCSC finishing in third place. The swim meet marked the highest attended event for a national women's meet and marked the final national meet for von Saltza and Indiana swimmer Becky Collins, both of whom were entering college.[89] Von Saltza was upset in the 100-meter freestyle by fourteen-year-old Robyn Johnson, though they both clocked in with the same time of 1:03.2.[90] Von Saltza withdrew from the 200-meter freestyle, which she had won the year prior, to allow her SCSC teammate Pokey Watson a shot at finishing in the top two for a spot on an upcoming European swim tour, though Watson was unsuccessful in her efforts.

Von Saltza was honored by her American teammates on a European tour of swimming competitions immediately following the national championship meet. The American swimmers, which also included Collins and de Varona, competed in six meets in Holland, Great Britain, and Germany.[91] By year's end, with von Saltza retired, de Varona was being hailed as the Queen of Age Group Swimming, with the top performance in fifteen different events for thirteen- and fourteen-year-olds.[92]

The retirement of von Saltza cleared the way for new aquatic stars at the next indoor national championships held at Sacramento's Arden Hills Club.[93] De Varona, swimming unattached, but committed to joining SCSC that summer, won three events (200-yard IM, 200-yard backstroke, 100-yard backstroke). SCSC won the team title with 46 points, led by Roby Whipple and diver Joel Lenzi O'Connell. Terri Stickles also swam unattached, but was planning to join de Varona and SCSC prior to the outdoor championship meet, making Haines's team a clear favorite to win the outdoor title with their new team members.[94]

Chris von Saltza and Donna de Varona, flanked by Susie Barkley (*left*) and Kristie Gimenez (*right*). *Courtesy International Swimming Hall of Fame.*

Still, there was room for surprises. In fact, one swimming insider predicted, "upsets will be the order of the day as another crop of brilliant newcomers challenge the incumbents."[95] Upsets there were. LAAC, led by Carolyn House and Sharon Finneran, beat SCSC by 6 points to claim the title in the Chicago pool. Five world records, ten American records, and eleven meet records were established at the meet.[96] House was the new face of women's swimming, for the time being.[97] The 1962 All-American team was named in early January 1963. American women had set fifty-three world records during 1962. Donna de Varona, "the 15-year-old mermaid from Santa Clara," was named an All-American in two events, and was credited with five new American records. Terri Stickles of San Mateo, and swimming for SCSC, was named an All-American in four events.[98]

Jack Clowser dubbed de Varona the "finest all-strokes swimmer" in the nation after the young swimmer led the SCSC to "an awe-inspiring triumph" at the National AAU Senior Women's Indoor Swimming Championships held in Middleburg Heights, Ohio. At the meet, de Varona set three American records and SCSC amassed 113 ½ points soundly drubbing their opponents (LAAC, the second-place team, had only 38 points), and claiming their eighth national title since 1957. Clowser called it a "Santa Clara rampage." At the age of fifteen, de Varona was the owner of eleven national titles. She and Stickles were the only double winners of the championship meet.[99]

The outdoor championships were set for High Point, North Carolina, which had hosted the previous version of the national event in 1941 and 1950. Only three remaining Olympians from 1960 were still actively competing in AAU swimming and would be at the meet, de Varona, House, and Patsy Willard, who all hoped to make the 1964 team heading to Tokyo.[100] This time, de Varona and Stickles were unable to lead SCSC to victory, losing to LAAC by a score of 70–64. De Varona was the high point winner of the meet, winning two events and finishing second in two, for 24 points.[101]

In the spring of 1964 it was announced that the AAU men's indoor meet would be held in conjunction with the World's Fair in New York, and would also serve as the Olympic trials for the men's swimming team. Haines was announced as the assistant coach for the men's team. The women were not afforded a similar stage, despite their successes.[102] Instead, the AAU Senior Women's Indoor Championship was held at the University of Pittsburgh, where Donna de Varona cemented her status as "unquestionably the greatest woman swimmer in the United States today." De Varona earned high points for the meet with 26 points, with three titles, and SCSC won their third consecutive indoor title with 130½ points, beating second place City of Commerce Swim Club by almost 80 points, and dominating the meet "like it had never been dominated." Other SCSC swimmers who added to the total included Jana Haroun, Claudia Kolb, Terri Stickles, Pokey Watson, and the newest SCSC member Sharon Finneran, who had moved north from southern California. Event records were set in every event, the first time this had occurred in women's swimming. The average age of the participants was fifteen and one-half years old.[103]

By 1964, SCSC was a recognized force in girls swimming, as Haines was heralded for his coaching acumen. His coaching and the success of the SCSC team attracted swimmers from other swim teams to join Haines, in many cases requiring their families to uproot to relocate closer to Santa Clara. Stickles, Watson, Finneran, and de Varona had all started their swim careers with other teams and made the decision to join Haines and his successful team. Haines's swimmers were considered "the finest collection of water bugs in the country," and as they sought to earn their Olympic berths, faced "the stiffest competition . . . right in their own pool."[104] De Varona, the youngest Olympian in 1960, was heralded as America's top swimmer. She appeared on the cover of national magazines, including *LIFE*, *Time*, *Look*, and *Sports Illustrated*, and was the most photographed female athlete of her era.[105] Her family, after shuttling her to SCSC for training on the weekends, finally relocated to Santa Clara in 1962, ending her lengthy commute across the Bay Area. Like other female swimmers, de Varona's commitment to her sport was noted in a feature that discussed her intense practice schedule, as well as her efforts to stay involved in school activities at Santa Clara High School.[106] In addition to de Varona, SCSC's roster was full of bonafide Olympic talent. Claudia Kolb appeared on the cover of the September issue of *Amateur Athlete*.

These SCSC stars were on display at the outdoor championships held in Los Altos, only the third time the men and women's championship meets were at the same site. In front of a crowd in excess of 2,000, the SCSC women and men's teams won titles, the first ever for the men, and the first outdoor title for the women's team since the "heyday" of von Saltza in 1960. De Varona was unstoppable, earning 29 points for high point honors, and her fourth straight crown in the 200-yard individual medley and fourth crown in the 400-yard individual medley in five years. Despite her accolades, the aging swimmer's "heir apparents" were also in attendance, including thirteen-year-old distance phenom Patty Caretto. Kolb was a double winner at the meet. SCSC dethroned LAAC after their two-year reign, accumulating 205 points to second place Commerce City's 150.[107]

Expectations for the American women for the long-awaited Tokyo Games were high, but not nearly as high as their male counterparts, who were considered "superlative." De Varona was expected to be the "aquatic queen" at the Games, leading a team of American girls that consisted entirely of teenagers, making her the "grand old lady" of the squad at seventeen years old.[108] One thing the women had over their male teammates? In addition to "being as deep, talented and potentially victorious," the "girls" had "the edge in one department . . . all of them are lovely."[109] The men lived up to the hype, winning nine of twelve events, with SCSC's Don Schollander dominating with four gold medals.[110] The American women, too, found great success, outshining their male teammates, winning seven of ten events and eighteen of thirty possible medals (five silvers and six bronzes).[111] De Varona led her American teammates to a sweep in the 400-meter individual medley in Olympic record time and added a gold in the 4x100-meter freestyle relay in their world record setting performance. De Varona's SCSC teammate, fourteen-year-old Claudia Kolb was a "marvel," winning a silver medal in the 200-meter backstroke behind the Soviet Union's Galina Prozumenshchikova, whose performance marked her country's ascension in the sport.[112] Pokey Watson, also fourteen years old and an SCSC swimmer, joined de Varona on the winning relay.[113] Watson started her swimming career with the Palo Alto Athletic Club, and moved to train with Haines after her coach John Williams suggested she would only get better by joining SCSC.[114] Sharon Finneran, who had relocated to northern California to train with Haines and SCSC, finished second to her new SCSC teammate de Varona in the 400-meter individual medley. Terri Stickles finished third in the 400-meter freestyle. The AAU was particularly pleased with the American women's performances, as all twelve who medaled had come out of age group swimming (as did the fifteen male medalists).[115] The AAU's Pacific Association celebrated the Bay Area's important role in America's aquatic dominance, and awarded de Varona their Outstanding Women's Swimmer Award, while awarding Schollander the Outstanding Male Swimmer Award along with their support for the Sullivan Award (to which de Varona was also nominated). Thirteen SCSC swimmers won gold medals at the 1964 Olympic Games, and there was no reason to think the club's success would not continue with another wave of talented swimmers.[116]

There was no let up after the Olympics. The 1965 AAU championships, both indoor and outdoor, provided evidence that the next wave of teen swimmers were primed and ready to go. Finneran and Kolb finished in first and second place in the 400-meter IM, but it wasn't enough for the SCSC, despite their loaded roster. Commerce City, led by Patty Caretto, won the indoor title where ten American records fell.[117] That summer, SCSC defended their outdoor title, with de Varona watching from the sidelines working for ABC. Pokey Watson, Claudia Kolb, Linda Hildreth, and Terri Stickles were victorious in the 400-meter medley relay. Kolb was the meet's only triple winner, with SCSC beating the second-place Vesper Boat Club by a score of 196 to 129. Five world records fell in front of 3,000 fans.[118] According to Steiger, the progress made by American swimmers was "amazing," and he noted that young swimmers in the ten-and-under and eleven-to-twelve age group were swimming within seconds of world and American records of twenty-five years prior, evidence of their advancement. These improvements were owed to better coaching, training, and facilities. He also noted that the women were outpacing their male counterparts in the rate of improvement.[119]

Many of these "amazing" swimmers were slated to compete in the 1966 national indoor AAU meet in Bartlesville, Oklahoma, which had last hosted the national event in 1960. There was great anticipation in the appearance of Olympians.[120] For all the anticipation, perhaps it came as little surprise to swimming insiders when Haines's SCSC women successfully defended their title, winning in the last event by one second over the second-place Vesper Boat Club, by a score of 94 to 86. The meet welcomed new faces, Olympic medalists, and twelve new meet records.[121] Finneran, at age twenty, was one of the oldest participants in the meet, and successfully defended her 400-meter individual medley title, and also won the 1,650-yard freestyle. Other swimmers to earn points for the SCSC included Kolb, Linda Hildreth, Sue Jones, Lisa Lewis, and Pokey Watson.[122]

That summer, a coed US delegation traveled to Moscow for a meet with Poland, Norway, Bulgaria, and their Soviet hosts.[123] The outdoor AAU national championships were held in Lincoln, Nebraska, where the SCSC women and men won team trophies and nine world records and fourteen American records fell.[124] SCSC's freestyle relay foursome of Kolb, Linda Gustavson, Nancy Ryan, and Pokey Watson set a world record in their event finishing in eight minutes and fifty-five seconds, besting the previous record by five seconds. It was one of five world records set at the meet. While SCSC women won the meet, two young teens from other clubs had notable performances. Karen Muir, fourteen, and Catie Ball, thirteen, both won events, marking their ascension in the women's ranks, with Ball besting Kolb in the 100-meter breaststroke.[125] Later that fall, the United States sent a delegation of eight swimmers to Mexico City to test run the aquatic facilities for the 1968 Olympic Games. The delegation included Ball and SCSC swimmers Watson and Kolb.[126] At the end of the year, SCSC swimmers littered the All-American list, with Watson being named in seven events, and Kolb in four events.[127]

At the 1967 AAU indoor national championships, Kolb led SCSC to their fourth indoor team title in five years, soundly beating Arden Hills Swim Club by a resounding 136 to 59 points, with seventeen swimmers. Kolb was the high point winner of the meet, with 22, with help from Sue Pederson, Lee Davis, and Pam Kruse, who joined her on the June cover of *Amateur Athlete*. The meet, which established twelve new records, was telecast on *ABC Wide World of Sports*, with de Varona as part of the telecast team. The meet also determined the Pan Am team. In addition to Kolb earning a spot on the Pan Am team, other SCSC swimmers selected to represent the United States included Pokey Watson, Lee Davis, Pam Carpenilla, Nancy Ryan, and Linda Gustavson.[128]

American teenage girls dominated the international swimming scene, with age group swimming getting the credit for the global takeover. Their youth was viewed as an asset, training as adult athletes, but not knowing "the limitations of speed, and being uninhibited by the time barriers," and as a result, setting "records that seem well beyond the grasp of the older girls." Most of the women retired by college, deciding to focus on academics and their "interest in boys," both of which "destroys their competitive edge," at least according to Albert Schoenfield, writing in *Amateur Athlete*. Such short-sighted thinking about female athletes in sport revealed that, despite the progressiveness of swimming in offering opportunities for female athletes, swimming was still viewed by many as an age-appropriate activity with an expected retirement upon entering college. For male swimmers, collegiate swimming was the expected next phase of their careers.[129] In any case, these teenage mermaids were the bulk of the American Olympic swim team for the second Olympiad in a row and were expected to achieve great things, and gold medals, on the world's largest athletic stage in Mexico City.

At the Pan Am Games in Winnipeg, only two weeks prior to the AAU outdoor meet, Kolb set two world records.[130] At the AAU nationals, Kolb finished with the high points award with 32 points, coming in with two first-place finishes, two seconds, and two world records. It was the fourth consecutive team title for SCSC with 203 over Vesper Boat Club's 105.5 and LAAC's 61.5 points. Pokey Watson was a part of all three winning SCSC relays. Debbie Meyer, a young swimmer from Sacramento, emerged as another California Olympic hopeful. Harry Hainsworth, AAU aquatics director, called the record-setting performances the "greatest day in the history of American swimming."[131] A team of women headed to Japan and England for a series of meets, with another contingent headed to Mexico City for another set of trial runs in the Olympic facilities. Later that year, a coed team swam in England, Sweden, and West Germany, including SCSC's Watson.[132]

By the start of the 1968 swim season, SCSC girls had won fifteen of the last twenty-two indoor and outdoor AAU titles.[133] Haines had over three hundred swimmers under his tutelage in the club's summer swim program, along with his elite team of Olympians. Kolb was the star of the SCSC squad, though she shared the spotlight with her equally talented teammates, such as fellow Olympian Pokey Watson, and future Olympic teammates Linda Gustavson, Jan Henne, and Jane Swaggerty. Pokey Watson, always a contributor for SCSC, hoped to win a gold medal at her second consecutive Olympics, a rarity in women's swimming, though she was unsure which stroke she would attempt to qualify for the team.[134] Kolb won three events at the indoor championships held at the University of Pittsburgh, including the 400-yard medley relay with teammates Jane Swaggerty, Jan Henne, and Linda Gustavson. The 400-yard freestyle relay team also won gold. Despite the impressive performance of Sacramento's fifteen-year-old Debbie Meyer, SCSC handily won the team title.[135]

Prior to the 1968 Games in Mexico City, expectations were high for SCSC swimmers, with experts predicting medal finishes for Jan Henne, Linda Gustavson, Jane Swaggerty, Pokey Watson, and Claudia Kolb.[136] The SCSC women were well represented, with Haines serving as the men's coach. Kolb and Watson, at eighteen years old, were considered "old folks" on the Olympic squad, but their experience paid off with both winning gold medals. Watson won a gold medal in the 200-meter backstroke in a world record, four years after winning a gold in the freestyle. Kolb won gold medals in the 200-meter and 400-meter individual medley, both in world record times.[137] Jan Henne joined Kolb as a double gold winner, in the 100-meter freestyle and 400-meter freestyle relay, as well as a silver and bronze. Joining Henne on the winning relay was Gustavson, who also garnered a silver and bronze in her individual freestyle events. Rounding up the SCSC medalists were Lynn Vidali placing second to Kolb in the 400-meter IM, and Jane Swaggerty with a bronze in the 100-meter backstroke. The next summer, both Kolb and Watson retired from the sport, ending prestigious careers and signaling the end of SCSC's team dominance in girls swimming and Olympic competition.[138] Much of this shift is also due to the rise of Debbie Meyer of Sacramento's Arden Hills Club and her Olympic performance at the 1968 Games, indicating that there were other California clubs that were able to produce dominant swimmers. Moreover, the 1968 Olympic performance of SCSC's Mark Spitz, along with the recent success of the SCSC men's team overall, also overshadowed the continued success by individual SCSC female swimmers.[139]

Conclusion

By the end of the 1960s, women's swimming had begun its subtle shift. Teenagers were still at the forefront, though more of them were continuing to swim and finding opportunities to compete for their colleges after aging out of age group swimming. The American women's swim team in 1972 had two SCSC gold medalists, Karen Moe and Keena Rothhammer, though it was clear that not only was the talent in women's swimming spread across the country, it was beginning to age. Moreover, other countries were posing a serious challenge to America's aquatic dominance.[140] With the advent of Title IX in 1972, women's swim teams appeared on college campuses in record numbers and national collegiate competitions became increasingly important with AAU swimming serving as the gateway for college, mimicking the men's model.

Much of the success of the Santa Clara Swim Club, and the concomitant media attention to girls swimming, and girls swimming in the Bay Area, begins with George Haines, whose legacy in women's swimming extends from youth teams in the 1950s to women's collegiate swimming in the 1980s, a legacy that is healthy and thriving in the 2010s in the Bay Area, with Cal coach Teri McKeever, with a long record of success at Cal, becoming the first woman to serve as head coach of the women's Olympic swim team in 2012. McKeever has led Cal to three national titles, while Stanford has won nine national titles, including one with Claudia Kolb at the helm (1979–80 season, AIAW title), and another with George Haines as the head coach (1982–83, NCAA title). When McKeever was hired in 1992, she replaced former SCSC standout and 1972 Olympian Karen Moe. Both schools started their programs in the mid-1970s, first competing in the AIAW championships and then in NCAA competition. Both schools boast long lists of All-Americans and Olympians, making the Bay Area one of the nation's most attractive destinations for aquatic stars.

In 2015, in a nod to the swim club's legacy, the International Swimming Hall of Fame decided to relocate its headquarters to Santa Clara and the Bay Area given the SCSC's role in the development of the sport. With the relocation of the International Swimming Hall of Fame to Santa Clara, the city and the sport hope to reconnect with the Santa Clara Swim Club's rich history. This is only fitting, as

Haines and a number of his female and male swimmers are honored in the Hall of Fame. Chris von Saltza was inducted into the second class of entrants of the International Swimming Hall of Fame in early 1967, making her the first SCSC swimmer to enjoy such an honor. The SCSC star was credited with helping "spark the current renaissance in U.S. swimming."[141] Two years later, von Saltza was joined by Donna de Varona, and George Haines was inducted in 1977.[142] The SCSC dynasty of the 1960s is well represented in the Hall, with Claudia Kolb (1975), Lynn Burke (1978), Jan Henne (1979) Pokey Watson (1984), and Sharon Finneran (1985).[143] In the decade prior to the passage of Title IX, when sporting opportunities for girls and women were severely limited, a team, comprised of teenage girls from California's Bay Area, the SCSC mermaids coached by George Haines, was a formidable dynasty of sport. Perhaps the relocation of the International Swimming Hall of Fame to Santa Clara, the home of the sport's greatest team, will renew interest in the successes of this Bay Area squad.

10

A Friendly Competition

The 1962 US-USSR Track Meet at The Farm

CHRIS ELZEY

John Thomas gripped the flagstaff. Above his head, the United States flag fluttered lightly in the breeze. It was a proud moment for the twenty-one-year-old high jumper. Minutes earlier, as standard-bearer for the American squad during the opening ceremony of the 1962 US-USSR track meet, he had led his team into a crowded Stanford University Stadium amid boisterous cheers. Now, spiffily attired in a white USA tracksuit and standing at midfield with fellow Americans, Olga Connolly, 1956 Olympic gold medalist, and miler Jim Beatty, Thomas listened to the "Star Spangled Banner" and gazed up toward the edge of the stadium set against the azure sky. What young athlete would not want to carry his national flag in what the *Palo Alto Times* would term the "[b]iggest, best dual meet ever"?[1]

To Thomas's left stood the Soviet contingent: Vera Krepkina, 1960 Olympic long jump champion; Victor Tsibulenko, winner of the javelin at the 1960 Rome Games; and Valeri Brumel, the outstanding high jumper and USSR flag-bearer whom *Time* magazine noted had "a matinee-idol grin." For the 72,500 in attendance, the juxtaposition of the two flags recalled a world roiled by ideological confrontation and the threat of nuclear war. But to Thomas and his fellow athletes that day—American and Soviet alike—the meet at The Farm, as Stanford is commonly known, afforded not only an opportunity to engage in spirited competition; it also offered a chance to chip away at Cold War suspicion and fear. For San Franciscans, the popular meet offered more—reaffirming the idea that the

Bay Area was a politically tolerant region and national track Mecca. Following the conclusion of the meet, few would be left disappointed.[2]

The 1962 matchup, held the weekend of July 21 and 22, was the fourth in a series of meets between the United States and Soviet Union that dated back to the late 1950s. In January 1958, the two Cold War foes had inked an agreement initiating exchanges in music, science, film, dance, and sport, among other activities. In large part, the agreement resulted from the easing of Cold War tensions, and the three meets prior to 1962—no competition was staged during the Olympic summer of 1960—reflected, particularly among American and Soviet competitors, the spirit of goodwill in which the accord was negotiated and signed.[3]

The competition at Stanford was the second US-USSR meet held in the United States. In 1959, following the previous year's dual meet in Moscow, Philadelphia had hosted the event. Though the Soviets appreciated the organization of the meet, they enjoyed themselves much less off the track. According to the meet report filed by the US State Department–supplied interpreter, Soviet team members groused that meals lacked black bread and fruit, and, after visiting "a rest stop between New York and Philadelphia," were flabbergasted that bathroom goers were charged to use the lavatories. In one of the more embarrassing incidents for meet planners, the Soviets showed up late to a gala because the drivers of the buses in which they rode had "got[ten] lost." Although the gala started at 7 p.m., attendees did not receive dinner until more than three hours later. The report described the evening as "a fiasco."[4]

Aware of the missteps, planners of the 1962 competition did all they could to ensure that the Soviets had a memorable visit. Helping lead this effort was Payton Jordan, Stanford's head track coach and director of the meet. Track was Jordan's life. A native Californian, Jordan was a star sprinter in high school and at the University of Southern California (USC). With his gazelle-like speed, he was practically a shoo-in for the 1940 Olympics, but he never got the chance to compete because the Games were canceled, due to the start of WWII. After serving as an officer on naval airbases in California and Iowa during the war, Jordan coached at Redlands High School and Occidental College in Los Angeles. In 1956, following a decade of success at Occidental, he was hired at Stanford. In the seven years since coming to The Farm, he had coached several All-Americans. Two of his teams came in fifth at the national championships.[5]

Jordan was familiar with Soviet track and field. As an assistant coach of the squad that traveled to Moscow in 1958 for the inaugural US-USSR meet (the 1961 meet would also be held in the Soviet capital), he had befriended several Soviet sports officials, including Gavriel Korobkov, the amiable and bespectacled coach of the national team. Jordan's experience in Moscow got him to thinking:

why not have Stanford host the meet? In February 1959, Jordan proposed that following that summer's dual competition in Philadelphia, a second meet be held at The Farm. The Stanford matchup, though, never occurred. The Soviets, apparently, did not want to participate in consecutive dual meets.[6]

A different proposal from Jordan was better received. Al Masters was Stanford's long-serving athletic director. Earlier, he had suggested to Jordan that Stanford host the 1960 Olympic track and field trials. Jordan dutifully submitted the request. Masters had experience with such things, having brought the 1932 trials to Stanford. Like Jordan, he believed that the 1960 meet would attract big crowds. He was right. An estimated 106,000 people came to watch the tryouts, making it "[America's] largest attendance for track since the 1932 Olympics at Los Angeles," one correspondent noted. According to *Los Angeles Times* sports editor Paul Zimmerman, receipts from the trials totaled $268,000.[7]

Like a catchy tune, the figure stuck in Masters's head—and for good reason. At the time, Stanford's athletic department was hurting financially, in large part because the football team that fall—it finished 0-10—failed to generate enough income. But cash had to be generated somehow. Given the success of the 1960 trials, and given Jordan's contacts in the Soviet Union and the US State Department (during the mid-1950s, Jordan had coached in Greece as part of a State Department–run program), an American-Soviet track meet was the obvious choice. On January 21, 1961, the *San Francisco Chronicle* reported that the Amateur Athletic Union (AAU), at its annual meeting in December, had given "[t]entative approval of the Stanford Stadium site" for the 1962 meet (the AAU would later fully sanction the event). As the administrative body for American track, the AAU was tasked with selecting the location of the meet.[8]

Publicly, Jordan and Masters exuded confidence whenever discussing the meet. Privately, though, they must have had their doubts. What if the large crowds failed to materialize? What if the weather was unseasonably cool? What if it rained? There was also the hefty financial commitment—$125,000—that Stanford pledged upfront to the AAU. If returns came in less than projected, it would be Stanford that suffered the most. In addition, roughly $53,000 of the meet's earnings was to be handed over to the State Department, which had covered the cost of sending the American team to Moscow in 1961 after the AAU said it did not have the funds to pay for the trip. Lastly, Stanford was required to share half the profits with the AAU. Masters was mainly the one who negotiated the terms for the university, and even though they may have seemed unfair, he was willing to take the risk.[9]

As for Jordan, he threw himself into his directorship duties with characteristic intensity. Overseeing a large staff and often attending to minor issues himself, he worked tirelessly, sometimes as many as fourteen hours a day. "My aim," he told *Palo Alto Times* columnist Walt Gamage, "is to make this [meet] the greatest track . . . meet ever held in this country." And Jordan believed he knew how, explaining to Gamage, "This meet will have the flavor of the Olympics with flags, bands and the teams marching into the stadium." The reference to the Olympics is revealing. Jordan wholeheartedly believed in the noble purpose of sport, and he envisioned that the meet would help erode Cold War enmity. As he explained to a reporter for the *Palo Alto Times*, "There's no other avenue like sports for breaking down international distrust. Music, art and drama are also important but they don't reach the vast number of people that sports can."[10]

Jordan's words were relevant—especially in 1962. During the previous two years, the downing of the American U-2 spy plane, the US-backed invasion of the Bay of Pigs, and the building of the Berlin Wall had poisoned the optimism of 1958 and 1959, heightening Cold War anxieties. A Gallup poll conducted in early 1962 found that 34 percent of Americans believed "it [was] . . . impossible to reach a peaceful settlement of differences with Russia." In December 1960, 27 percent of respondents professed the same belief.[11]

The first half of 1962 brought more troubling news. In 1958, the US and USSR had entered into formal talks on the abolishment of nuclear weapons testing. The parleying continued on and off for three years, during which time neither nation detonated a single nuclear device. But in September 1961, the Soviets, in part to bolster their stance in the evolving dispute over Berlin, began testing again, prompting the United States to follow suit, though its weapons, unlike the USSR's, were exploded underground. Not surprisingly, talks were broken off. By late April 1962, the US had restarted aboveground detonations, despite the resumption of talks seeking to ban nuclear testing. Three months later, the talks were discontinued yet again. Suddenly, the prospect of nuclear war seemed frightfully real. The Cuban Missile Crisis that fall underscored just how perilous that prospect was.[12]

With the Cold War intensifying, no one could be certain that the Stanford meet would not draw anti-USSR protestors. Masters, nevertheless, wanted to be prepared. In an April 1962 letter to Lyle M. Nelson, director of university relations, Masters downplayed the seriousness of several anti-Soviet letters sent to Stanford officials, but admitted: "I am more uneasy about the possibility of having a picket line here the two days of the Russian meet." To Masters, preventing the demonstrations would be easy enough. "My present feeling is that we ought to have some kind of 'flying' squad to move [the protestors] off campus, if they should convene here," he wrote. "What do you think about that?"[13]

Nelson took five days to respond, but not before running Masters's idea past Frederic O. Glover, executive assistant to Stanford president J. E. Wallace Sterling. Glover did not like the idea. Neither did Nelson. In his reply to Masters, Nelson wrote, "Both of us [Glover and Nelson] are quite hesitant to organize any kind of a flying squad," though Nelson did mention that "we will bring [the idea] up sometime at the President's staff meeting to see if we can get an opinion as to what our rights might be." As things turned out, no protests occurred. The biggest issue police faced was "keep[ing] tabs on the eight lost children who strayed from their seats in search of autographs and couldn't find their way back to their parents," the *Palo Alto Times* reported.[14]

On the evening of July 13, a Friday, the TWA Boeing 707 carrying the USSR team landed at San Francisco International Airport. In truth, the Soviets were fortunate to be there. Confusion over who was to fund the last leg of their trip from New York to San Francisco had nearly caused them to miss their flight. USSR officials were under the assumption that American organizers would pay for it. However, the AAU, which had negotiated the travel arrangements with Soviet authorities, argued that the agreement signed by US and USSR officials explicitly stated that the visitors were to cover all costs "to the site of the meet." The Soviets, however, interpreted the phrase as meaning simply to the United States.[15]

A quarrel ensued. Neither the AAU nor the Soviets would budge. So dire was the situation, it looked like Stanford would have to intervene. Masters, though, later described as "friendly yet tough as leather," refused to commit any money. He knew that the university was contractually bound to bear the expense of the Soviets' roundtrip transit between San Francisco airport and campus, not the trip to the West Coast. Finally, at the State Department's urging, the AAU scratched together the approximately $25,000 to cover the USSR team's airfare. Stanford planners exhaled a sigh of relief.[16]

Now, at the airport, all of that was forgotten. As USSR athletes, coaches, and officials exited the jetliner's rear door and made their way down the stairs to the tarmac, the contingent of Americans gathered beside the jet—including Payton Jordan and Chuck Taylor, Stanford's assistant athletic director and former football coach—started clapping. Within minutes, the groups mingled as if it were a family reunion. Casting perspective on the scene, a writer for the *Palo Alto Times* noted, "Soviet athletes bound for the Winter Olympics at Squaw Valley in 1960 were lustily booed by an airport crowd."[17]

The warm greeting on the tarmac presaged a week of friendly interaction. On July 17, a *Palo Alto Times* headline trumpeted, "Spirit of Olympics sweeping over Stanford." Ever since the Soviets had arrived on campus and checked into Stern Hall, the multiwing dormitory where the American squad also stayed, students and locals alike had treated the visitors with respect. Bert Nelson, cofounder of *Track and Field News*, the highly respected publication headquartered in nearby Los Altos, was struck by the openness and fraternization at Stern Hall. "I was surprised with the easy informality of the arrangements," Nelson later wrote. "No guards or keep out signs. Nothing at all to keep the two teams from intermingling, or to keep the press and public away." Less than two miles away, in Palo Alto, American and Soviet flags hung from shop windows and walls. Giving voice to the local mood, the *Palo Alto Times* headlined, "To Soviet Athletes: Welcome!" Years later, writer Garry Cavalli, in his fine article about the meet, "Cold War, Warm Welcome," quoted Jordan as saying: "Our philosophy was, let's entertain these people [the Soviets]. Let's treat them like human beings, like we want to be treated."[18]

Augmenting the goodwill, the Americans and Soviet teams held joint practices, in which coaches and athletes freely exchanged ideas and training tips. Combined workouts had been staged at the 1959 and 1961 meets, but the ones at Stanford were more numerous and easygoing, and better supported. Writing about the practices, Bill Leiser of the *San Francisco Chronicle* observed: "Angell Field"—the venue near Stanford Stadium where the two squads practiced the most—"has been flooded with as many as 6000 observers who stayed and looked on. . . . What they were watching was Russians and Americans getting along with each other." Earlier, Art Rosenbaum, the *Chronicle*'s sports editor, quoted a US competitor: "These are the most relaxed social contacts the teams have ever had in their four years of competition." Photos of US and USSR competitors training side-by-side, and Soviet athletes signing autographs for children, appeared in local papers.[19]

In addition to practicing, the Soviet squad was kept busy with activities organized by Stanford planners. USSR team members toured San Francisco, visiting the Golden Gate Bridge, Nob Hill, Chinatown, Fisherman's Wharf, and Sausalito. They were also shown around the Ford car factory in nearby Milpitas. According to the *Palo Alto Times* reporter who accompanied the team, questions about employee perks dominated the conversation with plant executives. At the factory, the Soviets ate lunch, which included "a cake decorated to read 'Welcome Russian Track Team.'" On Wednesday, there was a banquet hosted by the PALO club, and the next evening a trip to the Winterland Ballroom in San Francisco to watch the Ice Follies. The Soviets participated in informal activities, too, playing volleyball, basketball, and softball with Stanford undergrads and local residents. Dance parties with US and USSR athletes lasted late into the night. Jordan hosted several Soviet team members at his house.[20]

The Soviets' courteous behavior and relaxed manner caused many to rethink Cold War stereotypes. In a piece titled "Special Report: A Most Human Group," a writer in the *San Francisco Chronicle* commented, "The image that some Americans have of Russians being bearded, evil-looking Bolsheviks with a knife dripping blood in one hand and a cop of Das Kapital in the other has been dispelled by" the USSR track squad. The writer also quoted a Stanford student as stating, "The USC football team should be so nice." Readers of local papers learned that USSR athletes liked many things Americans did: cars, jazz, traveling, dancing, shopping, and watching TV. Two days after the meet, the sports editor of the *Sacramento Union* wrote, "Perhaps contrary to the expectations of some, the Russian men and women looked and acted very much like Americans."[21]

The roster that featured those men and women teemed with talent. A writer for the *Moscow News* termed it "an all-star outfit." The women's team, especially, was superb. In the three previous meets between the US and USSR, the Soviet women had dominated, and every prediction for 1962 called for the same. Although Vera Krepkina was the reigning Olympic long jump champion, it was her teammate, Tatyana Shchelkanova, who had won the event in the 1961 US-Soviet meet with a world-record leap. Eleven months later, just before the Stanford competition, Shchelkanova broke her own mark. The Press sisters, Tamara and Irina, both born in Kharkov, Ukraine, were expected to win their events as well. Irina, twenty-three, would be competing in the 80-meter hurdles, while Tamara, who was two years older, was scheduled to participate in the discus and shot put. Both were going into the Stanford meet defending world records.[22]

The men's team, too, had much to be proud of. Vasily Kuznetsov, a thirty-year-old decathlete, had competed in numerous international competitions, including the first American-Soviet meet in 1958. Pyotr Bolotnikov, labeled by Bert Nelson as "king of the 10,000 meter men," won a gold medal at the 1960 Rome Olympics. Victor Tsibulenko was a world-class competitor in the javelin. Vladimir Truseneyev had set a new world record in the discus in June 1962, only to have American Al Oerter break the mark several weeks later.[23]

But there were two athletes that stood out above the rest. Igor Ter-Ovanesyan was a twenty-four-year-old long jumper who was well known among American fans. A versatile athlete whose first taste of Olympic competition was at the 1956 Games in Melbourne, Ter-Ovanesyan had competed in every meet of the US-Soviet series and had participated in three indoor meets in New York in 1961. These appearances, though, were not what brought him fame. On June 10, 1962, in Yerevan, Armenia, he sailed 1'¼" past American Ralph Boston's 1961 record-setting leap of 27'2", making him and Boston at the time "the only 27-foot broad jumpers in history," the United Press International (UPI) wrote. US track observers took notice. Five days before the Stanford meet, a soaring Ter-Ovanesyan was featured on the cover of *Sports Illustrated*. Below the picture was the caption: "THE NEW RUSSIAN ASSAULT."[24]

Unquestionably, Ter-Ovanesyan's athletic prowess drew Americans' attention. But it was his personality that captivated them. He spoke English. He enjoyed jazz. He was friends with many US athletes, including Ralph Boston, with whom he developed an amicable rivalry. There was something un-Soviet about the USSR broad jumper. The UPI described him as "a slender, clean-cut youngster with dark, bushy hair and a liking for black knit neckties." Sportswriter Arthur Daley called him "the Russian Ivy Leaguer." So much did the Soviet long jump star seem to admire America that during the 1960 Rome Olympics, the CIA had encouraged him to defect.[25]

Ter-Ovanesyan's teammate, Valeri Brumel, may have had more star power. He was good-looking—a writer for the *New Yorker* thought "Brumel . . . resemble[d] a young Tyrone Power"—and the best higher jumper on the planet. As an eighteen-year-old, he had come in second at the 1960 Rome Olympics. But it would be a long time before anyone beat him again. Between June and August of 1961, he set three world records, the last of which—7'4½"—remained the world mark going into the Stanford meet. Brumel was not a showoff, but he was a showman. *Time* marveled in August 1962, "Standing in the Stanford gym before the meet, Brumel"—who measured 6'1"—"happily demonstrated his technique by leaping up under a 10-ft.-high basket and touching the rim with his right foot." His ability to defy gravity was the product of long hours in the gym. "The barbell and I are particular friends," he wrote in a 1963 *Sports Illustrated* article.[26]

The American team featured marquee names too. On the women's squad, sprinter Wilma Rudolph Ward—in 1961, she wed William Ward, also an athlete—was the biggest draw. Winner of three gold medals and recipient of the 1961 Sullivan Award for best amateur athlete, Rudolph, a student at Tennessee State University (TSU), where she ran for coach Ed Temple's legendary Tigerbelles, was easily the fastest and most recognizable woman in track and field. Also a Tigerbelle, Vivian Brown was predicted to be a top finisher in the 200 meters. (Three other Tigerbelles were also on the team.) Another contender was discus thrower Olga Connolly. But given the strength of the Soviet women, Donnis Thompson, the coach of the US women's team, knew her squad was overmatched. Still, she remained hopeful, stating, "We don't expect to win, but we'll cut in on [the Soviets'] point totals." Thompson, a Chicago native who coached track at the University of Hawaii, would later encourage Hawaiian congresswoman Patsy Mink to propose what eventually became Title IX.[27]

The American men, by contrast, were looking to continue their unbeaten streak against the Soviets. The sprinters—Bob Hayes, Roger Sayers, and Paul Drayton—were picked to win their events, as were the hurdlers. Shot putter Dallas Long, bronze medalist at the 1960 Rome Games, had set a new world record in May 1962, while discus thrower Al Oerter's came three weeks before the Stanford competition. Two months shy of twenty-six, Oerter, who stood 6'4" and weighed 240 pounds, was already a double Olympic gold medalist. Hammer thrower Harold Connolly, who, along with Oerter and seven other athletes, decided not to participate in the 1961 US-Soviet competition because the AAU demanded that they remain in Europe after the meet in Moscow to compete in additional competitions, had won an Olympic gold medal in 1956. Jim Beatty looked to have few challengers in the 1,500 meters. Ron Morris and John Cramer were favorites in the pole vault. Unlike Cramer, Morris used a fiberglass pole.[28]

Among the better-known athletes on the US men's team was Ralph Boston. A native Mississippian, the gregarious twenty-two-year-old had made headlines in 1960, shattering the long jump record established by Jesse Owens in 1935. Soon thereafter, a confident Boston claimed the Olympic gold medal in Rome. In 1961, he flew 27'½"—the first time anyone had jumped 27 feet, and in the US-USSR meet later that summer, he added 1'½" to the mark, beating Ter-Ovanesyan by nearly a foot. By the start of the Stanford meet, Boston and Ter-Ovanesyan's rivalry had grown, albeit lopsidedly. In their four previous matchups, Boston, who attended Tennessee State, had not lost. In July 1962, though, it was Ter-Ovanesyan who owned the world record.[29]

American John Thomas also had a friendly rivalry with his Soviet counterpart. The trouble was that Valeri Brumel dominated it. Before his duels with the Russian, the 6'5" Thomas had literally been a rising star. In 1960, as a gangly nineteen-year-old sophomore at Boston University, he set four world records in the span of two months, the last of which—a stratospheric leap of 7'3¾"—came during the 1960 Olympic trials at The Farm. But several weeks later, at the Games in Rome, he finished third behind Brumel and gold medalist Robert Shavlakadze, also from the USSR. From then on, Thomas seemed to be playing catch-up. In 1961, Brumel beat him four consecutive times. The next year, in a meet against Poland, Thomas mustered only 6'9¾", and finished third. In the run-up to the Stanford meet, people wondered if Thomas would be able to rekindle his magic from 1960.[30]

As the start of the meet approached, anticipation for what a *New York Times* writer called "[America's] biggest track and field extravaganza since the 1932 Olympics" ballooned. Bay Area newspapers ran articles daily about the upcoming Cold War showdown and Stanford officials worked long hours preparing for the massive crowds that were sure to arrive. Fans wanting to attend the meet could do so by plunking down $6 for reserved seats or half that for nonreserved. Attached to the envelope in which people were to insert their money when ordering tickets was the meet's schedule, below which a blurb advertised: "AN UNPARALLED OPPORTUNITY TO SEE SOME OF THE WORLD'S MOST FAMOUS TRACK AND FIELD STARS—BOTH DAYS ARE OF EQUAL INTEREST." Two athletes per team would compete in each event. Scoring would be based on a descending scale: 5 points to the winner, 3 to the runner-up, and 2 and 1 for third and fourth place, respectively.[31]

The buildup was tremendous. A crew from ABC-TV was scheduled to arrive later in the week, loaded down with "13 cameras, eight tape machines and two mobile units," according to a *Los Angeles Times* journalist. The crew's task would be made doubly difficult since Jordan insisted that the infield was to be as cable-free as possible and have just two mobile cameramen covering events. Walter Gamage noted on July 12 that Stanford's "concessionaire . . . has already ordered . . . 200,000 soft drinks, 50,000 hot dogs, 80,000 ice cream bars, 40,000 malted milks, 50,000 frozen orange juice sticks, 20,000 special pennants, 6,000 coolie hats and 100,000 programs." American men's coach John Oelkers, whose full-time job was coaching track at Tulane, told those attending a pre-meet banquet: "We have respect and admiration for the Russian team. And this is the best American team we have had. The meet should be the greatest in the series." Pressed to forecast a winner, Soviet coach Gavriel Korobkov said: "Predictions are for press men, not coaches. But [the meet] should be 50-50. We have a very strong team this year. I hold that the whole match will be the keenest ever."[32]

Despite the feeling of goodwill permeating Stanford's campus, the two teams were nevertheless Cold War rivals. An *Oakland Tribune* editorial published on the eve of the meet spoke to this inevitability while simultaneously belittling women's participation in sport. "International prestige is one of the fruits of victory when the United States and the Soviet meet in athletic competition," the editorial began. "This consideration comes alive every four years at the Olympic Games but it is an equal incentive in the lesser jousts, such as the men's track and field dual meet at Stanford University Stadium Saturday and Sunday." As if to reinforce the editorial's main point, an adjacent cartoon depicted a buffoonish Khrushchev sitting on the edge of a building and holding a sign that declared, "'A SHOWDOWN ON BERLIN IS NEAR!'" above which the caption stated: "HE'S CLIMBED BACK OUT ON THE LEDGE AGAIN!"[33]

Saturday, July 21, dawned bright and crisp. Temperatures hovered in the mid-50s, but soon shot up to a track-meet-perfect 78 degrees. Alongside The Farm, El Camino Real, a highway connecting Palo Alto to points north and south and one that provided access to Stanford's 90,000-seat stadium, was being expanded. A *Palo Alto Times* editorial advised, "Try walking to [the] meet." Near campus, hotels were booked solid. The previous night restaurants had closed later than normal to accommodate the ravenous swarms. But by 8 a.m., ticket buyers were queuing up. ABC technicians unloaded gadgetry and readied it for the national telecast on "Wide World of Sports," which would beam segments of the meet into peoples' homes, live—except in the Bay Area, where it would not be shown. To maximize attendance, Stanford officials had gotten ABC to agree not to televise the meet to surrounding cities and towns. (ABC paid just $25,000 for broadcast rights.) KCBS radio, though, would air the meet, and KGO-TV planned to provide a thirty-minute recap at night. In the Stern Hall refectory, American and Soviet athletes, seated apart from one another, ate breakfast in hushed voices.[34]

Around 12:30 that afternoon, fans began streaming into the stadium. The stands were awash in sunshine. The scoreboard, though, was blank. Earlier, electricity to the stadium and immediate vicinity had abruptly stopped, shutting down stoplights and aggravating motorists. Fortunately, the electricity returned just before 2 p.m. Jordan and his staff were relieved. The opening ceremony was slated to start at 3 p.m. "The power failure," the *San Francisco Examiner* explained the next day, was "presumably caused by the extra drain of television and radio equipment on hand for the international event." People were in a festive mood. Former Oregon State high jumper John Radetich, who attended the meet with his father as a thirteen-year-old, recalled there being "a picnic atmosphere" among fans.[35]

At approximately 3 p.m., under a bright, unblemished sky, the US and USSR teams strode into the stadium and made their way to the middle of the infield. Cheers and applause from the large crowd filled the air. The Americans wore white sweat suits with a AAU-USA patch on the upper left side of the tops. The Soviets were garbed in blue with white CCCP lettering sewn across the front of their warm-ups. Short speeches were given, and banners traded. The American and Soviet flags, held upright by John Thomas and Valeri Brumel, served as a focal point, drawing spectators' attention as the US and USSR national hymns played. Not far behind Thomas and Brumel were American and Soviet athletes. The ceremony lasted almost twenty-five minutes.[36]

Fifteen events—five women's and ten men's—comprised Saturday's program (the decathlon was contested both days). As expected, US sprinters and hurdlers finished 1-2 in their events, while Wilma Rudolph Ward, who had recently returned to competition, showed flashes of her Olympic self, winning the 100 meters in 11.5 seconds, three-tenths of a second faster than runner-up Maria Itkina, the thirty-year-old USSR sprint champion. Other American victories followed. US athletes in the men's 110-meter hurdles and 400 meters each claimed the top two spots. Watching the events, Art Rosenbaum, sports editor for the *San Francisco Chronicle*, sensed a gradual shift in the crowd's mood. "Bit by bit the polite cheers turned partisan," Rosenbaum noted, adding, "Pretty soon, the partisanship was almost as pronounced as in a Giant-Dodger series. The Russians were the Dodgers, naturally." Ron Morris's victory in the pole vault drew loud cheers.[37]

Meanwhile, on the west side of the infield, Ralph Boston and Igor Ter-Ovanesyan were limbering up for their duel in the long jump. Ter-Ovanesyan, however, was ailing. Earlier in the week, he had pulled a thigh muscle during practice, and was only able to compete now because he had been given several injections of Novocain. In the end, the poster boy of USSR track was unable to keep up with his American rival, and lost by 2¾". Boston, dubbed "the Tennessee jackrabbit" by John Dixon of the *Long Beach Independent Press-Telegram*, jumped 26'9", far shy of Ter-Ovanesyan's world mark, but good enough to ensure that his undefeated streak over the Soviet remained intact. (The next year, at the Millrose Games in Madison Square Garden, Ter-Ovanesyan finally defeated Boston.)[38]

The last four events of the day capped what had been so far a strong US showing. Dallas Long and Gary Gubner claimed first and second place in the shot put, respectively, and the men's and women's 400-meter relay teams thrilled the crowd, each finishing on top. Running the final leg, Rudolph Ward had to come from six feet behind to ensure the US win. Harold Connolly, whose Czechoslovakian-born wife, Olga, finished second to Tamara Press in the discus, grabbed headlines by winning the hammer throw with a world record-breaking toss of 231'10". In his lead the next day, *New York Herald Tribune* sportswriter Jesse Abramson beautifully captured the burly American's exploit: "Harold Vincent Connolly spun three times and hurled the 16-pound hammer 231 feet and 10 inches through golden California sunshine to a world record yesterday."[39]

Save for John Cramer's disastrous finish in the pole vault—he missed all three attempts and consequently was not awarded a point—the US team had had a good first day. The men held a 61–45 advantage, while the women, though behind, 30–22, had been more competitive than expected. Added together, the totals put the US ahead, 83–75.[40]

The US press happily reported the news. The *Independent Press-Telegram*'s John Dixon began his article: "It was a Black Saturday for the Reds." A *Washington Post* headline, ignoring the women's competition entirely, read: "U.S. Leads Russians in Track." Combining the men's and women's results, one California paper headlined, "U.S. JUMPS INTO 83–75 LEAD." Not all commentators, though, focused on the score. A writer for the *New York Times* quoted a Soviet journalist traveling with the USSR team as commenting: "[The trip] has been wonderful. Everyone has been so friendly. We will be sorry to say good-by."[41]

Sunday, July 22, brought another postcard-perfect day. Masters and Jordan must have been relieved knowing that they and their staff would not have to contend with rain and cooler temperatures. No doubt the athletes and the 81,000 onlookers who braved traffic backups and long lines to watch the US and USSR teams compete welcomed the nice weather. If the meteorological gods had ever blessed an event, they did so at Stanford.[42]

The performances by athletes that afternoon were as sparkling as the sunlight shimmering off San Francisco Bay. Vivian Brown, the Tennessee State Tigerbelle, won the 200 meters, and American Willie Atterberry took the 400-meter hurdles in 50.3 seconds, a new meet record. Also setting a meet record was thirty-two-year-old Pyotr Bolotnikov, who did so in the 5,000 meters. A day earlier, the inexhaustible Bolotnikov had won the 10,000 meters. Combined, the victories gave him a "Woolworth Double," a badge of honor among distance runners that was named after the popular five-and-dime retailer. Americans Paul Drayton and Roger Sayers swept the 200 meters, as did their teammates, Jerry Seibert and Jim Dupree, in the 800 meters. Tatyana Shchelkanova beat Tigerbelle Willye White in the long jump, and Vasily Kuznetsov finished first in the decathlon. In the 1,500 meters, Jim Beatty outkicked Ivan Byelitskiy to take the race. Beatty's time was three-tenths of a second faster than the American mark he set in 1961. The Press sisters took their events—Irina, the 80-meter hurdles, and Tamara, the shot put. The latter's heave of 57'¾" established a new meet record. Winning the 1,600-meter relay, the US men's team broke the meet record set in 1958.[43]

Fans sitting on the east side of the stadium had the best view of what was undeniably the most awe-inspiring athletic feat of the afternoon. During the Olympic trials two years earlier, in the same stadium, John Thomas had propelled himself over the bar and into the record books. Unfortunately for him, there would be no repeating of history. The highest mark he cleared was 6'10"—far below what his rival, Valeri Brumel, eventually scaled. Even Gene Johnson, whom Thomas had beaten at the AAU national meet in June, and the second Soviet jumper, Victor Bolyshov, finished ahead of the lanky African American.[44]

Brumel, meanwhile, was going strong. He easily bounded over heights that his fellow competitors struggled with. Eventually, he found himself alone in the competition. And still he climbed, catapulting over 7'1", 7'2", and 7'3". Then the bar was lifted to 7'5", half an inch higher than the reigning world mark he set in Bulgaria in 1961. A hush fell over the stadium. Eighty-one thousand pairs of eyes focused on the Soviet jumper as he readied himself for the leap.

Brumel slowly began his approach, picked up speed, and just before reaching the pit, planted his left foot firmly on the infield sod and blasted off like a *Vostok* rocket. With his limbs and torso working in perfect synchronicity, he brought his right leg over the bar, then his body, and finally his left leg, all the while looking downward. It was a perfectly executed "straddle" jump. (Not until the early 1970s did the Fosbury Flop, named after American Dick Fosbury, who had popularized the technique by flying over the bar backward at the 1968 Mexico City Olympics, become the acceptable style.) Immediately after spectators saw that Brumel had cleared the height—during the leap, he grazed the bar, causing it to waggle—"There was a thunderclap roar from the crowd . . . then a long, standing ovation," the UPI reported. With a wave of his right hand, a smiling Brumel acknowledged the cheers.[45]

The next day, Curley Grieve, sports editor of the *San Francisco Examiner*, wrote: "A slim Siberian-born Russian did something in Stanford stadium yesterday that Khrushchev couldn't hope to match," adding, "[Brumel] made 81,000 American fans stand up and applaud and this was no mild hand-clapping, a

Valeri Brumel, winner of the high jump at the 1962 US-USSR track meet, accepts congratulations from his rival and fourth-place finisher John Thomas. *Courtesy Stanford Athletics Photograph Collection.*

gesture of politeness. . . . It was an honest-to-goodness expression of admiration for a great performance by a great athlete." Grieve was not the only one impressed by Brumel. *Time* quoted one spectator as saying, "Now there is one Russian you can't help but like."[46]

Graciously, Brumel repaid the compliment, admitting to a writer for the *San Francisco Chronicle*: "I had no feeling [about the record leap before takeoff]. But the people in the stadium wanted me to do it. And that helped me to do it. This has been one of the pleasing results in my life, because I did it in a foreign country." Cordner Nelson of *Track and Field News* quoted the Soviet star: "I knew the people in the stands wanted a record so I tried extra hard."[47]

The most stirring moment of the meet, though, came at the end of the closing ceremony. After the festivities had concluded, the two squads should have left the infield and processed out the stadium. Instead, flag-carriers John Thomas and Victor Tsibulenko, hands clasped in a firm handshake, "marched shoulder to shoulder around the track," while their fellow team members trailed behind in two long queues, smiling, arms entwined. Many waved to spectators as the jaunty tune of "The Stars and Stripes Forever" could be heard coming from a Marine Corps band. "The Star Spangled Banner" and the USSR national hymn were also played. "Suddenly," a *Palo Alto Times* scribe penned, "81,000 pairs of hands were clapping, and it was then and there that a monumental and permanent dent was recorded in the Iron Curtain." Bob Brachman, hardly a sportswriter noted for his sentimentality, quoted Jordan as saying: "I cried, along with everybody else, during that spontaneous display at the end." The *Palo Alto Times* editorialized, "One wished the political leaders of the two nations could have linked arms and joined in that magnificent show of sportsmanship."[48]

Overall, the US squad fared well. Of twenty-two men's events, the Americans won fourteen. The US women's results were not as good—the Soviets took seven of ten events—but the Americans proved that they could hold their own against the best team in the world. In the final scoring, the US men defeated their USSR rivals, 128–107, while the Soviet women triumphed, 66–41. The victory of the American men was their largest in the dual meets to date. The US women, for their part, tallied their second-highest number of points since the track series started in 1958. The five TSU Tigerbelles on the seventeen-woman roster had been the heart of the US squad. Excluding the 20 points automatically earned by athletes who came in third and fourth, the Tigerbelles accounted for 18 of the Americans' remaining 21 points. For the Soviet women, Tamara Press herself was responsible for 10. Altogether, one Soviet, two world, three American, and fourteen meet records were broken.[49]

Given the competitive nature of the Cold War, it was no surprise that Americans and Soviets were unable to agree upon the results. This was nothing new.

Disagreements had arisen in all three previous American-USSR meets. The problem stemmed from how the two nations kept score: Americans refused to combine the points of the men's and women's meets, while the Soviets did. (The program for the meet, issued by Stanford, stated, "Separate team scores will be kept for the men's events and women's events.") The methods yielded different winners, since the USSR women had always posted larger margins of victory than did the US men. To the Soviets, the controversy was an issue of equality. As USSR coach Gavriel Korobkov remarked before the Stanford competition, "We do not discriminate against women. In Russia there are no separate meets for boys or girls or for men and women. . . . I, for example, am the coach of everybody here." However, many Americans believed that the Soviets adhered to their system so that they could say that they had prevailed.[50]

Predictably, in the days after the Stanford competition Americans and Soviets dueled over who beat whom. A banner headline in *Sovetskii Sport* announced, "FOURTH MATCH—FOURTH VICTORY," a subhead adding, "USSR national team—USA national team 173:169." *Pravda*, *Izvestia*, and *Sovetskaia Rossiia* likewise proclaimed that the USSR had triumphed. Stopping off in New York on his way home with the rest of the Soviet team, Korobkov stated, "By combined scores we won by four points." Three weeks after the meet, US State Department official Frank G. Siscoe noted in a letter to Robert E. Miller, Stanford's associate director of university relations: "Typical headlines [about the meet in the USSR] were 'Soviet Track Athletes Win Again,' 'Soviet Victory at Palo Alto,' 'Match of Giants Won by U.S.S.R.'"[51]

Americans disagreed. *Amateur Athlete* called the Cold War matchup "a smashing U.S. triumph." The *Chicago Daily Tribune* headlined on the first page, "U.S. DEFEATS RUSSIANS IN TRACK MEET." Ignoring the women's competition altogether, a headline in one Texas paper declared: "Americans Wallop USSR by the Largest Margin." The *New York Herald Tribune*'s Jesse Abramson took more of a jingoistic stance. "The week-end competition proved [that] . . . American coaching and training methods produce the world's best athletes and the Soviets, who admittedly borrowed our techniques from coaches, textbooks and movies, have not caught up," and that "[t]he American athlete who expends sweat, blood and tears to achieve world class can be trusted to attain top condition on his own responsibility. To see the entire U.S.S.R. squad assembled [at Stanford], all working out daily for a week under scads of coaches, while less than half the U.S. squad was in sight until the last day, was nerve-racking." Al Oerter, who set a new meet record in the discus, was quoted as admitting, "I was more interested in beating the Russians, than trying for a world mark."[52]

Americans cleverly found other ways to assert victory. The *Chronicle*'s Art Rosenbaum reminded readers, "The conventional distribution for dual meets is 5-3-1 and 5-0 in the relay. . . . On that basis . . . the final score would be . . . USA 139, USSR 137." Jack Murphy, who covered the meet for the *New Yorker*, focused on the scoring in the relays. "Had the American rule been in effect"—in other words, winner-take-all—". . . the Russians . . . would have dropped nine points and their victory," Murphy wrote. John Cramer's dismal result in the pole vault was also discussed. Substitute the zero he received with the three points he should have earned for coming in second—the position he was predicted to finish—and the Americans would have won, 172–171, commentators said. Former Stanford track coach Robert L. "Dink" Templeton noted "that [the US] could have tied the meet by running Wilma Rudolph in the 200 for a sweep with Vivian Brown."[53]

Despite the tussle over scoring, nearly everyone extolled the goodwill shown during the meet. Following the second day of competition, a page-one headline in the *San Francisco Chronicle* declared, "81,000 Cheer A Track Meet With No Losers," while a cartoon on the paper's op-ed page showed a high jumper with "SOVIET ATHLETES" scrawled across the back of his jersey leaping over a wall labeled "EAST-WEST TENSION." The *Examiner*'s Bob Brachman wrote: "No doubt after the treatment the Reds were accorded here, both sides hope with government blessing to perpetuate the rivalry which for 10 days at least stomped out all feelings of bitterness between peoples of opposing ideologies." The *New York Times* editorialized: "The [US and USSR] teams apparently met in a true spirit of brotherhood, too seldom found in the diplomatic arena. Perhaps the delegates in Geneva [negotiating nuclear testing] have something to learn from the young athletes who met in Palo Alto." Newspapers nationwide published a photo of USSR miler Ivan Byelitskiy kissing fellow competitor Jim Beatty on the cheek after Beatty won the 1,500 meters. In the USSR, *Pravda* observed that the meet witnessed "a remarkable atmosphere of friendship," and the *Moscow News* wrote that "an overall record in athletic friendship" had been set at Stanford.[54]

Those affiliated with the competition were especially impacted. "In my 30 years of coaching," USSR coach Gavriel Korobkov confessed, "I've never seen a meet where there was more good fellowship, competition, fun and enthusiasm than this one." Stated Pincus Sober, an AAU administrator, "I know the kids on this Russian team . . . will spread the word about the wonderful way they were treated here at Stanford. . . . When their acquaintances try to tell them that all Americans are warmongers, I'm inclined to think some of these athletes will put them straight." The American interpreter for the Soviet squad noted in his post-meet report, "I did not hear a single unfavorable comment or criticism [from USSR team members] on any point. . . . They were greatly impressed by the friendliness and sportsmanship of the American coaches and athletes and by the 80,000 spectators present each day of the competition."[55]

As could be anticipated, the meet was widely praised. Commentators called it "a splendid and entertaining show," the "[b]iggest, best dual meet ever," "one of the greatest athletic competitions in American history," and an "All Time Classic." A *Los Angeles Sentinel* headline, referencing the 1960 Rome Olympics, proclaimed: "USA-Russia Meet Rivals Rome." One Soviet journalist told Jordan, "[The meet] was undoubtedly the finest sports meeting I have ever attended. I doubt if I shall ever see another one like it," while the title of a *San Francisco Examiner* editorial simply read: "Great Job at Stanford." Even the upper echelons of US power applauded the way in which the meet was handled. In a letter to Stanford president J. E. Wallace Sterling, US secretary of state Dean Rusk wrote: "The friendly association of the American and Soviet athletes—all in a fine California setting—contributed significantly, I believe, to the development of international good will."[56]

The day after the meet, the Soviets again visited San Francisco and shopped. The US women's squad manager Eileen Goodnight and Joanne Terry, the TSU Tigerbelle who had come in fourth in the 80-meter hurdles, tagged along. Leather jackets were a popular item. The Soviets "also purchased shoes, bedding such as comforter, and records (Dinah Washington, Ray Charles and the Barry Sisters)," a reporter for the *Palo Alto Times* noted. "The men bought slacks and the interpreter purchased a suit." After returning from San Francisco, the Soviets dined at the International Cuisine in Stanford. Earlier, team members had "arrived en masse and were applauded as they entered the restaurant." Throughout the evening, diners asked the athletes for autographs and snapped pictures. Following the meal, the USSR team left for the airport. Among the meet planners to say goodbye were Jordan and Chuck Taylor.[57]

Everyone was sad to see the Soviets leave. Walt Gamage wrote: "When they departed . . . for Moscow [via New York and Paris] quite a few athletes cried openly. . . . And to be completely honest there were quite a few tears shed by the Stanford officials and others there to bid the Russians bon voyage." The next day in New York, the Soviets ate lunch at the New York Athletic Club (NYAC), shopped (again), and visited the city, including the United Nations and Rockefeller Center. They boarded an Air France plane later that night.[58]

Back in California, Al Wolf, the congenial sportswriter for the *LA Times*, estimated that Stanford stood to pocket approximately $85,000 from hosting the meet. The UPI predicted roughly the same amount. The Associated Press (AP) was more optimistic, reporting, "Stanford could receive as much as $100,000 for its share." Actually, the university's take came to nearly $113,000, with revenues surpassing $367,000. Masters, obviously, was thrilled. Ten days after the meet, he wrote President Sterling: "When I first told you I would guarantee the $125,000 estimated [before the meet], you had me a little worried when you kept quizzing me about whether or not I thought I could make it. Naturally I am glad the chance I took paid off handsomely for us."[59]

In the immediate afterglow of the meet, Stanford authorities sought to capitalize on the wild enthusiasm that had been generated by the USSR team's visit. Reports circulated that university officials were interested in having The Farm host the next US-USSR meet on American soil—which at the time was slated for 1965 but actually occurred a year earlier—as well as the 1964 US men's Olympic trials, and even the Olympic Games. Though the overtures were initially met with encouragement—a day after the meet, AAU administrator Pincus Sober, who had had misgivings about Stanford hosting the competition, confided to Walt Gamage, "Stanford [is] the logical place to hold the [1964] trials. . . . How can anyone argue against Stanford after watching the wonderful way this meet was staged here?" The Farm never again hosted the US-Soviet meet or the Olympic trials. The 1968 and 1972 Summer Games were held in Mexico City and Munich, respectively.[60]

But in the early 1960s, the San Francisco region was, in the words of *Track and Field News* writer Bert Nelson, "the track capital of the U.S." The dual meet at Stanford had proven that. San Francisco's claim as a prominent track and field hotbed was also borne out by history: The 1964 US-Soviet meet in Los Angeles had a two-day attendance of a little more than 106,000, and the next time the two Cold War foes competed in a dual meet in the United States, in 1969 in Los Angeles, only 30,340 spectators attended. The *Palo Alto Times* was correct when it editorialized a day after the 1962 dual competition, "[the meet's] success, coupled with that of the 1960 Olympic Trials at Stanford, stamps the Peninsula and Bay Area as a foremost track center."[61]

During those ten magical days in July 1962, San Franciscans pushed aside Cold War suspicions and embraced the Soviet squad. It was a feeling Payton Jordan shared. In a July 31, 1962, letter to Stanford president Sterling, Jordan wrote that being a part of the competition "was an exciting experience for me and I shall always cherish the memories of this fine meet. . . . Through the wonderful relationship that existed between the athletes of our nations during the competition, I am sure better understanding and closer friendships will be realized for the people of both countries." The meet at Stanford showed that Americans and Soviets could get along, even as international tensions were careening toward a breaking point. The sporting rivalry between the two superpowers was not just about antagonistic competition. Sometimes enduring friendships were forged.[62]

11

"Skate Fast, Hit Hard"

San Francisco Bay Bombers and Bay Area Roller Derby

BETH CAVALIER

In August 1935, the first-ever roller derby event took place at the Chicago Coliseum, drawing nearly 20,000 fans.[1] The brainchild of Leo Seltzer, the Transcontinental Roller Derby was an endurance roller skating race where skaters competed in a mock marathon event covering nearly 3,000 miles over a period of several weeks. Mirroring the success of the Depression-era dance marathons, the Transcontinental Roller Derby expanded to a national traveling league featuring teams of skaters with five men and five women at a time scoring points by passing opponents in a pack (the basic rule structure that still exists in modern roller derby today, without the mythical cross-country race).[2] The Roller Derby spent several weeks in various cities across the country, enjoying high attendance night after night. Public interest in roller derby waxed and waned from 1935 into the early 1970s, with short periods of near total collapse, and many periods of tremendous success, high attendance rates, and record television ratings before the existing league finally collapsed in 1973. As roller derby evolved, California acted as the hub for the sport and for the subsequent television broadcasts, and by the mid-1950s the organizational structure of roller derby was completely based in San Francisco and the surrounding Bay Area.

Roller derby is a unique sport that began in 1935 as coed, in contrast to most other sports that women participated in throughout that era. Women's participation in roller derby as equal athletes to their male counterparts subsequently framed the coverage of the sport. In the 1930s, San Francisco was ahead of its time in its acceptance of female athletes, with local papers regularly covering women swimmers, golfers, and tennis players in both the Sports and the Society pages of the *San Francisco Chronicle*. This chapter traces the path of roller derby in the Bay Area, as it became the epicenter of the sport, focusing particularly on the ways in which the media covered the skaters.

In July 1938, Transcontinental Roller Derby first appeared in San Francisco at the Civic Auditorium and the event was "quintessentially San Franciscan," with the mayor firing the starting gun, a bench-clearing brawl, and a skater "knocked out colder than December 22 in Minnesota."[3] There was extensive news coverage of the inaugural roller derby contest in San Francisco. For days leading up to the first night on July 6, the *San Francisco Chronicle* dedicated numerous space in the sports section covering the "goofy show" that would soon be coming to town. Referring to the event as the "nuthouse on wheels" and the skaters as "wheeled maniacs,"[4] columnists seemed perplexed and bemused about the appeal of the event. A 1936 *Time* article covering the first roller derby event at the Chicago Coliseum noted, "In 1928 it was tree-sitting. In 1930 it was dance marathons. In 1932 it was Walkathons. Last week, it appeared possible that in 1936 the U.S. appetite for preposterous endurance might take an even more eccentric form: The Roller Derby."[5]

One of the more popular endurance contests of the era was the six-day bike race organized by Eddie Saunders in San Francisco. The bike races were initially equally as unpopular with sportswriters as the roller derby. Bill Leiser, a *San Francisco Chronicle* columnist, argued that roller derby was purportedly "even more goofy, and more exciting, than the bike races, which San Francisco considered rather silly until Eddie Saunders put them on as they should be put on a few years ago. The bikemen now come West for one annual show, and Saunders would probably be mobbed in any year that he forgot to show it."[6]

Notably, the *San Francisco Chronicle* and other newspapers were unclear about how to cover roller derby, finding difficulty in distinguishing between sport and spectacle (an issue still faced by modern roller derby more than seventy years later). In 1939, a columnist for the *San Francisco Chronicle* declared it the "best news of the year" that roller derby would not be returning to Oakland on the next tour.[7] He described a night at the Oakland Auditorium as an event that involved elements of "football, wrestling, speed, and endurance skating, and the constant noise of a thousand workers drilling rivets into the steel of a ten story madhouse." Though it pained Leo Seltzer to have roller derby not taken seriously as a sport, he often advertised the matches next to movie listings in the papers, rather than in the sports section, contributing to the confusion between roller derby's status as sport or entertainment.[8]

However, the novelty of the first roller derby event in San Francisco garnered extensive coverage in the *San Francisco Chronicle*.[9] During the weeks-long event, there were photos, articles, and recaps every day in the sports pages, sometimes garnering multiple stories on the same day. Will Connolly, a longtime *Chronicle* columnist in the early days of his career in 1938, devoted a significant amount of column space decrying, and then eventually coming to terms with the popularity of roller derby in San Francisco. Five days after the inaugural event, Connolly wrote a column protesting his lack of understanding of the rules of roller derby.

> The chilling thought occurred to us that maybe sports writers are recruited from [a] mentally arrested class in grammar schools, a suspicion that the public has long entertained. It puzzles us how the average citizen and his wife or girl friend, or both, immediately catch on to the complicated rules of roller derbies, six-day bike races, and walkathons, while sports writers flounder in a morass of confusion as to what it's all about . . . I am beginning to wonder whether Joe Q. Fan is a shrewder observer of sports than the journalists paid to interpret it for him in the papers. Although the six-day bike races have been presented in our town by Eddie Saunders a number of times, it was only last winter that the great light dawned and I grasped something of the technique of the goofy sport. My public, if any, was way ahead of me.[10]

Nine days later, Connolly was prepared to acknowledge that roller derby was there to stay in San Francisco. He concluded that after "mature reflection we can understand why the goofy show had caught on . . . there is no excuse for the success of the roller skate derby except this town harbors the most expert and courageous roller skaters in the world among its private citizens, and they are turning out to see that the art is practiced properly."[11] By the mid-1930s, roller-skating was one of the most popular forms of recreation in America, a fact not lost on Leo Seltzer when he created roller derby. Seltzer determined that there would be financial revenue in roller derby after reading an article that declared, "roller skating is the country's biggest sport . . . nearly every American who isn't crippled skates at some time in his life, twenty million adults keep it up, and that the sale of roller skates corresponds to ninety-seven percent of the birth rate."[12]

After its initial success in the mid-1930s, the Transcontinental Roller Derby spent several years barnstorming the country, staying weeks at a time in cities while the skaters slept on cots at the rink after the matches. During World War II, as a cost-effective measure, the Derby was streamlined to a single touring unit based in New York City. During this streamline, roller derby did not appear in the Bay Area at all from 1942 to 1949, but it achieved significant national acclaim on the East Coast. After first being televised in 1946, CBS picked up roller derby in 1948 and began broadcasting live matches several nights a week, and ABC continued the coverage beginning in 1949.[13] The television coverage revived the Derby audience and by January 1950 roller derby was back in the Bay Area, playing several nights a week at the Oakland Auditorium in the newly formed National

Roller Derby League (NRDL). Despite the growing success of the sport, disputes with Leo Seltzer over the excessive coverage of roller derby on television led to a nonrenewal of the television contract in 1951, essentially collapsing the league in New York.[14] By 1954, the elder Seltzer relocated his family, the league, and the skaters to California, which he called "the one place that never let him down."[15] Roller Derby began in earnest on the West Coast, and cemented its epicenter in the greater San Francisco Bay Area.

In 1954, West Coast derby was based in Los Angeles, and the first version of the soon-to-be-iconic Bay Bombers began in San Francisco. The Bombers roster included any skater who was willing to travel to San Francisco from Los Angeles, and skaters wore jerseys with the San Francisco Bay Bridge emblazoned across the chest. Attendance was spotty in the mid-1950s, dwindling to as few as two hundred a night at the Cow Palace when the derby played in San Francisco. Leo Seltzer's son Jerry took over command of the NRDL in 1958 and began a revival of the sport that his father had popularized. He relocated the league headquarters to San Francisco and made the Bay Bombers the premier franchise. He negotiated for an independent Oakland television station (KTVU) to begin broadcasting games and set out on an ambitious promotional strategy, ultimately culminating in a renewed interest in the sport that lasted for two more decades before the league folded in 1973. Video technology made it possible for the NRDL to send videotapes of games to television stations around the country, which were then able to show matches at their convenience. At its height of popularity, even competing in a sports market in the Bay Area with professional football, baseball, basketball, and hockey, the Bay Bombers drew more than 1 million spectators annually by 1969.[16]

The Emergence of the Bay Bombers

Throughout the ups and downs of organized roller derby in the twentieth century the sport always seemed to find its way back to San Francisco where it was welcomed by enthusiastic fans. Hartlaub noted, in covering a story about renowned skater Ann Calvello, "I'm guessing [fan treatment] is why former roller derby stars often settle in the Bay Area. To generations of fans, they aren't a gimmick. They are sportsmen and sportswomen. These are idols."[17] Though fans were enthusiastic about roller derby, sports writers and media continued to frame roller derby as a "less-than" sport, confusing it with entertainment and spectacle. A 1950 feature in the *Saturday Evening Post* noted, "popular though it is, the Roller Derby has not been unanimously accepted as a bona fide sport. Many of the sports writers, particularly those in the New York area, treat it as a traveling circus. Others view with loftiness its extreme commercialism, its emphasis on violence and the touch of fakery which lies behind some of its highly touted feuds."[18]

Whatever ambivalence the sportswriters had for roller derby, the people of San Francisco did not share that sentiment. In 1969, thirty years after roller derby first debuted in San Francisco, Frank Deford did a feature story for *Sports Illustrated*. He traced the rise, fall, and eventual resurgence of roller derby in San Francisco and noted that in the Bay Area, "with the Giants, Raiders, Athletics, 49ers, Warriors, Oaks, Clippers, and Seals as neighbors, the Bombers have drawn almost one million spectators a year. There is no apparent reason why, as Seltzer hopes, a real national Roller Derby league cannot evolve, with franchises in all of the country's most populous areas."[19] Roller derby did evolve, faced extinction, and was revived time and time again, and continues to thrive today in San Francisco and across the globe.

Media Coverage of the Skaters

The Bay Bombers were the premier franchise of the NRDL. Scores of skaters passed through as members of the Bombers, on one of the away teams for home matches, or on one of the many national tours. These skaters were celebrities in their own right, with speculation about their personal lives discussed by the fans and in gossip columns. Many of these skaters are remembered today as the grandfathers and grandmothers of the modern roller derby, such as Ma Bogash, who was the first female inductee into the Roller Derby Hall of Fame. Ma Bogash was one of the first faces of roller derby in San Francisco, covered by the *San Francisco Chronicle* in the days leading up to the inaugural game in 1938. Ma and her son Bill both played on the black team in the early days of the Transcontinental Roller Derby, eventually playing on the Bombers later in the NRDL. Bay Bomber rosters changed frequently, with players skating for the home team, or occasionally donning the jersey for the away squads in Los Angeles, Chicago, or New York.

Roller derby both reinforced and challenged the racial norms of the era, as media coverage attests. While skaters of color were often stereotyped, space emerged in roller derby to challenge and push racial boundaries in a way that was not yet happening in broader society, at least not as depicted in mainstream entertainment. Jean Porter, known as "Jeannie Porter, the Indian Girl," was often asked to pose for photos with fans with a feather sticking out of her hair. Yet it was also Porter who became one of the most recognizable faces of roller derby, when she was featured in a 1949 Paramount short film *Roller Derby Girl*, shown in movie theaters before feature films.[20] Skaters like Fletcher Saunders and George Copeland broke the color barrier in roller derby as some of the first African American skaters in 1958. Roller derby was able to move past racial boundaries; whereas *American Bandstand* still prohibited interracial couples on its show in 1962, in that same year the NRDL sponsored a promotional derby dance contest at Berkeley's Ice Arena that was won by an interracial pair, "Peanuts" Meyer and Dewitt Quarles.[21] These events were nationally televised, suggesting an ethos of racial progress by the NRDL. Similar tones of racial equality seemed to also be present in the Bombers fan base. Seltzer and Coppage noted, "Bay Area skating audiences in particular seemed color blind, and fans of color supported their Bay Bombers and loathed their opponents no matter who they were."[22]

One of the most remarkable features of the coverage of roller derby was the fact that female skaters, for the most part, were treated as athletes first. Part of the attraction of roller derby in the late 1930s and early 1940s was the novelty of women competing in nontraditional spheres. While male and female skaters did not compete against one another they occasionally performed in coed promotional events before official matches. The presence of female skaters in the Transcontinental Roller Derby was reported matter-of-factly, even if language included terms like "gals" and "girls."[23] A 1938 story in the *San Francisco Chronicle* featuring Wes Aronson, a football player turned roller derby star, noted that as far as Aronson was concerned, the "girls who 'can take it' certainly deserve to be in the sport."[24] In fact, it was often the women on the track who received more fan attention and more coverage in the newspaper accounts of the sport. In the nearly month-long period that the sport was in San Francisco for the first time, nearly 80 percent of the photos in the sports section of roller derby action featured women skaters, frequently in action poses. Women were more likely to be discussed in the feature stories that did not simply report scores, and skaters such as Ma Bogash, Ivy King, and Honey Thomas were given significant column space in the *Chronicle*.

While female skaters were often treated as athletes there was no escaping the novelty of women competing on equal footing as men. A comic in the *Chronicle* in 1938 took aim at Leo Seltzer as an "[e]astern gentleman who knows all the answers for a big box office" by introducing sex appeal. "The sex appeal and simple rules evidently get results,"[25] the cartoonist concluded. The early success of the Transcontinental Roller Derby happened at a time when female athletes were just beginning to be taken seriously as athletes by the general public. For example, female golfers, swimmers, and tennis players were gracing the pages of the sports section. Around the same time as roller derby first came to San Francisco the public was enthralled with the budding tennis rivalry between "the two Helens," Helen Moody and Helen Jacobs. Following the success of her Olympic track and field career, Babe Didrikson was just beginning to play golf in 1938, and her upcoming wedding to wrestler George Zaharias was announced on the front page of the sports section, not the society pages.[26] The coed sport of roller derby had perfect timing, and the progressive politics of San Francisco served as the perfect site for the success of female skaters in a new sport.

Even those columnists who did not agree with the idea of women playing sports begrudgingly came to accept roller derby and the athletes who participated in it. Will Connolly, one of the *Chronicle*'s sports columnists, described himself as a "crusader against the fitness of women for violent athletics," but still conceded that as a child, "the girls on my block could skate as well as we superior males."[27] Connolly had a peculiar explanation for the success of the sport in San Francisco—the hilly terrain. The precarious hills made it necessary for children who were interested in roller-skating to be good at it "to save their precious necks." This intense focus on survival left little time for chivalry. "We weren't very gallant, what with the immediate concern of holding our balance on nauseating inclines. When a girl fell down, she had to get up without courtly assistance and brush herself off." Connolly's recollection of his childhood was that, ultimately, ability mattered more than sex appeal when it came to sports—especially roller skating. "We recognized the ladies as equals in choosing sides for team tag and snap the whip," he stated, adding, "If they couldn't skate we wouldn't choose them, no matter how pretty they were."[28]

At the peak of their popularity in the 1960s, NRDL games were broadcast on television nearly sixteen hours a week in some markets.[29] By 1973, however, popularity began to wane. Televised games were equal part commentating and promotion. A YouTube video of a 1973 match between the New York Chiefs and the Bay Bombers features commentary by the KTVU "voice of the Derby," Walt Harris, who was nearly as famous as Al Michaels or Howard Cosell, and color commentary by Jerry Seltzer. Seltzer, ever the promoter, took the opportunity at every turn to mention upcoming events in various cities and ways in which fans could get tickets, programs, and merchandise. In this limited sample, it was clear that the women skaters were treated similarly to their male counterparts. The only noticeable difference was that the referees let the men fight more physically and for longer periods of time than the women. The crowd loved the (likely staged) fights and cheered loudly whether the male or female skaters were fighting. When the women were on the track, Harris exclaimed, "Ortiz hammered by Sandy Dunn. It's a little rough out there. That's roller skating action! It's rough! Sandy Dunn wrapping Tucker. Grabs her in a headlock, slams her to the track! Everything is legal if no one is looking."[30] Harris did not use different descriptors for women or men, with the exception of referring to the skaters as "gals," while referring to the men as "men."

Roller derby provided unique economic opportunities for women in sport, especially in the beginning. The opening line of the *Roller Derby Girl* short film notes, "Roller Derby: it's a good way to make a living, especially for a girl." A roller derby girl could earn "75 or a hundred bucks a week, or more if you score points." These economic opportunities attracted "a kid fresh off the local roller rinks, a kid who maybe figures she's tired of the cows and chickens, or an assembly line, or slinging hash."[31] The economic incentive, especially for women, continued throughout the entirety of roller derby in both the Transatlantic Roller Derby and the NRDL. One author wondered about the appeal for women:

> What leads women, many of whom seem normally feminine and in some instances downright dainty, to spend their lives at this breakneck profession would probably constitute an enlightening psychological study. The phenomenon is easier to understand on the economic level. Twenty percent of the gross box office goes directly to the players. Of this, four fifths is split according to individual ratings as judged by the coaches. Seasoned players get at least $4000 a year, stars as much as $15,000. In any event, their contracts guarantee a minimum of $75 to $125 a week, plus all expenses except laundry. The balance of the 20 percent is salted away in a fund maintained by the players themselves to be dipped into on rainy days.[32]

There were few economic opportunities for women from the late 1930s through the 1960s, especially women who were unmarried. In *Roller Derby Girl*, the narrator uses the possibility of finding romantic partners as a lure for new female potential skaters. "If there's a wedding on your mind, there's the men's team. A roller derby girl has a good chance of meeting the right guy—a fellow with what they call 'similar interests.'"[33] The Bay Bombers, in particular, saw several inter-team romances blossom, leading to marriages (and the occasional divorce),[34] and children who grew up to also become involved in roller derby. Rosie Baker and Annis "Big Red" Jensen, who met in roller derby, were married in the early 1950s and had a daughter who also competed for the Bombers in the late 1960s. The original "First Family" of roller derby included brothers Tommy and Buddy Atkinson, who both skated in the earliest versions of the Transcontinental Roller Derby. Tommy was one of the early coaches of the Bay Bombers, but was killed in a car crash in 1958. Buddy married another skater, Bobbie Johnstone. The Atkinsons' son Buddy Jr., daughter-in-law Dru Scott, grandson Sean, and granddaughter Ali all competed in roller derby, and all played in the Bay Area at various times in their careers. Buddy Jr. also acted as a Bombers coach briefly in the early 1970s, and today works as a consultant for banked track construction.[35]

The Blonde Bomber, the Demon of the Derby, and Mr. Roller Derby

While there were numerous noteworthy skaters who thrilled audiences throughout the several decades of roller derby in the Bay Area, none were more renowned and revered than the trio of Joan Weston, Ann Calvello, and Charlie O'Connell. Weston and Calvello were contrasted as the age-old battle of good versus evil, hero versus villain, while O'Connell played the part of the sneering tough guy. It is not coincidental that these three became the most famous skaters of their time because they provided the necessary ingredients for a proverbial sporting passion play. Weston, the "sturdy, 5-foot-10-inch blonde who skates like a turbo-charged bulldozer,"[36] played the role of "golden girl," and was the fan-favorite in every arena she skated in, even if she was on the away team. Calvello, often called "Banana Nose" because of her repeated broken noses, was the aggressive, flamboyant, and loud villain with wild hair and even wilder behavior. O'Connell, the highest-paid skater in history, maintained his popularity despite an aloofness with the fans and other skaters. He maintained a "good guy" persona despite what was often perceived as "dirty" play. His masculinity was constantly reinforced through references to his good looks and charm with women. The gender dynamics of the media and fans' relationships with these three skaters reflect a larger cultural pattern. During roller derby's heyday from the 1950s to the 1970s, society was changing rapidly in every aspect, including family structure, sexual norms, and gender ideologies. Roller derby encapsulated the anxiety and also the thrill of these cultural changes, by appearing to challenge everything that was known about sport and athletes, while simultaneously reinforcing classic gender norms and dichotomies. Ultimately, however, the skaters, male or female, were appreciated for their athletic talent. Walt Harris, the longtime voice of the NRDL on KTVU, compared the heyday of roller derby in the 1950s and 1960s to one of the newer, more soap-opera-like version in the early 2000s. He noted, "The girls that skated then were skaters. They didn't have to be pretty as long as they had a personality. Annis Jensen and Joan Weston, of course, and Ann Calvello, they were all good, tough skaters and competitors. They weren't worried about cheesecake."[37]

Joan Weston (1935–1997)

Simply put, Joan Weston *was* roller derby. Known as the Blonde Bomber (or occasionally the Blonde Amazon or the Roller Derby Queen), Weston was, and remains, the most recognizable name in the Transcontinental Roller Derby and NRDL. After her untimely death in 1997 at the age of sixty-two, Frank Deford noted, "at her peak in the 1960's, Joanie Weston was as famous a female athlete as Billie Jean King and Peggy Flemming [*sic*]. But, of course, she was famous with the wrong people. It wasn't tennis whites or figure skates she wore. Joanie Weston was the star of the Roller Derby."[38]

Joan Weston became captain of the Bay Bombers in 1965 when Annis Jensen did not want to travel on the cross-country tours that the Bombers participated in during the 1960s. Perhaps conscious of the media appeal of Weston, Jerry Seltzer "quietly slipped Weston into the Bomber leadership for low profile road games and untelevised contests."[39] Her status as star of the beloved Bombers, along with her cultivated good girl persona, made her the most recognizable and most popular player for the legions of Bomber fans in San Francisco and around the country. Perhaps most importantly, Weston did not shy away from media coverage and was eager to participate in television coverage of the sport. Deford noted, "Joan Weston did a good television interview, was photogenic (during the period the girls sometimes unaccountably courted a dour image) and had a realistic approach to the game."[40] While Weston was certainly one of the talents of roller derby, her lasting legacy to the sport is less about her skating talent and more about her personality and willingness to do whatever it took to make roller derby successful. Deford's 1969 *Sports Illustrated* feature stated, "Derby players often say she was 'not a skater,' that is, she could maneuver the track acceptably but without much proficiency. But she connected, she sold the game, and since it was not a completely genuine sport, this is what mattered most. She was also, as smitten reporters would often comment, 'a really nice lady.'"[41] The fact that Weston drew in reporters by being "really nice" served to help promote the NRDL, and Jerry Seltzer was strategic in cultivating Weston as the face of the franchise, no matter what team she represented.

As the most recognizable face in roller derby, Weston had reach outside the sport itself and into the broader public consciousness, challenging notions of what women could do in sport. Deford argued in her obituary,

> Weston mattered a great deal to those who made her the heroine in their lives. Especially, she mattered to frustrated young athletic girls. In a very real way, in fact, it is Joanie Weston who best exemplifies the American athlete of this century. She had grown up in Southern California, proficient at every physical thing she tried. She hit .730 one softball season at Mount Saint Mary's College, surfed the Pacific without a wetsuit, and once, on a boyfriend's dare, threw herself off a waterfall.[42]

Like her contemporaries Billie Jean King, Peggy Fleming, and Wilma Rudolph, Weston was a symbolic representation of the changing face of athletics, one that showed that women could compete and be successful at what had previously been a male domain. Joan Weston took that a step further, excelling at a sport that mainstream America did not fully understand, but embraced anyway, even with its violence, spectacle, and competition, which was in stark contrast to the public conception of the "female athlete" at the time.

Like many former roller derby skaters, Weston returned to the Bay Area upon her retirement from the sport. She participated in a few revivals of roller derby in the 1970s and 1980s, and married another skater, Nick Scopas. She was a long-time San Francisco recreational softball player, and owned a bar with her husband in the Bay Area. She helped run a roller derby training school in Hayward until the International Roller Skating League (IRSL) folded in the 1980s.[43] Described as a "purist who dislikes the props, gimmicks, and ersatz violence that have made the sport reminiscent of TV wrestling," she used the Hayward School to teach the fundamentals of the sport she loved.[44]

Weston died in 1997 at age sixty-two from Creutzfeldt-Jakob disease, and the *New York Times* ran her obituary, highlighting her status as a beloved celebrity, but focusing primarily on her athletic ability. Curiously, they devoted significant time to her recreational and college softball career, lamenting that she "passed up a promising and respectable future in softball to become the gum-chewing, power-skating, hip-bumping golden girl of Roller Derby."[45] After her retirement from roller derby, she and Bomber teammates Cathy Read and Sandra Dunn opened up a lesbian bar, the Driftwood, on Mission Boulevard in Hayward. Although not gay, Weston did bartend at the Driftwood.[46]

Today, Joanie Weston remains one of the most remembered and revered former roller derby stars. In the end, Weston was less concerned with being remembered as an individual and more concerned that roller derby live on. She told Frank Deford in the *Sports Illustrated* feature, "all I want out of the Derby is to make good money, get out in one piece and, years from now, when I say I was in the Roller Derby, I want people still to know what it is. I want that."[47] Ultimately, her wish for roller derby to remain culturally relevant was realized, and continues to be true today.

Ann Calvello (1929–2006)

If Joan Weston was the roller derby queen, Ann Calvello played the role of the rival, the villain who stood as the contrast to Weston's angelic persona. Known as the "Demon of the Derby," she was the skater that, once she left the home team Bombers for the visiting team, every fan loved to hate. "Just as in professional wrestling, the 'villians' [*sic*] were the biggest stars"[48] in roller derby. It was impossible to ignore Ann Calvello; with her wildly painted hair, garish makeup, deep tan, and loud voice, Calvello was known especially for playing the role of agitator.

Calvello was one Leo Seltzer's original 1954 Bay Area Bombers, briefly acting as captain in the late 1950s when Annis Jensen was injured. She played on the Bombers from 1954 through 1959 and then skated for the Red Devils and the Braves as an opponent on the away team until the league folded in 1973, with the exception of one season in 1965 when she joined a rival league. She was the league's premier visiting skater, "enraging the fans that once adored her" when she had been on the home team.[49]

Roller derby, especially in its early days, relied upon the spectacle of the event as much as it relied upon the skill of the sport, and none relished the spectacle more than Ann Calvello. She particularly played up the rivalry between herself and Weston, reacting in an exaggerated fashion to any perceived slight on the track. This was mostly an act; while the two were not close off the track, they did not have any real rivalry that extended after the whistle blew. She received the most penalties in the history of roller derby—over 9,000 minutes over her entire career. In the latter stage of her career, she often mimicked the overt and staged violence popular in wrestling.

Calvello was a media favorite in San Francisco and nationally, culminating with her presence on the cover of *TV Magazine* in 1966. She was the subject of a 2001 documentary *Demon of the Derby: The Ann Calvello Story.* Her life provided regular fodder for the gossip columns in the local papers in San Francisco. It was rumored that she asked to be traded from the Bombers after her "calamitous" short-term romance with Charlie O'Connell ended.[50] She ultimately married a referee, Roy Langley, who was abusive; she later divorced him. They had one child, whom she gave up for adoption. In the 2001 documentary, it was suggested that part of the reason she gave her daughter up was to be able to meet the heavy demands for travel associated with roller derby.

When Jensen retired in 1969, Calvello became the oldest skater competing in roller derby. In fact, she remains the oldest woman to have been on any professional sports team. This was an honor she "relished, often comparing herself to George Blanda of the Raiders, a kicker considered an oddity when he was playing in his 40s."[51] Calvello skated in six decades over two centuries, beginning her career in the 1940s with the Transcontinental Roller Derby and skating through 1998 in the American Roller Skating Derby. In 2000, she returned to the track for one final time to skate a race against a fellow skater in RollerJam. In an interview in the documentary, she stated,

> I still skate because I know I can do it! I am 69 years old. My body's strong, my mind's strong, and I've never smoked. You've seen me skate. I don't go huffing and puffing at the rails. I could be off two, three, four years and go out and skate a whole game. And I've been doing it 50 years, six decades in this century. And if God wills it in the year 2000, if I even skate one game, one jam, it will be two centuries! You're never going to see an athlete like that. That never made any money, but I got a strong body and a strong mind thanks to him upstairs.[52]

Calvello was forced out of the American Roller Skating Derby in 1998 because of a brain tumor. She refused to stop skating, and organizers were forced to demand her retirement after fellow skaters complained about being scared to hit her. However, this forced retirement from the track was short lived, as RollerJam contacted her in 2000 and had her compete in a match race (which she won). She was unable to keep competing in RollerJam, as the league folded a short time later.

Throughout all of the tumultuous changes in the sport of roller derby, from the early days prior to the NRDL, to the attempts throughout the years to revive derby, including the IRSL, RollerJam, and even the A&E television show *Rollergirls*, Ann Calvello was a constant presence. She was "always happily associated with Roller Derby and something of an expert at self-promotion, Calvello was affiliated with innumerable skating units and promotions after Roller Derby ended. Her frank comments did not always endear her to fellow skaters and she was something of a loner among Derby women. Toward the end of her life, she was touched when contemporary roller girls hailed her as an inspiration and a pioneer for women in sports, and her loyal network of fans were in constant contact."[53] The championship trophy for the banked track league in Texas (the Texas Roller Derby, or TXRD) is called the Calvello Cup.

Ann Calvello stayed connected to the Bay Area for her entire life. In fact, she grew up in San Francisco, graduating from Presentation High School in 1947. She remained connected to the Bay Area throughout her career, returning to live in San Bruno until her death. She worked as a ticket taker in Candlestick Park until the early 2000s. Hartlaub noted that his mother used to go out of her way to get her ticket taken by "THE GREATEST DERBY STAR IN HISTORY." He argued, "for those who don't know much about Calvello, this would be like going to a roller derby match and getting your ticket taken by Willie Mays." Calvello died in 2006 at age seventy-six from liver cancer. In her obituary, Jim Fitzpatrick, a fellow skater turned referee said this of Calvello: "She was creative, way ahead of her time. People would say to her, "you're the Dennis Rodman of your era.' 'No, no, no,' she'd say. 'They're the Ann Calvello of their era.' She's the one who created all this stuff."[54]

Charlie O'Connell (1935–2015)

Charlie O'Connell was easily the best-known male skater, frequently playing the role of beloved hero for the Bay Bombers, despite an aloof persona toward the media and fans. Jerry Seltzer described him as "surly, and he wanted to be left alone. Scowling constantly, but what a great skater. He rarely would do interviews unless on our KTVU telecasts, and that only added to his persona."[55] While he was a bit of a "bad boy" in roller derby when he began as a rookie skating for the New York Chiefs in 1952, described by Seltzer as "young and cocky," he evolved into one of the major ambassadors of the sport. His good looks made him a fan favorite, especially with women, and his life was often the subject of much tabloid speculation (reaching a culmination when he briefly dated, and then had a public breakup with Ann Calvello). Known as "Mr. Roller Derby," or sometimes simply as "Charlie O.," he is remembered today as one of the definitive personalities of the sport.

Throughout his career in the NRDL, O'Connell seemed to have uneasiness with the tension between the sport and spectacle of roller derby and appeared uncomfortable with the role of women in roller derby, despite the fact that his grandmother introduced him to the sport.[56] He frequently served as the distraction from women's races by making his entrance into the arena during their races, knowing his entrance was sure to draw the attention of the crowd and the television audience. He begrudgingly accepted the promotional schemes cooked up by Seltzer to foster a passionate fan base. Deford described the mentality clearly, "so they are all, as Larry Smith says, schizophrenic, like the game itself, torn between the old-time buffoonery and the display of speed and muscle that marks real sport."[57]He was a feature in the 1971 documentary film *Derby*, which was financed by Jerry Seltzer and focuses on the seedy underworld of roller derby.

In his 1971 cult-classic book *Five Strides on the Banked Track*, Frank Deford described the different ways in which Weston and Charlie interacted with the fan base:

> As the Bombers come out, the attention is such that Joanie can hardly reach the track. At last she gets to this sanctuary, but the fans will not permit her to leave them, so she must stand, leaning over the rail throughout the warm-ups, signing wave after wave of autographs. Charlie, in his anti-hero fashion, bursts brusquely through the well-wishers, leaps onto the track, and thereafter just whirs around with half-speed five-strides, sneering out, spitting occasionally (nearly affectionately, it seems), and treating the whole adoring mob with contempt. They love it, and keep calling to him, no less than to Joanie, who keeps standing patiently and signing her name.

O'Connell's relationship to the fans was paradoxical. The more disdainful and arrogant he appeared, the more the fans adored his behavior. Deford described him, "though such widespread popularity attends him, O'Connell does little to encourage it. Of all modern athletes, he most resembles Ted Williams, who was also marked by determined independence and aloofness. In both cases, the cool distance only adds mystery and romance to the aura. On the track, Charlie makes himself particularly hard to like . . . He seems to laugh only when an opponent is in distress. Yet all the fans adore him."[58] After his death in 2015, the director of the National Roller Derby Hall of Fame noted, "he was the best skater on the track—he was the kingpin and he was what people were buying tickets for. And

Charlie knew it. He had a swagger about him. He didn't really care what other people thought. He was wild. The man loved Roller Derby and he loved his part in it."[59]

This fan support sometimes manifested itself in humorous ways. After his retirement, O'Connell opened a bar in the East Bay area with his wife, Judy (whom he married upon his divorce from his second wife and upon her divorce from teammate Mike Gammon). On a roller derby telecast, he mentioned that he opened the bar, and a group of Hell's Angels showed up in support of their favorite former Bay Bombers skater. Jerry Seltzer recalled, "Charlie told them he really appreciated it, but it would scare away his neighborhood customers. They understood, rode away, and suddenly came back; 'Charlie, would you like us to wreck the other bars around here?' Charlie thanked them and said no."[60]

The fan adoration, as well as his unmistakable prowess at the sport, made O'Connell the highest paid skater in history, earning him around $100,000 a season.[61] He was most grateful for the material rewards, including a house in Hayward with a pool and incredible view, received as a result of his skills and celebrity on the roller derby track. In the film *Derby*, he proudly shows his backyard pool exclaiming, "roller derby gave me all this." For all of the complaints the skaters had about their rigorous travel and painful sport, O'Connell was always the first to comment on how lucky he considered himself to be.

While the fans adored O'Connell, many of the players had an uneasy relationship with him. Deford describes this relationship: "The players are not so generous. They all respect him for his professional ability, but he is a controversial personality, and frankly disliked in some circles. He likes to kid other people where they tend to be sensitive, and many cannot take his ribbing. Also, before and between marriages, he broke a few hearts. He is always, however, loyal to those who are close to him—and quick to defend his friends. He is closemouthed and can be trusted. And he is unmistakably and always a leader."[62] Charlie tried to walk away from roller derby as a skater at the peak of his game in 1971. He took over as coach of the Bombers and lasted seven months on the bench before he came out of retirement to skate again.[63] He stayed with the Bombers until the demise of the NRDL in 1973. In 1976 he participated in a Roller Derby benefit game with many other former skaters, including Weston and Calvello. After the success of this game, he and other skaters started a league called the International Roller Skating League (IRSL) in 1977 that was short lived. He played on the 1977 season for the Bay Bombers at Kezar Pavilion in San Francisco. By 1978 that league was sold to a partner, and O'Connell left roller derby for good. O'Connell stayed out of the limelight more than other former roller derby stars and did not participate in any derby revivals in subsequent years or give many interviews about his time as a roller derby star. He died in 2015.

The Venues

One of the interesting features of the sport of roller derby is its ability to fit into a variety of venues and facilities. As long as there was enough floor space, the banked track could be constructed in any space that would hold it. Many of the venues used for roller derby in the early days are still standing in San Francisco, though some have been repurposed for other activities. In addition to the venues, the corporate offices for the NRDL were located in the Bay Area (relocating to the Oakland Mall in the early 1960s), and there were two major roller derby training centers in Alameda and Hayward.

The very first roller derby competition in San Francisco was at the Civic Auditorium in 1938. This auditorium still stands today, as part of the Civic Center complex a few blocks north of Market Street and Van Ness. Another popular venue in the early days of roller derby was the famous Winterland Ballroom at the corner of Post Street and Steiner Street. Roller derby played "nightly except Sundays" at the ballroom, which began as a skating rink when it was constructed in 1928. It was converted to a music venue in 1971 and torn down in 1985.

The most popular venue for roller derby in the San Francisco area was Kezar Pavilion in Golden Gate Park. Kezar Pavilion was built in 1924 and was a small venue for roller derby, seating only a few thousand spectators. Jerry Seltzer liked to show games from Kezar on television, as the small size of the venue made it look like fans were crammed to the rafters and hanging off of the bleachers. Fans would often stampede the track after a victory, which helped cultivate the reputation of the crazed atmosphere for the television audience. Kezar Pavilion was home to more roller derby games than any other location in the Bay Area, beginning in the 1950s. The Bombers used Kezar as their home arena from 1961 to 1973. The Bay Area Derby Girls (the flat-track modern roller derby team in San Francisco) skated a flat-track exhibition bout at Kezar in 2011, and the modern-day Bay Bombers (coed, banked-track roller derby) have continued to play at Kezar since 2007. Today, the Pavilion hosts roller derby, professional wrestling, high school basketball, and occasional concerts.

While the Bombers most often skated at Kezar Pavilion, they still occasionally held matches at other venues in and around the Bay Area throughout the 1950s. They occasionally skated at the Oakland Auditorium (owned and run by the city of Oakland) in the late 1950s. It was hard for the NRDL to get regular dates at the Oakland Auditorium because they had a contract with a wrestling organization that tied up the venue most of the time. The Oakland Auditorium changed names in 1984 to the Kaiser Convention Center and still stands today on Tenth Street in Oakland.

Another venue used by the NRDL was the San Francisco Armory in the Mission District on the eponymous street at 1800 Mission Street. The Armory served primarily as a boxing venue from the 1920s through the 1940s, in addition to housing the Coastal Artillery, Naval Militia, Signal Corps, Engineering Corps, and divisions of the California National Guard.[64] In his personal blog, Jerry Seltzer notes that he began his promotional career at the Armory, with "banked track skating five days a week, with an occasional break for National Guard training."[65] Eventually, the NRDL abandoned the Armory and became a more mobile touring unit. In 1978, the building was designated a San Francisco City Landmark. In 2013 and 2014, the Bay Area Derby Girls skated several bouts at the Armory, before relocating to their current space in Richmond.

Throughout the early 1960s, the NRDL played matches in several venues around San Francisco, including Berkeley's Ice Arena (which closed in 2007 and was quickly designated a national landmark) and Richmond Auditorium, where the Bombers usually played several dates a season (and still exists today at Civic Center Plaza in Richmond). They played a few outdoor bouts at Frank Youell Field, which was also the initial home of the Oakland Raiders while the Oakland Coliseum Stadium was being built. Youell Field was demolished in 1969 after the Raiders moved into the Coliseum Stadium.

In November 1966, the Oakland Coliseum Arena opened as part of the Oakland-Alameda County Coliseum complex. The first three events at the arena were Oakland Seals (NHL) games. Roller derby debuted the same week and was the fourth event ever at the venue. They drew 11,000 fans, surpassing the Seals for any game they had played up to that point and setting an indoor sports attendance record for Oakland. The Bombers played at Oakland Coliseum Arena fairly regularly from 1966 to 1973. In 1970, the NRDL broke their all-time attendance record by drawing 28,314 to an event.[66] The facility was renamed Oracle Arena in 2006 and is currently the home of the Golden State Warriors.

Finally, a favorite of the Bombers was the Cow Palace in Daly City. While Kezar Pavilion served as the home venue for the Bombers, they played many exhibition games in the Cow Palace throughout the 1950s and 1960s. The Cow Palace, with its maximum seating capacity of between 12,000 and 14,500, was the venue for the world championships of NRDL from 1959 through 1973. In addition to roller derby, throughout its history, the Cow Palace has hosted NBA games, NHL games, indoor soccer, concerts, livestock shows, circuses, rodeos, and political conventions.

The Bay Area Derby Girls currently play at Craneway Pavilion in Richmond. They hosted the Western region WFTDA playoffs in 2012 and are able to support a significant crowd in the 45,000-square-foot space.

Roller Derby's Legacy

In 1973, faced with rising gas prices, a crumbling economy, and increased costs, Jerry Seltzer made the difficult decision to dismantle the NRDL. He sold what was left of the franchises to a rival Southern California league, RollerGames. The NRDL skated their last game in December 1973. In the years that followed, several different attempts to revive roller derby emerged, and Ann Calvello was involved in nearly all of them. The Bay Bombers briefly returned in 1974 in a league called the International Skating Conference, but the league folds by 1975. In 1976, Charlie O'Connell, Joan Weston, Ann Calvello, and other skaters participated in a roller derby benefit match in a gymnasium at Cal Berkeley. The success of this event led to former skaters, including O'Connell and Mike Gammon, to form the International Roller Skating League (IRSL) in 1977. That version of roller derby only lasted for one year, before Don Drewery (a former skater turned rock promoter) took over the league in 1978 and continued it through the mid-1980s.

In 1996, a former roller derby fan named Dan Ferrari began a banked-track league called American Roller Skating Derby in San Francisco and revived the Bay Bombers. The league is moderately successful, and these modern-day Bombers still skate at Kezar Pavilion in San Francisco. Ann Calvello competed with this league until she was forced out by management in 1998. Other sports that shared similarities with traditional roller derby emerged, including RollerJam, which had a short stint on cable television from 1999 to 2000. Jerry Seltzer served as the commissioner of RollerJam prior to its folding in 2000 after the television contract was not renewed.

In is unclear why roller derby has experienced such highs and lows throughout its existence. Jim Fitzpatrick, a former skater, referee, and coach of the Bay Bombers in the ARSD, noted,

> I have a theory about that. Our popularity rises and falls in inverse relation to the times. Roller Derby came into being in the 1930s, when times were tough in the Great Depression. But when things improved, the sport went through its first valley. Then World War II came along, and people wanted to cheer for the good guys and boo the bad guys again. After the war, when times were better again, we went through another valley. Then came the Korean War, and the sport peaked again. And so on and so on, up and down through the rest of the century. Now we're in a war again, so the sport is popular again.[67]

Another significant development aiding the decline of roller derby in the mid-1970s were changes in the sports media landscape. Part of roller derby's success stemmed from its being paired with the immensely popular wrestling programs, while there were limited other options on television. The sports news giant ESPN was founded in 1978 and along with other structural media changes began to provide significantly more options for sports fans simultaneously flooding the marketplace with choices.

In 2001, another revival in Austin, Texas, led to the most recent and current "roller derby revolution." By 2003, the revival split into two factions—the Texas Roller Derby (TXRD), who skated a banked-track style similar to the early days of roller derby, and the Texas Rollergirls, who skated a flat-track version made more accessible because of their ability to play anywhere. By 2005, the handful of flat-track leagues around the country banded together to form the Women's Flat Track Derby Association (WFTDA), which has evolved to include 357 different member leagues in twelve countries by 2014. Bay Area Derby (B.A.D.) Girls formed in 2004 and models their league around the similar "home team" strategy of the Bombers of the past. They are currently ranked #3 in the world, and have teams in Berkeley, Oakland, Richmond, and San Francisco.

Unlike roller derby of the past, most modern-day roller derby is dominated by women—the handful of men's league are dwarfed by the sheer number of WFTDA member leagues. While men's roller derby has gained significant expansion in their organizational structure since 2007 when they formed the Men's Roller Derby Association (MRDA), for the most part roller derby in the twenty-first century has been an all-women affair. Roller derby began as a sport with significant space for female athletes to be successful, and it remains today as one of the only sports where women have been involved from the very beginning.

Throughout history San Francisco gained a reputation as the counterculture epicenter with the Beatniks, punks, hippies, and ravers all claiming the Bay Area as home, often long before the ideologies associated with those movements became mainstream. Roller derby was never a sport that conformed to social norms, whether through racial or gender dynamics, media coverage, rules, or the continued changes to the structure of the game. The Bay Area was a logical place for roller derby to take root and flourish into the twenty-first century.

Today's roller derby bears the most resemblance to the sport once pioneered by Leo Seltzer in the 1930s. Skaters today have retained the do-it-yourself spirit of the early days when skaters barnstormed the country, delighting audiences with their speed, force, and skill. It is clear from its history that the trajectory of roller derby was anything but traditional. Elements of struggle, as well as attempts toward legitimacy continue to define, sustain, and expand the sport into the twenty-first century.

12

Sons of Oakland

The Raiders and the
Raz/Rais(ing) of a City

MARIA J. VERI

Professional football came to Oakland, California, in 1960, when the city was granted an American Football League (AFL) franchise, which would compete against already established teams in Buffalo, Boston, Houston, Dallas, Los Angeles, Denver, and New York. Oakland was the eighth and final original franchise to join the upstart new league. Ideas for a team name were solicited from the East Bay community through a "Name Your Football Team" contest sponsored by the Oakland Junior Chamber of Commerce, the Oakland Boosters, and the *Oakland Tribune*. The new AFL franchise, subsequently dubbed the Raiders, had a moniker and a host city, but not a dedicated place to play during its inaugural season. In the absence of a suitable facility in Oakland, the team played its home games across the Bay at San Francisco's Kezar Stadium and Candlestick Park, much to the consternation of Oakland residents tired of languishing in the shadow of the City by the Bay.[1] In addition to commuting to the foggy environs of San Francisco for "home" games, the Raiders also struggled to win consistently and to develop a solid fan base in the team's first years of existence. Early support was so lacking, and team play deemed so poor, that an *Oakland Tribune* columnist later described those years as "a time when a guy took in a Raider game more out of community obligation than the entertainment it figured to provide."[2] Lackluster play notwithstanding, in 1962 the Oakland City Council voted to support a major sports complex development for football, baseball, and basketball within city limits, with Mayor John Houlihan declaring, "I consider this the day of the great breakthrough in the effort to get Oakland moving forward."[3] East Bay sports fans weighed in on the Coliseum proposal in the editorial pages of the *Tribune*, with one vocal partisan opining, "One would have to be completely lacking in common sense not to see the tremendous, far-reaching effects of a stadium."[4] With this vote, Oakland joined other major-league cities across the United States who cast their fate with the perceived civic and economic value of professional sports. The aim of this chapter is to detail how this decision, as popular as it was at the time, is one that ultimately failed the city and its residents, and exacerbated already growing disparities between working-class neighborhoods in the flatlands and wealthier neighborhoods in the Oakland hills and foothills.

The Raiders' 1963 campaign generated even more enthusiastic community support and was a defining moment in the early history of the club. The team, newly ensconced in a temporary downtown Oakland stadium, the 23,000-capacity Frank Youell Field, played exciting football, finished the season 10-4, and its young head coach, Al Davis, was named AFL Coach of the Year. Oakland was so caught up in the team's newfound success on the field that the city's chamber of commerce feted Davis with a celebratory dinner in January 1964. Davis's remarks to the sell-out crowd assembled that night at Goodman Hall in Jack London Square were perhaps the first in an ongoing series of carefully crafted public messages intended to forge a sense of collective identity among fans: "We were dedicated at the outset to one thing. We would build pride in our organization and in our community, remembering that this is not just a civic thing, but a national thing ... We want you to grow with this football team. It will take you a while to get full confidence in us and it will take us a while to get the confidence in you."[5] With these words, Davis laid the foundation for the burgeoning Raider Nation[6] sense of pride. It took the team's gritty and determined play of the 1970s for Raider Nation to fully develop into a distinctive and powerful fan culture—one cited by many as the first real fan Nation in the United States—and one uniquely bonded with its team's identity and its home city.

Indeed, any discussion of Raider Nation would be incomplete without a consideration of the city of Oakland itself—its history, its population, its politics—especially during the franchise's first two decades of existence. Notably, Oakland and its home county of Alameda devoted considerable public resources to maintain a privately owned professional football franchise at a time of major cultural upheaval and rising racial and economic disparities. Despite the cultivation of an intensely loyal fan base during this time period, the financial promise of professional football and a world-class sports complex fell considerably short.

A broader contextual consideration of Oakland's history illustrates how significantly the city and its identity changed over the course of the twentieth century. The Oakland of the 1920s was a very different city from the Oakland of the late twentieth century. It was comprised largely of white Protestants, concentrated among whom was a significant Ku Klux Klan presence that wielded strong social and political influence across the city. The 1930s and 1940s were characterized by union drives and a growing workers' rights movement among the still predominantly white population. A greater number of blacks settled in Oakland during the World War II era, many of whom migrated from the southern United States for expanding employment opportunities in the shipyards and railroads of the East Bay. This influx led to a rise in the city's black working and middle classes in the 1950s and 1960s and helped create the urban black communities that served as the base for much of Oakland's civil rights activism in the 1960s and 1970s.[7]

As urban studies scholars and social geographers have noted, the most significant political, economic, and spatial transformation in the post–World War II United States was the dual overdevelopment of suburbs and underdevelopment of inner cities.[8] In cities like Oakland, this transformation had an underlying racial dynamic—white flight from city districts and urban decline in those increasingly black communities. The population shift in Oakland during the Raiders' first two decades of play bears out this dynamic. In 1960, the total city population was 376,548, with whites representing 73.6 percent of that population and blacks 22.8 percent. By 1980, just two years before the Raiders relocated to Los Angeles, the total population of Oakland shrank by just over 28,000, with whites comprising 38.6 percent of the diminished population, and blacks 47 percent.[9] During these decades, government neglect of black neighborhoods, combined with continued race-based discriminatory practices in employment, housing, and law enforcement, stoked political activism and greater pushes for civil rights. Community organizers began promoting black candidates for city government, and grassroots groups rose up to help disenfranchised black neighborhoods—most notably, the Black Panther Party, which opened its first office in January 1967.[10]

During the 1960s, the city and its home county of Alameda committed to a number of redevelopment activities and regional planning initiatives, which were spurred on by a growth-oriented faction of civic leaders, despite a city council known as a "bastion of low-tax, minimal-government conservatism." The Oakland-Alameda County Coliseum, eventual home of the Raiders, was one of these initiatives, along with freeway and public transportation expansion projects.[11] In 1960, the same year as the Raiders' arrival in Oakland, the chamber of commerce initiated a planning study for a major-league stadium and sports arena complex. This study led to the formation of the nonprofit Oakland-Alameda Coliseum, Inc. in 1961. Promotional materials for the Coliseum promised a "fully integrated stadium, arena, and connecting concourse" that would "accommodate the range of recreational and cultural events which the East Bay community has a right to enjoy" and provide the "ultimate source of income to city and county."[12] *Oakland Tribune* sports editor George Ross lauded civic leaders for what he regarded as their progressive vision. Of the city's February 1962 vote in favor of the proposed development, Ross wrote, "The City of Oakland took a bold and unhesitant step forward . . . and pulled the entire Eastbay miles toward major league greatness." He went on to claim that the stride "generates momentum which can bring to Oakland and all her Eastbay neighbor cities a new economic and cultural pulse" and "place us in the family of great cities of America."[13] The Coliseum board was able to avoid the need to secure voter approval for the development project by negotiating a lease-purchase agreement in which the board would finance construction and operation of the projected $25 million complex in return for annual payments from the city and county. The project was further facilitated by the donation of the eventual 105-acre site by the Port of Oakland to the city.[14] This political maneuvering resulted in a complex that eventually featured the Raiders, Major League Baseball's Oakland A's, and professional basketball's Golden State Warriors. All three teams enjoyed considerable success in the 1970s, with an especially vibrant fan community galvanizing around the Raiders.[15] Fan fervor notwithstanding, the Coliseum and its anchor franchise did not become the panacea predicted, as the economic pulse of Oakland to which Ross alluded in 1962 was barely registering by the 1980s.

The story of Oakland during the intervening decades is very much a tale of two cities, with intertwining, even competing, narratives of urban decline and professional sport development. As the fortunes of the Raiders steadily rose from the late 1960s throughout the 1970s, Oakland itself seemed to be on a reverse trajectory. In many respects, the city and surrounding East Bay area benefited from a number of development projects, including the expansion of regional freeways and the Bay Area Rapid Transit (BART) public transportation system to serve the ever-growing Bay Area population. Upon closer inspection, the $792 million bond measure approved by the mostly white, middle-class Oakland and Alameda County electorate in 1962 funded a network built to shuttle mainly white suburbanites from home to work in downtown Oakland or San Francisco and then back. Moreover, urban black neighborhoods were razed in preparation for this network, and highway construction severed once-vibrant African American communities. It bears further mention that in 1964, the same year ground was broken on the Oakland-Alameda County Coliseum, Oakland was designated as an economically depressed area under the Federal Area Redevelopment Act.[16] That designation came at the end of a time period (1958–1966) in which Oakland lost over 9,000 manufacturing jobs, General Motors moved its major plant of operations south to Fremont, and unemployment in the flats averaged 12.9 percent. The unemployment rate for youth in those predominantly black census tracts was two to three times higher—an even more troubling statistic when educational attainment is considered. In 1960, 26.5 percent of Oakland residents aged twenty-five years or older (254,555 of 367,548) had completed four years of high school, compared to 51.5 percent for California and 41 percent for the United States.[17] Basketball great and hometown legend Bill Russell spoke out in pointedly sarcastic terms in response to the news that Oakland would not approve a bond issue to pay for high school extracurricular activities (including sports) in 1966: "Don't worry about Oakland, it'll be a great sports town, just like all the right-wing cities . . . this town builds anything for the amusement of the affluent but cares nothing for its poor."[18]

By the end of the decade, the public education system in Oakland was in dire straits due to years of neglect and underfunding. A 1969 *Oakland Tribune* editorial exhorted voters to approve an increase in the tax rate ceiling to assist city schools. The editorial lamented the largest class sizes in Bay Area schools, the inability of the district to attract and keep quality teachers, the shabby state of classrooms, and the termination of counseling services.[19] Three decades later, with a city population of 399,484, the high school graduation rate for residents twenty-five years and older (261,402) was a dismal 17.7 percent—a striking *decrease* of 9 percent from 1960, when that population totaled 254,555.[20] While Oakland was maneuvering to build cultural and economic capital through a professional sports team, the city was failing to fund a broad range of social services, and its citizens were suffering. The interests of white business leaders and middle-class homeowners were well represented in the development projects of the 1960s, but renewal initiatives in black neighborhoods were sparsely supported by city government, and when they were funded, moved at a relatively glacial pace or stalled outright. Instead, blacks in the most underrepresented neighborhoods had to rely on social service and criminal justice agencies for much-needed community assistance. The consequences of this dynamic were perhaps most acutely felt in west Oakland, the most depressed area in the city by the late 1960s, with one-third of its residents living below the poverty level, compared to 13 percent for the entire city. In 1970, black unemployment in low-income urban areas exceeded 20 percent. The youth rate in those areas was a staggering 48 percent.[21] Despite these disparities, there is little evidence of the intersection of community activism and the burgeoning Raider Nation—or the franchise itself.

The Raiders established residency in the Coliseum in September 1966, and by 1967, the team garnered Oakland national media recognition and became the focus of the city's civic identity.[22] After the team's convincing 2-0 start to its 1967 AFL championship season, in which the Raiders steamrolled their opponents by scoring 86 points while giving up only 7, *Oakland Tribune* sports columnist Ed Levitt hailed the Raiders as "a joy to behold" and "a precision football machine" capable of beating any top team in either professional league.[23] In 1970, the

AFL merged with the National Football League (NFL), and fans willingly followed their team to the grander stage of the NFL, as Al Davis shrewdly maneuvered the franchise to greater heights of glory in the ensuing decade.[24] Davis, in fact, credited the Raiders with not just unprecedented success on the football field, but, as reported in a 1968 *Sports Illustrated* feature, with working "a long time to build up this city's image and pride in itself."[25] Indeed, this is one of the key societal functions of professional sports—teams often foster civic pride and community identity. Popular representations of the Raiders reinforce this theme by portraying a unified community of fiercely loyal fans. For example, the HBO documentary "Rebels of Oakland" casts the Raiders fans of the 1960s and 1970s as a diverse group of blue-collar fans with a "Hell's Angels feel" that was in line with the rebelliousness and unrest of Bay Area counterculture politics.[26] In their ethnography of Raiders fan culture, Miller and Mayhew present Raider Nation as a multiethnic, blue-collar fan base with solid working-class roots and the unique ability to unite fans across racial, gender, regional, generational, and cultural lines.[27] Many of these fans identified with the players signed by Al Davis in the late 1960s and 1970s—a number of whom were rejected as troublemakers or cast-off as past-their-prime by other teams. It was one of these players, the quarterback Jim Plunkett, who secured the allegiance of Cathy Frazier, a central California resident and lifelong Raiders fan. As she explains, "once Plunkett came to the Raiders, he became everything a Raider was supposed to be." Plunkett was her generation's version of legendary quarterback/kicker George Blanda—whose exploits as an aging player captured the imagination of her father thanks to NBC broadcasts of his hometown Raiders on their 2-channel television in King City.[28] Southern California native Rod Medina, now in his fifties, became a Raiders fan in the early 1970s, when his siblings were attending San Jose State University and his family made frequent visits to the Bay Area to see them. The radio broadcasts of Raiders games they listened to during these drives piqued his interest. "As a little kid," according to Medina, "it was really neat that these old guys were playing in professional football in a young man's game. And I just got into an appreciation for that team because I knew even at that young age that this was unique."[29] The Raiders characteristic style of team play also appealed to its diverse fan base. Spurred on by Davis's "Commitment to Excellence" philosophy, the Raiders played a relentlessly tough, physically punishing brand of football. The team frequently led the league in penalties and suspicion of dirty play and for a time was considered the most feared one in sports.[30] As Medina explains, "back then being tough, being rough, being dirty was what football was about and the Raiders showed that more than any other team." For Frazier, the team was uniquely intimidating: "You didn't want to play the Raiders. They'd come in and thump you—play hard, take a lot of penalties—because the players did truly believe Al Davis's 'Just Win, Baby' motto." Local media echoed these sentiments, both in the Raiders' heyday and in retrospect. Sports columnist Ray Ratto viewed the 1970s Raiders as "all personality and swagger, talent and stubbornness"—traits also embodied by owner Al Davis and legendary coach John Madden. In addition to the Raiders' one Super Bowl victory in the 1970s, there were conference championships, numerous big game victories, and occasional disappointments; even in the team's nonchampionship seasons, Ratto noted, "nobody who won an AFC title . . . did so without going through the Raiders and their phalanx of stars."[31] This style of play became fused with the image of Oakland. As Medina attests, "part of the Raider culture was being from Oakland. The Bay Area is what made them. It's what made them unique, it's a small market, Oakland." Darrell Bailey, a Bay Area college athletics administrator who started following the Raiders as a boy in the mid-1970s, remembers how the players of that era "played to the crowd . . . they would always mention Raider Nation or the pride of being a Raider . . . they would talk about Oakland, being an Oakland Raider. It was always about pride."[32] Frazier claims, more to the point, "Oakland is a tough city. The Raiders tradition is that of toughness."

The Raider Nation community forged its identity around the team's hard-nosed style of play and Oakland's tough, blue-collar, underdog image. For Frazier, this community is characterized by a personality trait that extends beyond football: "It's a personality trait of someone who doesn't accept that he or she can't do something, or is too old, or doesn't have enough talent . . . it's a person with guts, no fear, and who is not intimidated by any thing or any one." At a time when Oakland was losing its manufacturing base and reeling from cuts to social services, decreases in educational funding, and the isolation or destruction of urban working-class neighborhoods, the Raiders of the 1970s offered fans an emotional refuge. Moreover, Raider Nation created a sense of belonging in an increasingly fragmented society, and in so doing helped to fill a social void by serving as an imagined community for fans.[33] The Raider faithful could project their desires and disappointments onto the team, which became a powerful symbol of what Oakland had been and still represented. Even though blue-collar, manufacturing-based livelihoods had all but vanished by the 1980s, that way of life was embodied in the Raiders' style of play on the field, and by many of the players themselves. Fans religiously followed their revered Raiders, and the greater the team's success, the stronger the fan affinity. Bailey's earliest memories as a Raiders fan coalesce around the team's 13-1 1976 season that culminated in a dominating 32–14 victory over the Minnesota Vikings in Super Bowl XI. The team's Super Bowl XI triumph cemented the allegiance of many others as well. As noted in the *Oakland Tribune* at the beginning of the 1977 season, "There's a strong bond between the Raiders and their followers. Together they've rejoiced after miracle victories and suffered after numerous near-misses. Now they've reached a new plateau: World Champions."[34] In fact, starting with the 1969 season, attendance at Raiders' games rarely dipped below 50,000, and fan support led to 137 consecutive Coliseum sell-outs throughout the 1970s.[35]

Raider Nation has also been celebrated for the strong bonds that develop between fans who recognize one another as part of the same collective. As Rod Medina's son, Tomas, explained, "You feel a bond with Raider fans. I see other teams' fans kind of interact with each other, but it's on a different level in comparison to Raiders fans. There is uniqueness there. The Raider Nation means unity, strength, going against the odds, pride."[36] For Marty Valdez, a retired college sports information director and East Bay native, Raider Nation means "one thing in common with a person you don't personally know. You're both Raiders fans, both right there. I got his back and he's got mine. Even when you go to home football games, the Raider fans have your back."[37] Tomas Medina likens this supportive dynamic to family: "Raiders fans will let you know exactly how they feel. But the environment and feeling you get out in the parking lot is somewhat of a homecoming. All the fans are there for one reason. So just knowing that is really comforting . . . I feel it's home." As Raider Nation developed, it also became an important public space for fans, alongside, or in place of the disappearing labor unions, community organizations, and neighborhood associations that have historically served that purpose. According to Rhomberg, public spaces function as key sites for the collective formation of social identity and political opinion in a civil society. They are spaces in which people can learn about, discuss, and form opinions on the social and political issues affecting their lives.[38] In another era, Valdez's and Medina's descriptions might just as easily have applied to a labor union or church group, with a notable exception—Raider Nation's function as a public space has been limited to galvanizing support around the team and fostering an imagined community among fans, not fomenting political activism that extends beyond the team. What activism Raider Nation has engaged in was mostly in response to the franchise's threatened and eventual relocation to Los Angeles. From 1979 to 1981 especially, fans publicly voiced their opposition to owner Al Davis's Southern California quest through letters to the editor, city council forums, protest parades, and strikingly, a five-minute boycott by a fourth of the Coliseum crowd at the beginning of a December 7, 1981, Monday-night football game.[39]

An "us-versus-them" mentality also emerged among the fans of Raider Nation, primarily in relation to San Francisco, fans of opposing teams, and the NFL. Oakland's image as San Francisco's poor, rowdy relation across the Bay positioned the former port town in terms of what it was not—a cosmopolitan cultural capital with a celebrated, tradition-laden sports history.[40] Prior to its professional sports windfall of the 1960s, Oakland was overshadowed by a San Francisco that also dominated the Bay Area sport scene. In the early years of the franchise, an attendant inferiority complex fueled fans' loyalty to the Raiders. Local sportswriters did their part to instill civic pride in the franchise by promoting the nascent Raiders and celebrating the Coliseum development project. Frank Deford, writing in *Sports Illustrated*, described *Oakland Tribune* sports editor George Ross as the "Mother Superior" to Oakland's professional teams, and noted the newspaper's ostensible inability to settle for praising Oakland's accomplishments when it could at the same time disparage its neighbor to the west.[41]

In addition to unfavorable comparisons to San Francisco, Raider Nation has been burdened by the same negative perceptions from opposing fans that have plagued Oakland, many of them grounded in thinly veiled racism and class prejudice that stemmed from stereotypical representations of the city's growing and relatively large African American population.[42] This dynamic also illustrates the symbolic power of professional sports to link team and place and the extent to which the identities of the city and the team have fused—for fans and detractors alike. As Rod Medina explained, "I just think Raiders fans get a bad reputation. I think it's because Oakland is a blue-collar town which has a majority of black people in it. You know Green Bay is a blue-collar town but they are adorable, they are the cheeseheads. The Raiders are looked down upon. Why? Because we have a lot of minorities."

Ironically, the racial bias cited by Medina and other members of Raider Nation was also seen in the white-controlled city of Oakland's neglect of its black population. Professional football undeniably brought civic pride to Oakland and unified its diverse fan base around the Silver and Black, but in reality neither the Raiders nor the communal bonds of Raider Nation did much to mitigate the substantial racial and economic disparities created by the city's neglect of low-income black neighborhoods in the 1960s and 1970s. The city prioritized the team at the expense of its poor and working-class constituency by devoting considerable legal, political, and financial resources to the Raiders while failing to fund much-needed social services like education, healthcare, housing, and employment assistance programs. As Danielson reminds us, "the image of unifying power of a professional team obscures socio-economic factors that separate fans along class, income, ethnic, racial lines."[43] For example, the $2.2 million Sixty-Sixth Avenue Interstate 80 freeway interchange opened in September of 1968 after five years of planning and a year and a half of construction. The new exit was designed to better accommodate Coliseum football traffic from the north and to make the complex more accessible from the Nimitz Freeway, the East Bay's main north-south thoroughfare. This project, touted as the "last major improvement [the Coliseum] needed to become the best engineered sports palace in the nation," cost the city of Oakland $1.59 million, with the difference covered by the state of California. William F. Knowland, the conservative, white editor and publisher of the *Oakland Tribune*, represented the Coliseum complex at the dedication ceremony—a conflict of interest ignored in the paper's coverage of the event.[44] Support for the freeway enhancement plan dovetailed with the *Tribune*'s continued promotion of the Coliseum and its anchor football franchise as the best way to move the city forward. Indeed, the media coverage of the interchange opening noted Coliseum traffic as the reason for the development, not the betterment of Oakland or the welfare of residents in the mostly minority, working-class surrounding neighborhoods. "The first real test of its efficiency," the *Tribune* reported, "will not come until Oct. 6, when the AFL Champion Raiders open their home season against the Boston Patriots."[45]

The interchange project also exemplifies how Oakland was able to take advantage of federal aid programs in order to improve the infrastructure that most served the city's downtown businesses, white middle-class neighborhoods, and professional sports teams. By applying for federal urban renewal aid, the city received credits for local expenditures on BART and the freeway system. Thus, Oakland avoided spending public money on its low-income black urban communities while at the same time securing government assistance for its development projects.[46] In this sense, federal funding for low-income areas was sought as a means to an end, not an end in itself. Despite the unifying power and palliative effects of Raider Nation, it is important to note the limitations of an emotional refuge based on shared allegiance to a publicly subsidized, privately owned professional sports franchise. The feeling of belonging created by Raider Nation might have helped fans cope with cultural change, but it was not responsible for any meaningful social transformations, as living conditions in Oakland remained much the same—or declined—throughout the 1970s.

As Oakland pumped more money into its professional sports palace, social and economic circumstances across the city worsened. The percentage of Oakland residents living below the poverty level was 16.6 percent in 1970; by 1980 this percentage increased to 18.5 percent. Unemployment rates also rose during that time period, from 7.8 percent in 1970 to 9.4 percent in 1980. While the percentage of adults over twenty-five years of age who completed four years of high school rose to 30 percent in 1970, by 1980 that percentage dipped to 27.4 percent—just one percentage point higher than it was in 1960.[47] The crime rate during this time compounded problems for the Oakland populace. By the end of the 1970s, the city's per capita murder rate was two times that of San Francisco or New York City.[48] The number of murders per year hit 100 in 1973; dipped to 91 in 1977, the Raiders' first Super Bowl victory year; rose to 108 in 1979; and reached a then-historic high of 123 in 1981, the year the Raiders won a second Super Bowl and were readying for relocation to Los Angeles.[49] Staggering unemployment rates and the loss of a blue-collar economy made Oakland's low-income black neighborhoods especially vulnerable to higher crime rates and an influx of drugs in the 1980s.[50]

Yet, during the preceding time period, Oakland's political elite embraced the Raiders, and the burgeoning Raider Nation rallied around its team, often calling on the city to maintain its support of the Raiders and Al Davis. As early as 1968—and in spite of considerable backing from Oakland—Davis began complaining about what he perceived as the city's disrespectful treatment of the Raiders, and declared that if an opportunity to move the franchise to another city arose, he would pursue it without guilt. This first threat to seek another home for the Raiders was mired in Davis's jealous reaction to Oakland's efforts to secure and promote its four other professional sports teams of the era.[51] In the mid-1970s, Davis's threats to relocate the team if Oakland did not meet his demands grew more serious. He sought additional city and county funding for Coliseum improvements, including luxury boxes, scoreboard upgrades, a state-of-the-art sound system, renovated locker rooms, expanded seating to accommodate growing ticket demand, and right of schedule over baseball's A's, the other major tenant of the Coliseum.[52] Additionally, Davis opposed the Coliseum board's plan to raise rent at the Coliseum as well as the team's practice field near the Oakland airport.[53] In the midst of this tension, the city of Los Angeles began negotiating with Davis in 1979 in hopes of luring the Raiders south to the LA Coliseum. Thus armed with a suitor for his franchise, Davis leveraged professional football to force Oakland to either agree to spend limited public funds on the privately owned Raiders or risk losing the team to another city. Faced with the threat of losing the franchise, Oakland and Alameda County leaders attempted to meet Davis's demands through new lease proposals that promised significant funding for the Raiders. Fans and local business owners rallied around the team, as did the *Oakland Tribune* and a number of city and county officials. Piedmont fan Eva Ewen blamed the Coliseum and county officials for not doing enough to keep the Raiders happy: "They dragged their feet too long. As soon as they had an inkling the Raiders might leave, they should have done something. This is a great loss for the City of Oakland." Mike Perfetto from San Ramon echoed Ewen's sentiments, stating, "I don't blame Al Davis at all. The Coliseum and county officials could have kept the Raiders here if they had been willing to pay the price. But they kept dragging things out." Hayward resident Nick Niacaris criticized Al Davis for his lack of loyalty to Raiders' fans, but pointed the blame at the Coliseum board, claiming, "the Coliseum used nothing but uncommon sense through the negotiations. Fans around here would have paid extra to have the team stay. They could have added a tax to the season tickets or something."[54]

Many hoteliers and restauranteurs also deplored what they saw as the city and county's meager efforts to keep the Raiders in Oakland. Mark Novak, general manager of a Travelodge near the Coliseum, said, "I'm very disappointed in the city. The Raiders have created a lot of business for us, so much that we can't readily measure it in dollars." Dewey Bargiacchi, owner of Francesco's, a popular Italian restaurant and hangout for players and fans, told a *Tribune* business columnist that the loss of the Raiders would be a "big setback for Oakland, with the whole area suffering." General managers of the downtown Hilton and Hyatt hotels estimated that the relocation of the Raiders would cost the hotels tens of thousands of dollars in team lodging and fan business, as well as lead to lay-offs of part-time and full-time employees.[55] Politicians were split on how much Oakland should subsidize the Raiders through the terms of a new lease. Of an initial ten-year lease offer including $8.5 million in stadium and practice field improvements for the team, Alameda County supervisor John George claimed, "I don't see any way I won't vote for it. I think it's in the best interests of the Eastbay. The Raiders are the Sons of Oakland. It would be a tragedy if we had to have an expansion team as a stepchild."[56] Sons of Oakland or not, there is little evidence to suggest that public financing of a privately owned sports franchise is an effective means of economic development.[57] Moreover, the seeming "tragedy" of a potential NFL expansion franchise certainly paled in comparison to Oakland's combination of soaring crime rates, steep unemployment, medically underserved communities, and negligent educational stewardship. Supervisors Valerie Raymond and Fred Cooper opposed the lease terms, citing Alameda County's projected 1980 budget deficit of $12.5 million. Cooper told the *Oakland Tribune*, "The Raiders have been making money ever since the Coliseum was built and I seriously question whether government should give them a further subsidy when they are clearly making money."[58] Despite the projected $12.5 million budget shortfall, the board of supervisors voted in favor of the $8.5 million lease package, leaving one to wonder where the county expected to find the financial means to back it, and what would go unfunded in order to do so. For all of its uniqueness, Raider Nation was no different than other professional sports fan bases whose unwavering and often uncritical support benefited already wealthy team owners more concerned with profit than the welfare of their fans and host cities.

The *Oakland Tribune*, like most major daily newspapers, had a vested interest in keeping the city's professional football franchise in town, as the Raiders' existence brought continual opportunities for journalists to cover big-time entertainment stories with national resonance.[59] Throughout the 1970s, the *Tribune* devoted significant space and column inches to year-round coverage of the Raiders. In addition to the usual reporting on team and player performances on the field, the paper promoted the Raiders through numerous human interest stories and favorable editorials. Stories such as a 1976 feature on the charity work of core players reinforced the team's connection to the Oakland community. The *Tribune* reported on Otis Sistrunk's work with local drug abuse programs and Gene Upshaw's efforts to raise funds for research on behalf of the Alameda County American Cancer Society.[60] By all accounts, many members of the Raiders contributed to the East Bay communities they lived in, and media acknowledgment of their contributions no doubt endeared them even more to the Raider Nation faithful. However, it bears mentioning that repeated stories of this kind also obscured the realities on the ground, especially in the underserved neighborhoods of east and west Oakland. Even as early as 1968, Deford cautioned Oakland that its reliance on professional sports to establish a national reputation would leave the city a "vague receptacle for the teams that play there."[61]

The only notable early community opposition to the city's subsidization of the franchise came from the Black Panther Party's 1973 political platform. The Panthers called for increased rental charges and fees at the Coliseum and city golf courses, as well as a 5 percent capital gains tax on income property transfers and the property of large corporations.[62] In highlighting Coliseum rental fees, the Black Panthers framed Oakland's patronage of the Raiders as part of the political and economic dynamic that contributed to the oppression of urban black neighborhoods. This platform mobilized Oakland's poor black electorate, who turned out in record numbers to cast votes for Bobby Seale, the Panthers' 1973 mayoral candidate. Seale came in second place with 19 percent of the vote, forcing a runoff before ultimately losing to the incumbent Reading. The Panthers' political momentum continued through 1975, when Elaine Brown was elected to a city council seat with 40 percent of the vote. In 1977, Panther outreach and financing helped Lionel Wilson become the first black mayor of Oakland, but polling numbers showed growing voter apathy, as Wilson won his campaign with 1,000 fewer votes than Seale's second-place showing four years earlier.[63]

As part of its continued show of support for the Raiders, the City of Oakland welcomed the team home after its 1977 Super Bowl victory with a celebration at the Coliseum that featured entertainment and a special ceremony with players and coaches. This celebration, open to the first 43,000 people through the gates, gave fans a collective opportunity to publicly rally around their newly crowned champions.[64] The Raiders had reached the pinnacle of success in professional football, and in so doing provided Oakland with a coveted jewel for the city's crown. The already fervently supported team's Super Bowl championship arguably made Oakland that much more determined to fight Al Davis's relocation bid two years later. At the beginning of new lease negotiations, Mayor Wilson informed the press, "The council has decided it wants to see everything done to keep the . . . Raiders in Oakland."[65] "Everything" eventually included the promise of millions of dollars in publicly funded stadium upkeep and improvements, a lease term for half the number of years of the NFL average, prolonged negotiations with a demanding Raiders management, and the outlay of additional millions in litigation costs to seek legal recourse once the Raiders refused the final lease offer and signed a notice of intent to relocate to Los Angeles. By March of 1980, there were eight lawsuits involving the Raiders in the courts. One suit resulted in a restraining order issued by the Alameda County Superior Court that prohibited the Raiders "from removing equipment, materials, or assets" from Bay Area counties. In another suit filed concurrently, the city brought an eminent domain action against the franchise. Attorney David Self, who represented Oakland in the proceedings, told reporters, "The Raiders have been the Oakland Raiders for 20 years. They were born in Oakland, they were bred in Oakland, they belong in Oakland." Self further justified eminent domain condemnation, claiming that the franchise "is a public use—it is important to the social, economic, sociological and psychological life of the city."[66] Supervisor Fred Cooper even solicited San Jose congressman Don Edwards's help in drafting a bill for federal legislation that would prohibit profitable NFL teams from relocating without the approval of three-fourths of league owners.[67] Oakland promised the Raiders that improvements to the Coliseum would be made "within financial restrictions and at the specifications of Al Davis and the Coliseum board jointly," but when the Raiders refused to commit to more than a three-year lease, the city drew the line. Supervisor Joe Bort, an early supporter of the Raiders in lease negotiations, wrote in a *Tribune* op-ed that "there is no way the coliseum or the city and county jointly, considering our financial picture, can spend the millions of taxpayer dollars required to build luxury suites if the Raiders are not willing to stay over the period of years required to amortize the suites."[68] Had the Raiders been willing to sign a longer-term lease, though, Bort implied that the city and county would have willingly emptied public coffers to finance the team's demands. All told, Oakland spent considerable sums of money to keep the Raiders in town during the protracted negotiation process, and after the Raiders refused all offers and moved to Los Angeles, the city spent millions of dollars in unsuccessful litigation to bring the franchise back to Oakland.

Remarkably, Raider Nation remained faithful to the Raiders after the team relocated to Los Angeles, a further testament to the strength of the fan allegiance that developed throughout the 1970s. Raider Nation became an imagined community for like-minded fans from a diverse social spectrum, but the benefits of the communal ties forged in the stands of the Coliseum and the sports bars of the East Bay did not seem to extend much beyond the personal. As Lipsitz argues, professional sports "provide a limited sense of place for contemporary urban dwellers, offering them a rooting interest that promises at least the illusion of inclusion and connection with others."[69] The Oakland Raiders moved the city forward in terms of its national sports reputation, yet by the late 1970s it was apparent to anyone who cared to notice that the promise of professional football for Oakland's economic development not only never materialized, but drove the city into greater racial and economic disparities. While their allegiance to the Raiders remained intact and fans advocated on behalf of keeping the entity around which their imagined community was built in town, they seemingly ignored the growing disenfranchisement of Oakland's actual communities, especially those that had been long underserved.

For their part, the Raiders were just as invested in crafting the Raider Nation image as the fans were in having it; the support of an intensely loyal fan base and partisan city and county government helped increase the franchise's profit margin and overall value throughout its tenancy in Oakland, relocation to Los Angeles, and move back to Oakland in the 1990s. However, the city the Raiders came home to in the 1990s was considerably worse off than when the franchise left in 1982. Some 12,000 manufacturing jobs had been lost in the 1980s, the unemployment rate was 9.5 percent for the city, yet 14.5 percent for black workers and 20 percent in West Oakland, and most census tracts in east, west, and north Oakland were designated as medically underserved by the Department of Health and Human Services.[70] The Raiders were not solely responsible for these deplorable conditions in Oakland, but given the city's acquiescence to the franchise's financial demands for public subsidization, one is left to question the cost of team affiliation and imagined community, especially as history repeats itself in 2015.[71] What legacy did the Oakland of the twenty-first century inherit from its decades-long, nearly hundred-million-dollar commitment to a privately owned professional football franchise?

13

Rebel with a Racket

Rosie Casals

RITA LIBERTI

In February 1988 tennis great Rosemary (Rosie) Casals teamed up with Martina Navratilova to win the Virginia Slims doubles championship in Oakland, California. The win, was Casals's last of 112 doubles championships over the course of her career.[1] The Bay Area victory for Casals was a fitting end, as her introduction to tennis, three decades earlier, occurred just miles from the Oakland Coliseum on the public courts of San Francisco's Golden Gate Park. The legacy of Casals's tennis career is far more, however, than the sum of her victories on the court. In many ways an examination of her experiences in tennis sheds light on a myriad of issues in play during the 1960s and 1970s around femininity and athleticism, as well as women's place in society more generally. Definitions of womanhood and athleticism were struggled over in the public sphere during this period, as gender relations on a broader scale were in flux. Described as a "classic rebel,"[2] Rosie Casals challenged norms, including gender conventions across the span of her entire career and in doing so offers us a valuable perspective on the much larger social world of the period.

Casals's nonconformist leanings began as an elementary school child and enabled her entrance into tennis. Raised in a working-class family in San Francisco's Western Addition neighborhood, Casals often trailed after her father, Manuel, who enjoyed playing tennis in nearby Golden Gate Park, the city's largest recreational space. Not content with watching the action or playing on the merry-go-round with the rest of the children, the younger Casals persisted and finally convinced her father of her desire to play rather than spectate. Rosie

Casals's superior athleticism was quickly in evidence as was her commitment to and passion for the game. The self-described "tomboy" was soon to spend hours each day running around the tennis courts in the park rather than the streets of San Francisco.[3]

Casals's desire to be physically active and engage in competitive athletics served to establish and partially define her status as "rebel." Sport, especially in the late 1950s and early 1960s, was largely the preserve of boys and men. Physical activity was accepted and encouraged for young boys though such was not the case for Casals and her female peers. Girls who ventured onto fields and courts, given the gender norms of the era, risked their femininity and even their status as women in the eyes of a scornful society. Aware of this gendered reality, Casals concedes as an adult, "I'm lucky that he [Casals's father] happened to play tennis, which was kind of an acceptable sport for a girl."[4] All female athletes however, including tennis players, were held to rigid societal understandings of femininity. Every expression by female athletes, on and off the court, was subject to surveillance by a public that deemed its appropriateness relative to the narrow boundaries of proper womanhood.[5] Amid these societal constraints, Casals's actions on and off the court often ran up against the confines of gender norms. Much like the city from which she was born and raised, Casals's irreverence on and off the court was integral, rather than a tangential element, to her identity.

Issues around gender were just part of Casals's resistance to the established social order. As a female, she was an outsider in the competitive athletic arena but Casals's position as "other" was also keenly marked by her socioeconomic class standing and ethnic identity in the largely upper-middle-class, white world of tennis. Initially however, on the public courts in a large urban area like San Francisco, Casals's exceptional ability was the only part of her identity that marked her as different. Those who played on Golden Gate Park's courts reflected San Francisco's diversity and thus, according to Casals, a girl of color from a working-class household, made it "the right place for me to fit in."[6] And fit in she did, as her game improved quickly. In 1961, less than five years after first picking up a racket, Casals won the National Hard Court Championship in thirteen-and-under singles competition. Just six years later, still a teenager and barely out of George Washington High School, Casals and Billie Jean King captured their first of five Wimbledon doubles crowns as a pair.[7]

As Casals rose within the circles of the game's elite, she quickly understood her identity as a working-class youngster of color was of consequence and mattered. While she blended seamlessly with other tennis enthusiasts on the public courts of San Francisco, this was not the case more broadly across the tennis world. Class difference was the most striking to Casals, who, even as an adolescent, recognized "those that had [financial means] and those that didn't," adding,

"I was [among] those that didn't." Her outsider status had a number of implications including a keen understanding that little could be taken for granted. Simply getting to some of her career's earlier tournaments was made more difficult given her family's humble surroundings. For instance, while other players' families had "nice cars" the Casals had an older model Studebaker, which she remembers pushing as much as actually riding in it. Fortunately, Casals adds, the street on which her family lived was on a slight hill making it much easier to push the car to get it started. "I'd double clutch [the car], go around the block, pick him [her father] up and off we'd go!" For young Casals the stress of an upcoming match was coupled with anxiety over arriving, let alone on time. A burden many of her tennis peers did not have to consider.[8]

Any number of incidents, both on and beyond the court, were markers to the young San Franciscan of the lower-class position from which her family came. Casals remembers, "I had all these hand-me-downs [including] tennis clothes and rackets." These material items were constant signifiers that "let me know where I was," she said. In the early 1960s Casals met Billie Jean Moffitt (later King) for the first time and her memories of the initial encounter are telling. Moffitt, an already established player in elite women's tennis, had according to Casals, "at least eight rackets" in hand and was wearing a Fred Perry tennis skirt with her initials on the shirt. "Whoa," Casals remembers thinking, "*this* is a tennis player."[9] Even as a youngster, Casals recognized that athletic skill was just one of the ways in which status in tennis was conferred.

For Rosie Casals, victories on the court, especially early in her career, undercut any doubts she may have had about belonging in that space or having earned the right to occupy it. Many of her tennis peers had expensive tennis dresses and cars, as well as memberships to the best private clubs in the nation. Beating the competition represented so much more than a win for Casals, who saw each victory as a "statement" or a "way of feeling equal" among a group of people who seemed to have everything they desired—except a win over her. Casals's familial history and class standing helps to explain the fierce determination with which she engaged tennis and her opponents.[10] In early 1965 the *San Francisco Examiner* ran a feature on sixteen-year-old Casals, the local rising star of women's tennis and comments about her personality rivaled those concerning athletic ability. Even at such a relatively young age, Casals's feisty, spirited, and outspoken persona, according to author Bill Hall, was cause for both concern and celebration. Casals's "ready tongue from an alert intellect" has caused critics to argue that she is "too cocky, too confident," Hall concedes. With a conciliatory tone, he adds, "Hers is a strong, determined personality." Foretelling a future that was to unfold in the coming years, the author concludes that Casals's energy and approach combined with great athleticism would equal a "colorful champion."[11]

San Francisco native Rosemary "Rosie" Casals, circa 1966. *Courtesy of the Bancroft Library, University of California, Berkeley.*

As her tennis skills advanced she was further removed from the public courts of Golden Gate Park. In so many ways Rosie Casals's world changed a great deal in a short span of time. What remained constant, however, were Casals's attitude and approach to the game and the world around her. Though unsettling to some both in and beyond the tennis establishment, Casals's powerful strokes on the court and her colorful and direct style off it symbolized the bold actions of many other folks within the various social movements taking place across the United States. Casals's various points of resistance to the status quo proved a reflection of social change happening during the era as well as a catalyst for it.

At the historical moment in which Rosie Casals's tennis achievements catapulted her onto the national and even international stage titanic cultural and social shifts were taking place within the United States. Throughout the 1960s and early 1970s historically marginalized groups asserted their rights, demanding a reshaping to the structures that created inequality. One of those campaigns for change was the women's rights movement. Emboldened by the civil rights movement across the nation, specifically the American South, as well as the peace movement, women's rights' leaders forged a concerted effort for change. Sexist ideologies and discriminatory structures pervaded early 1960s America. As a result there were, relative to men, a limited range of opportunities and rights afforded the nation's female citizens.[12] It is in this setting that those arguing the rights of women gained momentum and drew attention. Importantly, Casals's tennis career did not just parallel the women's rights movement, it also moved symbiotically with it.

In part, the growing gender consciousness and the rise of the women's rights movement through the first half of the 1960s was the result of rapidly increasing numbers of females in the paid workforce and the inequalities found there. Rising material expectations of an expanding middle class during the post–World War II era, combined with surging inflation rates translated into more women seeking paid employment outside the home. The increase was drastic so much so that from 1960 to 1966 the percentage of women working jumped from 30 to over 46 percent. However, the range of employment opportunities and wages for working women were limited. Females laboring beyond the home were overwhelmingly confined to relatively low-wage occupations in clerical, sales, and factory work. As a result, in 1966 female earnings were just 60 percent of men's wages. More women, either by necessity or desire, entered a workplace in the 1960s that was not necessarily eager to greet them.[13]

As a counter to this reality, liberal feminists, or those eager to work for change *within* current economic, legal, and political structures, demanded "equity" with men in the public sphere. Opportunities were being denied to women, liberal feminists argued, and this was, thus, at its core an issue of fairness. Women's rights advocates sought change in labor settings and numerous other public spheres, including educational, political, and legal campaigns for equity throughout the late 1960s and early 1970s.[14] However, the origin of the women's rights movement and its continuing energy throughout the period was due to more than a narrow range of issues resting on a liberal feminist platform. Rather, diverse perspectives advocating change were to be found across the movement. While liberal feminists viewed wage discrimination and greater access to opportunities as central components to/for the campaign, the movement was deeper and broader than that. There were more radical elements to those advancing the place of women, and these included a criticism of patriarchy. Those in this camp targeted societal understandings of femininity and masculinity, arguing that traditional, quite restrictive, ideas about gender fed discrimination and inequality of opportunity.[15] Regardless of the perspective, those championing women's rights and challenging the gendered status quo stretched to any number of corners throughout society, including women's sport and, more specifically, to tennis.

Facilitated by the feminist movement, women's sport entered a "dramatically new era" as the 1960s drew to a close.[16] Hurdles to access in women's sport that seemed insurmountable for the first several decades of the century were now within reach. The excitement stirring among many in the broader women's rights movement was echoed in athletics as expectations grew for greater female participation across all arenas in society. Within these wider currents of change, women's sport expanded and yet, like their nonsporting peers, female athletes faced ongoing discrimination to their full and unfettered involvement in athletics.

Women's tennis also rode this revolution that sought to alter the cultural landscape and not surprisingly Rosie Casals was at the rebellion's core. By 1966, at age seventeen, Casals was ranked the seventh-best female tennis player in the world. *World Tennis* could not hide its enthusiasm for the first-time Wimbledon participant, saying that she was the "most exciting player" at the tournament. The magazine's accolades continued, "she is the girl who has every shot in the book (plus two hitherto unknown)."[17] Rosie Casals is, according to *World Tennis* in 1966, "a name to remember."[18] The following year Casals made it difficult for fans to forget, as she won Grand Slam doubles titles at Wimbledon and the US Open, playing alongside Billie Jean King. Despite being at the top of her game and playing competitively among the world's greatest players, Casals and a number of her athletic peers thought it time to do what was happening in many different sectors of society—challenge the long-established order of things to change unequal relationships of power.

Tennis, through the 1960s, under the auspices of the United States Lawn Tennis Association (USLTA), was defined as an amateur game in which players could not compete—at least not openly—for prize money. Established tournaments and the Grand Slam events, thought to be among the game's most prestigious, were amateur-only affairs. As the decade neared its end a number of players in elite tennis, including Billie Jean King and Rosie Casals, voiced their displeasure with a system coined "shamateurism." In this context, tournament winners were paid "under the table," so not to violate the USLTA rule against formal payments to players. Eager to openly and unapologetically earn a living as tennis players, a number of top male and female athletes in the game challenged the ban on amateur-only tennis. The era, known as "Open tennis," professionalized the sport. The hope among supportive players was that the transition away from old system would not only bring bigger purses, but also greater transparency in relation to prize money than in the past. The enormous risk to "go pro" taken by many of tennis's greatest players was successful. Organizers of historically amateur-only tournaments quickly realized that in order to attract the best players to their events they needed to welcome entries from professional athletes.[19]

On April 1, 1968, the San Francisco press heralded the news of the game's top players moving away from their amateur standing with the headline, "Billie, Rosie Turn Pro" (Billie Jean King was living in Berkeley at the time). King, the article noted, was the top-ranked female player in the world and as such could earn up to eighty thousand dollars her first year, with other ranked players in the twenty-five-thousand-dollars-and-up range.[20] The potential earnings were significant, especially considering women in the full-time labor force in 1968 earned $4,460 a year. Indeed, all seemed good for the female tennis players who made the move to the professional ranks.[21]

However, professional tennis, if conceptualized as a workplace like any other, brought remarkably similar discriminatory practices and wage inequalities, based on sex, to those found in labor more broadly during this period in history. Making prize money more transparent also exposed gross inequalities, as earnings for the men's draw at tennis tournaments far outdistanced the women's, many times over.[22] Moreover, on some occasions women had to make it to the quarterfinal round of a tournament in order to see a cent in prize money, while such was not the case with men.[23] And finally, in addition to wage inequality, women's matches, even the finals, were sometimes held far from center court.[24] Women, it seemed, were being held to the periphery of professional tennis, both literally and figuratively. Frustration among Casals, King, and a few others built to the breaking point in late 1970 when the prize money for the Pacific Southwest Championship was announced. The men's tournament winner was to receive $12,500 and, in contrast, the women's champion, $1,500. Event organizer Jack Kramer stood firm against the female players' protests, arguing that men drew many more fans than women and thus his decision was not sexist, it was instead a sound business practice. Casals countered, arguing with her usual outspokenness, female tennis players she said, "expend the same amount of energy as the men. We practice as much. We play just as hard. We contribute our share to the success of a tournament."[25] The issues and the swirl of energy that so informed the larger women's movement in the nation were echoed in the voices of Casals, King, and the others.

The snub by Kramer at the Pacific Southwest Championship prompted nine of the elite female tennis players, including Casals, to start another tour beyond the boundaries of the USLTA. This action was both bold and radical, as players once again risked their careers in taking a step away from the USLTA and the many traditions on which it stood. Casals, King, and seven other female players became known as the "Original Nine," playing their first tournament in Houston—a competition won by Casals.[26] This was the beginning of what became a decades-long partnership with a major sponsor, tobacco giant and cigarette maker Philip Morris. Virginia Slims, a cigarette, targeted specifically to female audiences became the tennis tour's moniker. For some, the bond between this new venture of a professional women's tennis tour and more sweeping cultural shifts was inextricable. "You've heard of Women's Lib [women's liberation movement]" a Virginia Slims spokesperson quipped, "this is Women's Lob."[27]

The move to the professional ranks and the fledgling Virginia Slims Tour can be understood as a political act as much as a financial one for Casals and King. King's family, like Casals's, was not of financial means and the prospect of making money at tennis was less a luxury than an economic necessity. Casals expressed the gendered and classed dimensions, saying, "We were fighting for our livelihood. We wanted to earn a living; we wanted to play sports, be accepted. People looked at us and said 'why aren't you in the kitchen? Why aren't you raising children, getting married, etc etc?' We said, 'why should we?'"[28] Casals's words are significant in that they cut to the core of foundational elements of the larger feminist movement in the early 1970s and the athlete's resistance to prescribed dominant expectations of womanhood. Indeed, the feminist movement stirred intense apprehension about "the family," and criticism often was informed by these concerns.[29] Other women, too, like Casals, publicly defied gender assignments as they sought a path on which their identities were not defined by normative notions of family and motherhood.

Like so many other women across society during the period, Casals challenged the assumptions on which traditional conceptualizations of gender were built, as she was fervent about tennis as a career choice and not a hobby. She and King demanded a place in the male preserve of sport. They believed their commitment to the game and their superior athletic skills warranted, not only attention, but also respect from the tennis establishment. Casals's and King's incursion was met with resistance of its own from those who believed they overstepped appropriate boundaries of femininity and womanhood. Relaying the anxieties of some in society one observer noted that Casals and King were "A little too hungry, a little too eager for public recognition, a little too ready to make tennis their careers."[30] Detractors aside, Rosie Casals had confidence in the new tour, noting that elite women's tennis could "put fannies in the seats," as their matches had been doing so for years.[31] Her trust and that of her female tennis peers, in the enterprise, was well placed. Despite its critics, by 1971 the Virginia Slims Tour (or as King affectionately called it, the "Broads' Tour"[32]) secured a foundation. "In addition to making money," *Newsweek* reported, "the women's lobbers have found an identity and a following all of their own."[33] The respect and the credibility extended to them by a growing number of fans was crucial to a larger agenda in which they were "accepted as athletes not as freaks, as role models rather than as tomboys in a state of arrested development, as careerists rather than amateurs waiting to catch a husband."[34]

The growth of the Virginia Slims Tour, however, did not eradicate the many tensions around femininity and athleticism that persisted in sport and society. In fact, fears that sport masculinized women had deep roots and may have been fueled, not in spite of women's expanding role in society and sport, but because of it. Not surprisingly in this setting, gender served as a subtext in many of the media reports about Casals and the cohort of elite female tennis players throughout the period.

Even among allies, both of the players and the tour, reassurances about the athletes' gendered normalcy were always written into the text, competing and often overshadowing discussions of tennis and athletic skill. For example, according to one report, "Women pros were as nice to look at as they were to watch perform," for they remained "graceful, well-proportioned [and] tough without being mannish." Some female athletes, the author concedes were "beautiful [and] even cute."[35] For writers, compliments were shrouded in narrative layers that were sexist and infantilized women athletes. Soon after Casals's and King's first Wimbledon doubles title, Frank Deford of *Sports Illustrated* noted of the pair, "Good as these two young ladies looked . . . and both of them are good to look at—it was once again Rosie Casals, that sprightly Minnie Mouse in sneakers, who showed she is the biggest threat to Mrs. King's supremacy."[36]

Observers were fascinated with Casals, who embodied a status that, for some, seemed at odds with society's strict gender classification system of masculine *or* feminine. Casals was, according to *Newsweek*, "far more combative than cute,"[37] underscoring the narrow and simplistic boundaries of femininity to which women athletes were confined. It was not just her athleticism that drew attention for its perceived rupture of traditional notions of femininity, but a specific style of physicality. Casals and the tennis she played were described as "fiery," "explosive," "feisty," "aggressive," "attacking," and "powerful."[38] Most onlookers simply could not reconcile these terms, and the athleticism that inspired them, with a woman. Casals's serve was so strong, one commentator noted, it was "hard to believe Rosie is not a man."[39] Another said of Casals, she is a "jock first, woman second,"[40] with the definition of the former precluding the latter.

Characterizations of female athletes were sometimes extreme and the direction taken by commentators bordering on the absurd. A *Sports Illustrated* piece on women's tennis in 1972 by Edwin Shrake, for example, managed to address a number of societal preoccupations and fears when it came to female athleticism. Trying to find suitable descriptions to characterize the athletes and their behavior, the reporter resorts to stereotypes. He begins, "As the women, or girls—whatever you call a bunch of females . . . in their early 20s—gathered at a long table gossiping and laughing, there was the feeling of watching some postgraduate sorority affair." Shrake continues, describing who and what the women were in his view, as much as what they were not. The top athletes in the women's game he noted, in wonder, "were an amazingly good-looking group of people." The female athletes debunked cliché representations, as "nobody had a beard [or] looked or sounded like Ernest Borgnine." And if that was not enough to put readers' minds at ease, he added, "Nobody waddled, not a lumberjack in the group." While Shrake's comments provide convincing evidence to doubters that female tennis stars were not men, are they, however, really "normal" women? Several are married, he offers, but "few [female athletes] travel with their husbands," and Shrake concedes, "none have children." Indicators such as these among a group of strong, independent, and athletic women led to "inevitable speculations about homosexuality," for Shrake and certainly other observers as well.[41]

Female strength, including that which was displayed in athletics, was clearly threatening to some. However, attributes often displayed by women in sport that repelled a segment of the population were welcomed by others eager to make the connection between female physicality and empowerment. Such was the case for *Ms.* magazine in a 1974 article that claimed the denial of a woman's "physical powers"[42] was the most egregious act perpetrated by the patriarchy. Thus it instructed readers, "by developing her powers to the fullest, any woman from Olympic star to the weekend tennis player, can be a match for any man she chooses to take on. More importantly, she will inherit the essential source of human self-confidence—pride in and control over a finely tuned body. That alone would be a revolution."[43]

Rosie Casals was the exception, however, to the more general rule among female athletes, many of whom were reticent to make a claim about their relationship to the transformative changes happening throughout society. Never one to be described as timid, Casals thought a public alliance with the broader women's movement was important to advance women's tennis, a view not shared by many other players, at least not initially. In early discussions on the topic Casals and the game's top and most visible player, Billie Jean King, held opposing perspectives. King, according to Casals, was firm, saying, "We're not going with that bra-burning stuff," prompting Casals's counter, "I played without a bra anyway . . . I [was] all for it!"[44] Of course, King eventually warmed to the idea of positioning the cause of advancing women's rights on the court with those off it.

For many, Casals's commentary in the booth during the "Battle of the Sexes" match between Billie Jean King and Bobby Riggs in September 1973 cemented what they believed they already knew about her, that she was the "little broad with the big mouth."[45] Casals's "pointed, rapid-fire comments"[46] largely directed at Riggs, throughout the course of the nationally televised event, did not enamor her to many observers, who sent vitriolic mail in response. Letters to the Editor of *Sports Illustrated* after the King versus Riggs event illustrate the ire directed at Casals. On October 8, 1973, *Sports Illustrated* published six letters, three of which focused, not on King or Riggs, but on Casals's comments during the match. One letter writer characterized Casals's remarks as "venomous," as well as "childish and spiteful."[47] Others claimed Casals's comments in the booth "set Women's Lib back 10 years."[48]A final observer noted that while "Billie Jean King did the improbable when she beat Bobby Riggs [in] three straight . . . Rosie Casals accomplished the impossible when she made Howard Cosell [also in the booth] seem like the perfect gentlemen."[49]Male broadcasters' critical comments directed toward athletes were not unusual, nor did they signal a hostile response from the viewing public.[50] Such was not the case for Casals, and other "gender rebels," in this early 1970s moment, who had an "allure," according to Edward Miller, but were as often "forced to suffer for [their] difference."[51]If folks were ever neutral about Casals they certainly were not after the match, as she in a 1974 article was said to be a "symbol, however mistakenly of the women's movement and the image is bound to stay with her for awhile." Casals, who had been making "pointed, rapid-fire comments" for years, found the whole matter amusing, finding no reason to defend herself or the comments made during the telecast.[52]

It was not just a woman's outspokenness or even a public stance in support of women's rights that represented affinity with feminism and social change, however. Female athletes, especially those with a high profile like Rosie Casals, *embodied* resistance to the gendered status quo and as a result every stroke, serve, or smash was a very public feminist act. Casals's embodied agency was also expressed in other ways as she often ignored the rules guiding expected patterns of gendered behavior, both on and off the tennis court. In 1974 Catherine Bell writing for *Tennis* said Casals "hides behind no fluttering, mendacious 'femininity.'" Rather, Bell continues, it is as though Casals "collects everything that women are not allowed to be or feel and throws it all uncompromisingly beyond every stereotype."[53] This despite others on the tour who wrestled with societal tensions surrounding femininity and athleticism. As example, Virginia Wade noted that women have a tendency to become "desexed" if they spend too much time in female-only circles. Frankie Durr feared lifting weights would lead to bulky musculature and as a result refrained from such training, regardless of the on-the-court benefits from increased strength. Conversely, Casals remained unfazed by the boundaries of acceptable behavior or the implications of overstepping them, saying of female athleticism, "If someone says it's not feminine . . . I say screw it."[54] Even off the court Casals's actions failed to heed dominant ideas about gender and femininity. In a locker room press conference after a contest against Margaret Court, Casals, who took both a beer from a Virginia Slims official and a cigarette from an onlooker, joked, "a good athlete's got to puff."[55]

Casals's unapologetic behavior with regard to gender, and the controversy such displays raised, even extended to her choice of tennis dresses. Female players' attire on the court has long been a point around which issues of "decorum, social distinction, physicality, and femininity"[56] have been debated in public spaces. Tennis "whites" epitomized the game's upper-class roots, as the garments were "hard to launder and keep pristine [and thus] were the prerogative of the rich."[57] The sport's class origins, however, were far removed from Casals's reality, and in many ways her fashion choices communicated her unique subject position. On Casals's selection of sportswear one observer sarcastically noted, "for practice she wore a conservative outfit [a] psychedelic orange satin warm-up with black stripes down the arms and legs."[58]

The fashions worn by Casals, as well as a number of her athletic contemporaries in the 1970s, were the creation of Ted Tinling. Hired by the Virginia Slims Tour, Tinling had, for decades, made his career in women's tennis fashion. Intent on helping to reconcile ongoing tensions around gender and athleticism, Tinling believed his dresses would make athletes more attractive to a public eager for evidence of traditional femininity among its tennis stars. Tinling said that elite female tennis players were in need of a makeover, as he wondered, "why so many girls wish to look like second-class men."[59] Tinling's intentions for his costumes, however, were not always taken up and similarly understood by players, including Casals. Less about a display of a certain kind of femininity, the athletic apparel was much more about personal style for Casals, who notes proudly, "I was the rhinestone queen."[60] Others, however, saw the colorful and eye-catching designs as a direct challenge to tennis's established order.

In 1972 Casals appeared on the staid Wimbledon court with a dress "quartered in blue with a 'VS' [Virginia Slims] motif running throughout." And the next day she appeared on the number-one court for the women's doubles semifinal match with the "cigarette motif again boldly blazoned on the front." Instructed to adhere to Wimbledon's dress code of "predominantly" white outfits officials warned Casals would be banned from further play if she did not comply. Claiming Wimbledon officials' actions were "hypocritical," Casals added, "if they won't allow Virginia Slims advertising then they shouldn't allow the Fred Perry leaf on shirts, the British Leyland cars that take the players to their hotels, or the Commercial Union results board giving the placings to date."[61]

Others, too, were critical of Wimbledon's response to Casals, but for reasons other than it being an overreaction to a perceived fashion faux pas. In a searing satirical essay in *World Tennis*, Bud Collins mocked Wimbledon officials for their unyielding adherence to an outdated dress code for athletes. The incident on the Wimbledon courts symbolized, for Collins, uneasiness by tournament officials around issues of race and gender. In a parody of the event, set in Medieval England, Collins writes of observers' ambivalence expressed toward and about Casals. "Once upon a turf," he begins, "a soulful little girl named Rosie" captured the public's attention as her feats of "uncommon agility" were entertaining to many. However, a critical mass of others disliked her "carefree nature," believing it "unbecoming a female," exposing her "waywardness and wickedness" in the process. The gendered connotations were equaled, in Collins's view, by the racial dimensions of the dress controversy. The presence of a nonwhite dress threw the crowd into a "state of shock" as though they were seeing "a purple cow in Guernsey, a pink elephant in Tanzania, or a black legislator in South Africa."[62] Concluding the piece in the present-day moment Collins says of Wimbledon authorities, they "wouldn't be so gauche as to try to dictate to a young woman what she should or should not wear in the year 1972, would they?"[63] On one level Collins's remarks in reaction to Casals's attire reflect debates around equal rights and female independence that raged throughout society. Importantly, however, the discussions in women's tennis did not simply mirror these broader conversations, they contributed greatly to them.

Women's sport fashion often earned greater popular attention than the athlete, this being a case in point. The dress, like Casals, challenged rules of conduct on the court—and social convention off it. The attire was, for her, a form of self-expression, which personified a style she was eager to portray to a public not necessarily similarly keen on its exhibition. "I think my clothes look feminine enough," said Casals. Dismissively, and yet also subversively, she adds, "I go on the court to play, and whether people like it or not, I really couldn't care less."[64] Speaking years later about the ensemble that created the controversy, Casals quipped, "it became a famous dress and beat me to the Hall of Fame."[65]

Casals notes that for all of the actions and statements, listed above, believed to be transgressions, "I've been attacked, messed around, misinterpreted. Sometimes

I feel threatened." Ultimately, however, what drove her was a determined attitude she cultivated years earlier as a youngster on the public courts of Golden Gate Park. "So what?" she concludes, "I'm doing what I want to do."[66] This seemingly selfish comment obscures the many ways Casals advanced the cause of gender equality, furthered women's tennis, and strengthened the game for those who played it when she no longer did.

Not surprisingly, local media reports detailing the Virginia Slims Tour stop in Oakland in 1988 featured the game's then dominant player, Martina Navratilova. However, those accounts seemed as preoccupied with Navratilova's earnings for the weekend as they were with the athlete herself. "Guys, in the time it takes you to wash your car, vacuum it and Windex it inside and out," one local sports reporter quipped, "Martina Navratilova won $50,000."[67] Another noted that Navratilova's take for the week was actually $57,500 as she collected another $7,500 for winning the doubles title with Rosie Casals.[68] Ironically, Casals place was reduced to a footnote of sorts, this despite the fact that her efforts and those of a few contemporaries nearly two decades earlier made it possible for Navratilova's windfall.

Throughout history, especially in the 1960s and 1970s, female athletes' power, physical skill, determination, and boldness embodied the foundational tenets of women's liberation, giving observers a different, expanded understanding of womanhood's meaning.[69] In more recent years commentators have looked a bit more closely at Casals's role in furthering women's tennis and more favorably upon the gender misdeeds she was believed to have staged. Writing in 2005 Selena Roberts observes, "Rosie was also one of the few women on the tour who truly possessed what was known in the 1970s as va-va-va-voom. Crowds adored this feisty merrymaker. Bold enough to wear spangles and sequins. Never a conformist, she colored outside the lines. If Billie was the high-profile ringleader of the Original Nine, Rosie was the spirited core of its inner circle."[70]

In 2009 Joel Drucker of ESPN paid homage to Casals by recognizing both her great athleticism as well as her commitment to social change. In winning the first Virginia Slims tournament in 1970, Casals was "front and center, not just as a self-proclaimed militant activist but also a superb player."[71] The passage of time enables observers a different perspective on a past seen through another lens, one that recognizes Casals's influence as more expansive and profound than victories on the court. The frame through which Casals understands the contributions she made during her career share similar ground to the recent observations offered by others. Speaking to the relative freedoms female athletes experience in sport today as opposed to forty years ago, Casals reflects, "it's a lot easier being a [woman] athlete. There's more acceptance, more appreciation. I'd like to think that I contributed to that."[72] Indeed, Rosie Casals, the "classic rebel [and] pugnacious outcast from the wrong side of the tracks,"[73] did just that.

14

The Early Gay Games

The Bay Area Years

JUDY DAVIDSON

While the international gay and lesbian sport movement (most visibly and popularly manifested through events such as the Gay Games and OutGames) has become a global sport tourism success in the twenty-first century, the humble beginnings of this phenomena are found in the early to mid-1980s in San Francisco, California. Originally called the Gay Olympics, the first Gay Games were held in 1982, and were followed four years later by Gay Games II in 1986. Developed as a grassroots movement led by Dr. Thomas Waddell, the early games were touted as a celebration of socially progressive inclusion, where participation (rather than excessive competition) in sporting activities was stressed. The express invitation of these early games was to all of humanity to attend—not just individuals who identified as gay or lesbian.[1]

The Gay Games have since become major events. San Francisco was the site for the first two games (in 1982 and 1986) and Celebration '90 was staged in Vancouver. These games were the largest sporting event of its kind held in the world in 1990. New York City hosted Unity '94, which included the marking of the twenty-fifth anniversary of the Stonewall Riots (often heralded as the "birth" of the gay rights movement). Over ten thousand people participated in 1994. The games have subsequently been held in global cosmopolitan destinations such as Amsterdam, Sydney, and Chicago. The Federation of Gay Games (FGG), founded in 1989 to replace the original San Francisco organizing group, is the international governing body for this organization that claims to be the most inclusive major sporting event in the world.[2] In 2006, the OutGames were launched in

Montreal—a splinter organization from the parent event. These Olympic-style spectacles are fascinating mixtures of highly professionalized, rationalized organizations that legitimate an "alternative lifestyle" to a gathering of thousands of lesbians and gay men who play out contested identities and political agendas throughout the athletic event.

The Gay Games emerged in the 1980s, the decade that sexual minority rights became more popularly politicized, the AIDS epidemic took hold, and gay and lesbian communities established themselves in major metropolitan cities across North America. This chapter recounts some of the controversial struggles in which the early Gay Games found themselves. I suggest that these early gay rights struggles in which Games organizers and supporters were embroiled had, and continue to have, assimilationist effects for the current iteration of the large sporting spectacle. That is, large events like the Gay Games attempted to mainstream themselves and actively sought acceptance by normative society and its powerful sport institutions (like the USOC, the IOC, corporate media, etc.). It might be tempting to read my critique of the contemporary lesbian and gay athletic movement as suggesting that sexuality is no longer an issue in athletics. However, the reader is encouraged to grapple with the complex temptations and co-optations that increased corporate capitalism and the related impulses of professionalization subtly (and likely unavoidably) exerted on this successful sexual identity-based organization and movement over time. Even into the second decade of the twenty-first century, many, if not most, conventional, mainstream athletic contexts at all levels remain stubbornly homophobic, and conditions for queer athletes in these situations remain decidedly chilly. The Gay Games movement has importantly created a space where lesbian and gay sexualities are openly celebrated and performed in a serious sporting environment. Continuing to historicize and ask after how that contemporary festive space persists in continuing to reiterate other forms of economic, racial, national, and bodily privilege remains crucial to a struggle for social justice in a larger queer community—widely and broadly construed beyond its current configurations.

"Papa Games"

The first two Gay Games were held in San Francisco, California, in 1982 and 1986. The Bay Area, and by the 1980s, San Francisco's Castro Street community in particular, were home to one of the largest and most famous burgeoning gay subcultures in North America. Thousands of dishonorably discharged gay servicemen returned to San Francisco in the 1940s in the wake of World War II. The subsequent "white flight" to outlying suburbs in the 1950s meant that real estate in the working-class Castro Street district became very affordable, and the area was soon home to what would become a flourishing gay enclave. Independent gay businesses, bars, services, and community supports developed, and gay residents bought Victorian homes, renovated them, and stayed. Political tensions between assimilationist homophiles to radical gay liberationists to lesbian feminists and early queer transgender struggles were all present in this neighborhood. By the late 1970s, the Castro functioned as a small gay city within a city, developing its own street fair and theater district and drawing lesbians and gay men to immigrate to the city and area, a parallel economy that generated twenty-five to thirty million dollars a year. It was in this cultural and political context that Tom Waddell developed the dream of hosting an Olympic-type athletic event for gays and lesbians, and that dream was realized in 1982. By the second Gay Games in 1986, the AIDS crisis and epidemic was taking its toll on this community that had developed a thriving sexual subculture, and concomitantly, it was this unique queer kinship that mobilized health-care politics and policy, and importantly, alternative forms of community care and support.[3]

Dr. Thomas Waddell was the original driving force and obsessive organizer of the Gay Games. He literally single-handedly put together the first games against massive odds, including serious legal challenges, lack of financial support for an unproven cause, no experience in organizing large events, and a gay community reluctant to embrace the idea. Waddell consciously and unconsciously infused his personal history and values into the Gay Games. As many commentators have noted, he had very strong opinions and convictions of which he did not let go, and he would not back down from political or ethical challenges.[4] His cultural capital (and the implicit values held therein) is one crucial condition of possibility for the emergence and production of this event.

Gay Games I occurred between August 27 and September 5, 1982, in San Francisco. They attracted about 1,300 athletes from 179 cities around the world who competed in seventeen events.[5] Even though the event was literally organized around various kitchen tables, it was consciously styled after the modern international Olympics, combining athletic and cultural events for an international competition with a gay inflection. There were active outreach programs to attract "minorities" such as women, people of color, and gays and lesbians from small-town America as well as other countries. A trans-America torch run started in New York at the site of the Stonewall Inn and was used to light the flame of the Gay Games in San Francisco during the opening ceremonies.[6] To a large extent, Waddell influenced and created many of these "Olympic-style" touches for his event. His history and experiences inform not only the emancipatory thrust of the Gay Games, but much of its conservatism as well.

Waddell's life, in many ways, can be read to some extent like the stereotyped white American dream come true. He was born into poverty and a broken home, escaped it to spend his adolescence with sympathetic, liberal artists who nurtured in him a love for the finer things in life. He attended college and chose to pursue a medical degree. He was an all-round athlete in high school and college, competing on the football, gymnastics, and track and field teams. As a member of the US National Track and Field team, he traveled to countries in the global south, extolling the virtues of Americanized athleticism. In 1966, Waddell was drafted for the Vietnam War, and through a combination of charm, professional immunity, and back-room connections, he managed to avoid active duty, and instead trained and qualified for the 1968 US Olympic team. He placed sixth in the decathlon and spoke out against the racism that had Tommie Smith and John Carlos thrown off the US Olympic team for raising their defiant fists in the black power salute on the medal podium. After the 1968 Olympic Games, Waddell left the army and serious sporting competition. He worked for an international medical conglomerate and came out, wholeheartedly indulging in the 1970s gay male scene in San Francisco's Castro District.[7] His next serious battle was to be with the United States Olympic Committee (USOC).

Waddell had wanted the first games in 1982 to be called the Gay Olympics. The appropriation of the Olympic ethos of friendship, athletic achievement, and international participation was strategically paired with the invocation of gay identity. It was Waddell's mission to create space where gays and lesbians could be fully who they were in athletic contexts. Waddell was also committed to the event being a serious athletic competition, and the Olympics denoted that for him.

The Thwarted Gay Olympics

The initial planning for what was at that time called the Gay Olympics was produced and organized in various kitchens and living rooms throughout San Francisco between 1980 and 1982. The group went ahead and organized under the name San Francisco Arts & Athletics, Incorporated (SFAA) as a California nonprofit, public benefit corporation.[8] Organization for the first games proceeded. Local, national, and international gay and lesbian sporting groups were contacted, events and venues arranged, and fundraising was started in earnest. A board of directors was created and the organizational structure for the event was chaotically put together as the planning proceeded. Waddell was elected president and chair of the SFAA in the summer of 1981. Ad hoc committees got the nuts and bolts of athletic and cultural events cobbled together.[9] The Gay Olympic Games were getting their word out across the United States, effectively enough to catch the attention of official amateur sport organizations.

In late January 1982, the San Francisco gay and lesbian newspaper, the *Bay Area Reporter (BAR),* broke the story that the United States Olympic Committee

(USOC) had informed the Gay Olympic Games organizers that they could no longer use the word "Olympic." Lorch, writing in the *BAR*, reported, "Congress has voted that the USOC owns the word 'Olympic,' also 'Olympiad' and 'Citius Altius Fortius' or any combination or simulation thereof. Anything that would cause confusion, cause mistake, deceive, or falsely suggest a connection with the Corporation or any Olympic activity are prohibited as well."[10] The fledgling organization took a few days to assess its options. The American Civil Liberties Union (ACLU) declined to take up their cause, so the SFAA retained the *pro bono* counsel of Mary Dunlap, who would become the Gay Games' tireless attorney for the next five years.[11] Waddell wrote the USOC back, suggesting that both First Amendment guarantees of free speech and Fifth Amendment guarantees of equal protection under the law were violated in Miller's demand. On this latter charge, Waddell wrote, "There is a discriminatory action on the part of the USOC which has sanctioned the 'Junior Olympics' and the 'Special Olympics' but has looked the other way on the Armenian Olympics, the Xerox Olympics, the Crab-Cooking Olympics, the Diaper Olympics, the Rat Olympics, and the Dog Olympics, while at the same time takes exception to the term 'Gay Olympic Games.'"[12]

Over the next five years, this litany of not sanctioned, yet sanctioned Olympic events was to become the most oft-quoted and popularly used lament to illustrate what gay activists believed would be apparent—that the USOC was a homophobic and retributive behemoth. Waddell expressed hope that the dispute could be resolved amicably but quickly dispelled any idea that the gay group might back down. The Gay Olympics would go to court if necessary.[13] Nothing was heard from Colorado Springs for another seven months. The SFAA resumed using the word Olympic as it worked toward the ten-day athletic festival set for the late summer. There were defiant letters of protest to the editor published in the *Bay Area Reporter* and written to the USOC directly.[14] While the USOC had the legal right to sue the Gay Olympics, the gay community told the story of being singled out unfairly and subjected unconstitutionally to petty, homophobic discrimination.

About three weeks before the first Gay Olympics were to start, a court injunction banning the use of the word Olympic was placed on the SFAA. W. April, of the *Bay Area Reporter*, noted, "In a surprise eleventh hour move that threaten[ed] to turn the first Gay Olympic Games into the the Gay 'Bleep' Games, the International and US Olympic Committees obtained a federal court order . . . prohibiting the Gay Olympics people from using the word 'Olympic' or 'Olympiad.'"[15] Volunteers scrambled to literally scrape the offending word off the medals, change souvenirs and t-shirts, and destroy or black out posters and signs.[16] Until the changes could be made, button and t-shirt sales were suspended.[17] The event had to be referred to as the Gay Athletic Games or the Gay Bleep Games by the organizers. A note on the inside of the Official Program read "Due to the last minute court action taken by the U.S. Olympic Committee concerning the use of the word 'Olympic,' all references to that term had to be deleted from this program. The judge's decision on the permanent injunction had not been made by publication deadline. We apologize to the writers and advertisers whose articles and ads we had to change to comply with the court's original temporary restraining order."[18] The only fundraising tactic left to the event was to sell tickets to the opening and closing ceremonies. Estimates of the losses due to the last-minute court order ranged between $15,000 and $30,000, a substantial sum for the fledgling organization.[19]

Nonetheless, the games went on, very successfully. Politicians defiantly proclaimed the Gay Olympic Games open. Tina Turner performed for forty-five minutes to wildly cheering fans. People in the stands wept openly as over 1,300 gay and lesbian athletes from many different countries (claims vary between thirteen and nineteen) marched into the stadium. Various testimonials from fans talked about being in the closet or being out for the past twenty-five years and in either case, effused about how liberating being in the Gay Games opening ceremonies crowd was.[20] A Gay Olympics, cross-America torch run ended in Kezar Stadium, as two former US Olympians, George Frenn and Susan McGrievey, lit the Gay Games flame.[21] Participation in the athletic and cultural events produced a plethora of gay pride stories for the next four years. Tom Waddell had a hand in almost every aspect of putting together the inaugural games, and he pulled off an impressive event, under great stress. The games ended with Waddell announcing that they would occur again in four years time (the Olympiad time period) in San Francisco while they organized an international body to move the games out of San Francisco after 1986. They vowed to wage the court battle against the USOC.

Arguably, the USOC's last-minute court action became a crucial condition of possibility for the continued and inevitable long-term success of the Gay Games. Among other things, the legal claim garnered them national and international media attention. *Sports Illustrated* ran a short, supportive piece on August 16, 1982.[22] Similarly, the German weekly, *Der Spiegel,* sent a feature writer to cover the games; "We thought this was important to cover. It really attracted our attention when the USOC asked them to drop the 'Olympics' from the name."[23] Other commentators have suggested that if it had not been for the USOC's court challenge, the media might have completely ignored the first games.[24] Waddell claimed, "The USOC persecution drew our own community together and attracted mainstream press interest that we could never have bought."[25] The USOC, in its juridical challenge, produced the conditions for an incitement to discourse, which contributed to the entrenchment of a longer-term discursive formation known as the Gay Games. The local and global attention the prohibition garnered helped to sediment the continuation of this gay pride event. Ironically, rather than quash it, the sporting venture was given a better chance by the USOC.

However, while the court case may have produced the conditions of possibility for the Gay Games, it was a stressful, exhausting birth. The USOC was unrelenting in its pursuit of trademark protection. In February 1984, they were granted a permanent injunction against the Gay Games, meaning that the USOC "avoid[ed] a trial and a public airing of the issues in the case."[26] Later the same year, the USOC was awarded $96,600 in attorney's fees to be paid by the SFAA and Tom Waddell. A lien was placed on Tom Waddell's San Francisco home.[27] The SFAA continued to appeal the original 1982 injunction to higher court levels. Waddell mortgaged his historic Albion Street home in the Mission District of San Francisco to help pay for the legal costs in the battle.[28] In April 1985, the courts ordered that no further assets of SFAA or its directors could be seized. Gay Games II could be held with no threat of interference from the USOC.[29] Student groups protested at Stanford, leafletting an international soccer match.[30] Shawn Kelly, the Gay Games II executive director, sent out dense press releases, desperately explaining the complicated legal wranglings.[31]

The Gay Games itself was undergoing its own corporate rationalization process. Unlike the first games, which had been a kitchen-table organization cobbled together and headed up by Tom Waddell, Gay Games II was a much more community-planned event.[32] For health reasons, Waddell, who was now battling AIDS, was forced to delegate authority to various committees and individuals. The board hired a full-time executive director, all sporting events used US national or international rules and regulations, and the "Procession of the Arts" was more formally organized and integrated into the overall event. Discussions were held about which events should charge admission and for how much. Corporate fundraising techniques were put into place and a communications committee headed up all media relations. The group persevered despite having the court of appeals rule against them yet again in January 1986. Just before the opening of Gay Games II, Mary Dunlap and the SFAA announced they were appealing to the Supreme Court.[33] Gay Games II was held August 9–17, 1986, with approximately double the participants (+/-3,700) and double the budget (+/-$780,000). Waddell had just been released from hospital with pneumonia and had developed full-blown AIDS. He won the javelin competition. The event was considered a raving success yet again.[34]

In the fall of 1986, the Supreme Court announced that it would review the entire case. The SFAA board committed funds to the legal battle, and the ACLU agreed to defray 50 percent of their out-of-pocket expenses.[35] Mary Dunlap, their fiery and at times, polemic lawyer, donated hundreds of hours *pro bono* to the cause. The case was heard in Washington on March 24, 1987. The whole hearing was given thirty minutes. Dunlap thought it went well, but as an observer in the court, a sick Waddell was not so convinced. In late June 1987, the Supreme Court delivered its 7–2 decision (5–4 on the Fifth Amendment/state action claim) in favor of the USOC in all aspects of the case. While other groups borrowing the word Olympic remained untouched by the USOC, the US Supreme Court justices deemed there was no discriminatory action and granted the USOC exclusive and proprietary right to use of the word "Olympic." The USOC and the American legal system effectively colonized Olympic discursive space through commercial trademark law.[36] Three weeks later, Tom Waddell died of AIDS-related complications.

This early history of the Gay Games has been read as a heroic resistance struggle for the social justice cause of gay and lesbian sporting emancipation.[37] I argue that there is a corollary analysis to be made. Reading alongside this dramatic backdrop of struggle and loss (of an Olympic ideal and the death of a founder), I now highlight three particular incidents that emerge from this period of Gay Games history that are read as nascent indications of how the games would continue to secure their privileges of class, whiteness, and athletic normativities, even as they rhetorically struggled with questions of inclusion, nondiscrimination, and tolerance. These early forms of struggle produced assimilationist organizational responses by the SFAA and FGG. These responses foreshadow the subsequent transformation of the Gay Games toward an alignment with the hegemonic political formations and practices of Western dominance—particularly increasing corporatization and integration (or at least some acceptance) into powerful municipal, federal, and nongovernmental political machineries into the twenty-first century.[38]

The Riefenstahl Affair

At times, Tom Waddell's slavish commitment to the purity and transcendence of athletic performance blinded him to larger political issues. Prior to Gay Games I, in March 1982, Waddell organized a fundraising screening of Leni Riefenstahl's controversial film *Olympia*, a ground-breaking documentary of the 1936 Berlin Summer Olympics, at the Castro Theatre in San Francisco. As Waddell explained, "I chose to show the movie not for its minimal political content, but because it is a paean to the human body and to sports. Riefenstahl caught in her movie the athletes' will as well as their strength. The film focuses on the athletes and the sporting contests, demonstrating the beauty and positive nature of sport. It is in this spirit, the ideal of sport, in which the Gay Olympic Games of 1982 invite you to view the ineffable beauties of Olympic endeavour, Leni Riefenstahl's *Olympia*."[39]

While pioneering and revolutionizing sport film as art, Riefenstahl's film was also commissioned by Hitler and used for Nazi propaganda purposes. Waddell continued: "It may seem like a strange choice for kicking off an Olympics for people that the Nazis persecuted. BUT! This was the very first Olympic movie ever made, and it is still the best! Whether you agree or not with the slant of the message (and I doubt you will), you will nevertheless see a cinematic piece of history by an artistic genius. It was a peculiar and dangerous time for the world; the movie shows what sport can be and even more important SHOULDN'T be."[40]

The howls of protest were fast and furious. The recently formed Lesbian and Gay Jewish Activist League denounced the idea and leafleted Castro Street, urging people not to attend.[41] Critics were appalled that a gay event was willing to make money off of a Nazi propaganda piece, while others suggested Waddell was obsessed with a pornographic, fascist male body ideal.[42] Supporters cried censorship, that they were being denied the opportunity to see a classic film, and wanted to know who was going to replace the lost revenues.[43] The Riefenstahl film lived up to its notorious reputation as the games' board of directors made the decision to cancel the screening after Waddell received violent threats, and rumors circulated that he had been active in the Nazi party. Even in backing down, Waddell said, "I feel like I'm yielding to the same kind of censorship the Nazis themselves practised."[44] As Mary McDonald has suggested, following Pawas Bisht's work, it is a complicated, perhaps troubling, politics when one of the twentieth century's most iconic and horrifying collective memories gets mobilized to project a contemporary "trouble" onto another geopolitical moment and context, when they are not, in fact, analogous.[45] This collision of identity politics and liberal freedoms exposes the cracks in Waddell's philosophical rhetoric concerning what he wanted the games to do and how he could not grapple with the difficult political implications of deep, historical legacies of trauma.

The exaltation of an almost fascist body ideal at the Gay Games continues to haunt this event. In commenting on the 1990 Vancouver Games, critic Marusia Bociurkiw suggested that that event was a "paean to Weimar-esque notions of the body beautiful."[46] Gordon Waitt observed a decade later that the Sydney Gay Games in 2002 glorified the nationalistic fantasy of the perfectly sculpted, white, masculinist body and that that body ideal pervaded the event.[47] Indeed, the contemporary Gay Games is predominantly populated by a very particular kind of white gay masculinity.

Rallying against Visa

Tom Waddell died at home of AIDS-related complications in the summer of 1987. Among many other memorializations and commemorative practices for the Gay Games founder, there were two community-based protests that were mobilized. These resistances not only marked a grieving process for Waddell himself, but for a collective gay community anger at the USOC and the Olympics for not countenancing gay athletics in the wake of the Gay Games losing the fight to use the word Olympic at the Supreme Court. The first of these was a protest against a Visa credit card affinity program, and the second was the struggle to get strategic antihomophobic conditions imposed on a San Francisco/Bay Area bid for the 1996 Summer Olympics.

The earliest indications of a gay consumer boycott of companies who supported the USOC through fundraising campaigns appeared in the public media in May 1987, even before the Supreme Court had delivered its Gay Olympics decision. A letter written to a vice president at Merrill Lynch Realty asked the company to reconsider supporting a homophobic organization (the USOC) through a formal fundraising campaign. One letter to the editor read, "This has not been a civilized dispute about the Committee's right to expropriate for its exclusive use a part of our language, but an ill-tempted personal attack on a former Olympic champion who happens to be gay."[48] The letter writer then went on to comment that property owners in the Bay Area should know who Merrill Lynch was supporting, intimating that monied gay real estate buyers and sellers were discerning and discriminating customers.

In August 1987, the Visa company sent out their promotional newsletter, trumpeting a new, "no-hassle" USOC sponsorship program. With every transaction made with a Visa credit card within a certain time period, customers would automatically be donating a percentage of their purchases to the "good" cause of the United States Olympic Committee.[49] Yet another protest concerning the Gay Games was chronicled through the pages of *BAR*, first through letters to the editor, which then spread to a nationwide organized rally. Between August 1987 and February 1988, during the time in which the promotional campaign ran, pressure was exerted upon Visa to end their sponsorship of the USOC. Many people wrote letters to the banks that held their Visa accounts and copied them to *BAR*, where they were publicly reprinted. The letters all registered some form of opposition to the donation of their money to the USOC because of its homophobic attack on the Gay Olympics.

Grievances, threats, and conditions varied. Writers were outraged that credit card users were unwittingly being coerced into donating to a homophobic organization.[50] Suggestions were put forth that donations by Visa be made to the Gay Games (often still defiantly written as Gay Olympics) or to AIDS organizations.[51] Merchants in the Bay Area indicated they would draw their customers' attention to the problems with the sponsorship program and request they not use Visa.[52] Many letters[53] invoked the memory of Tom Waddell and his persecution by the USOC, pointedly described in one letter as a "campaign of judicial fag-bashing."[54] There were those who cited the amount of money Visa made from them, how Visa would make no more until the program was pulled, and wondered how Visa and their cooperating financial institutions were unaware of the very large gay and lesbian community in the Bay Area, some of whom were very large depositors.[55] Demands were made that Visa publicly apologize to the gay community.[56]

Sasha Alyson, of Alyson Publications based in Boston, Massachusetts, wrote an open letter in August 1987 condemning Visa's sponsorship program and sent it to 140 gay and lesbian newspaper editors across North America. In his letter he briefly outlined the history of USOC's discriminatory action against the Gay Games and urged readers to cut their Visa cards in half with instructions to send one half to the Visa Marketing Department (contact name and address included) and the other half to him. His intention was to find a gay artist who would sculpt a memorial to Tom Waddell with the remaining halves of the cut Visa cards.[57] Mary Dunlap wrote Visa and stated triumphantly, "Since [my clients, the Gay Olympics] can't use the word, I can't use my Visa card. Enclosed please find the half you may dispose of."[58] By December, several hundred snipped cards had been sent to Alyson.[59] His hope was to hurt Visa in the pocketbook. However, after several months of letter writing, Visa refused to end the sponsorship campaign, and an apology to the lesbian and gay community from the San Francisco-based company was never to be realized.

Late in the campaign, an alternative, social justice credit card affinity program called Working Assets got entangled in the protest. This program supported politically progressive nonprofit organizations, including the National Gay and Lesbian Task Force (NGLTF). Unfortunately, because of their association with Visa, they unintentionally and involuntarily got caught in the USOC promotion.[60] As a result of this, Working Assets publicly announced that they were making special donations of $1,000 to three national gay and lesbian organizations (NGLTF, National Gay Rights Advocates, and Lambda Legal Defense and Education Fund) to protest Visa's USOC program.[61] Members of the lesbian and gay community were encouraged to switch to a Working Assets Mastercard.

The Visa protest was an early appeal to a "pink" market, the nascent flexing of the gay market niche muscle. The message was one of "if you don't start listening to our political concerns in the civil rights arena, we will stop supporting your business with our dollars, which are becoming more and more substantial." The commodification of gay or lesbian identities started to become explicitly recognized by activists as useful for public causes and civil rights issues. In certain local contexts, the call to heed gay and lesbian buying power was heard and respected. In October 1987, the San Francisco Chamber of Commerce encouraged its members and associates to donate to the USOC to support the US

Olympic team going to Seoul. Gay members of the chamber reacted quickly and the director of the chamber did a quick reversal, recognizing the organization's insensitivity, and apologizing to the gay and lesbian community. O'Loughlin reported, "We need the gay community to be members of the chamber. We're belatedly sensitive to the community."[62] In Washington, DC, six months later, gay activists protested proposed municipal legislation which would have donated one dollar of every city residents' tax refund to the USOC.[63]

The large credit corporations took little or no heed of the gay-led USOC protest, despite the best efforts of the grassroots card cutters. In fact, Mastercard, which during the protest was touted to be the card to which to switch, overlooked AIDS charities in a "cause-related marketing" campaign that ran simultaneously in late 1987 with Visa's USOC drive.[64] The lesbian and gay niche market was not yet considered large enough, sufficiently influential, nor incorporated acceptably (in the capitalist economic sense of incorporation) to be fully embraced by corporate America. Once the lesbian and gay agenda curbed its loud and overt calls for justice, equality, and fair treatment, it was then welcomed with open arms by certain large businesses on their corporate terms starting in the early and mid-1990s. Ironically, in 1993, the Federation of Gay Games got an affinity credit card with Action Mastercard, with 0.5 percent of cardholder purchases going to the Federation Board.[65] The failure of the nationwide Visa protest was an interesting harbinger of the Gay Games' own commercialization trajectory. The triumph of capital is seen in this homonormative[66] course the Gay Games took into the 1990s and the twenty-first century.[67]

The (Supposed) Tyranny of the "Faggots of Frisco": Protesting the San Francisco/Bay Area 1996 Olympic Bid

Coinciding with the Visa protest and the Supreme Court deliberation and decision on the use of the word Olympic, the gay community and sympathetic municipal politicians succeeded in putting antihomophobia conditions on a San Francisco/Bay Area bid for the 1996 Summer Olympic Games. Supervisor Harry Britt, a dependable vote for gay causes, introduced legislation in early January 1987 to the San Francisco Board of Supervisors. It proposed "to remove the city from any efforts to bring the 1996 Olympics to San Francisco" until the USOC allowed the Gay Games to use the word Olympic and they ended their harassment of Tom Waddell.[68] The constituency of the gay community that was interested in this issue was already in protest mode. Letters were written to Mayor Feinstein, to the *Chronicle*, and to the *BAR* condemning the USOC's case against the Gay Games and its persecution of Waddell.[69] San Francisco was invoked as being a tolerant, open, and diverse community that should not sanction the kind of bigotry that the USOC persisted in perpetrating.[70]

In addition, writers suggested that bringing the Olympics to San Francisco would be nothing more than hosting a "mammoth boondoggle," which would see athletic events held in widespread facilities (with few new facilities being built in San Francisco proper), creating inconveniences for local residents, and stealing precious public funds away from desperately needed city services. While the promoters of the Bay Area bid invoked the multimillion-dollar windfall that the 1984 Los Angeles games generated (implying that San Francisco would enjoy the same fate), astute observers in the gay community noted that few, if any local LA businesses profited, and that most residents stayed home and watched the games on television.[71] Interestingly, these community criticisms echo the critical academic literature in sport sociology that questions the unmitigated "good" of Olympic-style sporting spectacles.[72]

The Britt legislation was revived again in September 1987. By then, the Gay Games had lost its court case to use the word Olympic and Tom Waddell had been dead for two months. The *San Francisco Chronicle* editorial staff, in keeping with its minimal and lukewarm support for the Gay Games and gay community, suggested that Harry Britt's legislation should not be fueled by a grudgeful revenge of Waddell's unfortunate death.[73] The matter had been decided by the court once and for all, and the *Chronicle* claimed over two-thirds of San Francisco's population supported the Olympics bid. State senator Quentin Kopp, chair of the BASOC, suggested that Britt's resolution was "manifestly unfair" to the hundreds of people who worked on the bid proposal and those who supported it.[74] Of course, Kopp's claim negated and made invisible how "manifestly unfair" the USOC's legal move was to the hundreds of volunteers and participants in the first two Gay Games. Rikki Streicher, an SFAA board member, noted that in the BASOC's promotional bid package they described major, successful events that had been hosted by the Bay Area over the last fifty years, indicating the area's ability to welcome the Olympic Games. Not once were the Gay Games mentioned as an athletic event worthy of note, although the smaller Super Bowl event held at Stanford was invoked. Streicher suggested that this was simply indicative of the entrenched homophobia of the Olympics and based on that alone, she could not support the bid.[75]

The jockeying for supervisor votes and support for the Britt legislation began and carried on until March 1988.[76] At a February 4, 1988, hearing on the subject, various arguments were heard. Quentin Kopp maintained that hosting the Olympics would result in two billion dollars of income for the Bay Area and that he had the support of six supervisors, forty-five Bay Area city councils, and three major Bay Area chambers of commerce.[77] Kopp also suggested that a member of the Olympic Site Selection Committee had indicated to him during a San Francisco visit that the Bay Area would be one of two places the USOC would consider (resedimenting Helen Lenskyj's arguments that Olympic site decisions are made through insider nepotism and corruption).[78] Additionally, another USOC member confided in Kopp that he had changed his mind and now supported San Francisco's bid after visiting the city.[79] Mary Dunlap also presented counterarguments at the hearing, reinvoking the unfairness of the USOC to allow other organizations to use the word Olympic when the Gay Games could not.[80] New mayor Art Agnos officially waded into the fray two days later, stating that he opposed the Olympic bid until the USOC recognized gays and lesbians as "part of the human family."[81]

The gay community was not "one big happy family" itself on this issue. The Golden Gate Business Association (GGBA), a sort of gay and lesbian "chamber of commerce" in San Francisco, polled its board members about their support for the Britt resolution, with a resounding majority opposing it.[82] However a week later, a letter to the editor in *BAR* from four past presidents of the GGBA wholly supported the Britt resolution on the basis that dignity and human rights were more important than commercial gain[83] and another letter urged GGBA members to withdraw from the organization.[84] Letters to the editor in *BAR* suggested that Britt and the gay community should let it go, that the Olympics were larger than the narrow mindedness of USOC bigotry.

These letters suggested that a better way to express gay pride was to have the Olympics come to the city so the gay community could showcase its intelligence, integrity, professionalism, and hospitality to an international audience rather than be known for pouting and petty squabbling.[85] Others proposed that by 1996 the USOC would have come around and that gays and lesbians would have no quarrel with them by then.[86] The liberal progressive politics in these letters (slow incremental change will occur and militant defiance should be avoided) did not sit well with certain Gay Games commentators. Will Snyder suggested in a *BAR* commentary that it was time for those in positions of power (such as the USOC) to start compromising, and that the time for gays and lesbians to compromise was over.[87] It seemed the San Francisco Board of Supervisors were about to agree.

Compromise was something that Mayor Art Agnos seemed to be able to broker between the BASOC and the gay community, including Quentin Kopp, Mary Dunlap, and Harry Britt. Agnos and his office had managed to get the USOC's ear during the 1988 Calgary Winter Olympics. While making no promises, the USOC "didn't tell [them] to go to hell either," and an Agnos spokesperson added that the authority of the San Francisco mayor's office siding with the gay lobby may have influenced the USOC's decision to engage in some form of dialogue.[88] Perhaps it was this reason that Quentin Kopp and the BASOC agreed to meet with Agnos and the gay community lobby group. The two constituencies sat down together for the first time and discussed their differences, producing a five-point proposal upon which all agreed would be written into the San

Francisco/Bay Area Olympic bid.[89] The Britt Resolution was revised accordingly to be put to a vote of the San Francisco Board of Supervisors.

Following the mediation meeting with the BASOC and members of the gay community, Art Agnos drafted a letter to the USOC through Ronald Rowan (who continued to act as general counsel for the USOC). The five-page letter was consumately written, conciliatory while simultaneously demanding. Agnos invoked Waddell as a personal friend, characterizing him as a hero for dignity and proposing that the unfortunate incidents between 1982 and 1987 had clouded what should be a good relationship between the gay and lesbian athletic community and the USOC. Recognizing that the USOC would be unlikely to return the word Olympic to the Gay Games, Agnos was happy to report that this was no longer a contingent demand. The mayor then outlined the five new requirements the Bay Area had of the USOC if San Francisco were to consider hosting the 1996 Summer Olympics Games.

These conditions were (1) An antidiscrimination statement that included sexual orientation. (2) A seat on the BASOC for a member of the lesbian and gay community. (3) A commitment to supply organizational and fundraising expertise to Gay Games organizers, and help organizing Gay Games III. (4) Support for the Amateur Sports Act amendment to exempt the Gay Games from that legislation. (5) Encourage the USOC to actively lobby for changes in immigration law to not exclude homosexual visitors from the United States. Agnos ended his letter by invoking the purposes and goals of the USOC, specifically drawing attention to the sections in which the organization was bound to promote amateur athletic opportunities for *all*, and that conflicts and disputes were to be resolved swiftly in the best interests of *all* amateur athletic participants. Agnos concluded, "Your mandate encourages us to believe that the US Olympic Committee has an open door to 'encourage' and support lesbian and gay athletic events just as it does for other sporting groups."[90]

The revised Britt resolution was finally voted on and barely passed in a 6–5 decision on March 7, 1988, almost one year since it had been first tabled. And the gay community, characterized by one newspaper as the "Faggots of 'Frisco,'" quickly became Quentin Kopp's and the mainstream media's scapegoat for the imminent loss of the Olympics bid, as the five requirements of the USOC took on the entire significance for the bid's failure.[91] Even after the USOC named Minneapolis/St. Paul and Atlanta as the two prospective US city sites, Kopp persisted in his divisive political grandstanding.[92] Four supervisors signed a petition for a ballot initiative that would welcome the Olympics to San Francisco without the "ridiculous" demands of the gay community.[93] Commentators suggested there were broad deficiencies in the Bay Area proposal notwithstanding the human rights issues.[94] This reasoned approach, however, was lost in the tirade of vitriolic moralism that a gay minority was putting its rights ahead of the entire area.[95]

Garnering and maintaining the gay bloc vote in San Francisco municipal politics was taken very seriously in the late 1980s.[96] The *Sentinel* and *BAR* were full of debate and controversy over which supervisor or mayoral candidates deserved the gay vote and who voted how on gay- and lesbian-related initiatives.[97] The 1996 Olympics issue prompted gay and lesbian staff and committee members to resign in protest when the elected officials for whom they worked voted against Britt.[98] The gay community was influential enough to make or break certain municipal political careers. For instance, letters were written to Quentin Kopp, clearly stating that he had hid his homophobic politics well and that he would lose volunteer time, money, and votes at the ballot box.[99] Various gay and lesbian clubs intended to support an alternative Democratic candidate in Kopp's district and in the upcoming election planned to actively campaign against the supervisors who voted with him, and to support supervisors who had supported the Britt resolution, especially those (predictably female) candidates whose reelection was questionable.[100] The amount of political pressure and heat that the mayor and all the supervisors took from the public on this issue was enormous, most of it hostile to losing the Olympic opportunity.[101]

Conclusion

Importantly for the trajectory of understanding the history of the Gay Games, two of the five demands in the revised Britt resolution became important impetuses for the Gay Games to start to gain institutional and political credibility with the USOC and the US federal government, respectively. In particular, an information sharing meeting between the FGG and the USOC finally took place in the mid-1990s, and an immigration waiver for homosexual and HIV-positive travelers was realized under the Clinton administration for the 1994 games in New York City.[102] And into the twenty-first century, building on these institution recognition strategies, gay and lesbian athletic movement activism has meant that the international Olympic movement has recognized the inclusion of LGBT identity issues through the formal countenancing of Pride Houses, starting with the 2010 Winter Olympics in Vancouver.[103] The Gay Games movement has paralleled many other mainstream lesbian and gay human rights organizations by engaging various political and economic institutions on their hegemonic terms.

What these last three examples (the Riefenstahl film controversy, the protests against Visa, and the USOC site selection process) foreground is that the gay athletic movement was, from its inception, an assimilationist project. Each of these protests centers and privileges a certain kind of subject—a white, professional middle-class masculinity that exalts and celebrates a particular kind of athletic embodiment, economic entitlement and influence, and finally a kind of masculinist social and political capital that eventually opened the doors of a variety of powerful political institutions. While using progressive inclusion themes, and garnering other kinds of critique in support, it is not surprising to find these early seeds of homonormative strategies, compromises, and directions for this fascinating incarnation of post-Stonewall gay and lesbian athletic pride. Like many of the other "battles" of the gay rights movement (such as the fight for gay marriage or the right of homosexuals to serve in the American military), powerful (ironically) traditional and conservative political rationalities held sway. Effectively, any complaint about the immorality or revulsion of gayness was neutralized or submerged in the face of maintaining a certain kind of patriotic citizenship or securing economic advantages. Particular gay men and fewer lesbians (both characterized by white professional, class privilege, and political and organizational entitlements, skills, and networks) were able to work for, organize, and sell the Gay Games as less threatening and profitably progressive to the changing face of powerful institutions in the United States such as the USOC and the White House. Contributing to this shift was the increasing entrenchment and acceptance of neoliberal market and political logics in the 1990s and into the new millenium. In this new landscape, the professionalized gay demographic was courted as one of the new, profitable niche markets.

On the one hand, this chapter has laid out a series of losses or failures for the Gay Games and the gay community of San Francisco (the loss of the word Olympic, the death of Tom Waddell, the failed attempt to show controversial films, the unscuccessful protest of Visa, or the watered-down compromise bid conditions). On the other hand, all of these defeats have proven to be extraordinarily productive in how they contribute to the continued trajectory of the highly successful and enduring international Gay Games movement. The question that needs to continue to haunt these athletic events is for whom they are produced, and with what effects for those (other, less normative queer) communities that are largely left out.

15

The Larry Krueger Incident

Sports-Talk Radio and the Consequences of Imagery

SAMUEL O. REGALADO

As the 2005 major league season plodded along into August, the San Francisco Giants were nowhere near the team that they were in the previous year, one in which they had won ninety-one games. And their key players from that 2004 season were all, by 2005, either disabled or having a subpar year. Jason Schmidt, the club's ace pitcher who had eighteen wins in 2004, won only twelve in 2005. And Barry Bonds, who clubbed forty-five homers in 2004, a year later, mired in injuries, went on to hit only five. Amassing a paltry forty-five wins by August, the local media, as expected, routinely echoed their frustration toward the team and its manager, Felipe Alou.[1] Mired in yet another slump, criticism of the Giants took an especially volatile turn when on the evening of August 3, Larry Krueger, host of the popular radio sports-talk program called "Sportsphone 680," lambasted Alou and his Latin American players. "You have a manager in Felipe Alou whose mind has turned to Cream of Wheat," Krueger said. Continuing, he aimed his venom at the players, "I cannot watch this brand of baseball any longer. A truly awful, pathetic, old team that only promises to be worse two years from now. It's just awful and bad to watch. Brain-dead Caribbean hitters hacking at slop nightly."[2] Though the next day the talk-show host apologized for his remarks, the matter, as Krueger and the station had hoped, did not quickly subside. In fact, his rant unleashed a firestorm of protest from which the loudest voice came from the skipper, himself.

Felipe Alou, the seventy-year-old manager, was understandably outraged. That his team had not lived up to its expectations certainly played into his anger. As such, his response was sharp and pointed. "I'm going to make sure that it is known worldwide," he retorted. "I had zero means when I was a 20-year-old kid in Louisiana, but I'm 70 now. I have the means now to identify people like that. They're going to know in my country tonight. (Even) the president of my country," he added.[3] When told of the apology, the skipper refused to accept it, instead referring to Krueger as "the messenger of Satan."[4] With the lines drawn, the San Francisco sport community entered into a fray, which spoke as much about the past as it did about the present.

Since the Giants' arrival to San Francisco from New York in 1958, the team had earned a reputation for having had a considerable Latino presence on its rosters. Indeed, even though superstar Willie Mays came with the team from New York, San Franciscans, perhaps in an attempt to "wash away" all traces of New York influence, that year selected rookie sensation Puerto Rican Orlando Cepeda as the team's "Player of the Year."[5] Within a short time after Cepeda's celebrated arrival and success, the team stocked its roster with several Latin players whose skills made the Giants contenders throughout much of the 1960s. Felipe Alou, along with his brothers Mateo and Jesus, Jose Pagan, and Juan Marichal were, among others, the most prominent in a wave of Latin players who played major league baseball in that era. But their success did not come easily. The trauma of cultural adaptation effected several players. Few of them could not read English and fewer still could speak it. Furthermore, this difficulty in communication made them easy prey for mainstream columnists who often portrayed these players in unflattering ways that reiterated decades-long stereotypes of the Latin people.

Roberto Clemente, the star right fielder for the Pittsburgh Pirates, did not take kindly to the demeaning characterizations of people like himself. Having emerged as a star by the early 1960s, Clemente was not shy about expressing his opinions especially when it came to Norte Americano views about Latin players. "The Latin player doesn't get the recognition he deserves. We have self-satisfaction, yes, but after the season is over nobody cares about us," he said.[6] And Clemente was not alone in his disenchantment.

Felipe Alou made his debut with the Giants in 1959. Born twenty-one years earlier in Haina, in the Dominican Republic, Alou's upbringing was one of abject poverty. "Every penny in hand meant that much more food in the belly," he recalled. [7] Signed to a contract with the then New York Giants in 1956, the Dominican spent his initial days as a professional in Louisiana and Florida. Both spots then had rigid segregationist policies that Alou experienced firsthand. At Lake Charles, Louisiana, his time there was short lived because of a law that forbade whites and blacks from competing with one another in athletics. In three days, the Giants shipped him to Florida. There, police authorities threatened him with arrest for ordering a late-night snack at a fast-food restaurant.[8]

As a big leaguer, the Dominican excelled and by 1960 was a fixture on the team's starting lineup. Within a few short years, his two brothers, Mateo and Jesus, joined him on the club. And to augment the North American fans' fascination with this arrangement, in a 1963 game the three shared the outfield with one another.

But the ever-observant older brother remained mindful of the difficulties Latinos, like himself, shared as professional baseball players in the United States. Coincidentally, Alou's emergence as a big leaguer came at a time when Roberto Clemente's voice on the issue of the Latino image had grown loud. "I live 250 miles from Miami. But some people think I live in the jungle," Clemente angrily testified.[9] Undoubtedly taken by the Pirates' star's outspoken defense on behalf of the Latinos, Alou joined Clemente's crusade and also expressed himself on the matter. In 1963, following a dispute he had with Commissioner Ford Frick, a man the Dominican argued, "never understood the Latins and their problems."[10] Later that year, he drew up a "Bill of Rights" that called for the baseball echelons to better address Latin concerns. In December of 1965, the commissioner's office took heed of Alou's protests and, under the tenure of William D. Eckert, appointed Cuban Bobby Maduro to act as a liaison on behalf of Latinos in the majors.[11] But, in reality, it was likely another incident that occurred in 1964 that precipitated the commissioner's move.

In July of that year, while the Giants were in New York for a series against the hometown Mets, Alvin Dark, the San Francisco manager, when asked about his team's character unleashed a harsh criticism toward his players of color. Black and Latin players, he assessed, were "not able to perform up to the white ball player when it comes to mental alertness." He went on to say that they were not "sharp mentally," and that black and Latin players did not carry with them the level of pride found in the white players.[12] Those close to the Giants were not surprised at his evaluation. His relationship with his Latin players was already a difficult one. Earlier that year, he created a clubhouse rule whereby all players had to speak English, including Latin players when they spoke to one another.[13] Understandably, his Spanish-speaking players were outraged. Orlando Cepeda declared, "I would feel foolish if I spoke to [Jose] Pagan in English."[14]

Condescending perceptions regarding the Latino intellectual capabilities had roots that reached into a time well before 1964. In 1940, in a poll taken by the Office of Public Information, only 15 percent of those surveyed believed that Latin people had any intellectual capabilities.[15] In baseball, the notion of a dumb Latino was already established a decade before the poll was released. In the 1930s, for instance, the press enjoyed printing Latino responses to questions phonetically or, at best, in broken English. Player and coach Miguel "Mike" Gonzalez from Cuba was a particular favorite of the writers. His "good field, no hit" phrase by which he echoed his assessment of players was baseball's early version of the Ricky Ricardo character seen on the *I Love Lucy* television of the 1950s. And this practice continued well into the 1960s until Roberto Clemente derided reporters for depicting his interviews in a similar manner. "Anytime a fellow comes from Puerto Rico they want to create an image. They say 'Hey, he talks funny!' But they go to Puerto Rico and they don't talk like us. I don't have a master's degree, but I'm not a dumbhead."[16] Orlando Cepeda, also victimized by similar images, weighed in as well. "Latin players are always labeled as being dumb. We have to do twice as much as the American players to earn respect and a place on the team," he claimed.[17]

Even though outside of baseball, opportunities for Latinos and blacks increased after the 1960s, in echelons of major league baseball, similar opportunities were sparse and this prompted questions. The issue of alleged intellectual incapacities of ethnics in the arena of baseball exploded on April 20, 1987, during an ABC interview that was initially designed to celebrate the fortieth anniversary of Jackie Robinson's breaking of baseball's color barrier. While in discussion with host Ted Koppel, Al Campanis, the vice president of the Los Angeles Dodgers, in response to a query about the lack of blacks in the baseball hierarchy, claimed that blacks lacked "the necessities" to hold such positions, and compounded his observations with other racial stereotypes that flabbergasted Koppel. The fallout was immediate. Within days the Dodgers fired Campanis and reaction to his comments came from a number of circles. Campanis, it should be noted, was not the first notable baseball figure to make such a statement. Remarkably with much less fanfare, in a 1963 interview, Alvin Dark, when asked about blacks as possible team managers, told the reporter "baseball is not ready for colored managers."[18]

Other perceptions of black athletes also emerged. Remarkably, less than a year after the Campanis debacle, in January 1988 CBS analyst Jimmy "the Greek" Snyder commented that black athletes were, since the antebellum period, "bred." As with Campanis, Snyder's remarks sparked outrage and CBS, after disavowing Snyder, fired him from his post on the football analyst team.[19]

Snyder, of course, was not the last football analyst to create controversy on the issue of race. Rush Limbaugh, the radio personality, who ESPN hired to provide commentary on the "Sunday NFL Countdown" show for games during the 2003 season, in one broadcast targeted Philadelphia Eagles' quarterback Donovan McNabb for his lack of stellar play. Claiming that the then three-time Pro Bowler and runner-up to the NFL "Most Valuable Player" award as a rookie was not that good from "the get go," Limbaugh charged that the star player benefited from the NFL's concern for political correctness and "the media [was] desirous that a black quarterback do well."[20] As a result of the outcry that followed, Limbaugh resigned from ESPN. In that same year, KNBR in San Francisco turned to an all-sport format.

Even before Limbaugh's short-term career as a television sport analyst unceremoniously ended, sports-talk radio was already developed as a forum for dialogue and biting exchange. Years earlier, Bill Mazer was the first to introduce an interactive format to his WNBC sports-talk radio show in New York City, one that aired on March 30, 1964. "My first caller was a kid who wanted to know who I thought was better: Willie Mays or Mickey Mantle," recalled Mazer.[21] Appearing only periodically in the WNBC schedule, station managers there and elsewhere were hesitant to commit more time to Mazer's format as most listeners then deemed such shows to be "boring and uninteresting."[22] In the 1970s, John Sterling's sports-talk programs, which also aired in New York City, introduced "combined subject knowledge and a unique brand of sarcasm" to his broadcasts.[23] Still, while his approach was more contentious than his predecessors, Sterling and others "maintained their poise and marked degree of decorum" so as not to embarrass their stations nor the teams in their regions.[24] In the 1980s, however, Pete Franklin, operating out of Cleveland with his show called "Sportline," drew attention for his more abrasive and critical assessment of teams and players, and biting exchanges with callers. Franklin's approach was such that his show landed a nationally syndicated spot on the airwaves.[25]

In 1987, WFAN in New York City adopted all-sport programming. So successful was this move that in the span of a decade the station reached the $50 million mark in advertising billing, the first to do so in radio.[26] By the early nineties, other all-sport programming appeared in several other cities, including those with limited access to high-profile teams. Salt Lake City, for instance, with only one professional team, the Utah Jazz of the National Basketball Association, in its locale, nonetheless, had four all-sport radio stations operating in its midst.[27] In 1992, ESPN, which had aired round-the-clock televised sport coverage since 1979, introduced "ESPN Radio" and aired it nationally from its base in Connecticut.

KNBR began its broadcasts of the Giants in 1979. Up until 2003, the station had regular music and news programming. However, in that year, with ratings having dipped, station managers opted to adopt an exclusive sports programming format. Larry Krueger had, to that point, been with the station since 1996. Three years later, the California State University, Sacramento, graduate was one of a number of those who commented on sports under the old system. But under the new format, the station promoted Krueger to sports director and his "Sportsphone 680" was his marquee program. As with other sports-talk show hosts around the country, Krueger's approach to guests and the targets of his criticism was aggressive and, at times, ruthless. Even before the 2005 fiasco with the Latinos, for instance, Krueger had lobbied to oust Felipe's Alou's predecessor, Dusty Baker.

Baker managed the club from 1993 through the 2002 season. During those years he captured an unprecedented three "Manager of the Year" awards, finished second place or higher on the National League's Western Division in all but two seasons, and came five outs away from winning San Francisco's first World Series title on the West Coast in 2002. Yet, this failed to impress Krueger, whose late-night rants targeted Baker on a seemingly nightly basis. Joan Walsh, a San Francisco resident and liberal political columnist, who in 2002 covered local issues, in a story about Baker's unceremonious firing that year claimed that Krueger's comments to her about Baker "skirted on the edges of racism."[28] Similar to Limbaugh's rants against McNabb in 2003, Krueger called Baker "overrated," and, as reported by Walsh, maintained the skipper was "a charismatic players' manager who relied on hunches, not baseball smarts, to run his game, was too loyal to his favorites, and got away with all of it because writers were reluctant to criticize a minority manager."[29]

Rhetoric that targeted political correctness was popular in the sport commentary world of talk radio. Inflammatory dialogue that seemingly had no boundaries was already popular in San Francisco and beyond. Bay Area listeners were not unfamiliar with this style even outside of sports. In fact, by 2005, a competing station, KSFO, then housed Michael Savage, who billed himself as being "To the right of Rush and to the left of God." Savage's acerbic political commentary on his "Savage Nation" broadcasts had a huge national audience. Thus, Krueger was quite in step with his contemporaries, as they fought to outdo themselves for ratings. Successful in his endeavors with Baker, the "Sportsphone 680" host approached Felipe Alou in a similar manner. Only this time, the results were not as Krueger had expected.

Baseball, by then, was already sitting on a minefield when it came to controversial and insensitive comments made by sportscasters. Only a year before, Steve Lyons, Fox Sports baseball television analyst and former major leaguer, launched a lengthy commentary on Shawn Green, then an outfielder for the Los Angeles Dodgers who was Jewish, for the player's decision not to play on Yom Kippur. "He's not even a practicing Jew," bellowed Lyons. "He didn't marry a Jewish girl. And from what I understand, he never had a bar mitzvah, which is unfortunate because he doesn't get the money."[30] Lyons continued in his capacity at Fox until the fall of 2006, when, in another stumble whereby he characterized Lou Piniella, Venezuelan ballplayer Marco Scutaro and, by extension, their Latin heritage with the habits of a thief, the Network fired him.[31]

However, as Krueger had demonstrated, sports-talk radio was, in many respects, even more susceptible than television to such on-air charges. Writing for *Slate* in 2006, Robert Weintraub reasoned that such behavior came as a result of "the sheer tonnage of live airtime."[32] With round-the-clock commentary on sports, accompanied with interviews and other related events, "it's no surprise that [discourse is] not all Daniel Webster-level oratory."[33] Weintraub went on further to attribute partial blame to the Internet, as it advanced easier fan access to sports programs. "The Internet has empowered citizen critics to fan the flames of outrage, spotlight offensive statements . . . and [possibly] have their voices heard by the networks," he wrote.[34] As well, boorish and extremely offensive language was also legally safe to express. Writing on the legal latitude afforded to sports broadcast discourse, Allison McDonald pointed out "the FCC [Federal Communications Commission] does not focus on language that includes racial, ethnic, religious or homophobic slurs."[35] Only comments of a "sexual nature" were outside of the bounds of legal protection. In short, she concluded, "The First Amendment does not protect feelings, only speech."[36]

Unwilling to sit by and simply absorb the comments, Alou and other Latinos exercised their own free speech rights and went on the offensive. After pulling his own talk-show program from the KNBR schedule, Alou told the press that "I heard [comments like these] in the South, and some other cities, but not here. It tells me that a man like me and the Latin guys have to be aware it's not over yet, or it is coming back."[37] Backing up their manager, Edgardo Alfonzo took aim at Krueger and claimed, "It was a stupid and racist comment. It would have to come from someone who's brain-dead himself."[38] Omar Visquel, among the most respected of all players in the big leagues, was "insulted" by the comments and called them worse than those made in 1999 by Atlanta Braves' pitcher John Rocker about ethnics.[39]

For its part, KNBR sought to minimize the damage by omitting the comments from the transcript and censoring any further discussion of the topic, which angered white ballplayer J. T. Snow. "It's kind of a double standard for a guy to be able to make those comments and for players not to be able to react to them," he said.[40] For two full days following the August 3 broadcast, the station seemed unsure about its direction. After Tony Salvadore, the station's vice president, initially declared Krueger to be "a terrific employee for the eight-plus years," he suspended Krueger for a week without pay.[41] But this action failed to satisfy Alou and his supporters like his son who weighed in and reminded the public of the larger scenario of the Latino experience, one that bore an uncanny resemblance of the past. "In the minor leagues, people think all Dominicans, Mexicans and Venezuelans are dumb," said an angry Moises Alou. "You think if a guy doesn't speak English it's because he's stupid."[42]

While Krueger sat at home awaiting his fate, *San Francisco Chronicle* writers began to weigh in. Columnist Gwen Knapp criticized the station for having stonewalled two days before taking action against Krueger and, pointing to Alou's history at confronting racial discrimination, added that the Giants' manager "had

50 years' worth of things to say."[43] But he challenged the critics who defended the "Sportsphone 680" host by painting him as a person victimized by political correctness. "Krueger isn't a victim of political correctness," she retorted. "The people who uttered the slur invariably look sympathetic, because they are individuals under attack, with microphones in the face and lots of explaining to do." Scott Ostler, on the contrary, maintained only that Krueger's rant was simply a "poor choice of words." And, in an attempt to balance blame, suggested that Alou had "slipped on a banana peel" when he refused to accept Krueger's apology.[44] By the end of the week, the story had gone national and was the butt of jokes. Comedy Central's *South Park* aired a comical version of the Krueger fiasco in one of its episodes. And *Saturday Night Live* did much the same in its "Church Lady" segment, reprising the Alou "messenger of Satan" comment.[45]

None of this amused Tony Salvadore. By then he was forced to patch up relations with the ball club itself, which had a financial interest in KNBR. Moreover, as the story drew national attention, Susquehanna Radio Corporation, which owned KNBR, grew very uncomfortable and dismayed that the story remained a news item.[46] On his own midmorning show, KNBR's Gary Radnich echoed the pressure seen at the station. "One more log on the fire with a big million-dollar corporation like this, you're talking FCC licenses, you're talking about a lot of repercussions."[47]

The end for Krueger came less than a week after his controversial broadcast. Along with the talk-show host, his program director and morning-show producer also were fired. Alou, who had earlier sent mixed signals about what should be done to Krueger, responded, "I think it is very unfortunate that a man, or a number of men, had to lose their jobs over a thing like this." In an effort to contextualize the episode, he added that his objective was to "make people aware that this is not to be tolerated, to degrade a race of people or people from a region."[48] The station simply refused to comment further on the matter. Salvadore, himself, returned no phone call and nor did Krueger immediately respond.[49] Some callers into the station reacted harshly. "Alou's got the blood of three families on his hands," said one.[50] A week past the firings, *Chronicle* writer Bruce Jenkins wrote a piece that, as Gwen Knapp had earlier observed, described Krueger as a victim of political correctness. Krueger, the family man, was now out of a job, Jenkins wrote. He went on to say, "The firestorm was justified and appropriate—for a while. Once Alou took it to the extreme with his satanic reference, it became a parade of lunacy."[51] To Jenkins, Krueger's absence left a "void" to the sports listenership in the Bay Area.[52]

Such sentiments, it should be noted, were absent when Dusty Baker lost his job three years earlier, in part a result of Krueger's campaign to get the manager fired. The Larry Krueger incident was, by 2005, then the most recent episode of racially laced connotations that did not begin with his August 3 comments, but had roots that reached well into the Giants' history in San Francisco with the most explicit example found in the Alvin Dark comments of the 1960s. Questions regarding the intellectual capacities of nonwhites was a consistent theme found not only in the Dark assessment, but had advocates who echoed this position well into the twenty-first century. And the roster of these proponents came from baseball management and high-profile media spokespeople, and some of whom worked outside of baseball. More so, the incident revealed, or at the very least highlighted the fact that critics of "politically correctness" had a comfortable home in the world of sports. Athletic competition, it appeared, gave radio commentators license to portray and illuminate aged-old stereotypes that targeted ethnic minorities for generations. "Trash talking" in a demeaning manner was clearly not confined to the field of play. And, in that sad respect, Larry Krueger was a product of his time.

Bill Mazer, who hosted the first interactive sports-talk program in 1964, passed away in 2013. While his segment was reasonably popular, not until the late 1980s did his format really catch fire. Unfortunately, its popularity grew not as a result of respectful discourse between fans and hosts, but because hosts intentionally sought to ignite controversy on topics that inflamed their listeners. As they contested for ratings and notoriety, their rhetoric often grew more bombastic and aggressive. As well, they often tapped into a segment of the public angry over issues related to what they complained to be "politically correct" and other such perceived sensitivities. As well, referring, as writer Michael Harrison did in *Talkers Magazine*, to sports-talk radio listeners as being "emotionally engaged," stations like KNBR tapped into an audience that was largely white and overwhelmingly male.[53] And it was this profile of listeners who found in "Sportsphone 680," and others like it, a sanctuary for their frustrations that their hosts played upon.

Seven years after his firing, Larry Krueger's exile came to an end when KNBR re-signed the former "messenger of Satan" to a two-year contract. Krueger, to his credit, spoke little of the 2005 controversy only to say that his own actions had caused his demise. Felipe Alou retired following the 2006 campaign. Shortly thereafter, Brian Sabean, general manager of the Giants, hired the former skipper to be his special assistant, a position that was, apparently, one to be held in perpetuity. Like Krueger, Alou remained mute on the infamous KNBR broadcast and its immediate and explosive aftermath. By 2012, both were once again part of the San Francisco baseball scene, as they were seven years earlier. Of course, it need be said that Bruce Bochy, a competent baseball manager who was white, replaced Alou and continues to manage the club today. With the club's fortunes having improved in recent years, along with the fresh memory of the Krueger incident, all remained peaceful in the waters of the San Francisco's baseball world, at least for now.

Notes

Introduction

1. "Parade, Large Rally Celebrate Warriors' Long-Awaited NBA Title," *ESPN*, June 19, 2015, accessed November 25, 2015, http://espn.go.com/nba/playoffs/2015/story/_/id/13115607/golden-state-warriors-parade-celebrate-nba-title.

2. "Thousands Celebrate Golden State Warriors in Oakland," *KCRA News*, June 19, 2015, accessed November 25, 2015, http://www.kcra.com/news/nba-champion-warriors-fans-ready-to celebrate/33674608. In 1962 the Philadelphia Warriors relocated the franchise to San Francisco and named the San Francisco Warriors. By the 1971–1972 season, the team was playing most of its games in Oakland and was renamed the Golden State Warriors.

3. Deane A. Lamont, "Pierre de Coubertin in San Francisco," *Journal of Olympic History* 13, no. 3 (November 2005): 38–42.

4. "Lenz' World Tour Awheel: From Siskyou to San Francisco," *Outing* 22, no. 4 (July 1893): 311.

5. Ibid. For more on Lenz and his cross-country trip, and his post-American bike ride, see David V. Herlihy, *The Lost Cyclist: The Epic Tale of an American Adventurer and His Mysterious Disappearance* (New York: Houghton Mifflin Harcourt, 2010).

6. Tom White, "California in Winter: San Francisco Area Puts Sports High on List of Its Activities," *New York Times*, December 15, 1940, Section 11, 7.

7. Dick Heller, "The Way It Was: A's Ruled Early '70s," *Washington Post*, October 13, 2009, accessed November 26, 2015, http://www.washingtontimes.com/news/2009/oct/13/the-way-it-was-no-disagreement-as-ruled-early-70s/?page=all. For more on the Oakland A's successes in the 1970s, see Bruce Markusen, *Baseball's Last Dynasty: Charlie Finley's Oakland A's* (Indianapolis, IN: Masters Press, 1998). For a more recent analysis of the Oakland A's, see Michael Lewis, *Moneyball: The Art of Winning an Unfair Game* (New York: W. W. Norton & Company, 2004).

8. There is no shortage of books written about the area's most renowned franchise. A search on Amazon for books about the San Francisco 49ers produces over 6,000 results.

9. The San Francisco Giants have won three World Series titles over the last five seasons. The team relocated to San Francisco for the 1958 season. Similar to the 49ers, there is no shortage for books about the baseball franchise. For just a sampling of articles written about the team's half-century history in California, see Robert F. Garratt, "Horace Stoneham and the Breaking of Baseball's Second Color Barrier," *NINE: A Journal of Baseball History and Culture* 22, no. 2 (2014): 42–53; Larry R. Gerlach, "Crime and Punishment: The Marichal-Roseboro Incident," *NINE: A Journal of Baseball History and Culture* 12, no. 2 (2004): 1–28. Professional baseball was a popular pastime prior to the arrival of major league baseball with the Pacific Coast League; for example, see Steve Treder, "Open Classification: The Pacific Coast League's Drive to Turn Major," *NINE: A Journal of Baseball History and Culture* 15, no. 1 (2006): 88–109.

10. The six universities currently competing at the NCAA Division I level are the University of California, Berkeley; Stanford University; Santa Clara University; San Jose

State University; Saint Mary's College of California; and the University of San Francisco. San Jose State athletics and its role in the 1968 Olympic Games, and the broader civil rights movement, have been well detailed in previous publications. For example, see Amy Bass, *Not the Triumph but the Struggle: The 1968 Olympics and the Making of the Black Athlete* (Minneapolis: University of Minnesota Press, 2002); Douglas Hartmann, *Race, Culture, and the Revolt of the Black Athlete: The 1968 Olympic Protests and Their Aftermath* (Chicago: University of Chicago Press, 2004); Herbert G. Ruffin II, "'Doing the Right Thing for the Sake of Doing the Right Thing': The Revolt of the Black Athlete and the Modern Student-Athletic Movement, 1956–2014," *Western Journal of Black Studies* 38, no. 4 (2014): 260–78; Maureen M. Smith, "Frozen Fists in Speed City: The Statue as Twenty-First-Century Reparations," *Journal of Sport History* 36, no. 3 (2009): 401–20. The University of San Francisco's heyday in athletics came with their two NCAA basketball titles in 1955 and 1956, led by Basketball Hall of Famer and local star Bill Russell. For more on Russell's life growing up in Oakland and attending USF, see Aram Goudsouzian, *King of the Court: Bill Russell and the Basketball Revolution* (Berkeley: University of California Press, 2010).

11. "Cardinal Athletics," http://facts.stanford.edu/campuslife/athletics, accessed November 29, 2015.

12. The Bay Area Sports Hall of Fame is one local organization that honors and recognizes athletes and coaches who were born and raised in the Bay Area, as well as those who competed for Bay Area teams. While many of the inductees are honored with plaques at the San Francisco International Airport, Terminal 3, other plaques are located at Bay Area sporting facilities. The hall of fame welcomed their first class of inductees in 1980. With over 150 members, the hall of fame includes female and male athletes and coaches, introducing many visitors to the area to less familiar female athletes who've not been written about as much as their male counterparts, including tennis star of the 1920s Helen Wills Moody, swimmer Ann Curtis, Olympic and ABL/WNBA basketball star Jennifer Azzi, and Olympic ice skater Peggy Fleming. Two hall of fame members are written about in this collection, tennis player Rosie Casals (Class of 2003) and Olympic swimmer Donna de Varona (Class of 1987); see Rita Liberti "Rebel with a Racket: Rosie Casals," and Maureen M. Smith and Matthew R. Hodler "Pioneers in the Pool: The Santa Clara Swim Club Mermaids of the 1950s and 1960s," respectively.

13. Mel Scott, *San Francisco Bay Area: A Metropolis in Perspective* (Berkeley: University of California Press, 1985), 2–22.

14. Katia Savchuk, "California Has More Billionaires Than Every Country Except the U.S. and China," *Forbes*, March 4, 2015, accessed November 28, 2015, http://www.forbes.com/sites/katiasavchuk/2015/03/04/california-has-more-billionaires-than-every-country-except-the-u-s-and-china/. For additional readings on the recreational, sporting, and physical activities of the citizens of the greater Bay Area, as opposed to professional athletes and teams, see, for example, Chandra Bhat and Allison Lockwood, "On Distinguishing between Physically Active and Physically Passive Episodes and between Travel and Activity Episodes: An Analysis of Weekend Recreational Participation in the San Francisco Bay Area," *Transportation Research Part A: Policy and Practice* 38, no. 8 (2004): 573–92; Robert Cervero and Michael Duncan, "Walking, Bicycling, and Urban Landscapes: Evidence from the San Francisco Bay Area," *American Journal of Public Health* 93, no. 9 (2003): 1478–83; Esther M. John, Pamela L. Horn-Ross, and Jocelyn Koo, "Lifetime Physical Activity and Breast Cancer Risk in a Multiethnic Population: The San Francisco Bay Area Breast Cancer Study," *Cancer Epidemiology Biomarkers & Prevention* 12, no. 11 (2003): 1143–52; Susan G.

Zieff, Mi-Sook Kim, Jackson Wilson, and Patrick Tierney, "A 'Ciclovia' in San Francisco: Characteristics and Physical Activity Behavior of Sunday Streets Participants," *Journal of Physical Activity & Health* 11, no. 2 (2014): 249–55.

15. Alyssa Cymene Howe, "Queer Pilgrimage: The San Francisco Homeland and Identity Tourism," *Cultural Anthropology* 16, no. 1 (2001): 38.

16. Anthony Ashbolt, *A Cultural History of the Radical Sixties in the San Francisco Bay Area* (London, England: Pickering & Chatto, 2013), 30.

17. Nan Alamilla Boyd, *Wide-Open Town: A History of Queer San Francisco to 1965* (Berkeley: University of California Press, 2003), 3.

18. Ryan Bort, "The Tech Industry Is Stripping San Francisco of Its Culture and Your City Could Be Next," *Newsweek,* October 1, 2015, accessed November 28, 2015, http://www.newsweek.com/san-francisco-tech-industry-gentrification-documentary-378628. See also, Julie Carrie Wong, "Dropbox, Airbnb, and the Fight over San Francisco's Public Spaces," *New Yorker,* October 23, 2014, accessed November 30, 2015, http://www.newyorker.com/tech/elementsdropbox-airbnb-fight-san-franciscos-public-spaces.

19. For more on the region's hiking and use of outdoor space, see Rita M. Liberti, "Trailblazing in Marin: Women's Dipsea Hikes, 1918–1922," *California History* 81, no. 1 (2002): 54–65. For more on the history of San Francisco's parks, see Richard Walker, *The Country in the City: The Greening of the San Francisco Bay Area* (Seattle: University of Washington Press, 2009); Terence Young, *Building San Francisco's Parks, 1850–1930* (Baltimore: Johns Hopkins University Press, 2004).

20. Steven A. Riess, "Historical Perspectives on Sport and Public Policy," *Policy Studies Review* 15, no. 1 (1998): 5.

21. Fred Farmer, "Movement Now in Full Swing to Construct Municipal Stadium for San Francisco," *San Francisco Bulletin,* October 13, 1920, 20.

22. Roger W. Lotchin, "California Cities and the Hurricane of Change: World War II in the San Francisco, Los Angeles, and San Diego Metropolitan Areas," *Pacific Historical Review* 63, no. 3 (1994): 398.

23. Lawrence E. Davies, "Spirited Politics in San Francisco," *New York Times,* May 24, 1959, L53.

24. John Cote, "Behind the 49ers Stadium Mess," July 12, 2009, accessed November 29, 2015, http://www.sfgate.com/49ers/article/Behind-the-49ers-stadium-mess 3224387.php.

25. The coeditors of this collection have both written previously about various sporting locations in the Bay Area. For example, see Liberti, "Trailblazing in Marin." Maureen M. Smith, "Willie Mays Plaza, McCovey Point, and the Dominican Dandy in Bronze: (De) Constructing History at AT&T Park in San Francisco," *Journal of the West* 47, no. 4 (2008): 60–69; Maureen M. Smith, "From 'The Finest Ballpark in America' to 'The Jewel of the Waterfront': The Construction of San Francisco's Major League Baseball Stadium," in *The Rise of Stadiums in the Modern United States: Cathedrals of Sport* (Sport in the Global Society), ed. Mark Dyreson and Robert Trumpbour (London: Routledge, 2009).

26. Kathleen S. Yep, *Outside the Paint: When Basketball Ruled at the Chinese Playground* (Philadelphia: Temple University Press, 2005).

27. Susan G. Zieff, "From Badminton to the Bolero: Sport and Recreation in San Francisco's Chinatown, 1895–1950," *Journal of Sport History* 27, no. 1 (2000): 1–28.

28. Roberta J. Park, "Sport and Recreation among Chinese American Communities of the Pacific Coast from Time of Arrival to the 'Quiet Decade of the 1950s,'" *Journal of Sport*

History 27, no. 3 (2000): 445–80; Roberta J. Park, "German Associational and Sporting Life in the Greater San Francisco Bay Area, 1850–1900," *Journal of the West* 26, no. 1 (1987): 47–64; Roberta J. Park, "San Franciscans at Work and at Play, 1846–1869," *Journal of the West* 22 (1983): 44–51; Roberta J. Park, "Time Given Freely to Worthwhile Causes: Anna S. Espenschade's Contributions to Physical Education," *Research Quarterly for Exercise and Sport* 71, no. 2 (2000): 99–115; Roberta J. Park, "From Football to Rugby—and Back, 1906–1919: The University of California-Stanford University Response to the Football Crisis of 1905," *Journal of Sport History* 11, no. 3 (1984): 5–40.

29. Deane Anderson Lamont, "Oakland: The Bay Area's Playing Field," *Journal of the West* 48, no. 1 (2009): 58–72. Also see Deane A. Lamont, *America's "Healthiest" City: A History of Early Oakland, California* (Saarbrücken, Germany: VDM, 2010).

1. Oakland's Nineteenth-Century Parks and Resorts: "Lungs of the City," Commercial Sporting Venues, and Instruments of Civic Boosterism

1. Frank Clinton Merritt, *History of Alameda County, California* (Chicago: S. J. Clarke, 1928), 220, and *Alameda County Illustrated: Eden of the Pacific* (n.p., Oakland Tribune, 1898). The second publication listed above is a part of the collection held in the Bancroft Library at the University of California at Berkeley, hereafter cited as BLUC.

2. John R. Betts, "Public Recreation, Public Parks, and Public Health before the Civil War," in *Proceedings of the Big Ten Symposium on the History of Physical Education and Sport*, ed. Bruce L. Bennett (Chicago: Athletic Institute, 1971), 46–47.

3. Lemuel Shattuck, *Report of the Sanitary Commission of Massachusetts, 1850* (Cambridge, MA: Harvard University Press, 1948), 166, and *Promotion of Public and Personal Health* (Boston: Dutton & Wentworth, 1850).

4. Steven A. Riess, *City Games: The Evolution of American Urban Society and the Rise of Sports* (Urbana: University of Illinois Press, 1991), 42.

5. John Duffy, *The Sanitarians: A History of American Public Health* (Urbana: University of Illinois Press, 1991), 33. A number of those engaged in the mid-century urban park movement also thought that exercise in the outdoors was necessary for the maintenance of optimal health. This notion allied them with the numerous antebellum health reformers who were pushing the efficacy of various forms of gymnastics and calisthenics at that time. This tacit alliance was well described in 1857 by Egbert Viele, a civil engineer and planner of New York City's Central Park, who declared that both "air and exercise" were a "necessary sanitary provision." "Public Recreation, Public Parks, and Public Health before the Civil War," 41–47.

6. Shattuck, *Report of the Sanitary Commission of Massachusetts, 1850*, 166.

7. Duffy, *The Sanitarians*, 33, and Riess, *City Games*, 42–46. In 1856, Olmstead formed a partnership with Calvert Vaux. Together, in competition with thirty-two others, they submitted their design for the creation of New York's Central Park. Their plan was awarded first prize. Raymond H. Clary, *The Making of Golden Gate Park: The Early Years, 1865–1906* (San Francisco: California Living Books, 1980).

8. Clary, *The Making of Golden Gate Park*, 2. See also, *Golden Gate Park* (San Francisco: Golden Gate Media Productions, 1987), 6. Additionally, John P. Young, *San Francisco: A History of the Pacific Coast Metropolis* (San Francisco: S. J. Clarke, 1912), 581–82.

9. Frederick Law Olmstead's plans for Mountain View Cemetery are to be found in the Oakland Miscellany Collection (vol. 3) in the BLUC. See also "Historic Cemetery Bears

Architect's Vision," *Oakland Tribune*, December 10, 1995, and Clary, *The Making of Golden Gate Park*, 2.

10. See John Heinitz, "The Early Development of Lake Merritt, Oakland, California: 1852–1907" (Master's thesis, California State University, Hayward, 1992).

11. DeWitt Jones, ed., *Oakland Parks and Playgrounds* (Oakland: Oakland Free Library, 1935), 16.

12. "Annual Message of W. R. Andus, Mayor of the City of Oakland, Cal.," in *Supplement* to the *Oakland Daily Evening Tribune*, February 4, 1879.

13. Edgar J. Hinkel and William E. McCann, ed., *Oakland 1852–1938: Some Phases of the Social, Political and Economic History of Oakland, California* (Oakland: Oakland Public Library, 1939), 749.

14. Mayor Davis's vision would not be completed until well into the first decade of the following century. For details of the development of Lake Merritt, see "The Early Development of Lake Merritt, Oakland, California: 1852–1907."

15. "Message of William R. Davis, Mayor of Oakland," in *Oakland Daily Evening Tribune*, October 4, 1887. For detailed information on Oakland's self boosterism, see Deane A. Lamont, "Sport and Leisure in the Building of an Urban Community: The Case of Oakland, California 1850–1906" (Doctoral diss., University of California at Berkeley, 1996), particularly chapter 5, "City Building."

16. *Oakland Daily Evening Tribune, Special Illustrated Edition*, January 20, 1887, in Elizabeth L. Bagwell, *Oakland: The Story of a City* (Novato, CA: Presidio Press, 1982), 123–26.

17. Jones, *Oakland Parks and Playgrounds*, 21–22.

18. *A Directory of the City of Oakland* (Oakland: Strickland & Company, 1878), 71.

19. Bagwell, *Oakland*, 157.

20. The site of the trotting park and the later adjacent resort is in modern-day Emeryville that was incorporated as a neighboring town to Oakland in 1896. Frank Clinton Merritt, *History of Alameda County, California* (Chicago: S. J. Clarke, 1928), 156.

21. Donald Hausler, "The Emeryville Horse Race Track: 1871–1915," *Journal of the Emeryville Historical Society* 5, no. 1 (1994): 3–6. For general comments, see also Jones, *Oakland Parks and Playgrounds*, 240–42.

22. *Oakland Tribune*, February 20, 1934.

23. *Oakland Daily Transcript*, August 17, 1874.

24. "The Emeryville Horse Race Track: 1871–1915," 6–7.

25. *Oakland Tribune*, February 20, 1934.

26. The first field day had been held at "Oakland's Cricket Grounds" (possibly Badger's Park). *The Blue and Gold* (Oakland: Daily Evening Tribune Steam Printing House, 1880), 28.

27. *The Pacific Life*, November 27, 1880. Also, 1880's *The Blue and Gold*.

28. Hausler, "The Emeryville Horse Race Track," 7–9. See also Donald Hausler's article "Emeryville's Black Turfmen" in the winter 1991 newsletter of the Northern California Center for Afro-American History and Life.

29. Hinkel and McCann, *Oakland 1852–1938*, 755.

30. Hausler, "The Emeryville Horse Race Track," 7–13. Also, Leon F. Litwack and Winthrop D. Jordan, *The United States: Becoming a World Power* (Englewood Cliffs, NJ: Prentice-Hall, 1991), 569–82.

31. For details regarding militias in the Bay Area during the second half of the nineteenth century, see R. A. Burchell, *The San Francisco Irish: 1848–1880* (Berkeley: University

of California Press, 1980), and Roberta J. Park, "German Associational and Sporting Life in the Greater San Francisco Bay Area, 1850–1900," *Journal of the West* 26 (1987).

32. Jones, *Oakland Parks and Playgrounds*, 240–42. One such club was the *Deutcher Krieger Verein*.

33. Ibid., 242–44. Also, "German Associational and Sporting Life in the Greater San Francisco Bay Area, 1850–1900."

34. Jones, *Oakland Parks and Playgrounds*, 242–44.

35. Ibid., and for a map image, visit http://oaklandhistory.tumblr.com/post/76951244001/badgers-grand-central-park.

36. Jones, *Oakland Parks and Playgrounds*, 247–49.

37. *Oakland Morning Times*, May 17, 1879. The track at times may have featured races, but the Badger's Park facility seems more often to have served as a site for training horses destined to run at Oakland Trotting Park. The absence of regular competition was probably due to city anti-betting ordinances.

38. Jones, *Oakland Parks and Playgrounds*, 249–50. See also, "Sea Captain Paved Way for Oakland's Lake Festivities," *Oakland Tribune*, June 4, 1995. There are many baseball histories that capture the rise of the sport in northern California. See for example: D. Dobbins and J. Twichell, *Nuggets on the Diamond: Professional Baseball in the Bay Area from the Gold Rush to the Present* (San Francisco: Woodford Press, 1994); F. W. Lange, *History of Baseball in California and Pacific Coast Leagues, 1847–1938* (Oakland: n.p., 1938); and K. Nelson, *The Golden Game: The Story of California Baseball* (San Francisco: California Historical Society Press, 2004).

39. Jones, *Oakland Parks and Playgrounds*, 249–50. Also *Oakland Tribune*, June 4, 1995.

40. For an example of the social (including the role of the beer garden) and work lives of Germans in a nineteenth-century American city, see Kathleen Neils Conzen, *Immigrant Milwaukee, 1836–1860: Accommodation and Community in a Frontier City* (Cambridge, MA: Harvard University Press, 1976).

41. Jones, *Oakland Parks and Playgrounds*, 261–63.

42. Douglas S. Brookes, "The Early Years of the Dimond District," *Oakland Heritage Alliance News* 6, no. 3 (1986). See also, Jones, *Oakland Parks and Playgrounds*, 261–63.

43. Merritt, *History of Alameda County*, 533.

44. Jones, *Oakland Parks and Playgrounds*, 252–53. See also, *Montclarion*, December 19, 1995.

45. *Oakland Daily Evening Tribune*, January 20, 1887.

46. Jones, *Oakland Parks and Playgrounds*, 266.

47. Robert Sibley, ed., *The Golden Book of California* (Berkeley: California Alumni Association, 1937).

48. Jones, *Oakland Parks and Playgrounds*, 267–69, and the *Oakland Daily Evening Tribune*, January 20, 1887. Jeffries was goaded out of retirement in 1910 only to be defeated by Jack Johnson the first black world heavyweight champion in arguably the most notorious world championship fight ever held. It was originally planned that the fight would take place at the former Oakland racetrack, but legal concerns saw it moved to San Francisco and then Reno, Nevada. Johnson defeated Jeffries in the fifteenth of forty-five scheduled rounds in the sweltering heat on July 4, 1910. For details of the fight's planning, see the *San Francisco Call*, May 19, 1910.

49. Lois Rather, *Oakland's Image: A History of Oakland, California* (Oakland: Rather Press, 1972), 56.

50. Between 1870 and 1880, Oakland had grown from a city with some 14,000 inhabitants to a population of over 42,000; yet, it remained far from the 250,000 residents that San Francisco, the Pacific Coast's commercial center, had attained by 1880.

51. For useful summaries of Lewis's work, see Fred E. Leonard and George B. Affleck, *A Guide to the History of Physical Education* (Philadelphia: Lea & Febiger, 1947), 255–67; James Whorton's *Crusaders for Fitness,* 275–81; and Harvey Green's *Fit for America.*

52. Dioclesian Lewis, *Oakland (California): Its Climate, Etc.* (San Francisco: Cubery & Company, 1877). The pamphlet that contains Lewis's "Address to the Oakland Real Estate and Merchant's Exchange of March 31, 1877," BLUC.

53. Lewis's attachment to the East drew him out of his California "retirement" after only three years. He died in Yonkers, New York, on May 21, 1886. *A Guide to the History of Physical Education*, 255–67.

54. Hinkel and McCann, *Oakland 1852–1938*, 130–32.

55. Ibid., 133–34. Though the improvement of Lake Merritt was planned and desired by many for years, it wasn't until 1898 that construction of the boulevard around the lake finally began.

56. Lois Rather, *Oakland's Image: A History of Oakland, California* (Oakland: Rather Press, 1972), 56.

57. A special edition of the *Oakland Morning Times*, September 2, 1886.

58. Ibid., September 3, 1886.

59. A special edition of the *Oakland Daily Evening Tribune*, January 20, 1887.

60. *Oakland, California* (n.p.: Oakland Board of Trade, 1886), 1–5, BLUC.

61. *Catalogue and Price List of Oakland Real Estate* issued by William J. Dingee (Oakland: Pacific Press, 1887), 4–6.

62. Advertisement in special edition of *Oakland's Daily Evening Tribune*, January 20, 1887.

63. Because Oakland was located at the base of foothills whose streams and rivers emptied into a tidal lake and estuary much of the effluvia produced by its inhabitants was washed out into the San Francisco Bay.

64. *Oakland Tribune Illustrated Special Edition*, January 1888, 17.

65. Hinkel and McCann, *Oakland 1852–1938*, 145. Though the Exchange espoused encouragement for "immigration" to Oakland, not all ethnicities were welcomed. Just as other merchant groups in the 1870s had been concerned with Chinese street merchants operating in their city, so too was the Exchange worried that the Chinese (many of whom seemed to come daily from San Francisco) were taking their trade and paying "not a cent of rent or license."

66. *Facts & Figures of Oakland*, 1896 (n.p., n.d.), BLUC.

67. George W. Calderwood and G. T. Loofbourow, *Oakland: "Athens of the Pacific"* also *Facts and Figures of Alameda County*, 81. See page 91 regarding the racetrack's spectator capacity. A booklet, BLUC.

68. *Alameda County Illustrated: Eden of the Pacific* (n.p., *Oakland Tribune*, 1898), BLUC.

69. Hinkel and McCann, *Oakland 1852–1938*, 139–45. In 1910, the Oakland Chamber of Commerce revived the sightseeing idea. In that year, twice daily around the city automobile tours were introduced.

70. *Oakland Enquirer*, November 13, 1905.

71. Rather, *Oakland's Image*, 62–69.

72. With regard to the half-million figure, see Hinkel and McCann, *Oakland 1852–1938*, 161. See also the Oakland Chamber of Commerce *Bulletin* 1 (4), April 1910, BLUC.

73. Oakland Chamber of Commerce *Bulletin* 1 (4), April 1910, BLUC.

74. For an example, see *Oakland, California.* A magazine featuring a lavish color frontispiece was "issued" by the Oakland Chamber of Commerce, though "published" by the Sunset Magazine Homeseekers' Bureau of Information, circa 1911, BLUC. This publication contains a comprehensive survey of Oakland's various recreational attractions.

75. Oakland Chamber of Commerce *Bulletin* 1 (9), September 1910, BLUC.

76. This information is drawn from Hinkel and McCann, *Oakland 1852–1938*, 826–27, and Peter Thomas Conmy, *The Beginnings of Oakland, California* (Oakland: Oakland Public Library, 1961), 45. See also the data concerning Oakland in the eighth (1860) through the thirteenth (1910) United States Census reports. The information concerning Oakland's parks and playgrounds is from *Oakland, California* (n.p.: Oakland Chamber of Commerce) and the *Sunset Magazine* (n.p.: Homeseekers' Bureau of Information, c. 1911).

2. Boosterism, Boxing, and the Battle for the Bay: The Jeffries-Johnson Fight in the Bay Area

1. "Jeffries Retains World Heavyweight Championship," *San Francisco Call*, August 15, 1903.

2. "It's 'Up to You' Champion Jeffries," *Los Angeles Times*, October 29, 1903.

3. "Public Refuses to Accept Color Line," *Los Angeles Times*, October 22, 1903.

4. "Jim Jeffries Turns Down Offer to Fight Big Jack Johnson," *New York Evening News*, December 18, 1903.

5. "It's 'Up to You' Champion Jeffries," *Los Angeles Times*, October 29, 1903.

6. "Jack London Describes the Fight and Jack Johnson's Golden Smile," *San Francisco Call*, December 27, 1908.

7. For information about progressive in San Francisco, see Gerald Woods, "A Penchant for Probity: California Progressives and the Disreputable Pleasures," in *California Progressivism Revisited*, ed. William Deverell and Tom Sitton (Berkeley: University of California Press, 1994), 99–116.

8. "Horsemen form a Town," *San Francisco Call*, October 10, 1896; "Name of a Town," *San Francisco Call*, October 27, 1896.

9. "Two Ideas of Jim Jeffries," *Los Angeles Herald*, May 28, 1903.

10. "Jeffries Wants to Go Fishing," *Baltimore American*, April 23, 1905.

11. "The Superiority of the Black," *New York Age*, December 31, 1908.

12. Jim Jeffries, "My Story of My Life," *Oregonian*, March 20, 1910.

13. Natalia Molina, *Fit to Be Citizens: Public Health and Race in Los Angeles, 1879–1939* (Berkeley: University of California Press, 2006), 34.

14. Jeffries, "My Story of My Life."

15. "Jolts from John L.," *North Carolina Observer*, May 21, 1905.

16. "Two Ideas of Jim Jeffries," *Los Angeles Herald*, May 28, 1903.

17. "Life Story of Jack Johnson," *Oregonian*, May 9, 1909.

18. Jack Johnson, *In the Ring and Out: The Autobiography of Jack Johnson* (New York: Carol Publishing Group, 1992), 38–39.

19. "Charity Loses Childs Cash," *Los Angeles Express*, October 23, 1902.

20. C. E. Van Loan, "I'll Rush from the Start," *San Francisco Examiner*, June 26, 1910.

21. "Fights to Rest Title from Negro," *Memphis Scimitar*, December 17, 1909.

22. "Richmond in the Field for Championship Belt," *Oakland Tribune*, March 3, 1910; "Salt Lake Offer Is Still Being Considered," *San Francisco Examiner*, March 2, 1910.

23. "Richmond in the Field for Championship Belt," *Oakland Tribune,* March 3, 1910.
24. "High Time for Rickard and Jack Gleason to Get Together on a Location," *San Francisco Chronicle,* March 6, 1910.
25. "Gleason and Rickard in Position to Agree," *Oakland Tribune,* March 4, 1910. "Cost Too Much to Hold Fight Here," *San Francisco Chronicle,* March 14, 1910.
26. "Immense Arena to Be Erected in the Infield," *San Francisco Examiner,* March 9, 1910.
27. Ibid.; "Race Track Convenient," *Oakland Tribune,* March 20, 1910.
28. "Emeryville Will Be Seen of Jeffries-Johnson Fight," *Oakland Tribune,* March 8, 1910.
29. "Immense Arena to Be Erected in the Infield," *San Francisco Examiner,* March 9, 1910.
30. "Ordinance Which Authorizes Heavy Weights to Fight," *Oakland Tribune,* March 30, 1910.
31. "Emeryville Gets the Jeffries-Johnson Fight," *San Francisco Call,* March 9, 1910. It is not clear what fire Christie was referring to.
32. "Emeryville Will Be Scene of Jeffries-Johnson Fight," *Oakland Tribune,* March 8, 1910.
33. "Championship Battle Will Spread City's Fame," *Oakland Tribune,* March 19, 1910.
34. Ibid.
35. Ibid. In the meeting, the chamber also supported the baseball team, the Oakland Oaks.
36. "Deasy Asks for Fight Money to Come Here," *San Francisco Chronicle,* March 23, 1910.
37. "Barry and Burns Are Ready for Heavy-Weight Fight on Tuesday Night," *San Francisco Chronicle,* March 27, 1910.
38. "Oakland Ministers Appeal to Officers to Stop Big Fight," *Sacramento Star,* April 5, 1910.
39. "Clergy's Plan Outlined for Stopping the Fight," *Oakland Tribune,* April 9, 1910.
40. "Gillette Unable to Prohibit Fight," *Oakland Tribune,* April 26, 1910.
41. Ibid.
42. "Moran and M'Carthy Are Both of Irish Descent," *Oakland Tribune,* April 28, 1910.
43. "Novice Tommy McCarthy Boxes Past Master Moran To-Night," *San Francisco Examiner,* April 29, 1910.
44. "Fighter's Skull Fractured in Ring," *San Francisco Examiner,* April 30, 1910; "Promoters Say Great Fight Will Go On," *San Francisco Examiner,* May 1, 1910; "M'Carthy's Death Was Accident, Says Jury," *San Francisco Examiner,* May 6, 1910.
45. See Steven A. Riess, *Sport in Industrial America, 1850–1920* (Wheeling, IL: Harland Davidson, 1995), 147–49.
46. "Jack Johnson Arrives and Predicts a Victory," *Oakland Tribune,* April 30, 1910.
47. "Jeff Puts in Strenuous Work," *San Francisco Examiner,* May 1, 1910.
48. "Ministers Battle against Big Fight," *San Francisco Examiner,* May 1, 1910; "Pastor Urges His Flock to Oppose Big Prizefight," *Oakland Tribune,* May 2, 1910.
49. "Divines Decry Prize Fights from Pulpits," *San Francisco Examiner,* May 2, 1910.
50. "Governor Helpless," *San Francisco Examiner,* May 6, 1910.
51. "Boxing Bouts in Oakland Limited to 10 Rounds," *Oakland Tribune,* May 4, 1910.
52. "Predicts Big Movement against Fight," *Oakland Tribune,* May 5, 1910.
53. "Statement Made by Thomas H. Williams," *Oakland Tribune,* May 17, 1910.
54. "Richmond to Fore with Offer to Promoters," *Oakland Tribune,* May 18, 1910.
55. See Barbara Berglund, *Making San Francisco American: Cultural Frontiers in the Urban West, 1846–1906* (Lawrence: University Press of Kansas, 2003.)

56. "What Fight Means to the City," *San Francisco Chronicle*, May 22, 1910.

57. "Recommends Granting of the July Permit after Exchange of Amenities," *San Francisco Chronicle*, May 25, 1910.

58. James N. Gillett Collection, The California State Library, Sacramento. This extensive collection is held at the California State Library and has eight alphabetized boxes of letters sent to Governor Gillett on a variety of issues. Out of the supposed thousands of letters sent to him about the fight, he kept only three letters.

59. *Los Angeles Times*, May 6, 1910.

60. "Governor Gillett Says Fight Cannot Be Stopped," *San Francisco Chronicle*, May 19, 1910.

61. "Fight Is a 'Frame-Up' Says Gillett," *Sacramento Star*, June 2, 1910.

62. "I Made That Statement," *Sacramento Star*, June 3, 1910.

63. "Governor Gillett's Stop Fight Letter Starts War," *San Francisco Examiner*, June 16, 1910.

64. "Gillett's Supporters Give Other Side; The Fair Name of California Is Safe," *San Francisco Examiner*, June 16, 1910.

65. "Gillett Is Silent about His Motives," *San Francisco Examiner*, June 16, 1910.

66. "Views of Numerous Prominent Citizens," *San Francisco Examiner*, June 16, 1910.

67. "Tremendous Loss to City: Kirk Harris," *San Francisco Examiner*, June 16, 1910.

68. "I'm Not Concerned Asserts Fickert," *San Francisco Examiner*, June 17, 1910; "Fickert vs. Gov. Gillett: District Attorney Is Hurt," *San Francisco Examiner*, June 17, 1910; "No Fight Here That Is Settled," *San Francisco Examiner*, June 16, 1910.

69. "Gov. Gillett Is Scored by Kelly," *Sacramento Star*, June 18, 1910; *San Francisco Examiner*, June 16, 1910; "McCarthy Will Not Discuss Politics," *San Francisco Examiner*, June 19, 1910.

70. "Attorney-General Webb Declares He and Governor Will Use Strongest Measures within Their Power if 'Necessary to Stop Fight,'" *San Francisco Examiner*, June 17, 1910.

71. "Restraining Order Refused against Langford-Kaufman Go," *San Francisco Examiner*, June 18, 1910; "Ruling of Judge Van Nostrand," *San Francisco Examiner*, June 18, 1910; "Everything up to Martin; He'll Enforce Law; Fickert," *San Francisco Examiner*, June 18, 1910; "I'm Going Ahead, Insists Blot; I'll Charge Each Soldier $100," *San Francisco Examiner*, June 18, 1910; "Blot Gives Up with Never a Gun Fired," *San Francisco Examiner*, June 19, 1910.

72. *Marysville Daily Appeal*, May 23, 1910.

73. "Threatened Fight on Fair a Motive?" *San Francisco Examiner*, June 16, 1910; "Panama Exposition vs. the Prizefight," *San Francisco Chronicle*, June 16, 1910.

74. "Gillett Thought of Fair Is the Claim," *Sacramento Star*, June 16, 1910; "Enthusiastic Citizens," *San Francisco Chronicle*, June 17, 1915.

75. *San Francisco Examiner*, July 5, 1910.

76. "7,000 Riot in the Capital of the Nation," *Sacramento Star*, July 5, 1910.

77. For a history about prizefight films, and a good overview of Jack Johnson on film, see Dan Streible, *Fight Pictures: A History of Boxing and Early Cinema* (Berkeley: University of California Press, 2008).

78. "Fight Pictures Prohibited Here by Mayor," *San Francisco Chronicle*, July 7, 1910; "Mayor's Ax Is Ready for the Fight Film," *San Francisco Examiner*, July 8, 1910. Across the Bay Oakland politicians wrote a city ordinance to ban all brutal films.

79. "Fight Picture Men Threaten Litigation," *San Francisco Examiner*, July 7, 1910.

80. "Censors Oppose Pictures," *San Francisco Chronicle*, July 7, 1910.

81. "Noted Clubwomen Join in War on Fight Pictures," *San Francisco Examiner*, July 10, 1910.

82. "Citizens Join in Opposition to Pictures," *San Francisco Examiner*, July 9, 1910.

83. "Censors Place a Ban on All Fight Films," *San Francisco Examiner*, July 12, 1910.

3. Reforming the Big Game: The Bay Area Rugby Experiment of 1906–1919

1. Benjamin Ide Wheeler, "Shall Football Be Ended or Mended?" in *The Abundant Life*, ed. Monroe E. Deutsch (Berkeley: University of California Press, 1926), 113–15; originally published in *American Monthly Review of Reviews* (January 1906), 72–73.

2. The standard account of the West Coast rugby experiment is Roberta J. Park, "From Football to Rugby—and Back, 1906–1919: The University of California-Stanford University Response to the 'Football Crisis of 1905,'" *Journal of Sport History* 11, no. 3 (1984): 5–40. See also John Sayle Watterson, *College Football: History, Spectacle, Controversy* (Baltimore: Johns Hopkins University Press, 2000), 93–98; Brian M. Ingrassia, *The Rise of Gridiron University: Higher Education's Uneasy Alliance with Big-Time Football* (Lawrence: University Press of Kansas, 2012), 61–67. On transnational reform movements during the Progressive Era, see Daniel T. Rodgers, *Atlantic Crossings: Social Politics in a Progressive Age* (Cambridge, MA: Harvard University Press, 1998). On California progressivism, see George E. Mowry, *The California Progressives* (Berkeley: University of California Press, 1951); Tom Sitton and William Francis Deverall, editors, *California Progressivism Revisited* (Berkeley: University of California Press, 1994).

3. On the early years of the Stanford-Cal rivalry, see John Sullivan, *The Big Game: A Game-by Game History of America's Greatest Football Rivalry* (West Point, NY: Leisure Press, 1982), 11–81.

4. See Ingrassia, *Rise of Gridiron University*, 50–51.

5. David Starr Jordan, "University Tendencies in America," *Popular Science Monthly* 63 (June 1903), 147.

6. On the 1905 controversies and the NCAA, see Ingrassia, *Rise of Gridiron University*, 56–61.

7. "Wheeler Says Game Must Be Made Over or Go," *San Francisco Chronicle*, November 27, 1905, 4. On Wheeler, see Kevin Starr, *Inventing the Dream: California through the Progressive Era* (New York: Oxford University Press, 1985), 227.

8. "Jordan Has Cure for 'Dirty Football,'" *San Francisco Chronicle* (hereafter *SFC*), December 7, 1905, 8.

9. Waldemar Young, "The Football Fuss: Its Application to Play and Value of Criticism in the Far West," *SFC*, November 19, 1905, 41; "Movement Begun for Football Reform," *SFC*, December 5, 1905, 8 (Wheeler quotation); Park, "From Football to Rugby," 15.

10. "Movement Begun for Football Reform," *SFC*, December 5, 1905, 8. See also "No More Football," *Los Angeles Times* (hereafter *LAT*), November 29, 1905, I1.

11. "Faculty Committees Sound Doom of the Old Game," *SFC*, December 12, 1905, 8 (quotations).

12. Wheeler to Hadley, December 11, 1905, RU 25, YRG 2-A, Series I, Box 91, Folder 1796; Hadley to Wheeler, December 18, 1905, RU 25, YRG 2-A, Series II, Box 108, Letterbook July–December 1905; Arthur Twining Hadley Papers, Yale University Manuscripts and Archives Division, New Haven, Connecticut.

13. "Rugby to Be Substituted for American Game," *SFC*, March 23, 1906, 8. See also "Rugby Game Is Finally Adopted," *Daily Palo Alto* (hereafter *DPA*), March 22, 1906, 1; "Reach Quick Decision," *DPA*, March 23, 1906, 4. The *DPA* was Stanford's student newspaper.

14. Orrin Leslie Elliott, *Stanford University: The First Twenty-Five Years* (Stanford, CA: Stanford University Press, 1937), 234–35; "Rugby Match Saturday," *DPA*, February 7, 1906, 1; "Experts Play Rugby," *DPA*, February 12, 1906, 1. On the NSWFC invitation, see H. Chesney White to Jordan, 1 June 1907, David Starr Jordan Papers (hereafter DSJ), Reel 55, Frame 015, Stanford University Archives, Stanford, California (hereafter SUA). On Jordan's background, see Michael L. Smith, *Pacific Visions: California Scientists and the Environment, 1850–1915* (New Haven, CT: Yale University Press, 1987), 130–36.

15. "Rugby Game Is Popular," *LAT*, September 23, 1906, III2.

16. "Wheeler on Rugby," *SFC*, March 24, 1906, 8. The origin of the term "battleball" is recounted in Frank Angell, "Rugby Football on the Pacific Coast," *The Independent*, January 27, 1910, 195–98.

17. "Rugby Game Is Popular," *LAT*, September 23, 1906, III2.

18. Wheeler, "Shall Football Be Ended or Mended?" 113–15.

19. David Starr Jordan, *The Days of a Man: Being Memories of a Naturalist, Teacher and Minor Prophet of Democracy* (Yonkers, NY: World, 1922), 2:193. On Jordan's ideas about eugenics and pacifism, see Paul Crook, *Darwinism, War and History: The Debate over the Biology of War from the "Origin of Species" to the First World War* (Cambridge: Cambridge University Press, 1994), 119–24. On the nervous system's manly and imperialistic implications, see Kristin Hoganson, *Fighting for American Manhood: How Gender Politics Provoked the Spanish-American and Philippine-American Wars* (New Haven, CT: Yale University Press, 1998), 88–106.

20. Jordan to Camp, January 20, 1908, Walter Camp Papers, Yale University Manuscripts and Archives Division; microfilm copy in the University of Illinois Library, Urbana, Illinois, Reel 11, Frame 322; Camp to Jordan, January 8, 1908; DSJ, Reel 58, Frames 81–85, SUA.

21. See "Stanford Eleven Will Not Play Rugby" and "Wheeler on Rugby," *SFC*, March 24, 1906, 8; "Football or Nothing," *LAT*, May 27, 1906, III3.

22. Howard M. Johnson, "Students Down on Rugby Game," *SFC*, September 16, 1906, 2 (quotation); "High Schools Reject Rugby," *LAT*, September 23, 1906, III2.

23. James to Jordan, c. April 20, 1906, DSJ, Reel 49, Frame 168; "Jordan Addresses Students," *DPA*, April 21, 1906, 4, SUA. On natural disasters as catalysts for rebuilding, see Kevin Rozario, *The Culture of Calamity: Disaster and the Making of Modern America* (Chicago: University of Chicago Press, 2007), esp. 101–33.

24. "Great Rally at Stanford," *SFC*, September 8, 1906, 8 (quotation); Howard M. Johnson, "Berkeley Undergraduates Take Kindly to the New Game of Rugby Football," *SFC*, September 9, 1906, Sports 2.

25. See "Loyal to California," "Stanford Roots Hard," and Archie Rice, "Blue and Gold Thrice Beaten," *SFC*, November 11, 1906, 38.

26. "Stanford Team Defeats the University of California," *SFC*, November 11, 1906, 38.

27. Archie Rice, "Veteran Football Critic Says Make New Game for the West," *SFC*, November 18, 1906, S1.

28. S. H. Baskerville to David Starr Jordan, December 10, 1906; DSJ, Reel 52, Frames 482–85, SUA. Based on the records at Stanford, it appears that Jordan and Baskerville corresponded extensively regarding the latter's proposal to coach the team.

29. "Rugby Football to Be Retained," *LAT*, January 17, 1907, I7.

30. "Oppose the Game," *LAT*, December 20, 1907, I6; "Jordan Meets Chill Silence," *LAT*, December 21, 1907, I6; "Sporting Comment on Timely Topics," *LAT*, December 22, 1907, VIII3; "Dr. Jordan Flays American Football," *New York Times* (hereafter *NYT*), December 22, 1907, S1. See also Jordan, *Days of a Man*, 2:193.

31. Jordan to Van Hise, February 5, 1908, RG 4/10/01, Folder 6-76, and Van Hise to Jordan, February 13, 1908, RG 4/10/01, Folder 6-76, University of Wisconsin Archives, Madison, Wisconsin. On the response to Jordan's proposal, see Brian M. Ingrassia, "A Department of the Modern University: Discipline, Manliness, and Football in American Colleges, 1869–1929" (Ph.D. diss., University of Illinois at Urbana-Champaign, 2008), 122–23, 133n102. On the rationale behind Van Hise's response, see Ingrassia, *Rise of Gridiron University*, 64–66.

32. Angell, "Rugby Football on the Pacific Coast," 195–98. See also Angell, "Rugby vs. Intercollegiate Football," *Sequoia*, December 1908, 113–14; Angell, "The Passing of the Paid Coach," *Sequoia*, March 1911, 183–84; and Angell to Jordan, July 22, 1915; DSJ, Reel 92, Frame 1087, SUA. On Angell's background, see Ingrassia, *Gridiron University*, 85–86. Stanford's current track stadium is named after Angell.

33. "To Offset English Football in West," *NYT*, March 11, 1909, 7. On California high schools' piecemeal adoption of rugby, see Park, "From Football to Rugby," 31.

34. "California Team Off for Vancouver," *NYT*, December 21, 1909, 10; "Sporting News in Brief," *NYT*, May 19, 1910, 11 (quotations); "All-Americans Beaten at Rugby," *NYT*, June 19, 1910, S1; Park, "From Football to Rugby," 23.

35. "No Changes to Be Made in Football," *NYT*, December 30, 1914, 9.

36. "Football in the West," *NYT*, November 23, 1913, FS11; "To Play Football on Coast," *NYT*, December 10, 1912, 13.

37. "Warning to California Eleven," *NYT*, November 2, 1912, 14; Sullivan, *Big Game*, 111–14.

38. "Don't Know How to Play Rugby," *NYT*, October 15, 1913, 9.

39. "Finds Rugby a Failure," *NYT*, April 9, 1914, 9.

40. "War Spoils International Sports," *NYT*, September 23, 1914, 10.

41. Sullivan, *Big Game*, 119–22; Park, "From Football to Rugby," 9; "Eastern Elevens for Exposition," *NYT*, February 14, 1915, S2; "Effort Made to Bring Universities Together," *SFC*, September 13, 1915, 6.

42. Park, "From Football to Rugby," 33; "Rugby Doomed in America," *NYT*, October 17, 1915, S3 (quotations); see also "Colleges Break on Rugby," *NYT*, May 21, 1915, 11.

43. "Close Vote Saves Rugby," *NYT*, May 4, 1916, 13; "Hard Knock for Football," *NYT*, October 27, 1916, 10 (quotation).

44. "Football Schedule Includes American and Rugby with California," *DPA*, October 23, 1918, 1; Editorial, *DPA*, October, 23, 1918, 3 (quotation).

45. "Terse News of Sports in Town and Out," *NYT*, August 6, 1919, 16; Jordan, *Days of a Man*, 2:194–95; Elliott, *Stanford University*, 234–35.

46. "American Football Is Decided by the Athletic Board," *DPA*, February 12, 1919, 1; "Herbert Hoover Accepts Responsibility for Tuition Ruling and Supports Move," *DPA*, October 16, 1919, 1.

47. On stadiums at Stanford and Cal, see Ingrassia, *Rise of Gridiron University*, 149–51. On the rejection of rugby as "foreign," see Park, "From Football to Rugby," 20–21.

4. Bay to Breakers: The Original Fun Run

1. Marty Post, "Bay to Breakers '84," *Runner's World,* May 1984, 18A.

2. Ibid.

3. Len Wallach, *The Human Race: Bay to Breakers: Largest Run for Fun in the World* (San Francisco: Hearst, 1978), 186.

4. Only two other races in the United States have tenures that rival that of the Bay to Breakers: the Boston Marathon and the Dipsea Race. The Boston Marathon, first run in 1897, altered its format in 1918 as a result of World War I, and the Dipsea Race, first run in 1905, ceased operation in 1932 and 1933 due to the Great Depression, and from 1942 to 1945 due to World War II. "Boston Marathon History: Boston Marathon Milestones," *Boston Athletic Association*, accessed June 30, 2015, http://www.baa.org/races/boston-marathon/boston-marathon-history/boston-marathon-milestones.aspx; Barry Spitz, *Dipsea: The Greatest Race* (San Anselmo, CA: Potrero Meadow, 2010), 52, 65.

5. Clint Pumphrey, "How Bay to Breakers Works," *How Stuff Works*, accessed June 2, 2015, http://adventure.howstuffworks.com/outdoor-activities/running/events/bay-to-breakers.htm.

6. "History," *Bay to Breakers*, accessed July 29, 2014, http://www.baytobreakers.com/history/.

7. John Brant, "Break Away Barrios," *Runner's World,* September 1990, 99; Anthony Ashbolt, *A Cultural History of the Radical Sixties in the San Francisco Bay Area* (Brookfield, VT: Pickering & Chatto, 2013), 30.

8. Data used here is for the 5k, 10k, half marathon, and marathon distances, those race distances most commonly run in the US. "Statistics," *Running USA*, accessed July 29, 2014, http://www.runningusa.org/statistics.

9. Wallach, *The Human Race*, 186.

10. Francis J. Mannix, "Cross-City Races Take Precedence as Biggest Feature in Athletics," *San Francisco Bulletin*, December 25, 1916.

11. Wallach, *The Human Race*, 32; "San Francisco Earthquake, 1906," The Center for Legislative Archives, accessed June 11, 2015, from http://www.archives.gov/legislative/features/sf/.

12. Michael Oriard, *Reading Football: How the Popular Press Created an American Spectacle* (Chapel Hill: University of North Carolina Press, 1993), 61.

13. Spitz, *Dipsea*, 1, 4.

14. Francis J. Mannix, "The Bulletin Arranges a Big Cross City Race," *San Francisco Bulletin*, December 6, 1911.

15. Ibid.

16. Ibid.

17. "Entry Blank for the Bulletin's Annual Cross City Race," *San Francisco Bulletin*, December 25, 1916.

18. "Brief Items of Local Interest," *Sausalito News* (Sausalito, Calif.), December 16, 1911, 3.

19. Wallach, *The Human Race*, 34, 176.

20. Benjamin D. Rader, *American Sports: From the Age of Folk Games to the Age of Televised Sports* (Upper Saddle River, NJ: Pearson Education, 2009), 78; Wallach, *The Human Race*, 35.

21. Wallach, *The Human Race*, 196.

22. Ibid., 17.

23. "Course Info & Map," *Bay to Breakers*, accessed on June 11, 2015, from http://www.baytobreakers.com/course-info/.

24. "Large Entry List for the Cross City Race," *San Francisco Call*, January 1, 1912, 15.

25. "Brief Items of Local Interest," *Sausalito News*, December 16, 1911, 3.

26. "Cross City Race Novelty Features," *San Francisco Call*, December 31, 1911, 35.

27. "Large Entry List for Cross City Race," *San Francisco Call*, January 1, 1912, 15.

28. William Unmack, "R. Vlught of St. Mary's College Wins by Two Seconds in Heartbreaking Sprint," *San Francisco Call*, January 2, 1912, 11.

29. "No Fair Riding in the Cross City Race," *San Francisco Call*, January 5, 1912, 11.

30. "Vlught First in Cross City Race," *San Francisco Call*, January 2, 1913, 14.

31. Cathy Tallyn, "Mary Sealy's Grandfather Won the First Bay to Breakers," *Rossmoor News* (Walnut Creek, Calif.), May 11, 2011, http://www.rossmoornews.com/articles/2011/05/11/news/community_news/mary%20sealys%20grandfather.txt.

32. Bishop Hanna, "Department of Commerce Exercises Will Be Held This Evening," *San Francisco Call*, June 11, 1913, 5.

33. Wallach, *The Human Race*, 204–7.

34. Ibid., 61, 68, 204–11.

35. Ibid., 69, 91.

36. Ibid., 99.

37. Rader, *American Sports*, 82; According to the 1920 U.S. Census, the white population of California was 94 percent and included individuals with British, Irish, German, Italian, Spanish, Scandinavian, Portuguese, Slavic, French, and "Other" heritage. The remaining 6 percent of the population included individuals who identified as American Indian (1 percent), Chinese (1 percent), Japanese (2 percent), African American (1 percent), and "All other" (less than 1 percent). Robert W. Cherny, Gretchen Lemke-Santangelo, and Richard Griswold del Castillo, eds., *Competing Visions: A History of California* (Boston: Wadsworth, 2014), 211.

38. Rader, *American Sports*, 72.

39. Wallach, *The Human Race*, 35, 39, 41, 44, 48, 88.

40. Ibid., 75.

41. "Elite Runner Info," *Bay to Breakers*, accessed June 18, 2015, from http://zappos baytobreakers.com/runner-info/elite-runner-info/.

42. "Large Entry List for the Cross City Race," *San Francisco Call*, January 1, 1912, 15.

43. Wallach, *The Human Race*, 70.

44. Ibid., 80.

45. Ibid., 96.

46. Ibid., 59; "Results," *Bay to Breakers*, accessed June 18, 2015, from http://btb.onlineraceresults.com/search.php#restop.

47. Wallach, *The Human Race*, 69, 202–5.

48. Ibid., 87, 95.

49. Ibid., 109.

50. *United States Jaycees v. San Francisco Jr. Cham. of Com.*, 354 F. Supp. 61 (N.D. Cal. 1972), August 9, 1972, http://law.justia.com/cases/federal/district-courts/FSupp/354/61/1380295/; Wallach, *The Human Race*, 144.

51. Ashbolt, *A Cultural History of the Radical Sixties*, 38–39.

52. Wallach, *The Human Race*, 103, 122.

53. Prescott Sullivan. *San Francisco Examiner*, March 22, 1947.

54. Wallach, *The Human Race*, 87, 127, 139, 158.

55. Ibid., 150.

56. Ibid., 141, 206.
57. Ibid., 208.
58. Ibid., 166, 176.
59. Ibid., 160.
60. Walt Daley, "Cross City Run Today," *San Francisco Examiner*, May 22, 1966, 2; Wallach, *The Human Race*, 209.
61. Wallach, *The Human Race*, 166.
62. Pamela Cooper, *The American Marathon* (Syracuse, NY: Syracuse University Press, 1998), 104.
63. Gerald R. Gems, Linda J. Borish, and Gertrud Pfister, *Sports in American History: From Colonization to Globalization* (Champaign, IL: Human Kinetics, 2008), 300.
64. Darcy C. Plymire, "Running, Heart Disease, and the Ironic Death of Jim Fixx," *Research Quarterly for Exercise and Sport* 73, no. 1 (2002): 41.
65. Rader, *American Sports*, 243.
66. Ibid., 243.
67. Wallach, *The Human Race*, 162, 171, 176, 188.
68. "Craig Virgin First of 27,000 in Bay to Breakers Race," *New York Times,* May 18, 1981, 11.
69. "Bay to Breakers History," *Bay to Breakers*, accessed June 30, 2015, http://web.archive.org/web/20070908170537/http://www.ingbaytobreakers.com/about_us/history.html.
70. Wallach, *The Human Race*, 193.
71. Carle Nolte, "Lenard Wallach, B2B Director, Dies," *San Francisco Chronicle*, June 4, 2010, http://www.sfgate.com/bayarea/article/Leonard-Wallach-B2B-director-dies-3186150.php.
72. Joe Henderson, "From Soldiering to Writing to Directing the World's Largest Footrace, Len Wallach Has Always Led the Way," *Runner's World,* December 1983, 25.
73. Jim Harrington, "Flashing Back to the Summer of Love," *Inside Bay Area* (Calif.), February 11, 2007.
74. Henderson, "From Soldiering to Writing," 25.
75. Wallach, *The Human Race*, 25.
76. "A Noted Veteran Race Director Speculates on the Future of Megaracing," *Runner's World,* April 1984, 134.
77. "Filling the Streets of San Francisco," *Runner's World,* July 1977, 49.
78. "A Noted Veteran Race Director Speculates on the Future of Megaracing," *Runner's World,* April 1984, 134.
79. Jim Webster, "Fun in the Sun; How a Scrap of Paper Started a Tradition," *Sun Herald* (Sydney, Australia), August 13, 1995, 57.
80. "The Untold Story of the City 2 Surf," The Sun-Herald City to Surf, accessed June 2, 2015, http://www.city2surfbook.com.au/.
81. Wallach, *The Human Race*, 176.
82. "Bay to Breakers Set for May 20," *Oakland Post,* April 20, 1980, 5; "Carroll Resents His Atlanta Exclusion," *Sydney Morning Herald,* April 13, 1996, 51.
83. For example, see Susan K. Cahn, *Coming on Strong: Gender and Sexuality in Twentieth-Century Women's Sports* (Urbana: University of Illinois Press, 1994), 2, 265.
84. Patricia A. Vertinsky, *The Eternally Wounded Woman: Women, Doctors, and Exercise in the Late Nineteenth Century* (Urbana: University of Illinois Press, 1989), 2; Cahn, *Coming on Strong*, 58–59.

85. Cahn, *Coming on Strong*, 115.

86. Pamela Cooper, "Marathon Women and the Corporation," *Journal of Women's History* 7, no. 4 (1996): 65.

87. Darcy C. Plymire, "A Moral Exercise: Long-Distance Running in the 1970s" (PhD diss., University of Iowa, 1997), 43, ProQuest (UMI No. 9731858).

88. Cooper, *The American Marathon*, 173.

89. "Barbara Preston: Death Notice," *San Francisco Chronicle*, November 24–28, 2010, accessed June 2, 2015, from http://www.legacy.com/obituaries/sfgate/obituary.aspx?pid=146796647.

90. Katie Harrar, "Bay to Breakers: Out of the Ashes a Famous Race Is Born," *Active.Com*, accessed June 2, 2015, from http://www.active.com/running/articles/bay-to-breakers-out-of-the-ashes-a-famous-race-is-born.

91. "Bay to Breakers 12k," accessed June 30, 2015, http://www.arrs.net/HP_BtB12.htm.

92. Cooper, *The American Marathon*, 161.

93. "Women in Sports," *Off Our Backs* 2, no. 2 (October 1971): 13.

94. "Bay to Breakers 12k," accessed June 30, 2015, http://www.arrs.net/HP_BtB12.htm.

95. Dan Giesin, "Kenyans Conquer Hayes St., Breakers—Kimani, Omoro Win Easily," *San Francisco Chronicle*, May 19, 1997, E1; "Bay to Breakers 12k," *Running in the USA*, accessed June 2, 2015, http://runningintheusa.com/Race/View.aspx?RaceID=2025.

96. Mark Winitz, "Centipede Participant's & Spectator's Guide," *California Track & Running News*, April/June 2009, 18–19; "This and That," *Northern California Running Review*, Spring 1979, 19.

97. Ibid.

98. Winitz, "Centipede Participant's & Spectator's Guide," 21–23.

99. Ron Hansen, "Bay-To-Breakers," *Runner's World*, August 1981, 62.

100. Jim Harmon, "Just Another Mainiac," *Runner's World*, September 1985, 59.

101. "Breakers: The Magazine of the Examiner Bay to Breakers," *San Francisco Examiner*, May 11, 1986, 1–54.

102. Henderson, "From Soldiering to Writing," 32.

103. Susan Steade, "What Makes 60,000 Run? Two Very Different Races Find the Formula to Draw Fields the Size of Santa Fe," *San Jose Mercury News*, March 12, 1998, 14D.

104. "Breakers: The Magazine of the Examiner Bay to Breakers," *San Francisco Examiner*, May 11, 1986, 12.

105. C. W. Nevius, "A Little Outing for 100,000—Humphrey, Halley's and Some Serious Runners," *San Francisco Chronicle*, May 19, 1986, 1.

106. Caroline Scarborough, "A Breakers for the Books—Eyestone, Waitz Top a Field of 100,000," *San Francisco Chronicle*, May 19, 1986, 59.

107. Henderson, "From Soldiering to Writing," 25–26.

108. Caroline Scarborough, "Rundown of Bay to Breakers," *San Francisco Chronicle*, May 19, 1986, 86.

109. George A. Hirsch, "The Second Running Boom," *Runner's World*, April 1997, 12; "2014 State of the Sport—Part III: US Race Trends," *Running USA*, July 9, 2014, http://www.runningusa.org/2014-state-of-the-sport-part-III-us-race-trends?returnTo=main.

110. "2014 State of the Sport—Part III: US Race Trends," *Running USA*, July 9, 2014, http://www.runningusa.org/2014-state-of-the-sport-part-III-us-race-trends?returnTo=main.

111. "Company Overview," *Citizens for the Preservation of Bay2Breakers,* accessed June 9, 2015, from https://www.facebook.com/citizensf/info?tab=page_info.

112. Zoë Corbyn, "Is San Francisco Losing Its Soul?," *Guardian*, February 23, 2014, accessed August 10, 2015, from http://www.theguardian.com/world/2014/feb/23/is-san-francisco-losing-its-soul.

113. James Raia, "Racers to Celebrate Recovery in Bay Area," *New York Times*, May 14, 1990, C11.

114. "Bay to Breakers," *Association of Road Racing Statistics*, accessed June 9, 2015, from http://more.arrs.net/raceSeries/404.

115. "Bay to Breakers," *Association of Road Racing Statistics,* accessed June 10, 2015, from http://more.arrs.net/raceSeries/404; "Kenyan Sammy Kitwara Wins 98th Annual ING Bay to Breakers 12K," *PR Newswire* (New York), May 17, 2009.

116. "Bay to Breakers," *Association of Road Racing Statistics*, accessed June 9, 2015, from http://more.arrs.net/raceSeries/404.

117. Dan Giesin, "Bay to Breakers Notes: Coogan Wins National Title," *San Francisco Chronicle,* May 20, 1996, E8; Dan Giesin, "Breakers, USATF at Odds," *San Francisco Chronicle,* May 17, 1997, B3.

118. "Chapter 2: How Did Bare-2-Breakers Begin," *BARE-2-BREAKERS,* accessed June 10, 2015, from http://www.baretobreakers.com/Main3.html.

119. Bare breasts are not prohibited in public spaces. "San Francisco Nudity Ban, A Balance of Interests," *Golden Gate University Law Review,* April 2, 2015, accessed October 31, 2015, from http://ggulawreview.org/2015/04/02/san-francisco-nudity-ban-a-balance-of-interests/.

120. Bob Egelko, "Public Nudity Is Not Free Speech," *San Francisco Chronicle,* January 30, 2013, E1.

121. Josh Richman, "San Francisco Orders Nudists to Put Their Pants On," *Contra Costa Times* (Calif.), November 21, 2012; Michael Cabanatuan, "Naked Protesters Decry S.F. Nudity Ban on 2nd Anniversary," *SFGate*, February 1, 2015, accessed October 31, 2015, from http://www.sfgate.com/bayarea/article/Nude-protesters-gather-in-S-F-to-decry-nudity-ban-6055522.php.

122. Kevin Evans, Carrie Galbraith, and John Law, eds., *Tales of the San Francisco Cacophony Society* (San Francisco: Last Gasp Publishing, 2013), xi, 207.

123. Blane Bachelor, "Bay to Breakers: A Race Like No Other," *Runner's World*, May 15, 2014, accessed June 4, 2015, http://www.runnersworld.com/races/bay-to-breakers-a-race-like-no-other.

124. Bruce Adams and Steven A. Chin, "From Ito to Groucho, There Was Something for Everyone," *SFGate*, May 22, 1995, accessed June 4, 2015, http://www.sfgate.com/news/article/From-Ito-to-Groucho-there-was-something-for-3146968.php.

125. Blane Bachelor, "Bay to Breakers: A Race Like No Other," *Runner's World*, May 15, 2014, accessed June 4, 2015, http://www.runnersworld.com/races/bay-to-breakers-a-race-like-no-other.

126. Peter Sinton, Edward Epstein, Carolyn Said, and William Carlsen, "Examiner Sold," *San Francisco Chronicle,* March 18, 2000, A1.

127. Chris O'Brien, "New Owner Vows to Revive Paper; Denver Billionaire Buys S.F. Examiner," *San Jose Mercury News,* February 20, 2004, 1F.

128. Eric Young, "San Francisco's Bay to Breakers Race Has New Owner," *San Francisco Business Times*, October 2, 2013, accessed June 10, 2015, from http://www.bizjournals.com/sanfrancisco/news/2013/10/02/bay-to-breakers-aeg-wasserman.html?page=all.

129. "Craigslist Sponsors Bay To Breakers for 2013 Race," *Huffington Post,* April 4, 2013, accessed June 10, 2015, from http://www.huffingtonpost.com/2013/04/04/craigslist-sponsors-bay-to-breakers_n_3016072.html.

130. Phil Matier and Andy Ross, "Bay to Breakers Porta-Party Turned Wild—And Very Wet," *San Francisco Chronicle,* May 21, 2008, B1.

131. Phil Matier and Andy Ross, "Sponsor ING Drops Bay to Breakers," *SFGate,* May 26, 2010, accessed June 10, 2015, from http://www.sfgate.com/bayarea/matier-ross/article/Sponsor-ING-drops-Bay-to-Breakers-3187604.php.

132. Will Kane, Ellen Huet, and Vivian Ho, "Bay to Breakers: Partier Dies in Roof Plunge," *San Francisco Chronicle,* May 21, 2013, C3.

133. Matier and Ross, "Bay to Breakers Porta-Party Turned Wild"; Steve Rubenstein, "More Portable Toilets, Sobering Spaces, Trash Crews at This Year's Run," *San Francisco Chronicle,* May 16, 2015, C1.

134. Meredith May, "Alcohol, Float Bans Ease Bay to Breakers Cleanup," *San Francisco Chronicle,* May 19, 2009, B1.

135. John Coté, "Plans for Bridge Tours Scrapped," *San Francisco Chronicle,* April 3, 2010, C1.

136. Will Kane, "Brakes Put on Booze as Patience Runs Dry," *San Francisco Chronicle,* May 11, 2011, A1.

137. "About," *Citizens for the Preservation of the Bay2Breakers,* accessed June 11, 2015, from https://www.facebook.com/citizensf/info?tab=page_info.

138. Steve Rubenstein, "More Portable Toilets, Sobering Spaces, Trash Crews at This Year's Run," *San Francisco Chronicle,* May 16, 2015, C1; John Wildermuth; "Party on the Run, But Not Too Much," *San Francisco Chronicle,* May 15, 2010, C1.

139. "Bay to Breakers," *Association of Road Racing Statistics,* accessed June 11, 2015, from http://more.arrs.net/raceSeries/404.

140. "Boston Marathon Bombing Injury Total Climbs to 264, Officials Say," *Reuters,* April 23, 2015, accessed October 31, 2015, from http://www.huffingtonpost.com/2013/04/23/boston-marathon-bombing-injury-total_n_3138159.html.

141. Victoria Colliver, "Manning Pick Furor Won't Easily Subside," *San Francisco Chronicle,* April 30, 2013, C1; Will Kane, "It's Still Our Wacky Rite of Spring, But Security Now Bigger Concern," *San Francisco Chronicle,* May 17, 2013, A1.

142. Zoë Corbyn, "Is San Francisco Losing Its Soul?" *Guardian,* February 23, 2014, accessed August 10, 2015, from http://www.theguardian.com/world/2014/feb/23/is-san-francisco-losing-its-soul.

5. Protecting the People's Mountain: Hiking in Marin County and the Roots of American Environmentalism

1. I would like to thank the staff at the Mill Valley Public Library for their guidance through their wonderful collection of local history, Diane Patterson at the County of Marin Board of Supervisors, Rita Liberti for support and camaraderie during the writing process, Jim Kaufman for his terrific outsider's eye, and Rita Liberti (again) and Maureen Smith for inviting me to be a part of this anthology.

Sausalito Times, August 7, 1920; minutes of the Marin County Board of Supervisors, Tuesday, August 3, 1920.

2. *Marin Journal,* June 24, 1920, 1.

3. Clipping from *Mill Valley Record,* August 31, 1950. Outdoor Club Art File, Lucretia Little History Room, Mill Valley Public Library, Mill Valley, California.

4. "Conservation Measures and the Tamalpais Conservation Club," *California Out-of-Doors,* August 1919, 161.

5. See Abraham Hoffman, "Mountain Resorts and Trail Camps in Southern California's Great Hiking Era, 1884–1938," in *Southern California Quarterly* 58, no. 3 (1976): 381–406. Term used by Hoffman to denote a casual day-tourist visiting to hike, as distinguished from locals or regular members of established hiking clubs.

6. This chapter speaks in some sense to the literature on roots of environmentalism in the United States. The hiking clubs proceeded the Civilian Conservation Corps, for example, the group that Neil Maher sees at the root of the modern environmentalist impulse for their close work in tending to open spaces. In historian John Walton's 2007 article on conservation in Big Sur, he discusses the role of citizen activism in preserving local open space that predates environmentalism of the 1960s in Big Sur; the hiking clubs in Marin contribute to this concept. See Neil Maher, *Nature's New Deal: The Civilian Conservation Corps and the Roots of the American Environmental Movement* (Oxford: Oxford University Press, 2009); John Walton, "The Land of Big Sur: Conservation on the California Coast," *California History* 85, no. 1 (2007): 44–64.

7. Rebecca Solnit, *Wanderlust: A History of Walking* (New York: Penguin, 2001), 3.

8. Ibid., 6.

9. The spur had been built into the Sausalito–Corte Madera line shortening the trip from San Francisco to the Mount Tamalpais / Mill Valley region considerably. See Ron Olson, "The History of Mount Tamalpais: It's Divided Ownership, Administration and Planning" (Master's thesis, California State University, 1985), 37.

10. See ibid., 37.

11. Melanie Kliewe, interviewed by Dorothy Killion, Mill Valley, CA, September 1972, 6. Literature on the Crookedest Railway cites 281 curves on the 8.5-mile route between Mill Valley and a tavern at the upper terminus. See Barry Spitz, *To Save a Mountain: The 100 Year Battle for Mt. Tamalpais* (Create Space Independent Publishing, 2012), 32; Fred Runner, *Mount Tamalpais Scenic Railway* (Charleston: Arcadia Publishing, 2009).

12. Spitz, *To Save a Mountain,* 32–33.

13. Keith McClellan, interviewed by Betsy Andresen, Mill Valley, CA, May 8, 1972, 5; Shayer Oswin Lancelot Robinson, interview by Helen Dreyfus, Mill Valley, CA, October 1979, 10.

14. Robinson interview, 7–8.

15. William Henry Close, interviewed by Karl Mosher, Mill Valley, CA, April 24, 1979, 12.

16. George R. Pimlott, interviewed by Betsy Andresen, Mill Valley, CA, March 25, 1975, 8.

17. John and Virginia George, interviewed by Karl Mosher, Mill Valley, CA, August 22, 1979, 20; Pimlott interview, 13; McLellan interview, 10.

18. Karen Lundqvist Connelly, interviewed by Betsy Andresen, Mill Valley, CA, April 7, 1972, 7.

19. Robinson interview, 9–10.

20. Kliewe interview, 2. An understanding of Mill Valley's growing popularity in the Bay area—especially in terms of hiking—would not be complete without a note about the Dipsea Race, which began in 1905, and in 1918 was opened to women. The race was more or less run along the Dipsea trail, a local favorite, and the event was recently described by a local historian as "unsurpassed among the world's footraces of its length for combination of stunning scenery, physical challenge and colorful history." It is a seminal part of hiking

history in the area, an annual draw for area crowds, and an interesting chapter in the history of gender and sport in the way women, who were active participants in early-twentieth-century hiking culture, were able to use this trail, this race, and this hiking culture as a venue for acceptable female athleticism. See Rita M. Liberti, "Trailblazing in Marin: Women's Dipsea Hikes, 1918–1922," in *California History* 81, no. 1 (2002): 54–65; and Barry Spitz, *Dipsea: The Greatest Race* (San Anselmo, CA: Potrero Meadow, 1993).

21. McLellan interview, 4.
22. Pimlott interview, 10, 8; Connelly interview, 14.
23. McClellan interview, 5
24. Connelly interview, 6–7.
25. Pimlott interview, 8; Ralph Sterner, interviewed by Ruth and Joe Wilson, Mill Valley, CA, October 1970, 1, 4, 14.
26. Approximately $45 in 2014 dollars. Advertisement in *California Out-of-Doors* 1, no. 5, 55.
27. *Sausalito News*, May 13, 1922.
28. *California Out-of-Doors* 1, no. 12, 109.
29. Ibid., no. 9, 1.
30. Ibid.
31. Ibid., no. 3, 18.
32. Ibid., March 1917, 132.
33. "The Discovery of the Out-of-Doors," *California Out-Of-Doors* 1, no. 1 (December 1914), 2.
34. Pimlott interview, 8.
35. Close interview, 12.
36. McClellan interview, 5.
37. George interview, 22–23.
38. Recounted in *California Out-of-Doors*, August 1918, 148.
39. George interview, 23.
40. Connelly interview, 16.
41. *Marin Journal*, June 10, 1920.
42. *Sausalito News*, February 19, 1921.
43. *Sausalito News*, June 26, 1920; *Marin Journal*, June 24, 1920. Also noted in the article, "Among the plans suggested as a . . . remedy were: To stop questionable parties at the San Francisco Ferry building; to establish a military patrol under federal supervision and to secure the co-operation of various hiking organizations." Among the organizations represented at the meeting were The Travelers' Aid Society for the Prevention of Cruelty to Children; YWCA, Juvenile Protective Association; State Board of Charities; Recreation League; Tamalpais Conservation Club; Outdoor Art Club of Mill Valley; Sausalito Women's Club; and nearly a dozen others.
44. Richard A. Walker, *The Country in the City: The Greening of the San Francisco Bay Area* (Seattle: University of Washington Press, 2008), 5.
45. Walker, *The Country in the City*, 19.
46. Marguerite Shaffer, *See America First: Tourism and National Identity, 1880–1940* (Washington, DC: Smithsonian Books, 2001), Kindle edition, introduction.
47. Shaffer, *See America First*, ch. 3.
48. *California Out-of-Doors*, January/May 1916, 121, 124.
49. Connelly interview, 16.

50. *Mill Valley Record* August 31, 1950
51. *Tamalpais Magazine* 1, no. 3 (March 1913).
52. Spitz, *To Save a Mountain*, 41.
53. *California Out-of-Doors* 1, no. 11, 103. Ralph Sterner was a San Franciscan who was a longtime renter at Barth's Retreat and claimed over 2,000 trips across the Dipsea Trail alone. See Sterner interview.
54. Harold Atkinson, "Early History of the Tamalpais Conservation Club, 1912–1926," Folder 1, Papers of Harold Atkinson, Lucretia Hanson Little History Room, Mill Valley Public Library, Mill Valley, CA.
55. Atkinson, "Early History of the Tamalpais Conservation Club," 3.
56. Membership included the Sierra Club, Cross Country Club, Sight-Seers Olympia Club, California Alpine Club, and the Coyotes.
57. Atkinson, "Early History of the Tamalpais Conservation Club," 59.
58. Ibid., 60.
59. *California Out-of Doors*, March 1917, 132.
60. Olson, "The History of Mount Tamalpais," 36. For more details, see Spitz, *To Save a Mountain*.
61. While John Muir saw this as a betrayal, Kent countered the public (in this case civic) control of Hetch Hetchy was a lesser evil than private acquisition. See Roderick Nash, "John Muir, William Kent and the Conservation Schism," in *Pacific Historical Review* 36, no. 4 (November 1967): 423–33.
62. William Kent, "Marking Off a Tamalpais Park," in *California Out-of-Doors* 1, no. 5 (1915): 45.
63. *California Out-of Doors*, March 1917, 132.
64. Ibid., January 1918, 1.
65. Atkinson, "Early History of the Tamalpais Conservation Club," 30, 35.
66. Ibid., 62.
67. *California Out-of-Doors*, August 1919, 161.
68. H. A. Hertenstein, "The New Function of the Tamalpais Conservation Club," in *California Out-of-Doors*, September 1924.
69. "Notes and Rules," in *California Out-of-Doors* 1, no. 4 (1915): 33.
70. Atkinson, "Early History of Mount Tamalpais," 22–23.
71. *California Out-of-Doors*, April 1923.
72. "Prevent Vandalism and Devastation on Mt. Tamalpais," *California Out-of-Doors*, October 1919, 166–67.
73. Taken from headlines in the TCC newsletter and mouthpiece *California Out-of-Doors*, from 1919 through 1926.
74. *California Out-of-Doors*, July 1922, 210.
75. Ibid., July 1925, 1.
76. Jesse K. Brown, "Tamalpais Is Your Mountain; Take Care of It," *California Out-of-Doors*, August 1923, 1.
77. C. G. Meyers, in *California Out-of-Doors*, August 1919, 162; "Making Friends with Nature," *California Out-of-Doors*, January 1923, 1.
78. Alice Eastwood, "A Plea for the Protection of Wild Flowers," *California Out-of-Doors*, April 1921, 190.
79. Noreen M. Breakey and Hugh E. Breakey, "Tourism and Aldo Leopold's 'Cultural Harvest': Creating Virtuous Tourists as Agents of Sustainability," in *Journal of Sustainable Tourism*, published online, June 23, 2014, accessed on July 15, 2014.

80. See Adam Rome, *The Bulldozer in the Countryside: Suburban Sprawl and the Rise of American Environmentalism* (Cambridge: Cambridge University Press, 2001).

81. See Walker, *The Country in the City*, 87–99.

82. *California Out of Doors*, January 1918, 1.

6. All in the Same Boat: Ky Ebright, Masculinity, and Cal Crew in the 1920s

1. Wythe Williams, "California's Eight Wins Olympic Title in a Stirring Race: Sweeps over Finish Line Half a Length Ahead of British as 10,000 Cheer," *New York Times*, August 11, 1928, 1. By comparison, the coxswain for the competing team against Cal, the British Thames Rowing Club, George Sulley, encouraged his rowers with the more sedate, "Up, up, up." See also Dwight Chapin, "He Hollered U.S. Rowers," *San Francisco Chronicle*, July 20, 1996; Jim Lemmon, *The Log of Rowing at the University of California, Berkeley, 1870–1987* (Berkeley: Western Heritage Press, 1989), 22.

2. Don Blessing, "Ebright: Friend, Tough Coach," *Daily Californian*, November 3, 1999; Katy Klinedinst suggests that Ebright was "perhaps the most successful coach Cal has ever had"; see Katy Klinedinst, "Directing a Dynasty," *Daily Californian*, November 3, 1999.

3. The intersection of politics, gender, and sports, as well as sport's relationship to masculinity, class, religion, and ethnicity, are complex, and there are some wonderful works utilizing the social constructivist model in history; see Bryan E. Denham, "Social Views of Masculinity Related to Sport," in *Sociology of Sport and Social Theory*, ed. Earl Smith (Champaign, IL: Human Kinetics Press, 2011), 143–52, and the works of Michael Messner, an excellent primer being *Power at Play: Sports and the Problem of Masculinity* (Boston, MA: Beacon Press, 1992).

4. Early collegiate rowing had English roots at Oxford and Cambridge where highly refined sport rules meant that "the notion of winning at any cost was unthinkable. The concepts of fairness, good manners, and being a good sport were central to their code of conduct. If a competitor suffered an accident at the beginning of a contest, it wasn't sporting to continue down the course alone." See Bryan Volpenheim, "Winning at All Costs: A Historical Perspective," in *Rowing Faster: Serious Training for Serious Rowers*, ed. Volker Nolte (Champaign, IL: Human Kinetics Press, 2011), 9.

5. For the popularity of crew in American society from the late nineteenth to the early twentieth century, see http://www.rowinghistory.net/cornell.htm, accessed April 14, 2014. Ebright's compensation was ten thousand dollars a year as coach, a sizable amount that increased yearly as Berkeley continued to win championships; see Blessing, "Ebright: Friend, Tough Coach."

6. Jim Lemmon, *The Log of Rowing at the University of California, Berkeley, 1870–1987* (Berkeley: Western Heritage Press, 1989), 18. See also Blessing, "Ebright: Friend, Tough Coach."

7. Russ Nagler had been coxswain for Washington University in 1921 and followed Ebright to Berkeley. Nagler worked as assistant to Ebright and as the freshman coach until 1951 when Nagler went to pursue a career in real estate. See Lemmon, *The Log of Rowing*, 18–19. For Ebright's strategy for recruiting team members, see Emmett Watson, "To Win, You Need a Guy Who Gives: So Says One Coach Whose Crew, Like a Dozen Others, Will Give All They've Got at Syracuse," *Sports Illustrated*, June 18, 1962. See also Carroll "Ky" Ebright, "Ky Ebright: Crew Coach for the University of California and the Olympics," Interview by Arthur M. Arlett, Regional Oral History Office, University of California

Bancroft Library (1968). http://www.archive.org/stream/crewcoachforucoly00ebririch/crewcoachforucoly00ebririch_djvu.txt, accessed July 31, 2014.

8. Brown, in *The Boys in the Boat*, details the crew team from the University of Washington in the 1936 Olympics in Berlin. Brown outlines the relationship between Ebright and the Washington team as well as the relationship between Ebright and the boat-builder George Pocock. See Brown, *The Boys in the Boat*, 86.

9. For more on Ebright's coaching style, see Lemmon, *The Log of Rowing*, 18–49, 94–95. For Ebright's strict dietary and abstinence policy, see Don Blessing, "Ebright: Friend, Tough Coach."

10. For crew management at Cal, see Lemmon, *The Log of Rowing*, 105.

11. Katy Klinedinst, "Directing a Dynasty," *Daily Californian*, November 3, 1999.

12. Ibid.

13. For Ebright's encouragement and rewards for his team, see Lemmon, *The Log of Rowing*, 95.

14. For Cal's progress in the 1920s, see http://www.californiagoldenblogs.com/2011/5/8/2102921/cal-crew-the-oldest-and-grandest-of-golden-bear-sports, accessed August 27, 2014.

15. John A. Lucas, "USOC President Douglas MacArthur and His Olympic Moment, 1927–1928," *OLYMPIKA: The International Journal of Olympic Studies* 3 (1994): 112.

16. John A. Lucas, "Architects of the Modernized American Olympic Committee, 1921–1928: Gustavus Town Kirby, Robert Means Thompson, and General Douglas MacArthur," *Journal of Sport History* 22, no. 1 (1995): 43.

17. Ibid., 113.

18. Quoted from "1928 Medalist Remembers the Glory," accessed July 7, 2014, http://www.berkeley.edu/news/berkeleyan/1996/0605/medalist.htm.

19. Chapin, "He Hollered U.S. Rowers."

20. For a detailed account of the 1928 homecoming and Ebright's mantra for California Olympic Gold, see Cal Crew: The Oldest and Grandest of Golden Bear Sports, accessed August 24, 2014, http://www.californiagoldenblogs.com/2011/5/8/2102921/cal-crew-the-oldest-and-grandest-of-golden-bear-sports.

21. Calvin Coolidge, Address to the American Society of Newspaper Editors, Washington, DC, January 17, 1925, accessed August 27, 2014, http://www.presidency.ucsb.edu/ws/?pid=24180.

22. A great many articles exist from the 1920s that indicate the level of interest the public had in American business; for a good example of business structure and mentality for recruiting potential business leaders, see Charles M. Schwab, "What Carnegie Looked for in Men," *System: The Magazine of Business*, July 1922, 41.

23. See Gary Fishgall, *Gregory Peck: A Biography* (New York: Simon and Schuster, 2002), 41.

24. Percival White, "The Almighty Minute," *Atlantic Monthly*, July 1920.

25. As the economist Kenneth Galbraith described the corporate man, which certainly calls to attention Ebright's insistence on abstinence of alcohol and intensity of training, "Any consideration of the life and larger social existence of the modern corporate man . . . begins and also largely ends with the effect of one all-embracing force. That is *organization* [italics mine] . . . it is to this, at the expense of family, friends, sex, recreation and sometimes health and effective control of alcoholic intake, that he is expected to devote his energies." See John Kenneth Galbraith, "Corporate Man," *New York Times*, January 22, 1984.

26. The correlation between height and income has been the source of multiple scientific studies. See Dave Gilson, "Don't Feel Bad for Tall People on Planes: They Probably Make More Money Than You," *Mother Jones*, August 28, 2014, http://www.motherjones.com/mojo/2014/08/tall-people-make-more-money-short-people, accessed August 28, 2014. Of the 1928 and 1932 Olympian crew teams, all crew members received University of California degrees; the majority ended up in careers in business or as professionals. One notable exception, crew member in the 1928 Olympic boat, John "Jack" Brink, was murdered by a teenage hitchhiker at the age of twenty-five, found in front of his car from a bullet wound to his temple in Falfurrias, Texas, in 1934. See Scott Harrison, "The Crew of '32," *Los Angeles Times*, August 7, 2012, accessed August 20, 2014, http://framework.latimes.com/2012/08/07/the-crew-of-32/. Also see Lemmon, *The Log of Rowing*, 92–93.

27. John Kenneth Galbraith, *The Great Crash, 1929* (Boston: Houghton Mifflin, 1955), 5.

28. Ebright held suspicions that Pocock favored the University of Washington crew team and would build superior equipment for them as well as his belief that Pocock harbored a fondness for the Washington crew team members over the Cal ones; see Brown, *The Boys in the Boat*, 88.

29. Lemmon, *The Log of Rowing*, 97–98. See Brown, *The Boys in the Boat*, 242.

30. Lemmon, *The Log of Rowing*, 49.

31. See Drew Desilver, "U.S. Income Inequality, on Rise for Decades, Is Now Highest Since 1928," Pew Research Center, December 5, 2013, http://www.pewresearch.org/fact-tank/2013/12/05/u-s-income-inequality-on-rise-for-decades-is-now-highest-since-1928/, accessed August 28, 2014.

32. Bruce Barton retold the Gospels and the life of Jesus Christ in terms of American business development and preached a modern interpretation of business as religion, encapsulating his and some Americans' philosophy in his bestseller *The Man Nobody Knows*. Barton contended that "Surely no one will consider us lacking in reverence if we say that every one of the 'principles of modern salesmanship' on which businessmen so much pride themselves are brilliantly exemplified in Jesus' talk and work," or how, according to Barton, Jesus "picked up twelve men from the bottom ranks of business and forged them into an organization that conquered the world," made sense to Americans who looked at the perceived prosperity of the nation as divinely inspired. See Bruce Barton, *The Man Nobody Knows* (New York: Macmillan, 1987).

33. For comments made by President Kerr, see Lemmon, *The Log of Rowing*, xi.

34. Based on the NCAA® Sports Sponsorship and Participation Rates Report, 2012–13, http://www.ncaapublications.com/productdownloads/PR2014.pdf, accessed August 28, 2014, 50–51.

35. See D. C. Charbuck, *The Book of Rowing*, 4th ed. (Woodstock, NY: Overlook Press, 2007), viii.

7. Off the Bench: Asian Americans and Sport in the Santa Clara Valley during the Mid-Twentieth Century

1. Joel S. Franks, *Asian American Basketball: A Century of Sport, Community and Culture* (Jefferson, NC: McFarland, 2016), ch. 2; http://www.bayareacensus.ca.gov/cities/SanJose50.htm, accessed December 11, 2014.

2. "Chicago Huskies First Amateur Cagers to Invade Local Courts," *San Jose Mercury*, December 3, 1949, 9.

3. "All Oriental Cage Tourney at SJS," *San Jose Mercury*, December 20, 1949, 21; "Oriental Cage Team Arrive," December 21, 1949, 19; "Oriental Cagers Open Tournament Tonight," December 22, 1949, 23.

4. "Hawaii Captures Oriental Tourney," *San Jose Mercury*, December 26, 1949, 12.

5. Edward Said, *Orientalism* (New York: Vintage, 1979); John Kuo Tchen, *New York before Chinatown: Orientalism and the Shaping of American Culture, 1776–1882* (Baltimore: Johns Hopkins University Press, 2001; Ronald Takaki, *Strangers from a Different Shore: A History of Asian Americans* (Boston: Back Bay Books, 1998).

6. Joel S. Franks, *Crossing Sidelines, Crossing Cultures: Sport and Asian Pacific American Cultural Citizenship* (Lanham, MD: University Press of America, 2009).

7. Josephine Lee, *Performing Asian America: Race and Ethnicity in the Contemporary Stage* (Philadelphia: Temple University Press, 1998).

8. I will focus on the middle decades of the twentieth century. In part, this is done to keep the chapter's length in check. It is also a reminder to readers that there is nothing novel about Asian American involvement in sport.

9. Renato V. Rosaldo and William V. Flores, "Ideology, Conflict and Evolving Latino Communities: Cultural Citizenship in San Jose, California," in *Latino Cultural Citizenship: Claiming Identity, Space, and Rights*, ed. William V. Flores and Rina Benmayor (Boston: Beacon Press, 1997.)

10. Cecilia M. Tsu, *Garden of the World, Asian Immigrants and the Making of Agriculture in California's Santa Clara Valley* (New York: Oxford University Press, 2013); Sucheng Chan, *The Bittersweet Soil: The Chinese in California Agriculture, 1860–1910* (Berkeley and Los Angeles: University of California Press, 1986); Takaki, *Strangers*.

11. Ibid.; Carey McWilliams, *Factories in the Field: The Story of Migratory Labor in California* (Boston: Little, Brown, 1939).

12. Ibid.; Tsu, *Garden*; Yukio Ichioka, *The Issei: The World of First Generation Japanese Immigrants, 1885–1924* (New York: Free Press, 1988); Timothy J. Luke and Gary Okihiro, *Japanese Legacy: Farming and Community Life in California's Santa Clara Valley* (Cupertino: California History Center, 1985); Takaki, *Strangers*; McWilliams, *Factories*.

13. Pinoy is a term used among Filipinos to men of Filipino descent. Pinay refers to females of Filipino descent.

14. Takaki, *Strangers*, 342; Carlos Bulosan, *America Is in the Heart: A Personal History* (Seattle: University of Washington Press, 1973), 205–9.

15. In 1880, Chinese immigrants comprised 7.7 percent of Santa Clara Valley's population. Forty years later, less than 1 percent of the county's population was Chinese American. In 1900, well below 1 percent of the county's population were Issei. By 1930, Japanese Americans comprised about 3 percent of those living in Santa Clara County. As for Filipinos, throughout the interwar years, they constituted only a slice of 1 percent of the county's settled population, although migrant workers from the Philippines moved in and out of the region. After World War II, the population of Asian Americans remained small. Only 872 Japanese Americans lived in the city of 95,000 in 1950 or less than 1 percent. The population of Chinese had declined to but 0.2 percent of San Jose residents. Filipinos were not counted but lumped into "other races." The next decade San Jose experienced growth, as it became more of a bush league Los Angeles, drawing upon the resources of the postwar "military-industrial" complex, gobbling up unincorporated areas adjacent to it, and extending suburban development. In 1960, San Jose could boast of over 200,000. Nearly 3,000 of these were Japanese Americans, while Filipino Americans now

counted as a separate category, comprised a population of 745 and Chinese Americans, 585. See Tsu, *Garden*, 8; http://www.bayareacensus.ca.gov/cities/SanJose50.htm, accessed November 13, 2014.

16. Steven Misawa, ed., *Beginnings: Japanese Americans in San Jose, 8 Oral Histories* (San Jose, CA: San Jose Japanese American Community Senior Service, 1981), 14.

17. Ralph M. Pearce, *From Asahi to Zebras: Japanese American Baseball in San Jose, California* (San Jose: Japanese American Museum of San Jose), 5–19; "Jap Pitches Hitless and Runless Baseball," *San Jose Mercury*, April 2, 1915, section 2, 16; Misawa, *Beginnings*, 16; "30,000 Yen Offered to Ruth for Baseball Tour of Japan," *New York Times*, June 17, 1925, 17.

18. Jack Graham, "Caught on the Fly," *San Jose Mercury*, May 7, 1922, 21.

19. San Jose's Buddhist Church, meanwhile, sponsored a female team of young adults—a team called the Purplettes because their uniforms bore the purple and white colors of the Buddhist Church. "Japanese Five Wins over Santa Clara Hi," *San Jose Mercury*, January 17, 1934, 14; "Local Japanese Boast Clear Slate," *San Jose Mercury*, January 18, 1934, 18; http://sjzebra.org/web/public/site/pages/about.html, accessed April 29, 2013.

20. George Kinoshita, "Sports Tidbits," *Heart Mountain Sentinel*, January 9, 1943, 7; "Broncs, Zebras Score Triumphs," *Heart Mountain Sentinel*, April 17, 1943, 7; Ted Yano, "Sports Tidbits," *Heart Mountain Sentinel*, May 9, 1943, 7. Indoor facilities for basketball were eventually built at the Heart Mountain camp. See Kunio Otani, "Sport Tidbits," *Heart Mountain Sentinel*, November 13, 1943, 7.

21. Ibid.; "GAA Wins Over Powell Sextette," *Heart Mountain Sentinel*, April 8, 1944, 7; "L'il Yokums Face 'Poops' in 6th Canto," *Heart Mountain Sentinel*, April 8, 1944, 7; Franks, *Asian American Basketball*, ch. 1.

22. Pearce, *From Asahi to Zebras*, 75–84, 96; Samuel O. Regalado, *Nikkei Baseball: Japanese American Players from Immigration and Internment to the Major Leagues* (Urbana: University of Illinois Press, 2013), 91–115; Joel S. Franks, *Asian Pacific Americans and Baseball: A History* (Jefferson, NC: McFarland, 2008), 62–63; "Zebra Nine Tackles Santa Barbara Sunday," *San Jose Mercury*, August 15, 1947, 11.

23. At the same time, a significantly less publicized female team was sponsored, like the Zebras, by San Jose's Buddhist Church. These female hoopsters would compete as the Alphas until the 1970s when they were renamed the Zebraettes. See http://sjzebra.org/web/public/site/pages/about.html, accessed April 29, 2013;
"Adult Basketball Teams Continue Loop Play Monday," *San Jose Mercury*, January 6, 1946, 14; "Adult Basketball," *San Jose Mercury*, February 7, 1946, 14; "21 Teams Compete in Cage Tourney," *San Jose Mercury*, March 3, 1946, 14; "San Jose Zebras Win Cage Tourney," *San Jose Mercury*, December 7, 1949, 19; "City Basketball," *San Jose Mercury*, December 2, 1949, 16; "Tom Ross Tops City Cagers," *San Jose Mercury*, December 25, 1949, 20; US Census Bureau, Manuscript Schedules, City of San Jose and County of Santa Clara, 1940.

24. "San Jose Beats Watsonville," *Chinese Digest*, January 17, 1936, 13; "San Jose Defeats Missouri," *Chinese Digest*, January 24, 1936, 12; "Young Chinese Host Beat San Jose," *Chinese Digest*, January 31, 1936, 12; "Basketball Results," *San Jose Mercury*, February 14, 1936, 21; "San Jose Hopes," *San Jose Mercury*, March 2, 1950, 22; "Filipino-American Cage Tourney Today," *San Jose Mercury*, March 4, 1950, 8; "Filipino Title Won by Vallejo," *San Jose Mercury*, March 5, 1950, 38; Peter Jamero, *Vanishing Filipino Americans: The Bridge Generation* (Lanham, MD: University Press of America, 2011), 23.

25. "Tennis Tournament Starts Saturday," *Chinese Digest*, July 24, 1936, 12; Vincent Chinn, "Thomas Wong, Thomas Leong Enter Quarter Finals," *Chinese Digest*, August 7, 1936,

12; "Sport Shorts," *Chinese Digest,* August 7, 1936, 13; US Census Bureau, Manuscript Schedules, City of San Jose and County of Santa Clara, 1930.

26. "Local Bowlers Hold Top Spots in Nisei Tourney," *San Jose Mercury,* August 12, 1947, 9; March 3, 1951, 9; "Maple Splinters," *San Jose Mercury,* July 26, 1953, 38; "Lucy Minimishi Rolls 665 Series," *San Jose Mercury,* December 2, 1960, 12; http://www.bowlingdigital.com/bowl/node/1978, accessed October 7, 2014.

27. Linda España-Maran, *Creating Masculinity in Los Angeles's Little Manila: Working-Class Filipinos and Popular Culture, 1920s–1950s* (New York: Columbia University Press, 2006), 103; Franks, *Crossing,* 33; *San Jose News,* August 16, 1936, 10.

28. Valerie J. Matsumoto, *Farming the Home Place: A Japanese Community in California, 1919–1942* (Ithaca, NY: Cornell University Press, 1993); Kathleen S. Yep, *Outside the Paint: When Basketball Ruled at the Chinese Playground* (Philadelphia: Temple University Press, 2009).

29. The GAA was significantly undermined by the passage and enforcement of Title IX. See Bruce Howard, "Female Pioneers in State Associations Lead Growth of Girls Sports," http://old.nfhs.org/content.aspx?id=6925, accessed November 17, 2011; Robert Pruter, *The Rise of American High School Sports and the Search for Control, 1880–1930* (Syracuse: Syracuse University Press, 2013), 246–49, 321–22.

30. http://www.niseibaseball.com/html%20articles/Women%20in%20Baseball/ women.html, accessed June 14, 2014; Jack Graham, "Around the Valley," *San Jose Mercury,* July 15, 1933, 17. See also San Jose High School Yearbook, 1931, www.classmates.com, accessed December 2, 2011; 1933, www.classmates.com, accessed March 26, 2014; 1936, www.ancestry.com, accessed July 22, 2014; 1939, www.classmates.com, accessed December 2, 2011.

31. Mountain View High School Yearbook, 1919, www.ancestry.com, accessed June 10, 2014; Santa Clara High School Yearbook, 1935, www.classmates.com, accessed July 24, 2014; Los Gatos High School Yearbook, 1936, www.ancestry.com, accessed July 19, 2014; Campbell High School Yearbook, 1940, www.ancestry.com, accessed June 18, 2013.

32. With the aid of the GI Bill and the booming postwar military-industrial economy in the region, many Japanese Americans and other Asian Americans were able to escape the economic and social segregation they suffered before World War II. See Takaki, *Strangers,* 406; Sucheng Chan, *Asian Americans: An Interpretive History* (Boston: Twayne, 1991), 139–40.

33. San Jose High School Yearbook, 1951, www.classmates.com, accessed March 26, 2014; James Lick High School Yearbook, 1954, www.ancestry.com, accessed June 27, 2014; US Census Bureau, Manuscript Schedules, City of San Jose and County of Santa Clara, 1940.

34. San Jose High School Yearbook, 1925, www.ancestry.com, accessed May 31, 2014; 1928, www.ancestry.com, accessed May 31, 2014; 1930, www.ancestry.com, accessed May 31, 2014; 1934, www.worldvitalrecords.com, accessed February 13, 2011; 1940, www.ancestry.com, accessed October 31, 2013; 1942, www.ancestry.com, accessed October 31, 2013; "San Jose Cagers Open League Season at Redwood City Tonight," *San Jose Mercury,* February 14, 1930, 26; Leonard Herman, "Loss of Stars by Graduation Impairs Records of Local Preps," *San Jose Mercury,* February 4, 1935, 11; Franks, *Asian American Basketball,* ch. 3.

35. "Milpitas Going Strong," *San Jose Mercury,* February 4, 1930, 19; February 10, 1930, 24; Jack Graham, "Santa Clara Cardinals Defeat P.M. Tossers," *San Jose Mercury,* February 18, 1930, 18; "Basketball," *San Jose Mercury,* January 19, 1933, 13.

36. "Bulldogs Begin PAL Cage Slate against Cougars," *San Jose Mercury,* January 6, 1950, 11; *San Jose Mercury,* March 6, 1950, 15; "Vikings Land Four on All-PAL Grid Team," *San*

Jose Mercury, December 6, 1950, 14; "'51 All Cage Team," *San Jose Mercury*, March 3, 1951, 9; Bob Kohn, "S.J. Hill Meet; W.G. Plays Lick," *San Jose Mercury*, January 19, 1960, 16.

37. "S.P. to Face Southside," *San Jose News*, May 28, 1946, 6; *San Jose Mercury*, September 22, 1950; Franks, *Asian Pacific Americans and Baseball*, 75; Ellen Wu, *The Color of Success: Asian Americans and the Origins of the Model Minority* (Princeton, NJ: Princeton University Press, 2014); Cindy I-Fen Cheng, *Citizens of Asian America: Democracy and Race during the Cold War* (New York: New York University Press, 2013).

38. Doug Moe, *Lords of the Ring: The Triumphs and Tragedy of College Boxing's Greatest Team* (Madison: University of Wisconsin Press, 2005), 85–86; Franks, *Crossing*, 44–45.

39. Dick Friendlich, "'47 Edition Spartans Ready for Hilltoppers," *San Francisco Chronicle*, September 18, 1947, 3h; Howard Hagen, "Loop Title, Bowl Bid on Block," *San Diego Union*, November 16, 1946, 16; "Montezumans Selected on All-Loop Team," *San Diego Union*, December 12, 1946, b4.

40. Franks, *Asian American Basketball*, ch. 5; Franks, *Asian Pacific Americans and Baseball*, 75; Franks, *Crossing*, 47, 45, 50, 134; "Spartan Boxers Leave on Northwest Trip," *San Jose News*, February 5, 1940, 7; Fred Merrick, "H-S Offense Baffles Spartans," *San Jose Mercury*, October 3, 1946, 12; "SJS Drills on Offense," San Jose Mercury, November 1, 1955, 15; "Local Boxers in Ring Trails," *San Jose Mercury*, April 21, 1960, 61; "Spartans Open Grid Practices Tomorrow," *San Jose Mercury*, April 24, 1960, 62; "Spartans Stomp on Hawaii, 34–0," *San Mateo Times*, September 24, 1955, 14; San Jose State College Yearbook, 1937, www.worldvitalrecords.com, accessed July 14, 2012; Stanford vs. San Jose State, Football Program, Stanford Stadium, Palo Alto, November 14, 1953; Stanford vs. San Jose State, Football Program, Stanford Stadium, Palo Alto, October 13, 1956.

41. Franks, *Crossing*, 156; "Pacific Citizen Sports," *Pacific Citizen*, December 9, 1950, 6; "Goto Tallies Eight," *Pacific Citizen*, December 9, 1950, 6; Stanford University Yearbook, 1937, www.ancestry.com, accessed April 15, 2014.

42. Santa Clara University Yearbook, 1950, www.ancestry.com, accessed January 31, 2013.

43. "Broncos Win: Pacific Pulls Triple Play," *San Jose Mercury*, March 5, 1950, 37; Franks, *Asian American Basketball*, ch. 5; Santa Clara University Yearbook, 1950, www.ancestry.com, accessed January 31, 2013.

44. Franks, *Crossing*; Wu, *Color of Success*; Cheng, *Asian American Citizens*.

45. Raj Jayadev, "Electronics Assembly for Poverty Wages: Behind Silicon Valley's Instant Millionaires," http://labornotes.org/1999/10/electronics-assembly-poverty-wages-behind-silicon-valleys-instant-millionaires?language=en, accessed December 3, 2010; http://aaci.org, accessed November 7, 2014.

8. San Francisco 49ers: The Romance of Memory

1. Robert F. Jones, "The Prime of Mr. John Brodie," *Sports Illustrated*, September 20, 1971, accessed December 29, 2014, http://www.si.com/vault/1971/09/20/612417/the-prime-of-mr-john-brodie.

2. Pierre Bourdieu, *Distinctions: A Social Critique of the Judgment of Taste Richard Nice*, trans. Richard Nice (Cambridge, MA: Harvard University Press, 1986).

3. Alex Schafran, "Origins of an Urban Crisis: The Restructuring of the San Francisco Bay Area and the Geography of Foreclosure," *International Journal of Urban and Regional Research* 37, no. 2 (2013): 666–67.

4. Gray Brechin, *Imperial San Francisco: Urban Power, Earthly Ruin* (Berkeley: University of California Press, 2006), xxiv.

5. Ibid.; Chester Hartman, *City for Sale: The Transformation of San Francisco, Revised and Updated Edition* (Berkeley: University of California Press, 2002).

6. Brechin, *Imperial San Francisco*; Philip J. Dreyfus, *Our Better Nature: Environment and the Making of San Francisco* (Norman: University of Oklahoma Press, 2008).

7. Brechin, *Imperial San Francisco*; Richard A. Walker, "Industry Builds out the City: The Suburbanization of Manufacturing in the San Francisco Bay Area, 1850–1940," *Journal of Historical Geography* 27, no. 1 (2001): 121–23.

8. Dreyfus, *Our Better Nature*, 63–64.

9. Walker, "Industry Builds out the City," 44.

10. Jasper Rubin, *A Negotiated Landscape: The Transformation of San Francisco's Waterfront since 1950* (Chicago: Center for American Places at Columbia College, 2011).

11. Dreyfus, *Our Better Nature*, 74.

12. Brechin, *Imperial San Francisco*; Dreyfus, *Our Better Nature*; Walker, "Industry Builds out the City."

13. Brechin, *Imperial San Francisco*, 121–23.

14. Michael Kazin, *Barons of Labor: The San Francisco Building Trades and Union Power in the Progressive Era* (Urbana-Champaign: University of Illinois Press, 1989).

15. Robert W. Cherny, "The Making of a Labor Radical: Harry Bridges, 1901–1934," *Pacific Historical Review* 64, no. 3 (1995): 378.

16. Ibid., 380.

17. David F. Selvin, *A Terrible Anger: The 1934 Waterfront and General Strikes in San Francisco* (Detroit, MI: Wayne State University Press, 1996), 11–12.

18. Jeffrey J. Safford, "The Pacific Coast Maritime Strike of 1936: Another View," *Pacific Historical Review* 77, no. 4 (2008): 585.

19. Bruce Nelson, "Unions and the Popular Front: The West Coast Waterfront in the 1930s," *International Labor and Working-Class History* 30 (1986): 63.

20. Walker, "Industry Builds out the City," 44.

21. Ibid.; Brechin, *Imperial San Francisco*; Schafran, "Origins of an Urban Crisis."

22. Walker, "Industry Builds out the City," 44.

23. Hartman, *City for Sale*, 3.

24. Ibid.

25. Maureen M. Smith, "From 'the Finest Ballpark in America' to 'the Jewel of the Waterfront': The Construction of San Francisco's Major League Baseball Stadiums," *International Journal of the History of Sport* 25, no. 11 (2008): 1529–30.

26. Brechin, *Imperial San Francisco*, 157–58.

27. Joyce Kuo, "Excluded, Segregated and Forgotten: A Historical View of the Discrimination of Chinese Americans in Public Schools," *Asian American Law Journal* 5, no. 7 (1998).

28. Hartman, *City for Sale*, 32.

29. Ibid.

30. Douglas S. Massey and Eric Fong, "Segregation and Neighborhood Quality: Blacks, Hispanics, and Asians in the San Francisco Metropolitan Area," *Social Forces* 69, no. 1 (1990); Schafran, "Origins of an Urban Crisis."

31. Dan Levy, "Hard Sell Ahead in Bayview: Few Believe They'll Reap Benefits of Mall-Stadium," *San Francisco Chronicle*, February 6, 1997, accessed January 2, 2015, http://www.sfgate.com/cgi-bin/article.cgi?file=/chronicle/archive/1997/02/06/MN38838.DTL.

32. Manuel Castells, *The Rise of the Network Society: The Information Age: Economy, Society and Culture*, Vol. I (Malden, MA: Blackwell Publishers, 1996).

33. Lonnie Bell, *The History of the San Francisco 49ers* (Mankato, MN: Creative Education, 2005), 4.

34. John Wiebusch, ed., *San Francisco 49ers, Great Teams' Great Years* (New York: Ridge Press, 1974), 18.

35. Bell, *The History of the San Francisco 49ers*, 6.

36. Bruce Lee, "Chicago Rolls in Second Half: Field Goals Highlighted," *San Francisco Chronicle*, September 25, 1950.

37. Bill Leiser, "49ers Woes Result from Growing Up," *San Francisco Chronicle*, September 6, 1950, 1H; Bruce Lee, "Chicago Rolls in Second Half: Field Goals Highlighted," *San Francisco Chronicle*, September 6, 1950.

38. Will Connoly, "Bless St. Mary's, 49ers for Bringing Good Teams to Town," *San Francisco Chronicle*, September 27, 1950, 3H; Bruce Lee, "Chicago Rolls in Second Half: Field Goals Highlighted," *San Francisco Chronicle*, September 27, 1950.

39. Bill Leiser, "Any City Will Support a Winner—the Test Is to Back a Loser, Too," *San Francisco Chronicle*, September 17, 1950, 1H; Bruce Lee, "Chicago Rolls in Second Half: Field Goals Highlighted," *San Francisco Chronicle*, September 17, 1950.

40. Bell, *The History of the San Francisco 49ers*.

41. Darrell Wilson, "49ers to Play Eagles," *San Francisco Chronicle*, September 19, 1964, 41.

42. Darrell Wilson, "49ers' Battered Knees," *San Francisco Chronicle*, October 21, 1964, 54.

43. Darrell Wilson, "St. Mary's Picks Up Lisbon," *San Francisco Chronicle*, October 19, 1964, 59.

44. Tex Maule, "Three for the Money," *Sports Illustrated*, December 16, 1957, http://www.si.com/vault/1957/12/16/605643/three-for-the-money.

45. Ron Fimrite, "From Dark Ages to Dynasty: The 49er Fans of Today See a Perpetual Powerhouse—but It Wasn't Always So," *Sports Illustrated*, February 16, 1995, accessed December 29, 2014, http://www.si.com/vault/1995/02/16/133323/from-dark-ages-to-dynasty-the-49er-fans-of-today-see-a-perpetual-powerhouse—but-it-wasnt-always-so.

46. Ron Fimrite, "Mind You, This Time It's Not All Over: For the Author, Who Long Ago Learned That Even if His Beloved 49ers Were Ahead They Were Doomed, the Frustration Has Ended," *Sports Illustrated*, January 25, 1982, accessed December 29, 2014, http://www.si.com/vault/1982/01/25/540931/mind-you-this-time-its-not-all-over.

47. Fimrite, "From Dark Ages to Dynasty."

48. Darrell Wilson, "Cards Soar—Fans Sore as Scrappy 49ers Lose, 23–13," *San Francisco Chronicle*, September 28, 1964, 47, 49.

49. Dick Friendlich, "Kezar No Place for Babies: Tempo Makes Huge Men Mean," *San Francisco Chronicle*, September 28, 1964, 49.

50. Jones, "The Prime of Mr. John Brodie."

51. Dwight Chapin, "Kezar Memories: Seagulls and Brawls," *San Francisco Chronicle*, http://football.ballparks.com/NFL/SanFrancisco49ers/oldindex.htm; Ron Fimrite, "Way to Go, and the Way It Went," *Sports Illustrated*, December 23, 1974, http://www.si.com/vault/1974/12/23/628160/way-to-go-and-the-way-it-went, accessed January 6, 2015; Fimrite, "Mind You, This Time It's Not All Over"; Fimrite, "From Dark Ages to Dynasty"; Jason Turbow, "West Coast Brew Gave Kezar Stadium Its Color," *New York Times*, January 21, 2012, accessed December 29, 2014, http://www.nytimes.com/2012/01/21/sports/football/colorful-history-of-kezar-stadium-49ers-former-home.html?mwrsm=Email&_r=0.

52. Chapin, "Kezar Memories"; also Turbow, "West Coast Brew."

53. Fimrite, "Way to Go, and the Way It Went."

54. Clifford DeOca, personal correspondence, January 10, 2015.

55. Al Moss, "Fights Flare up as Links Rip Bal, 51–3," *San Francisco Chronicle*, October 2, 1964, 56.

56. Ibid.

57. Al Moss, "Fights Could End Prep Grid," *San Francisco Chronicle*, October 8, 1964, 56.

58. See Norbert Elias and Eric Dunning, eds., *Quest for Excitement: Sport and Leisure in the Civilizing Process* (Oxford: Basil Blackwell, 1986); John Williams, Eric Dunning, and Patrick Murphy, *Hooligans Abroad: The Behaviour and Control of English Fans in Continental Europe* (London: Routledge & Kegan Paul, 1984).

59. See Chapin, "Kezar Memories"; Fimrite, "Way to Go, and the Way It Went," "Mind You, This Time It's Not All Over," and "From Dark Ages to Dynasty"; Dick Friendlich, "'Worst Field'—Cas," *San Francisco Chronicle*, January 3, 1965; Jones, "The Prime of Mr. John Brodie"; Pat Sullivan, "Kezar Memories: Setting Sun and Soaring Suds," *San Francisco Chronicle*, http://football.ballparks.com/NFL/SanFrancisco49ers/oldindex.htm; Turbow, "West Coast Brew."

60. Gwen Knapp, "Harbaugh: Unapologetic Attitude Is Defining Team," *San Francisco Chronicle*, accessed January 6, 2015, http://www.sfgate.com/49ers/knapp/article/Harbaugh-Unapologetic-attitude-is-defining-team-2326940.php, emphasis added.

61. Ibid.

62. "Dualism," Stanford University, http://plato.stanford.edu/entries/dualism/, accessed January 7, 2015.

63. Rick Telander, "Walsh's Boys Go Head to Head: San Francisco's Joe Montana and Cincinnati's Ken Anderson Are Both Students of the Same Pass Maste," *Sports Illustrated*, January 25, 1982, accessed December 27, 2014, http://www.si.com/vault/1982/01/25/540930/walshs-boys-go-head-to-head.

64. Cited in Kenny Moore, "To Baffle and Amaze: In 1979 Bill Walsh Brought His Iconoclastic, Unpredictable and Wide-Open Brand of Football to the Lowly San Francisco 49ers. Three Seasons Later They Were Super Bowl Champions," *San Francisco Chronicle*, Jnly 26, 1982, accessed December 27, 2014, http://www.si.com/vault/1982/07/26/624667/to-baffle-and-amaze.

65. Ibid.

66. Bill Walsh and Glenn Dickey, *Building a Champion: On Football and the Making of the 49ers* (New York: St. Martins Mass Market Paper, 1992).

67. Moore, "To Baffle and Amaze."

68. Vince Lombardi and George L. Flynne, *Vince Lombardi on Football* (New York: Galahad Books, 1973).

69. Walsh and Dickey, *Building a Champion.*

70. Paul Zimmerman, "Armed for the Playoffs under Scholarly Bill Walsh, the 49ers Have Been a Quick Study in Winning," *Sports Illustrated*, December 21, 1981, accessed December 21, 2014, http://www.si.com/vault/1981/12/21/826227/armed-for-the-playoffs-under-scholarly-bill-walsh-the-49ers-have-been-a-quick-study-in-winning; Moore, "To Baffle and Amaze"; Michael Lewis, *The Blind Side: Evolution of a Game* (New York: W. W. Norton & Company, 2007).

71. Paul Zimmerman, "Going Places with New Faces Rookies Are Proving That, with Parity in the NFL, Fresh Blood Can Turn around a Team's Fortunes," *Sports Illustrated*, November 23, 1981.

72. Walsh and Dickey, *Building a Champion.*

73. Craig Neff, "And This Too Has Come to Pass: The New Strategy Is Victory through Air Power . . . Even in the Big Ten," *Sports Illustrated*, November 8, 1982, accessed December 27, 2014, http://www.si.com/vault/1982/11/08/628031/and-this-too-has-come-to-pass.

74. Moore, "To Baffle and Amaze."

75. Rick Telander, "To Be Accurate, He's Not Inaccurate," *Sports Illustrated*, December 21, 1981, accessed December 27, 2014, http://www.si.com/vault/1981/12/21/826226/to-be-accurate-hes-not-inaccurate.

76. Lewis, *The Blind Side*, 108, 109.

77. Zimmerman, "Armed for the Playoffs."

78. Lewis, *The Blind Side*, 111.

79. Don Pierson, "A Big Win for Smash 'Em, Bash 'Em Football," *Chicago Tribune*, January 29, 1991, accessed on December 27, 2014, http://articles.chicagotribune.com/1991-01 29/sports/9101090324_1_ottis-anderson-coaches-giants-organization.

80. Cited in Tom Canavan, "Smashmouth Football Back at Giants Stadium," *SouthCoast Today*, accessed December 27, 2014, http://www.southcoasttoday.com/apps/pbcs.dll/article?AID=/20010104/NEWS/301049957&emailAFriend=1 .

81. Pierson, "A Big Win for Smash 'Em," emphasis added.

82. Hank Hersch, "Tale of Four Cities: For Giant Fans in Two Bay Areas, It Is the Best of Times, It Is the Worst of Times," *Sports Illustrated*, August 24, 1982, accessed December 27, 2014, http://www.si.com/vault/1992/08/24/127025/tale-of-four-cities-for-giant-fans-in-two-bay-areas-it-is-the-best-of-times-it-is-the-worst-of-times.

83. Steve Heimoff, blog, January 23, 2012, accessed December 27, 2014, http://www.steveheimoff.com/index.php/2012/01/23/how-the-right-turned-brie-and-chablis-into-an-epithet/.

84. Pat Buchanan, "In Darkest Pennsylvania," Creators.com, http://holidaymathis.creators.com/opinion/pat-buchanan/in-darkest-pennsylvania.html, accessed December 27, 2014.

85. Filip Bondy, "San Francisco 49ers Fans Are Soft Compared to Ny Giants Fans, Just Like the Bay Area Is Soft Compared to Cold New York City: 10 Reasons to Never Fear 49ers Fans," *Daily News*, accessed December 27, 2014, http://www.nydailynews.com/sports/football/giants/san-francisco-49ers-fans-soft-compared-ny-giants-fans-bay-area-soft-compared-cold-new-york-city-article-1.1008943.

86. Castells, *The Rise of the Network Society*; David Harvey, *The Condition of Postmodernity: An Enquiry into the Origins of Cultural Change* (Cambridge, MA: Blackwell, 1990); Fredric Jameson, *Postmodernism: The Cultural Logic of Late Capitalism* (Durham, NC: Duke University Press, 1991); Jeffrey Montez de Oca, "A Cartel in the Public Interest: NCAA Broadcast Policy during the Early Cold War," *American Studies* 49, no. 3/4 (2008): 157–94.

87. Robert J. Antonio and Alessandro Bonanno, "A New Global Capitalism?: From 'Americanism and Fordism' to 'Americanization-Globalization,'" *American Studies* 41, no. 2/3 (2000): 33–77; Pierre Bourdieu, "The Essence of Neoliberalism: Utopia of Endless Exploitation," http://mondediplo.com/1998/12/08bourdieu; Elizabeth Martinez and Arnoldo Garcia, "What Is Neoliberalism?: A Brief Definition for Activists," accessed December 27, 2014, http://www.corpwatch.org/article.php?id=376; Caroline Ratcliffe and Signe-Mary McKernan, "Childhood Poverty Persistence: Facts and Consequences," in *The Urban Institute's Low-Income Working Families Project* (Washington, DC: Urban Institute, 2010); Schafran, "Origins of an Urban Crisis."

88. Lois Weis, *Class Reunion: The Remaking of the American White Working Class* (New York: Routledge, 2004); Philippe I. Bourgois, *In Search of Respect: Selling Crack in El Barrio* (New York: Cambridge University Press, 2002).

89. Susan Jeffords, *Hard Bodies: Hollywood Masculinity in the Reagan Era* (New Brunswick, NJ: Rutgers University Press, 1994); Michael S. Kimmel, *Manhood in America: A Cultural History*, 3rd ed. (New York: Oxford University Press, 2012); Michael A. Messner, *Power at Play: Sports and the Problem of Masculinity* (Boston: Beacon Press, 1992).

90. Jeffords, *Hard Bodies*; George Lipsitz, "Whiteness and War," in *The Possessive Investment in Whiteness: How White People Profit from Identity Politics* (Philadelphia: Temple University Press, 1998); Joakim Nilsson, "Take Me Back to the Ball Game: Nostalgia and Hegemonic Masculinity in Field of Dreams," *Canadian Review of American Studies* 30, no. 1 (2000): 52–72.

91. Nilsson, "Take Me Back to the Ball Game."

92. Jeffords, *Hard Bodies*; Lipsitz, "Whiteness and War"; Nilsson, "Take Me Back to the Ball Game."

93. Dean V. Baim, *The Sports Stadium as a Municipal Investment* (Westport, CT: Greenwood Press, 1994); Dennis Coates and Brad R. Humphreys, "The Effect of Professional Sports on Earnings and Employment in the Services and Retail Sectors in US Cities," *Regional Science and Urban Economics* 33 (2003); Roger G. Noll and Andrew Zimbalist, eds., *Sports, Jobs, and Taxes: The Economic Impact of Sports Teams and Stadiums* (Washington, DC: Brookings Institute Press, 1997).

94. Fimrite, "Mind You, This Time It's Not All Over."

9. Pioneers in the Pool: The Santa Clara Swim Club Mermaids of the 1950s and 1960s

The authors extend their thanks to Wayne Wilson and the staff at LA84; the staff at the California History Room at the California State Library; and Ivonne Schmid at the International Swimming Hall of Fame.

1. Ledecky is often compared to Janet Evans, who as a seventeen-year-old won three gold medals at the 1988 Olympics. Evans was also a world champion in the 1,500-meter freestyle, an event not offered for women at the Olympic Games. Even decades prior to Evans's dominance in the distance events, American teen girls were the world's best in these events, with Ledecky continuing an American tradition of sorts.

2. Fleishhacker Pool was constructed in 1925 adjacent to the Great Highway. It was one of the country's largest heated salt-water pools, pumping salt water in directly from the Pacific Ocean. It closed in 1971 and was demolished in 2000. See Kevin Starr, *The Dream Endures: California Enters the 1940s* (Oxford: Oxford University Press, 2002). The Crystal Plunge, which opened in 1924 as the Crystal Palace Salt Water Baths, was located at Lombard and Taylor. The salt-water pool pumped salt water from Fisherman's Wharf and closed in 1956 after the building was condemned. The Fairmont Hotel was the setting of the Fairmont Plunge, opening in 1929 and closing in 1945. Also see Dwight Chapin, "When Plunge Was a Splash," *SFGate.com*, July 26, 2005, http://www.sfgate.com/sports/article/WHEN-PLUNGE-WAS-A-SPLASH-2652696.php; Peter Hartlaub, "Shrinkage: The Vanishing Swimming Pools of San Francisco," *SFGate.com*, August 2, 2012, accessed December 24, 2014, http://blog.sfgate.com/thebigevent/2012/08/02/shrinkage-vanishing-swimming-pools-of-san-francisco/.

3. In addition to Ann Curtis's success, the Athens Water Follies, a synchronized swim team from Oakland, dominated the sport for many years in the 1950s. For example, see

"PGCC to Host AAU Swim Meet," *San Mateo Times*, June 4, 1954, 13. For more on the development of women's swimming in the United States, see Lisa Bier, *Fighting the Current: The Rise of American Women's Swimming, 1870–1926* (New York: McFarland, 2011). Bier argues that the female swimmers from this time period were the trailblazers of the sport. Our use of "pioneer" in the title is marking the SCSC swimmers as pioneers of a new era of sport, American society, and international sport, including the Olympic Games.

4. Swim history in the Bay Area extends to earlier than the 1950s, with the construction of several swimming pools in the 1920s (see note 3 for examples). However, the focus of this chapter is post–World War II, another period of growth in pool construction, swim clubs, and amateur swimmers.

5. In terms of swimming pool construction, California was at the forefront of the growth. According to the National Swimming Pool Institute, there were 10,800 swimming pools in 1948, of which 2,500 were residential. By 1965, there were over 566,800 pools in the United States, of which 396,800 were residential, 81,350 were at hotels, 29,100 were swim clubs, and 15,300 community and municipal pools. California led the nation in 1965 with 189,750 public and private swimming pools. See Ted Smits, "The AAU Age Group Program: A Steady Flow of Champions," *Amateur Athlete*, November 1965, 8–9, 37. Smits also notes $3.6 billion spent on public swimming pools.

6. In fact, swimming had long been viewed as a female-appropriate activity. Bier discusses the status of women's swimming at the turn of the twentieth century. Also central to the acceptance of women's swimming in the first half of the twentieth century was Louis deBreda Handley, swimming journalist and coach of the 1924 Women's Olympic swim team, and considered the father of American women's swimming. DeBreda's writings on swimming, including five books, contributed to the sport's popularity as well as changes in the sport, such as the flutter kick. As a coach during the era of Women's Swimming Association, deBreda influenced American women's swimming for close to four decades.

7. The AAU had organized national competitions prior to 1952, though much smaller in nature and not organized by age groups as established by Bauer. Bauer helped revamp the novice and junior swimming divisions. Kaufman quickly joined with Bauer's plan and helped spread the age group program in California and the AAU's Pacific Association, and soon enough, around the nation. The age group program offered divisions for swimmers ages eight to eighteen. See Tony Zonca, "For Swimming, Of Course," *Reading Eagle*, September 17, 1961, 49; "No End in Sight for U.S. Swimming Supremacy," *San Bernardino County Sun*, August 23, 1966, 8; "Building Swim Team to Host Meet at City Park Pool," *Daily Times-News*, August 1, 1976, 16. Also see Bauer and Kaufman's biographies on the International Swimming Hall of Fame website.

8. Rose Mary Dawson, "The Success and Danger of Age Group Swimming," *Amateur Athlete*, July 1961, 12–13, 33.

9. For example, see Rose Mary and Buck Dawson, "Why Your Daughter Should Swim," *Amateur Athlete*, December 1962, 16–17. In this article, the Dawsons encourage parents to get their daughters involved in swimming, which offers physical and emotional benefits—and aligns with the White House emphasis on fitness. Also see Dawson, "The Success and Danger of Age Group Swimming," 12–13, 33; Louis J. Fisher, "AAU Leads in Youth Fitness," *Amateur Athlete*, May 1962, 6, 38. For more on Eisenhower and Kennedy's physical fitness programs, see Craig Allen, *Eisenhower and the Mass Media: Peace, Prosperity, & Prime-time TV* (Chapel Hill: University of North Carolina Press, 1993); Robert L. Griswold, "The 'Flabby American,' the Body, and the Cold War," in *A Shared Experience: Men, Women, and the History of Gender*, ed. Laura McCall and Donald Yacovone (New York: New York

University Press, 1998); Kurt E. Kemper, *College Football and American Culture in the Cold War Era* (Champaign: University of Illinois Press, 2009).

10. *Amateur Athlete*, January 1957, 13.

11. Beth Kaufman, "Age Group Swimming Has Banner Year," *Amateur Athlete*, November 1958, 19.

12. Rose Mary Dawson, "A Better Philosophy on Age Group Swimming," *Amateur Athlete*, December 1958, 19.

13. Ibid. Also see Harold O. Zimman, "MEMO from the Publisher," *Amateur Athlete*, May 1963, 3. Zimman viewed international competition as one end product, but also argued for girls to be engaged in swimming for the "same physical, mental, moral and emotional benefits that men derive from amateur athletics."

14. "Participation Is What Counts," *Amateur Athlete*, November 1961, 12–13. This article notes the retirement of Kaufman from the chairmanship of the AAU swim committee.

15. Jack Clowser, "Boost the Women," *Amateur Athlete*, September 1959, 37. *Amateur Athlete* was a major voice for amateur sport in America. Published monthly, the magazine covered a variety of sports, both female and male athletes. It began publication in 1921 as *The Athlete*.

16. George P. Meade, "Women Swimmers vs. Men," *Amateur Athlete*, December 1957, 18. These sorts of comparisons became the norm. For example, see Ernst Jokl, MD, "The Athletic Status of Women," *Amateur Athlete*, May 1962, 14–15, 23. Jokl compares the times of Chris von Saltza in 1960 with male medalists in 1932. He uses the data to dispel myths about girls in sports and contends that countries that allow women to compete in sport and participate in the Olympic Games are ahead of their peers in other areas as well. Also see Ernst Jokl, MD, "The Athletic Success of Young Girls," *Amateur Athlete*, January 1963, 20–21. In this article, Jokl uses comparative data to help argue for girls to begin serious training prior to the onset of puberty. The medical doctor takes the training of female athletes as a serious endeavor worthy of study and celebration.

17. Zimman, "MEMO from the Publisher," 3.

18. Elliot Almond and Mark Emmons, "A Mentor to Olympians and Kids," *San Jose Mercury News*, May 2, 2006, 1.

19. Coles Phinizy, "The Best in Any Tank, By George!" *Sports Illustrated*, July 22, 1968.

20. "Crack Northern California Swimmers Enter Marin Meet," *Independent Journal*, July 31, 1952, 9.

21. "PA Team Nabs Olympic Title," *Oakland Tribune*, November 12, 1952, 49.

22. "Swimming Meet Opens Tonight," *Daily Review*, January 16, 1953, 6. To provide a sense of how swimming was developing, see "Heinrich: Hayward's '54 Swim Best Ever," *Oakland Tribune*, January 5, 1954, 6. This article details the upcoming Hayward meet, which would feature new AAU events, including breaststroke events for boys and girls. It was stated that the meet was among the first to differentiate between breaststroke and butterfly events. It was also noted that these new events were recently sanctioned by FINA, the world governing body for aquatics.

23. "Barbara Stark Upset in Swimming Meet," *Oakland Tribune*, May 4, 1953, 30.

24. "Barbara Stark Betters Mark in S.F. Meet," *Oakland Tribune*, August 31, 1953, 29.

25. "Phebe Cramer, Barbara Stark in Race Finals," *Oakland Tribune*, April 15, 1954, 57; "Barbara Stark Again Cops U.S. Swim Title," *Oakland Tribune*, April 16, 1954, 37. Stark was unable to defend her title in the 100-yard backstroke. See "Barbara Stark Defeated in 100-Yard Backstroke," *Oakland Tribune*, April 17, 1954, 13.

26. "East Bay Met [*sic*] Championships Set at Albany," *Daily Review*, May 1, 1954, 5. Also see "245 to Compete in Swim Meet," *Oakland Tribune*, April 29, 1954, 55.

27. "Records Fall in East Bay Swim Meet," *Daily Review*, May 3, 1954, 4; "Carol Tait Sets Mark in East Bay Swimming Meet," *Oakland Tribune*, May 3, 1954, 36.

28. "Marin Girl Cracks Two Swim Records," *Independent Journal*, May 24, 1954, 6. Doll is identified as a student at Tamalpais High School who swims for the Santa Clara Swim Club. Also see "Nine PA Swim Marks Set in Berkeley Meet," *Oakland Tribune*, May 24, 1954, 30.

29. "Five PA Swim Marks Broken," *Oakland Tribune*, June 7, 1954, 41.

30. Russ Newland, "Palo Alto's Carol Tait Eyes 1956 Olympics," *San Mateo Times*, June 23, 1954, 19.

31. "Five U.S. Swim Records Broken," *Oakland Tribune*, July 17, 1954, 13. The next day, the newspaper identified Elsenius as being from Berkeley. See "Berkeley Girl on U.S. Swim Team," *Oakland Tribune*, February 27, 1955, 52A.

32. "Two Bay Girls May Be on Pan Am Swim Team," *Oakland Tribune*, February 26, 1955, 15.

33. "600 Registered for AAU's Swimming Meet," *Independent Journal*, August 24, 1955, 15. Also see "Carol Tait Defends AAU Swim Titles," *San Mateo Times*, April 7, 1955, 25.

34. "Walter Reed Wins Swim," *Oakland Tribune*, April 8, 1956, 54A.

35. "Four U.S. Swim Records Broken," *Oakland Tribune*, May 27, 1956, 57A.

36. "San Leandro Relays Draw Top Female Swimmers," *Daily Review*, June 7, 1956, 14.

37. "World Swim Mark Set at Santa Clara," *Oakland Tribune*, June 25, 1956, 34. Other newspapers of the time period note that there is no recognized world record for the women's 500-yard freestyle. For example, see "Doll Slips to Fifth in AAU Swim Finals," *Independent Journal*, April 18, 1957, 12.

38. *Amateur Athlete*, May 1956, 6; August 1956, 6. Sylvia Ruuska, swimming for Berkeley YMCA, thirteen years old. Qualifies for Olympic team. Ruuska was also a member of the 1956 All-America Women's Swimming team in two events, the 500-yd/400-m freestyle and the 880-yd/800-m freestyle. See *Amateur Athlete*, January 1957, 7.

39. *Amateur Athlete*, January 1957, 13.

40. Ibid., May 1957, 9, 30. Also see "Doll Slips to Fifth in AAU Swim Finals," *Independent Journal*, April 18, 1957, 12; "Paula Myers Wins Diving Championship," *Independent Journal*, April 19, 1957, 13; "Sylvia Sets Second U.S. Swim Record," *Oakland Tribune*, April 18, 1957, 45, 46; "Records Fall in Women's Swim Meet," *Oakland Tribune*, April 19, 1957, 43D. Also see "Miss Ruuska Victor in Swim," *New York Times*, April 18, 1957, 40.

41. Betty Baldwin, "New Faces Expected to Star in AAU Women's Swim Meet," *Amateur Athlete*, July 1957, 13; "Women Swimmers in National Meet," *Los Angeles Times*, April 16, 1957, C1.

42. For more on various swim meets in 1957, see "San Jose to Host AAU Swim Stars," *Daily Review*, February 21, 1957, 10; "Leandro Swim Clubs in Huge Albany Meet," *Daily Review*, March 1, 1957, 10; "Top Swim Stars to Compete in AAU Meet at Marin Pool," *Independent Journal*, May 20, 1957, 9; "Six National Records Broken in Los Altos Swimming Meet," *Oakland Tribune*, May 27, 1957, 36E; "AAU Meet Opens in Tiburon Tomorrow," *Independent Journal*, May 31, 1957; "Harrison Sets New Mark," *Oakland Tribune*, June 23, 1957, 58; "Top Age-Group Swimmers to Vie in 5th San Leandro Relays," *Daily Review*, June 28, 1957, 22; "Chris von Saltza Stars in San Leandro Relays," *Daily Review*, July 1, 1957, 8.

43. Jean Hoffman, "Sylvia Ruuska, Swim Phenom, Started Competition at Nine," *Amateur Athlete*, August 1957, 3.

44. "Myers Eyes Diving Throne," *San Mateo Times*, August 16, 1957, 12. Also see "Top Women Swim Stars in AAU Test," *Oakland Tribune*, August 11, 1957, 57. Also see *Amateur Athlete*, August 1957, 12; "Three Marks Set in U.S. Swimming," *New York Times*, August 15, 1957, 25.

45. *Amateur Athlete*, September 1957, 8–9.

46. "Swim Stars, Golfer to Get Doten Awards," *Oakland Tribune*, August 18, 1957, 63. The four swimmers were also named to the AAU All-American Swimming team for the year. See "Five Local Swimmers on All-American Team," *Oakland Tribune*, January 26, 1958, 54.

47. "Sylvia Ruuska Named Outstanding Athlete," *Oakland Tribune*, October 26, 1957, B13. Also see "Sylvia Ruuska to Be Honored Here," *Oakland Tribune*, November 21, 1957, D57.

48. "Sylvia Nabs Point Honors in S.F. Meet," *Oakland Tribune*, December 16, 1957, D45.

49. "Von Saltza Smashes Three More Marks," *Independent Journal*, February 17, 1958, 6.

50. "Sylvia Ruuska Sets World Record," *Daily Review*, February 22, 1958, 8.

51. *Amateur Athlete*, February 1958, 23; *Amateur Athlete*, April 1958, 27.

52. Ben York and Betty Baldwin, "Indoor Records Take a Beating at Women's Title Swim in Texas," *Amateur Athlete*, May 1958, 16–17; "Santa Clara Girl, 14, Breaks Swim Record," *Los Angeles Times*, April 11, 1958, C5.

53. "Women's Swim Record Set," *San Mateo Times*, April 10, 1958, 1.

54. "Chris von Saltza Breaks Own Record," *San Mateo Times*, April 12, 1958, 1; "Eight Marks Set in AAU Swimfest," *Los Angeles Times*, April 13, 1958, C7.

55. "Heinrich Sets 4 PA Swim Marks," *Daily Review*, April 28, 1958, 8.

56. Ben York, "Santa Clara Retains Senior Women's Title," *Amateur Athlete*, September 1958, 16–17. Also see "Von Saltza Shoots for 2nd Record," *San Mateo Times*, August 2, 1958, 8; "Chris Von [*sic*] Saltza Sets World Mark," *New York Times*, August 2, 1958, 14.

57. "Best Ever AAU Swim for Women," *San Mateo Times*, August 4, 1958, 19.

58. "Bay Area Gals Seek Laurels in Nat'l Meet," *Daily Review*, August 1, 1958, 6. Also see "Swim Meet in Opener," *Independent Journal*, August 1, 1958, 14.

59. "Top Swimmers Entered in Berkeley Show," *Oakland Tribune*, November 10, 1958, D40.

60. "Von Saltza Smashes Five Swim Records," *Independent Journal*, January 26, 1959, 7; Also see "Chris Von [*sic*] Saltza Breaks Two Marks," *Oakland Tribune*, January 25, 1959, 51.

61. "Von Saltza, Ruuska on Australian Tour," *Amateur Athlete*, January 1959, 17; "On Tour in Australia," *Amateur Athlete*, April 1959, 14–15. Also see "Chris, Sylvia to Vie in Australia," *Independent Journal*, January 26, 1959, 7; "Bay Girls to Face Aussie Swim Aces," *Daily Review*, January 30, 1959, 14.

62. "Bay Area Girl Sets Aussie Mark," *Oakland Tribune*, February 5, 1959, 42.

63. "2 American Girls Win Aussie Titles," *New York Times*, February 18, 1959, 42.

64. Ben York, "Florida's Big Splash," *Amateur Athlete*, May 1959, 7, 33.

65. "The Ladies Move Outdoors," *Amateur Athlete*, June 1959, 19, 25.

66. Hank Solomon, "The Incredible Sylvia Ruuska," *Amateur Athlete*, July 1959, 10.

67. Wally Willis, "Berkeley Y Wins AAU Swim Title," *Oakland Tribune*, July 20, 1959, 35, 37.

68. "Swim Team Dunks Coach," *Oakland Tribune*, July 20, 1959, 37.

69. "The Challenge from Redding," *Amateur Athlete*, August 1959, 15.

70. "Chris Wins 3rd Swimming Title," *Oakland Tribune*, September 6, 1959, 13; "Chris Von [*sic*] Saltza Excels at Games," *New York Times*, September 6, 1959, S1; "Chris Von [*sic*] Saltza Wins Fourth and Fifth Gold Medals in Games," *New York Times*, September 7, 1959, 21. The trials for the Pan Am Games were held a month prior in East Lansing, Michigan. See "Chris Von [*sic*] Saltza Gains 3d Victory," *New York Times*, August 12, 1959, 21; "Chris von Saltza Wins Two Events," *Los Angeles Times*, August 9, 1959, C5; also see "10 All-America Swim Berths to von Saltza," *Los Angeles Times*, December 7, 1959, C7.

71. For example, see "Santa Clara Miss Cracks Own Record," *Oakland Tribune*, January 31, 1960, 58; "Chris von Saltza Cracks Own Mark," *Oakland Tribune*, February 28, 1960, 61.

72. "Phillips Co. Hosts Senior Women's Title Swim Meet April 14–16," *Amateur Athlete*, March 1960, 24.

73. "The Baroness Deserves a Medal," *Amateur Athlete*, March 1960, 19, 21, 22.

74. "Berkeley Girls Compete in National Swim Meet," *Oakland Tribune*, April 10, 1960, 60; "AAU Swim Meet Opens Tomorrow," *Oakland Tribune*, April 13, 1960, D41.

75. Chris Von [*sic*] Saltza Sets Three Marks," *Los Angeles Times*, April 17, 1960, C7; "Records Fall in Women's AAU Swim," *Independent-Journal*, April 15, 1960, 10; "Sylvia Breaks Swim Record," *Oakland Tribune*, April 15, 1960, D43; "Chris Smashes Second AAU Mark," *Oakland Tribune*, April 16, 1960, B13.

76. Joseph M. Sheehan, "Drills (Not Pills) Put Pep in the U.S. Swim Team," *New York Times*, August 10, 1960, 40. This article also detailed the regimented training of the SCSC under Haines's leadership, such as year-round training, double workouts, six-day-a-week practices, land drills, etc. Haines also dismisses the accusations of other coaches and swimmers that he provided his swimmers with pep pills.

77. "Miss Chris Again," *Amateur Athlete*, May 1960, 8, 42. Also see "Chris von Saltza Is First Again in A.A.U. Women's Final," *New York Times*, April 16, 1960, 13.

78. Betty Baldwin, "The Girls Come of Age," *Amateur Athlete*, July 1960, 7.

79. Ibid., 8.

80. "Von Saltza, Burke Spark Swim Victory," *Los Angeles Times*, July 18, 1960, C6.

81. Ben York, "The Young Woman Went West," *Amateur Athlete*, August 1960, 15. Also see "Gals Maul Records in AAU Swimming; Ruuska Is Upset," *Independent-Journal*, July 16, 1960, 7; "Chris VonSaltza [*sic*] Nabs 2nd AAU Title; Ann, Too," *Daily Review*, July 17, 1960, III, 4; "Chris Von [*sic*] Saltza Clips Mark," *New York Times*, July 17, 1960, 143; "Von Saltza, Burke Spark Swim Victory," *Los Angeles Times*, July 18, 1960, C6. The third world record was set by Becky Collins in the 200-meter butterfly.

82. George Haines, "Balance Is the Best," *Amateur Athlete*, September 1960, 26.

83. Allison Danzig, "Chris Von [*sic*] Saltza Takes Heat in 100," *New York Times*, August 27, 1960, 13; "Chris von Saltza Smashes Mark," *Daily Review*, August 26, 1960, 22. Despite winning the most medals of the American female Olympians, von Saltza's accomplishments were overshadowed by track star Wilma Rudolph, who won three gold medals. For more on the media portrayal of von Saltza and Rudolph, see chapter 2 in Rita Liberti and Maureen M. Smith, *(Re)Presenting Wilma Rudolph* (Syracuse, NY: Syracuse University Press, 2015).

84. "The Competition at Rome," *Amateur Athlete*, October 1960, 12; Huston Horn, "Girls on the Go-Go-Go," *Sports Illustrated*, July 25, 1960; Arlie W. Schmidt, "Four Long Days in Pressure City," *Sports Illustrated*, August 15, 1960.

85. See *Amateur Athlete*, February 1961, 16–17.

86. "New Look at Hialeah," *Amateur Athlete*, May 1961, 8–9. Von Saltza was featured on the cover of this issue. The event was held in an outdoor pool following indoor standards.

There was some concern as to the youth of swimmers. In the ten years since the start of the AAU Age Group swimming program, the number of swimmers had exploded to over 800,000.

87. "Chris von Saltza Gains Fourth Individual Crown in A.A.U.'s Women Swim," *New York Times*, April 9, 1961, S5. Also "Chris VonSaltza [*sic*] Sets Second Record," *Daily Review*, April 7, 1961, 21.

88. These comments indicate the worry about younger girls beating their senior swimming counterparts, women who were older than eighteen and no longer part of age group swimming. Rose Mary Dawson, "The Success and Danger of Age Group Swimming," *Amateur Athlete*, July 1961, 12–13, 33. Dawson was writing specifically about girls. While teen boys found some success in the Olympic Games, they also had opportunities that extended beyond their swim clubs, including high school teams, but more importantly college teams. Their swim careers were not viewed as needing to end once they entered college. It was believed that age group swimming helped strengthen college programs. For example, see Harold W. Henning, "The Best Is Good Enough," *Amateur Athlete*, December 1961, 10–11, 34, 38.

89. "LAAC's Carolyn House Becomes New American Swimming Queen," *Los Angeles Times*, August 14, 1961; C. Robert Paul, "The New Rule at Philadelphia," *Amateur Athlete*, September 1961, 6–9.

90. "Chris Von [*sic*] Saltza Upset; Mark Falls in Women's AAU Swimming," *Los Angeles Times*, August 12, 1961, A7.

91. These sort of trips were reminiscent of von Saltza and Ruuska's trip to Australia; however, the new focus seemed to be on exchanging ideas about training and in some ways, generating interest in getting other countries to begin their own age group swimming programs. See Ben York, "The Girls Take a Grand Tour," *Amateur Athlete*, October 1961, 8–9, 32; Rose Mary (Mann) Dawson, "Our Age-Group Swimmers Go Abroad," *Amateur Athlete*, September 1961, 17–19, 38. Dawson served as a chaperone-coach of a June trip to Japan with four California teen swimmers, de Varona, Kerry Haines (daughter of George, age thirteen), SCSC swimmer Dick Roth (age thirteen), and Tom Jamison (age thirteen). The young squad swam in eleven meets over nineteen days as guests of Nippon-Suisei, the Japanese Amateur Swimming Federation. Dawson claimed the invitation demonstrated "what high regard the amateur sports world now has for the AAU program that did so much to bring the United States back to the top in Olympic swimming."

92. "Age Group Swim Records Tumble," *Amateur Athlete*, December 1961, 16–17, 31. This same moniker was bestowed a year later. See Harold W. Heller, "Gary Hall 1962 King of Age Group Swimming," *Amateur Athlete*, December 1962, 30–31.

93. "National Indoor Swim Championships Set," *Amateur Athlete*, March 1962, 24; "Swimmers Are 'Go' for National Championship," *Amateur Athlete*, April 1962, 32.

94. Marco Smolich, "Robyn Flies at Sacramento," *Amateur Athlete*, June 1962, 10, 36; "Three Teenagers Break Women's Swim Marks," *Los Angeles Times*, April 21, 1962, A2; "Two Teenagers Takes Triple Swim Crowns," *Los Angeles Times*, April 22, 1962, C10; Barbara Heilman, "Still on Top at 14," *Sports Illustrated*, April 16, 1962.

95. "Swimmers Set for AAU Championships," *Amateur Athlete*, August 1962, 24.

96. "A Record House Sees a House Record," *Amateur Athlete*, September 1962, 8–9; "Finneran, House Pace LAAC to Women's AAU Swim Title," *Los Angeles Times*, August 20, 1962, B1.

97. Tim Horgan, "The 1:20 Pound Champion," *Amateur Athlete*, October 1962, 20–21.

98. "All American Swimming Teams," *Amateur Athlete*, January 1963, 14–15.

99. Jack Clowser, "Queen of the Pool Haul," *Amateur Athlete*, May 1963, 6–7, 31; "Finneran Girls Set 2 Swim Records," *Los Angeles Times*, March 29, 1963, C4; "Santa Clara Mermaids Rout Field in AAU," *Los Angeles Times*, April 1, 1963, B8; "Santa Clara Swim Ace Sets Swim Mark," *Los Angeles Times*, March 30, 1963, A3.

100. "Women's Championships Revisit High Point," *Amateur Athlete*, July 1963, 22; Jack Houghteling, "Their Eyes Are on Tokyo," *Amateur Athlete*, August 1963, 14.

101. "Ellis, de Varona Smash Records, LAAC Leads," *Los Angeles Times*, August 17, 1963, A3; "LAAC Gains Title; Relay Record Set," *Los Angeles Times*, August 8, 1963, I2; Bill Hodges, "The Robyn Wings at High Point," *Amateur Athlete*, September 1963, 8–9, 28. According to Hodges, de Varona was headed to participate in the US-USSR meet in the Soviet Union, though the sporting monthly did not cover this event.

102. Dr. Harold W. Henning, "Olympic Swim Trials Set for New York," *Amateur Athlete*, April 1964, 22.

103. Jimmy Jordan, "AAU Swim a Record-Setting Success," *Amateur Athlete*, May 1964, 12–13, 37; "de Varona and Talmage Make Quite a Splash!" *Los Angeles Times*, April 20, 1964, B5; "de Varona Sets Mark, Finneran Loses 500," *Los Angeles Times*, April 19, 1964, C4; "Ferguson, Stouder in Record Swim Victories," *Los Angeles Times*, April 18, 1964, A4; "Finneran Sets Record, Easily Wins AAU 1650," *Los Angeles Times*, April 17, 1964, B4.

104. William Trombley, "For God, Country and the Santa Clara Swim Club," *Saturday Evening Post*, July 25, 1964, 66. Twombley discusses de Varona's family relocating to Santa Clara for her swimming. Twombley also notes that fifteen years prior, there had been only 25,000 amateur swimmers in the United States, and the country now boasted over 500,000, with 10,000 in the Bay Area alone. He referred to age group swimming as the "underwater equivalent of Little League."

105. *LIFE*, October 9, 1964; *Sports Illustrated*, April 16, 1962.

106. Tim Horgan, "The Solid Gold Donna de Varona," *Amateur Athlete*, June 1964, 13–15.

107. Ken Bishop, "The Tidal Wave Hits Los Altos," *Amateur Athlete*, September 1964, 10–11, 32; Ken Bishop, "The Wreck of the Old 57," *Amateur Athlete*, September 1964, 12–15, 30; "Stouder, Rose Shatter World Swim Standards," *Los Angeles Times*, August 3, 1964, B1, B6.

108. "Almost as Good, and Much Prettier," *Amateur Athlete*, October 1964, 18.

109. Ibid. This emphasis on the beauty and aesthetics of the women is similar to earlier coverage of female swimmers in the 1920s. For example, see Mark Dyreson, "Icons of Liberty or Objects of Desire? American Women Olympians and the Politics of Consumption," *Journal of Contemporary History* 38, no. 3 (2003): 435–60.

110. "The U.S. Caught Gold in Yoyogi," *Amateur Athlete*, November 1964, 17–19; Paul Zimmerman, "Schollander Brings U.S. First Gold Medal," *Los Angeles Times*, October 13, 1963, B1.

111. "U.S. Aquatic Queens Rule Tokyo," *Amateur Athlete*, November 1964, 20–23; "Americans Take Olympic Lead with 5 Medals, 4 in Swimming and Diving," *New York Times*, October 13, 1964, 52; "Miss Stouder Wants Fourth Gold Medal and Then Fun," *New York Times*, October 17, 1964, 21; "Records Come Splashing Down in Tokyo Pool," *New York Times*, October 14, 1964, 56; "U.S. Athletes off to Strong Start," *New York Times*, October 12, 1964, 40; "U.S. Swimmers Lower Records on Way to Gold Medals," *New York Times*, October 15, 1964, 47; Gwilym S. Brown, "A Dominant Swimmer for a Dominant Country," *Sports Illustrated*, October 26, 1964.

112. "U.S. Aquatic Queens Rule Tokyo," *Amateur Athlete*, November 1964, 22.
113. Watson also swam in the preliminary heat in the 4x100-meter medley relay, but during this time period only swimmers who swam in the finals received a medal.
114. Bob Merrill, "Pokey Watson, World Traveler," *Amateur Athlete*, December 1967, 20–21, 32.
115. "AAU Age Group Swim Program Rates Gold Medal," *Amateur Athlete*, December 1964, 16–17, 35. The AAU touted the age group success of the swimmers, noting de Varona's thirty-three firsts in age group swimming. Pokey Watson held nine firsts in the ten-and-under group, added nine more first the next year, two firsts and three seconds the next year, and one third in the thirteen- to fourteen-year-old age group. Terri Stickles won six titles and four Junior Olympic titles in a three-year period. Sharon Finneran held eleven first in age group, including seven in 1961 as a fifteen-year-old. Claudia Kolb had two firsts in 1962, and two more age group titles the next year. All of these 1964 Olympic swimmers were training at SCSC.
116. "16 Stars Vie for '64 Sullivan Award," *Amateur Athlete*, January 1965, 6–7, 42; "AAU Pacific Association Honors Olympians at San Francisco Award Dinner," *Amateur Athlete*, January 1965, 22–23, 30. California dominated Junior Olympics competition. In 1965, the western state won 56 of 144 titles with thirty-eight swimmers. See "AAU Junior Olympians," *Amateur Athlete*, December 1965, 14–15.
117. Shavenau Glick, "High School Girls Toss Record Hop," *Amateur Athlete*, May 1965, 12–13, 27. This was also reportedly the first AAU championship meet where the flip turn was used. For more on Caretto, see Shavenau Glick, "Patty Caretto—The Champion Who Shouldn't Be," *Amateur Athlete*, October 1965, 16–18. There was no reason to see an end to America's dominance in international swimming. According to Smits, "the failure of other countries to copy" America's age group swimming program all but assured the United States of continued success in the medal count. Smits compared American swimming to a factory with replaceable parts. See Ted Smits, "The AAU Age Group Program: A Steady Flow of Champions," *Amateur Athlete*, November 1965, 8–9, 37. For additional accounts of the indoor championships, see "Jeanne Hallock Victor in AAU 100 Freestyle," *Los Angeles Times*, April 10, 1965, A1; Braven Dyer, "Patty Caretto, 14, Breaks Women's Distance Record, Commerce Girls Save Best for Last, Win Swim Title," *Los Angele Times*, April 12, 1965, B3. Dyer's writing about women's swimming was quite graphic. For example, in this account of the record-setting performances, he used the phrase "climaxing an orgy of record smashing with four more new American marks" to describe the athletic excellence of teenage girls. Also see "Santa Clara Aces Dominate Meet," *Los Angeles Times*, July 24, 1965, A4.
118. Ned Braunschweiger, "Women Swimmers Wreck Old Adage," *Amateur Athlete*, September 1965, 10–11; "Randall, Kolb Shatter World Swim Records," *Los Angeles Times*, August 16, 1965, C5; "Krause, Moore Erase World Swim Records," *Los Angeles Times*, August 16, 1965, B1.
119. Gus Steiger, "Swimming's New Wave Is 'Amazing,'" *Amateur Athlete*, February 1966, 20–22.
120. "Many Olympians Plan to Swim in Sr. Women's Swim Championships," *Amateur Athlete*, April 1966, 27, 32.
121. George E. Durham, "Santa Clara Retains Swim Crown," *Amateur Athlete*, May 1966, 12, 31; "Santa Clara Mermaids Break American Mark," *Los Angeles Times*, March 13, 1966, I4.

122. "2 More Marks Set," *New York Times*, April 17, 1966, Sports, 4; "Finneran Leads Record Assault," *Los Angeles Times*, April 18, 1966, B2; "Randall, Ball Set American Swim Records," *Los Angeles Times*, April 17, 1966, H2; "Women's Swimming Winds up in Splurge of National Records," *New York Times*, April 18, 1966, 40.

123. Yevgeny Pozdnyakov, "Schollander Shows the Way," *Amateur Athlete*, September 1966, 10–11, 25.

124. Curt Mosher, "Fastest Water in the West," *Amateur Athlete*, October 1966, 6–7.

125. Curt Mosher, "Youth—Ah, It's Wonderful," *Amateur Athlete*, October 1966, 9; "Santa Clara Swim Club Breaks World Record in Women's Free-Style Relay," *New York Times*, August 21, 1966, Sports, 6; "Santa Clara Swim Club Girls Set Relay Record," *Los Angeles Times*, August 21, 1966, C11; "UCLA Sophomore, Miss Caretto Smash World Record Swim Marks," *Los Angeles Times*, August 22, 1966, B1; "U.S. Olympic Swimming May Improve on '64 Triumphs," *Los Angeles Times*, August 23, 1966, B4.

126. Harry Hainsworth, "U.S. Water Wizards Pace 17 Gold Medalists at Mexico's 'Olympics,'" *Amateur Athlete*, December 1966, 11, 34. For more on Catie Ball, see Terry Smith, "That's C-A-T-I-E Ball, Spelled with a C, as in Champion," *Amateur Athlete*, November 1967, 20–21, 34; Sandy Pawde, "Catie Has the Perfect Put-Down," *Amateur Athlete*, May 1968, 27.

127. "All-America Swimming Squad Lists Pokey Watson in Seven Spots," *New York Times*, December 16, 1966, 84; "1966 AAU All-America Women's Swimming Team," *Amateur Athlete*, February 1967, 16.

128. Dennis Lustig, "Claudia Paces Women's Swimming," *Amateur Athlete*, June 1967, 4–5; "Sue Pederson, 13, Sets New Medley Mark," *Los Angeles Times*, April 15, 1967, A4; "3 American Records Fall in Women's Swim Meet," *Los Angeles Times*, April 14, 1967, C9.

129. Albert Schoenfield, "Age Group Teens Dominate Women's Swimming World," *Amateur Athlete*, August 1967, 19, 31. For one example of how "older" swimmers were written about, see Bill Kreifeldt, "No Rocking Chair for Cynthia," *Amateur Athlete*, January 1968, 15, 34. Goyette, at age twenty-one, was considered the "old lady of competitive swimming." While attending college, Goyette still competed for her club team, but also began to swim in college meets for women.

130. Noah David Gurock, "Pan-Am Swimmers Submerge 14 Standards," *Amateur Athlete*, September 1967, 12–14.

131. "Five World Records Shattered in Women's AAU Swimming Meet," *Los Angeles Times*, August 20, 1967, H8; Harvey Pollack, "Happy Homecoming for Debbie," *Amateur Athlete*, October 1967, 4–5, 36. Meyer was also on the cover of the October issue. For more on Meyer, see Sherman Chavoor, "Debbie Meyer Is a Copy Cat," *Amateur Athlete*, January 1968, 16. Chavoor was Meyer's coach. Also see "Debbie Meyer, Catie Ball Smash World Swim Marks," *Los Angeles Times*, August 21, 1967, 5; George P. Meade, "And a Little Girl Shall Show the Way . . ." *Amateur Athlete*, May 1968, 26. Meade compares Meyer with male swimmers at the 1928 Olympic Games.

132. Harry Hainsworth, "U.S. Swimmers Honed Razor-Sharp for Olympics," *Amateur Athlete*, December 1967, 24.

133. Coles Phinizy, "The Best in Any Tank, By George!" *Sports Illustrated*, July 22, 1968. Phinizy wrongly states the SCSC women had won twenty-one of the last twenty-three championship meets. Fifteen of twenty-two is an equally impressive feat.

134. Bob Merrill, "Pokey Watson, World Traveler," *Amateur Athlete*, December 1967, 20–21, 32.

135. Harvey Shapiro, "Debbie and Claudia Co-Queens of Trees Pool," *Amateur Athlete*, June 1968, 14–15, 28; "Three American Records Clipped in Women's A.A.U. Swim Finals," *New York Times*, April 19, 1968, 60; "Debbie Meyer Breaks Own 1650 Record," *Los Angeles Times*, April 21, 1968, C10; "Claudia Kolb Breaks Mark in 400 Medley," *Los Angeles Times*, March 17, 1968, C7; "Debbie Meyer Breaks 1650 Freestyle Mark," *Los Angeles Times*, March 18, 1968, B3.

136. For more on the outdoor championships and the Olympic Trials, see "Arden Hills Sets World Relay Record," *Los Angeles Times*, August 4, 1968, B7; "Burton and Debbie Meyer Capture 1,500-Meter Events of AAU Title Swim," *New York Times*, August 5, 1968, 54; "Debbie Sets 3rd World Record in Swim Trials," *Los Angeles Times*, August 29, 1968, D3; "Girl Swimmer Breaks Three World Records," *Los Angeles Times*, August 26, 1968, E1; "Hutton, Meyer Just Miss World 1500 Records," *Los Angeles Times*, August 5, 1968, E5; "World 100-Meter Mark Barely Eludes Pedersen, Pedersen Wins," *Los Angeles Times*, August 26, 1968, D1.

137. Paul Zimmerman, "Pokey, Claudia Give U.S. 2 More Gold Medals," *Los Angeles Times*, October 26, 1968, D1.

138. "Olympic Swim Aces Watson, Kolb Retire," *Los Angeles Times*, June 29, 1969, C2.

139. For examples of the coverage of the men's team in the late 1960s, see Kim Chapin, "Old and New Pool Their Talent," *Sports Illustrated*, August 21, 1967; Anita Verschoth, "Santa Clara Holds a Splashdown," *Sports Illustrated*, July 21, 1969.

140. At the Olympic Games in 1972, there were fourteen events for women; the US won eight of those events, and a total of seventeen medals (accounting for 40 percent of the total medals in swimming). In 1976, that American dominance would be dismantled by East Germany.

141. "A Swimming Success at Lovely Fort Lauderdale," *Amateur Athlete*, February 1967, 20–23.

142. "12 Elected to Swimming's Hall of Fame; Miss de Varona and Mrs. Drake Head Coaches' Choice," *New York Times*, June 6, 1969, 49.

143. Other female SCSC stars have also been inducted into the Hall of Fame, such as Karen Moe and Keena Rothhammer, as well as a number of SCSC male swimmers, such as Don Schollander, Mark Spitz, Dick Roth, and Steve Clark, making the swim club the most represented club in the Hall of Fame.

10. A Friendly Competition: The 1962 US-USSR Track Meet at The Farm

1. "Biggest, best dual meet ever," *Palo Alto Times*, July 23, 1962, 16. San Francisco's two mainstream papers published a picture of the opening ceremony on page one. See *San Francisco Chronicle* and *San Francisco Examiner*, July 22, 1962, 1.

2. "Topping the Kangaroo," *Time*, August 3, 1962, 43.

3. For more on the meets, see Joseph M. Turrini, "'It Was Communism Versus the Free World': The USA-USSR Dual Track Meet Series and the Development of Track and Field in the United States, 1958–1985," *Journal of Sport History* 28 (Fall 2001): 427–71, and Rostislav Orlov, "Twenty-Four Rounds of the 'Match of the Giants,'" in *USSR-USA Sports Encounters*, ed. Victor Kuznetsov and Mikhail Lukashev, trans. by John Williams (Moscow: Progress, 1977), 33–55.

4. Report of 1959 meet in J. E. Wallace Sterling Papers (hereafter JEWSP), Box A26, Folder 18, Special Collections, Stanford University Libraries, Stanford, CA.

5. John B. Scott and James S. Ward, *Champions for Life* (Columbus, OH: Nicholas Ward, 2004), 7–13, 17, 19, 23, 43.

6. Art Rosenbaum, "Jordan Seeks Games Trials for Stanford," *Los Angeles Times*, February 24, 1959, sec. 4, 4.

7. Joseph M. Sheehan, "Brass Sets Mark for Pole Vault; Norton Wins 200," *New York Times*, July 3, 1960, sec. 5, 1; Paul Zimmerman, "Track Meet Big Business," *Los Angeles Times*, July 23, 1962, sec. 3, 2.

8. "Stanford Gets US-Russ," *San Francisco Chronicle*, January 21, 1961, 26.

9. Contract negotiations in JEWSP, Box A26, Folder 18.

10. Quoted in Walt Gamage, "Sport Shots," *Palo Alto Times*, July 17, 1962, 16, and Paul Emerson, "Stanford track coach follows own rule in demanding best," *Palo Alto Times*, July 12, 1962, 15.

11. *The Gallup Poll: Public Opinion 1935–1971, vol. 3, 1959–1971* (New York: Random House, 1972), 1755, 1699.

12. Walter LaFeber, *America, Russia, and the Cold War, 1945–1992*, 7th ed. (New York: McGraw-Hill, 1993), 219; Aleksandr Fursenko and Timothy Naftali, *Khrushchev's Cold War: The Inside Story of an American Adversary* (New York: Norton, 2006), 410; and Deborah Welch Larson, *Anatomy of Mistrust: U.S.-Soviet Relations during the Cold War* (Ithaca, NY: Cornell University Press), 140–41.

13. JEWSP, Box A26, Folder 18.

14. Ibid.; "Palo Alto has two days of 'Big Game' crowds," *Palo Alto Times*, July 23, 1962, 1.

15. Al Wolf, "Russians Demand AAU Pay Expenses," *Los Angeles Times*, July 15, 1962, sec. 4, 3. See also "Russ refuse to pay NY to SF air fare," *Palo Alto Times*, July 14, 1962, 1, and "AAU Picks Up $30,000 Soviet Track Travel Bill," *Washington Post*, July 15, 1962, C1.

16. Description of Masters in "An Athletic Era at Stanford Ends," *Christian Science Monitor*, September 3, 1963, 14. Refusal of Masters in JEWSP, Box A26, Folder 18. For additional coverage of dilemma, see Jesse Abramson, "Sale Hits 110,000 for Soviet Track," *New York Herald Tribune*, July 19, 1962, 23.

17. Peter Shaw, "60 Soviet athletes arrive at Stanford," *Palo Alto Times*, July 14, 1962, 1. The *Palo Alto Times* printed several photographs of the team's arrival. For example, see July 14, 1962, 11.

18. Dink Templeton, "Spirit of Olympics sweeping over Stanford," *Palo Alto Times*, July 17, 1962, 13; Bert Nelson, "USA-USSR Highlights," *Track and Field News*, August 1962, 4; Flags in Mrs. Thomas Rilea, "Russia at Stanford," *Chicago Daily Tribune*, August 1, 1962, 20; "To Soviet Athletes: Welcome!" *Palo Alto Times*, July 17, 1962, 14; Garry Cavalli, "Cold War, Warm Welcome," *Stanford Magazine*, May/June 2005, 53.

19. Bill Leiser, "High Jump Looms as Top Event," *San Francisco Chronicle*, July 20, 1962, 42, and Art Rosenbaum, "U.S. Stars Oerter, Grelle Ailing," *San Francisco Chronicle*, July 18, 1962, 43.

20. David Cowger, "Workers' fringe benefits interest Russ track stars," *Palo Alto Times*, July 18, 1962, 17.

21. Peter Grothe, "Special Report: A Most Human Group," *San Francisco Chronicle*, July 20, 1962, 42. For pictures, see *Palo Alto Times*, July 17, 1962, 8; July 18, 1962, 17; and July 19, 1962, 8, and *San Francisco Chronicle*, July 16, 1962, 52. Pat Frizzell, "Sports Patter . . . ," *Sacramento Union*, July 24, 1962, 6.

22. Victor Kruprianov, "Headlines and Highlights," *Moscow News*, July 15, 1962, 16. For information on women's team, see Gerald Lawson, *World Record Breakers in Track &*

Field Athletics (Champaign, IL: Human Kinetics, 1997), 375–76, 406, 415, 418–19; Peter Matthews, *Historical Dictionary of Track and Field* (Lanham, MD: Scarecrow Press, 2012), 170.

23. Bert Nelson, "Reds loaded with stars," *Palo Alto Times*, July 17, 1962, 19.

24. UPI quoted in "Ter-Ovanesyan of Soviet Union Sets World Record in Broad Jump," *New York Times*, June 11, 1962, 43; *Sports Illustrated*, July 16, 1962, cover. *Sports Illustrated* also published a short memoir by Ter-Ovanesyan. See Igor Ter-Ovanesyan, "A Soviet Champion Tells His Own Story," *Sports Illustrated*, August 6, 1962, 16–19, 52.

25. UPI in "Armenian Leaps 27 Feet 3 Inches," *New York Times*, June 11, 1962, 43; Arthur Daley, "Assembling the Talent," *New York Times*, June 22, 1962, 38. For CIA and defection, see David Maraniss, *Rome 1960: The Olympics That Changed the World* (New York: Simon & Schuster, 2008), 25–26, 28, 114, 144, 257–58.

26. Jack Murphy "Lipstick, Hair Ribbons, and Bright-Green Shorts," *New Yorker*, August 18, 1962, 76; "Topping the Kangaroo," *Time*, August 3, 1962, 43. For more on Brumel, see Gerard Elensky, "Thirteen Spells Victory," *Moscow News*, August 4, 1962, 15; Lawson, *World Record Breakers*, 182; and Valeri Brumel, "The Big Jump: A Siberian Champion Tells His Story," *Sports Illustrated*, February 4, 1963, 38–41; quote from p. 39.

27. Thompson quoted in "Yank Girls: We'll Make Things Close," *San Francisco Chronicle*, July 17, 1962, 37.

28. Records of Long, Oerter, and Connolly in Lawson, *World Record Breakers*, 239, 255, 267. For athletes' nonparticipation in 1961 meet, see Joseph M. Turrini, *The End of Amateurism in American Track and Field* (Urbana: University of Illinois Press, 2010), 57.

29. Lawson, *World Record Breakers*, 216–17, and Maraniss, *Rome 1960*, 222–23.

30. Matthews, *Historical Dictionary of Track and Field*, 200–201; Lawson, *World Record Breakers*, 181–82; and Maraniss, *Rome 1960*, 118–19. See also Hal Higdon, "204' 10 1-2" for Oerter," *Track and Field News*, July 1962, 1–2.

31. Joseph Sheehan, "Americans Figure to Win 14 Events," *New York Times*, July 21, 1962, 33. JEWSP, Box A26, Folder 18.

32. Hal Humphrey, "Track Fans Will Have Field Day," *Los Angeles Times*, July 18, 1962, sec. 4, 11; Jordan TV demands in Walt Gamage, "Sport Shots," *Palo Alto Times*, July 17, 1962, 16; Concessionaire in Walt Gamage, "Sport Shots," July 12, 1962, 16; Oelkers quoted in Dick O'Connor, "Russian athletes go to an American sports banquet," *Palo Alto Times*, July 19, 1962, 17; Korobkov quoted in John Dixon, "I, P-T Track Expert Selects U.S. over Russia," *Long Beach Press-Telegram*, July 19, 1962, C1.

33. "Prestige on the Line," *Oakland Tribune*, July 20, 1962, 23.

34. "Try Walking to Meet," *Palo Alto Times*, July 20, 1962, 16; Information on morning of meet in "Throng views track meet," *Palo Alto Times*, July 21, 1962, 1.

35. "Power Snafu before Russ Track Meet," *San Francisco Examiner*, July 22, 1962, 1; Author's telephone interview with John Radetich, June 25, 2015.

36. Cordner Nelson, "Track Talk," *Track and Field News*, August 1962, 17; "Stanford track meet to attract 85,000," *Palo Alto Times*, July 20, 1962, 1; and Bob Brachman, "Russ-U.S. Spectacular at Stanford Today," *San Francisco Examiner*, July 21, 1962, 42.

37. Art Rosenbaum, "U.S. Soviet Games off on Right Foot," *San Francisco Chronicle*, July 22, 1962, 1, 20.

38. John Dixon, "U.S. Victor, Russian Hero in 'Greatest' Dual Spikefest," *Long Beach Press-Telegram*, July 22, 1962, C1.

39. Jesse Abramson, "World Mark Falls; U.S. Leads Soviet," *New York Herald Tribune*, July 22, 1962, B1.

40. For scores, see Bob Brachman, "U.S. Men Lead Russians, 61–45; Girls Trail, 30–22; Connolly World Record," *San Francisco Examiner*, July 22, 1962, sec. 3, 1, and Bill Leiser, "American Men—8 Firsts to 2," *San Francisco Chronicle*, July 22, 1962, 33, 35.

41. John Dixon, "World Mark to Connolly; Lead, 61–45," *Long Beach Independent Press-Telegram*, July 22, 1962, C1; "U.S. Leads Russians in Track," *Washington Post*, July 22, 1962, C1; "U.S. Jumps into 83–75 Lead," *Pasadena Independent Star-News*, July 22, 1962, A1; and Wallace Turner, "Soviet Track Official Forecasts 100 More Meets in This Series," *New York Times*, July 22, 1962, sec. 5, 3.

42. "Palo Alto has two days of 'Big Game' Crowds," *Palo Alto Times*, July 23, 1962, 1.

43. Results in "Russian-U.S. Track Results," *San Francisco Examiner*, July 23, 1962, 51, and Cordner Nelson, "2 World Marks Broken," *Track and Field News*, August 1962, 1–3.

44. For high jump competition, see Murphy, "Lipstick, Hair Ribbons, and Bright-Green Shorts"; Bob Brachman, "A Brumel Mark: 7–5; Soviet Girls Triumph," *San Francisco Examiner*, July 23, 1962, 49, 51; and Nelson, "2 World Marks Broken," 1–3. Following paragraph from same sources.

45. UPI story in "Brumel Sets World Mark on First Try," *Chicago Daily Tribune*, July 23, 1962, B1.

46. Curley Grieve, "81,000 Stand Up to Cheer Brumel's Record Effort," *San Francisco Examiner*, July 23, 1962, 49; "Topping the Kangaroo," *Time*, August 3, 1962, 43.

47. Peter Grothe, "Russian Cheered for Leap," *San Francisco Chronicle*, July 23, 1962, 49; Cordner Nelson, "U.S.A. 128, U.S.S.R. 107," *Track and Field News*, August 1962, 2.

48. Dick O'Connor, "Dramatic end to track meet," *Palo Alto Times*, July 23, 1962, 17, 2; Bob Brachman, "Russ Agree: 'Stanford Meet Great,'" *San Francisco Examiner*, July 24, 1962, 47; "Biggest, best dual meet ever," *Palo Alto Times*, July 23, 1962, 16.

49. Results of past meets in Turrini, "'It Was Communism Versus the Free World,'" 434. Women results in *Track and Field News*, August 1962, 3. Records in *Palo Alto Times*, July 23, 1962, 15.

50. "4th USSR-USAR Dual Track and Field Meets for Men and Women," 12, in archival collection, LA84 Foundation, Los Angeles, CA. Korobkov in Al Wolf, "Russ Coach Claims Team Best Ever," *Los Angeles Times*, July 16, 1962, sec. 3, 3.

51. "Fourth Match—Fourth Victory," *Sovetskii Sport*, July 24, 1962, 4–5; "Soviet Press Lauds 'Friendship' on Farm," *Pravda* in (Hayward, CA) *Daily Review*, July 25, 1962, 9. *Izvestia* in Ernest B. Ferguson, "Russian Newspaper Claims Total Track Meet Triumph," *Baltimore Sun*, July 24, 1962, 22. *Sovestkaia Rossiia* in "'We Won Meet,' Soviet Paper Claims," *San Francisco Examiner*, July 25, 1962, 49. Korobkov quoted in "Russkie Coach: We Won," *Oakland Tribune*, July 25, 1962, 35. Siscoe letter in JEWSP, Box A26, Folder 18.

52. Harold O. Zimman, "The Best of Track and Field," *Amateur Athlete*, August 1962, 4; "U.S. Defeats Russians in Track Meet," *Chicago Daily Tribune*, July 23, 1962, 1; Jack Stevenson, "Americans Wallop USSR by the Largest Margin," *Wichita Falls Times*, July 23, 1962, 12; Jesse Abramson, "Reds Still Running in Place," *New York Herald Tribune*, July 24, 1962, 19; Oerter quoted in Joe Hendrickson, "Beatty's Plan Works," *Pasadena Star-News*, July 23, 1962, 17.

53. Art Rosenbaum, "A Few 'Ifs' to Change Score," *San Francisco Chronicle*, July 24, 1962, 42; Murphy, "Lipstick, Hair Ribbons, and Bright-Green Shorts," 80; Dink Templeton, "U.S. could have won overall meet from Soviets," *Palo Alto Times*, July 24, 1962, 16.

54. Art Rosenbaum, "81,000 Cheer A Track Meet With No Losers," *San Francisco Chronicle*, July 23, 1962, 1, 34; Bob Brachman, "Russ Agree: 'Stanford Meet Great,'" *San*

Francisco Examiner, July 24, 1962, 47; "The U.S.-U.S.S.R Track Meet," *New York Times*, July 25, 1962, 32. For picture, see *Bridgeport (CT) Post*, July 23, 1962, 12; *Cedar Rapids (IA) Gazette*, July 23, 1962, 13; *Long Beach Press-Telegram*, July 23, 1962, C1; *San Francisco Chronicle*, July 23, 1962, 48; and *Pasadena Star-News*, July 23, 1962, 16. *Pravda* quoted in "Soviet Press Lauds 'Friendship' on Farm," (Hayward, CA) *Daily Review*, July 25, 1962, 9. "Headlines and Highlights," *Moscow News*, July 28, 1962, 16.

55. Korobkov quoted in Walt Gamage, "Sport Shots," *Palo Alto Times*, July 23, 1962, 17. Sober quoted in Walt Gamage, "Russian athlete deeply touched by treatment they received here," *Palo Alto Times*, July 25, 1962, 23. Interpreter's report in JEWSP, Box A26, Folder 18.

56. Descriptions in Murphy, "Lipstick, Hair Ribbons, and Bright-Green Shorts," 84; "Biggest, best dual meet ever," *Palo Alto Times*, July 23, 1962, 16; and Bob Brachman, "A Brumel Mark: 7–5; Soviet Girls Triumph," *San Francisco Examiner*, July 23, 1962, 49, and Bob Brachman, "U.S.-Russian Meet All Time Classic," *San Francisco Examiner*, July 24, 1962, 49. Celes King III, "USA-Russia Meet Rivals Rome," *Los Angeles Sentinel*, July 26, 1962, A19. Journalist quoted in Bill Leiser, "Russ Return Meet Seen in '65," *San Francisco Chronicle*, July 24, 1962, 41. "Great Job at Stanford," *San Francisco Examiner*, July 24, 1962, 28. Rusk letter in JEWSP, Box A26, Folder 18.

57. Carolyn Gray, "Russians enjoy farewell dinner," *Palo Alto Times*, July 24, 1962, 8.

58. Gamage, "Russian athletes deeply touched by treatment they received here," 23; Frank Litsky, "Brumel Predicts High Jump of 7–6," *New York Times*, July 25, 1962, 38.

59. Al Wolf, "$85,000 Net to Stanford," *Los Angeles Times*, July 24, 1962, sec. 3, 2. UPI in "Stanford Seeks Rerun of Russ Meet in 1965," *Los Angeles Times*, July 24, 1962, sec. 3, 5. AP in "U.S.-Soviet Meet Exceeds Expectations," *Washington Post*, July 24, 1962, A19. Balance sheet and Masters letter to Sterling in JEWSP, Box A26, Folder 18.

60. Sober quoted in Walt Gamage, "Sport Shots," *Palo Alto Times*, July 23, 1962, 17.

61. Bert Nelson, "Track Topics," *Palo Alto Times*, July 26, 1962, 21. "Biggest, best dual meet ever," *Palo Alto Times*, July 23, 1962, 16.

62. Jordan letter in JEWSP, Box A26, Folder 18.

11. "Skate Fast, Hit Hard": San Francisco Bay Bombers and Bay Area Roller Derby

1. National Roller Skating Museum, accessed October 30, 2015, http://www.rollerskatingmuseum.com/rollerderby.html.

2. "Wheels Whirl at Auditorium: Ma and Sonny Skate in Roller Derby," *San Francisco Chronicle*, July 3, 1938, 4H.

3. Jerry Seltzer and Keith Coppage, *Bay Area Roller Derby* (Charleston: Arcadia Publishing, 2012).

4. Bill Leiser, "Nuthouse on Wheels: Skaters Go Tonight," *San Francisco Chronicle*, July 6, 1938, 1H.

5. "Roller Derby," *Time*, February 3, 1936, 26.

6. Leiser, "Nuthouse on Wheels."

7. Seltzer and Coppage, *Bay Area Roller Derby*.

8. Ibid.

9. By the 1950s, the luster of roller derby had worn off in the newspapers. This is likely related to the extensive television coverage of tape delay games and the proliferation of television sets in homes.

10. Will Connolly, "Roller Skate Addicts, They're Bright Minds," *San Francisco Chronicle*, July 11, 1938, 1H.

11. Will Connolly, "Roller Derby Fans Aren't Green at Game," *San Francisco Chronicle*, July 20, 1938, 1H.

12. John Kobler, "Madness on Skates," *Saturday Evening Post*, February 4, 1950, 22.

13. Keith Coppage, *Roller Derby to Rollerjam: The Authorized Story of an Unauthorized Sport* (Santa Rosa: Squarebooks, 1999).

14. Ibid.

15. Seltzer and Coppage, *Bay Area Roller Derby*.

16. Frank Deford, "The Roller Derby," *Sports Illustrated*, March 3, 1969.

17. Peter Hartlaub, "Six Decades of Roller Derby in the Bay Area," *San Francisco Chronicle*, March 10, 2011, accessed October 7, 2014, http://blog.sfgate.com/parenting/2011/03/10/six-decades-of-roller-derby-in-the-bay-area-photos/.

18. Kobler, "Madness on Skates."

19. Deford, "The Roller Derby."

20. "Roller Derby Girl," YouTube video, 5:21, posted by "RollerDerbyStars," January 17, 2012, https://www.youtube.com/watch?v=Nnf8wgmJFKI.

21. Seltzer and Coppage, *Bay Area Roller Derby*.

22. "Color blindness" is not necessarily "racial progress" per se, but given the 1962 social norms, treating skaters as athletes only regardless of race or gender was a fairly unique experience.

23. Incidentally, male skaters were occasionally referred to as "boys."

24. Art Rosenbaum, "Aronson Can Block—Coach Prefers Tall Girl Skater," *San Francisco Chronicle*, July 14, 1938, 5H.

25. Morie Morrison, "Round and Round," *San Francisco Chronicle*, July 11, 1938, 3H.

26. "Babe Didrikson to Wed Zaharias," *San Francisco Chronicle*, July 22, 1938, 1H.

27. Connolly, "Roller Derby Fans Aren't Green at Game."

28. Ibid.

29. Martin Snapp, "Roller Derby's Revival Has Official Skating on Air," *McClatchy-Tribune Business News*, November 26, 2007.

30. "(1973) Roller Derby Chiefs v Bombers (1st Half)," YouTube video, 47:50, posted by "Goldenclassictv," February 5, 2014, https://www.youtube.com/watch?v=Fx7JqGsNIeE.

31. "Roller Derby Girl," YouTube video.

32. Kobler, "Madness on Skates."

33. "Roller Derby Girl," YouTube video.

34. Many of the skaters married other skaters, including teammate couples such as Tommy and Bobbie Atkinson, Russ "Rosie" Baker and Annis "Big Red" Jensen, Gloria Mack and Billy Gardner, Joan Weston and Nick Scopas, and Charlie O'Connell and Judi McGuire (who divorced another skater, Mike Gammon, before marrying O'Connell). Charlie O'Connell and Ann Calvello had a brief romantic relationship, which provided fodder for the gossip magazines, and Calvello married and subsequently divorced Roy Langley, a roller derby referee.

35. Seltzer and Coppage, *Bay Area Roller Derby*.

36. Carrie Dolan, "Crash! Bang! Smash! Roller-Derby School Is Now in Session—Skating Star Is Trying Hard to Rid Sport of Fakery; Dyed Hair & Five Tattoos," *Wall Street Journal*, July 15, 1987.

37. Rodney Foo, "'Voice' of Roller Derby's Past Sneers at Today's Sport," *Knight-Ridder Tribune*, May 19, 2006.

38. Frank Deford, "Joan Weston—The Blonde Bomber," *Derby Memoirs*, 1997, accessed on September 29, 2014, http://derbymemoirs.bankedtrack.info/mem_Weston_Joan.html.

39. Seltzer and Coppage, *Bay Area Roller Derby.*

40. Deford, "Joan Weston."

41. Frank Deford, "The Roller Derby," *Sports Illustrated*, March 3, 1969.

42. Deford, "Joan Weston."

43. Joe Blenkle, "Many Derby Stars Would Return to the Banked Track," *Sacramento News and Review*, August 21, 1991.

44. Dolan, "Crash! Bang! Smash!"

45. Robert McG. Thomas Jr., "Joanie Weston, 62, a Big Star in the World of Roller Derbies," *New York Times*, May 18, 1997, accessed October 31, 2014, http://www.nytimes.com/1997/05/18/us/joanie-weston-62-a-big-star-in-the-world-of-roller-derbies.html.

46. Barbara Hoke, "Lesbian Bars in the San Francisco East Bay—Owned by Women for Women," (n.d.), accessed on October 30, 2015, http://www.cappellettidesigns.com/tellherstory/Bars.htm.

47. Deford, "The Roller Derby."

48. Snapp, "Roller Derby's Revival Has Official Skating on Air."

49. Seltzer and Coppage, *Bay Area Roller Derby.*

50. Ibid.

51. Ibid.

52. *Demon of the Derby: The Ann Calvello Story*, Directed by Sharon Rutter (2001), Fireproof Productions.

53. Seltzer and Coppage, *Bay Area Roller Derby.*

54. Claire Noland, "Obituaries: Ann Calvello, 76, Popular Skater for S.F. Team in Roller Derby," *Los Angeles Times*, March 17, 2006.

55. Jerry Seltzer, "Roller Derby Jesus," accessed on October 30, 2014, www.rollerderbyjesus.com.

56. Frank Deford, *Five Strides on the Banked Track* (New York: Little, Brown, 1971).

57. Deford, *Five Strides on the Banked Track*, Kindle edition, location 1948.

58. Ibid.

59. Steve Rubenstein, "Charlie O'Connell, Roller Derby Hall of Famer, Dies," *San Francisco Chronicle*, March 6, 2015, accessed on October 30, 2015, http://www.sfgate.com/bayarea/article/Charlie-O-Connell-Roller-Derby-Hall-of-Famer-6120341.php.

60. Seltzer, "Roller Derby Jesus."

61. Deford, *Five Strides on the Banked Track.*

62. Deford, "The Roller Derby."

63. In his time on the bench, he still frequently engaged in fights with rival skaters. See Deford, *Five Strides on the Banked Track.*

64. Armory Studios website, accessed October 30, 2015, http://www.armorystudios.com/history/.

65. Seltzer, "Roller Derby Jesus."

66. Deford, *Five Strides on the Banked Track.*

67. Snapp, "Roller Derby's Revival Has Official Skating on Air."

12. Sons of Oakland: The Raiders and the Raz/Rais(ing) of a City

1. Jim McCullough, *Pride and Poise: The Oakland Raiders of the American Football League* (Bloomington, IN: Author House, 2006); "Oakland Raiders Chronology," *San Francisco Examiner*, June 24, 1995, A12; "History of Raiders," *Oakland Tribune*, May 8, 1982, D1, 5.

2. Ed Levitt, "Terrific Football," *Oakland Tribune*, September 20, 1967, E41.

3. George Ross, "Oakland on the Move," *Oakland Tribune*, February 28, 1962, E35.

4. George Ross, "Come Hear the Fans," *Oakland Tribune*, April 20, 1962, E35.

5. George Ross, "Man Who Shook AFL Charms Oakland," *Oakland Tribune*, January 21, 1964, E33.

6. Raider Nation is the collective name given to the team's global fan base. The term was conceived in 1995 by Raiders fan Jim (Jimbo) Hudson and used to rally fans around the team upon its return to Oakland from Los Angeles. While the term is a mid-1990s invention, and judging by a key word subject search of the *San Francisco Chronicle's* online archive, wasn't used in that paper until 1996, the sense of fan affiliation that is associated with "Raider Nation" developed in the 1970s. In this chapter, I follow the precedent set in other sources and use Raider Nation to refer to the team's fan culture—both past and present—as the fan pride and identity conveyed by the term was evident well before the 1990s. See Jim Miller and Kelly Mayhew, *Better to Reign in Hell: Inside the Raiders Fan Empire* (New York: New Press, 2005), and Roger Mills, "Raider Nation: No Matter How Far-Flung Raider Fans Are, They Remain United by a Fierce and Belligerent Loyalty," *St. Petersburg Times*, January 25, 2003.

7. Chris Rhomberg, *No There There: Race, Class, and Political Community in Oakland* (Berkeley: University of California Press, 2007).

8. Rhomberg, *No There There*; Robert O. Self, *American Babylon: Race and the Struggle for Postwar Oakland* (Princeton, NJ: Princeton University Press, 2003).

9. Metropolitan Transportation Commission-Association of Bay Area Governments, *Bay Area Census: City of Oakland*, www.bayareacensus.ca.gov/cities/Oakland70htm.

10. Rhomberg, *No There There*; Self, *American Babylon*.

11. Rhomberg, *No There There*.

12. Oakland-Alameda County Coliseum, Inc., *Plans for an Integrated Stadium and Arena* (brochure, Oakland History Room vertical files, Oakland Public Library, Oakland, CA, 1961).

13. Ross, "Oakland on the Move."

14. Rhomberg, *No There There*.

15. Notably, baseball's A's experienced considerable success in the early 1970s, with three consecutive World Series championships (1972, 1973, 1974) and marquee talent like the young slugger Reggie Jackson and the dominant pitcher Jim "Catfish" Hunter. Fans rallied around the A's during these years, and the city of Oakland remained committed to keeping its MLB franchise, but not to the same extent that fans and civic leaders supported the Raiders. While there was overlap among fan groups for these professional teams, the Raiders' fan base stood out as a unique entity. A rooting interest in the Raiders did not necessarily coincide with fan commitment to the A's or Warriors. For more on the A's and Warriors during the 1970s, see Ray Ratto, "The 1970s: Oakland Rules. The Success of the A's, Raiders and Warriors Made It the City of Champions," *San Francisco Examiner*, October 10, 1999, D1; see also Frank DeFord, writer, "Rebels of Oakland: The A's, the Raiders, the '70s," (New York: Home Box Office, 2003).

16. Rita Liberti and Alicia St. John, "Imagining Oakland: Race, Representation, and the Raider Riots" (paper presented at the North American Society for Sport Sociology, Montreal, Canada, November 2003); Rhomberg, *No There There*; Self, *American Babylon*.

17. US Bureau of the Census, *1960 Census of the Population: Volume 1, Characteristics of the Population; Part 6, California* (Washington, DC: GPO, 1960).

18. Frank DeFord, "A City of Complexes," *Sports Illustrated*, April 1, 1968.

19. "Oakland Schools: Do We Dare Pinch Pennies Any Longer?" *Oakland Tribune*, May 18, 1969, 34.

20. CensusScope, *Educational Attainment, 1990–2000: Oakland, CA* (Social Science Data Analysis Network) http://www.censusscope.org/us/s6/m5775/chart_education.html; US Bureau of the Census, 1960.

21. Rhomberg, *No There There*.

22. Ibid.

23. Ed Levitt, "Terrific Football."

24. "Oakland Raiders Chronology," 1995; Ratto, "The 1970s."

25. Frank DeFord, "A City of Complexes."

26. DeFord, "Rebels of Oakland: The A's, The Raiders, the '70s."

27. Miller and Mayhew, *Better to Reign*.

28. Cathy Frazier, interview with the author, August 2014. All interviews cited were conducted specifically for this chapter. Interviewees are individuals known to either the author or her research assistant, Mark Cordes, who has roots in the Oakland/East Bay Area and has maintained a long-term affiliation with the Raiders that began in the 1970s.

29. Rod Medina, interview with Mark Cordes, April 2014.

30. DeFord, "Rebels of Oakland."

31. Ratto, "The 1970s."

32. Darrell Bailey, interview with Mark Cordes, April 2014.

33. Miller and Mayhew, *Better to Reign*.

34. Dave Newhouse, "Raiders Kick Off '77 Season," *Oakland Tribune*, September 18, 1977, 23.

35. Tom Weir, "The Raiders: A Battle since Day One," *Oakland Tribune*, August 17, 1980, H1, 6.

36. Tomas Medina, interview with Mark Cordes, April 2014.

37. Marty Valdez, interview with Mark Cordes, April 2014.

38. Rhomberg, *No There There*.

39. Miller and Mayhew, *Better to Reign*; Tom Weir, "City Moves to Get New Raiders Lease," *Oakland Tribune*, January 9, 1980, F1, 12.

40. Liberti and St. John, "Imagining Oakland"; Martinez, "Oakland Loses Its Grip," *Los Angeles Times*, February 3, 2003, 9.

41. Deford, "A City of Complexes."

42. Liberti and St. John, "Imagining Oakland."

43. Michael N. Danielson, *Home Team: Professional Sports and the American Metropolis* (Princeton, NJ: Princeton University Press, 1997).

44. "Something New for Coliseum," *Oakland Tribune*, September 25, 1968, E17.

45. Ibid.

46. Rhomberg, *No There There*.

47. US Bureau of the Census, 1960; US Bureau of the Census, 1970, *Census of Population and Housing: Census Tracts, San Francisco-Oakland, Calif.* (Washington, DC: GPO, 1970); US Bureau of the Census, 1980, *Census of Population and Housing: Census Tracts, San Francisco-Oakland, Calif.* (Washington, DC: GPO, 1980).

48. Heather MacDonald, "Jerry Brown's No-Nonsense New Age for Oakland," *City Journal*, Autumn 1999, http://www.city-journal.org/html/9_4_a2.html.

49. City of Oakland, *Summary of Part 1 Crime Offenses, 1969–2008*, http://gismaps.oak-landnet.com/crimewatch/pdf/Historical Data.htm.

50. Rhomberg, *No There There.*

51. DeFord, "City of Complexes."

52. Leon F. Mead, "Raiders: $72 Million, City of Oakland: 0 . . . Was That the Final Gun—A Story of Intrigue, Suspense and Questionable Reasoning," *Loyola of Los Angeles Entertainment Law Review* 9 (1989): 401–24.

53. Tom Weir, "City Moves to Get New Raiders Lease," *Oakland Tribune*, January 9, 1980, F1.

54. Peter Clark, "Oakland Feels 'Used' by Raider Owner: 'He's the No. 1 Culprit,'" *Oakland Tribune*, March 2, 1980, C1, 5.

55. Cliff Pletschet, "Loss of Raiders, A's Would Hit Hotels," *Oakland Tribune*, January 14, 1980, D6, 9.

56. Tom Weir, "Raiders Rap New Lease Offer," *Oakland Tribune*, February 6, 1980, F1.

57. See, for example, Joanna Cagan and Neil DeMause, *Field of Schemes: How the Great Stadium Swindle Turns Public Money into Private Profit* (Monroe, ME: Common Courage Press, 1998); George Lipsitz, "The Silence of the Rams: How St. Louis School Children Subsidize the Super Bowl Champs," in *Sports Matters: Race, Recreation, and Culture*, ed. John Bloom and Michael Nevin Willard, 225–45 (New York: New York University Press, 2002); Roger Noll and Andrew Zimbalist, eds., *Sports, Jobs, and Taxes: The Economic Impact of Sports Teams and Stadiums* (Washington, DC: Brookings Institution Press, 1997).

58. Tom Weir, "Raider 'Blackmail' Worries Supervisor," *Oakland Tribune*, January 23, 1980, F2.

59. Danielson, *Home Team.*

60. Tom LaMarre, "Three Raiders Who Make Life Better for Those in Need," *Oakland Tribune*, October 21, 1976.

61. DeFord, "City of Complexes."

62. Rhomberg, *No There There.*

63. Ibid.

64. "Raider Victory Celebration at Coliseum," *Alameda Times Star*, January 10, 1977.

65. Tom Weir, "City Moves to Get New Raiders Lease," *Oakland Tribune*, January 9, 1980, F1.

66. Robert Lindsey, "Oakland Cites Eminent Domain in Effort to Regain Football Team," *New York Times*, May 17, 1983, http://www.nytimes.com/1983/05/17/us/oakland-cites-eminent-domain-in-effort-to-regain-football-team.html.

67. Danielson, *Home Team*; Mead, "Raiders"; Tom Weir, "A Bill to Block the Raiders," *Oakland Tribune*, March 27, 1980, D1.

68. Joseph P. Bort, "What Will It Take to Keep the A's and Raiders?" *Oakland Tribune*, August 30, 1980, A13.

69. Lipsitz, "The Silence of the Rams," 241.

70. Rhomberg, *No There There.*

71. Once again, the Raiders are threatening to move to Los Angeles if Oakland does not provide a suitable stadium for the franchise. In response, the city of Oakland has cleared the way for a new sports development project, despite a nearly $100 million debt remaining from Coliseum renovations when the Raiders returned to Oakland in the 1990s and a projected $100+ million price tag for the new development. See, e.g., Mike Blasky, "Oakland Clears Path for Coliseum City Development," *Contra Costa Times*, April 1, 2015; Joe Nocera, "Football's L.A. Trick Play," *New York Times*, February 20, 2015.

13. Rebel with a Racket: Rosie Casals

I wish to thank Dr. Joan Johnson for the invaluable assistance she provided in the early stages of this project and Rosie Casals for taking the time to share her memories with me.

1. Joel Drucker, "Casals Far More Than King's Sidekick," accessed June 15, 2014, http://sports.espn.go.com/espn/womenshistory2009/news/story?page=Rosiecasals.

2. Grace Lichtenstein, *A Long Way, Baby: Behind the Scenes in Women's Pro Tennis* (New York: Morrow & Company, 1974), 52.

3. Rosemary (Rosie) Casals, interview by Rita Liberti, January 23, 2014, San Rafael, CA.

4. Ibid.

5. Susan K. Cahn, *Coming on Strong: Gender and Sexuality in Twentieth-Century Women's Sport* (New York: Free Press, 1994), 141–206.

6. Casals, interview.

7. For a good overview of Rosie Casals's career, see the Women's Tennis Association webpage, accessed June 20, 2014, http://www.wtatennis.com/players/player/1195.

8. According to Casals, tournament wins meant increased travel and, consequently, more costs incurred as a result. In an effort to make it possible for Casals to compete and to lessen the financial burden on her family the "Golden Gate Friends of Rosie" was established to defray travel costs and other expenses. Casals, interview.

9. Ibid.

10. Ibid. See also, Alida M. Thacher, *Raising a Racket: Rosie Casals* (Milwaukee: Raintree Editions, 1976), 17.

11. Bill Hall, "Rosemary Casals: She Fully Expects to Be the Nation's Best Woman Tennis Player," *San Francisco Examiner,* February 28, 1965, 1.

12. Anne Enke, *Finding the Movement: Sexuality, Contested Space, and Feminist Activism* (Durham, NC: Duke University Press, 2007); Terry H. Anderson, *The Movement and the Sixties: Protest in America from Greensboro to Wounded Knee* (New York: Oxford University Press, 1995); Ruth Rosen, *The World Split Open: How the Modern Women's Movement Changed America* (New York: Viking Penguin, 2000).

13. Rosen, *The World Split Open,* 78–79.

14. Rosemarie Tong, *Feminist Thought: A More Comprehensive Introduction* (Boulder, CO: Westview Press, 2009), 23–47.

15. For a good overview of radical feminism during the period, see Alice Echols, *Daring to Be Bad: Radical Feminism in America, 1967–1975* (Minneapolis: University of Minnesota Press, 1989).

16. Cahn, *Coming on Strong,* 246.

17. "Rosemary Casals: No. 1, Northern California," *World Tennis,* August 1966, 56.

18. Joseph McCauley, "World Rankings," *World Tennis,* December 1966, 25.

19. For historical context on events leading up to the Open Era in tennis, see Kevin Jefferys, "The Triumph of Professionalism in World Tennis: The Road to 1968," *International Journal of the History of Sport* 26, no. 15 (2009): 2253–69.

20. "Billie, Rosie Turn Pro," *San Francisco Chronicle,* April 2, 1968, 47.

21. US Census Bureau, "Current Population Reports: Consumer Income," Series P-60, No. 63, September 8, 1969, http://www2.census.gov/prod2/popscan/p60-063.pdf (accessed August 15, 2014).

22. Billie Jean King, *Pressure Is a Privilege: Lessons I've Learned from Life and the Battle of the Sexes* (New York: Life Media, 2008), 147–49.

23. Billie Jean King with Kim Chapin, *Billie Jean* (New York: Harper & Row, 1974), 100.

24. Ibid., 99.

25. Casals quoted in "Sport: Women's Lob," *Time*, December 7, 1970, 88.

26. King, *Billie Jean*, 105.

27. "Sport: Women's Lob," 88. For good background information on the start of the Virginia Slims tour and women's professional tennis, see Mary Jo Festle, *Playing Nice: Politics and Apologies in Women's Sports* (New York: Columbia University Press, 1996), 142–64.

28. Casals quoted in Selena Roberts, *A Necessary Spectacle: Billie Jean King, Bobby Riggs, and the Tennis Match That Leveled the Game* (New York: Crown Publishers, 2005), 78.

29. Natasha Zaretsky, *No Direction Home: The American Family and the Fear of National Decline* 1968–1980 (Chapel Hill: University of North Carolina Press, 2007), 14.

30. Lichtenstein, *A Long Way, Baby*, 56.

31. Casals, interview.

32. "Women Lobbers," *Newsweek*, May 3, 1971, 90.

33. Ibid.

34. Lichtenstein, *A Long Way, Baby*, 153.

35. Ibid., 13.

36. Frank Deford, "Some Beer for Newk, A Waltz for Billie," *Sports Illustrated*, July 17, 1967, 23.

37. "Teeny Tennis Bopper," *Newsweek*, January 2, 1967, 48.

38. As "feisty," see Pete Axthelm, "Tennis: A Triumph for Women's Lob," *Newsweek*, June 26, 1972, 56; as "explosive," see Bud Collins and Zander Hollander, eds., *Bud Collins' Tennis Encyclopedia* (Detroit, MI: Visible Ink Press, 1997), 461; as "fiery," see "Casals Cited for Assault," *San Francisco Chronicle*, May 24, 1977, 45; as "attacking, aggressive, and powerful," see Alida M. Thacher, *Raising a Racket: Rosie Casals* (Milwaukee: Raintree Editions, 1976), 6.

39. Kim Chapin, "A Bright Future for Little Miss Bombshell," *Sports Illustrated*, October 24, 1966, 69.

40. Lichtenstein, *A Long Way, Baby*, 87.

41. Edwin Shrake, "A Long Way, Bébé," *Sports Illustrated*, March 6, 1972, 35–36, 38, 41–42.

42. Ann Crittenden Scott, "Closing the Muscle Gap," *Ms.*, September 1974, 49.

43. Ibid., 89.

44. Casals, interview.

45. Jim Bainbridge, "The Essential Rosemary Casals," *San Francisco Examiner*, March 31, 1974, 24.

46. Roberts, *A Necessary Spectacle*, 124.

47. Ann N. Epes, "Noblesse Oblige," *Sports Illustrated*, October 8, 1973, 99.

48. David W. Bryant, "Noblesse Oblige," *Sports Illustrated*, October 8, 1973, 99.

49. David J. Timmer, "Noblesse Oblige," *Sports Illustrated*, October 8, 1973, 99.

50. Roberts, *A Necessary Spectacle*, 124.

51. Edward D. Miller, *Tomboys, Pretty Boys, and Outspoken Women: The Media Revolution of 1973* (Ann Arbor: University of Michigan Press, 2011), 72.

52. Bainbridge, "The Essential Rosemary Casals," 24.

53. Catherine Bell, "Rosie Casals: Why Hasn't She Lived Up to Her Potential?" *Tennis*, November 1974, 40.

54. Axthelm, "Tennis," 60.

55. Lichtenstein, *A Long Way, Baby,* 65.

56. Jaime Schultz, *Qualifying Times: Points of Change in U.S. Women's Sport* (Champaign: University of Illinois Press, 2014), 16.

57. Patricia Campbell Warner, *When the Girls Came Out to Play: The Birth of American Sportswear* (Amherst: University of Massachusetts Press, 2006), 52.

58. Lichtenstein, *A Long Way, Baby,* 52.

59. Quoted in Mary Hardwick, "Teddy Tinling Wins June Marlboro Award," *World Tennis,* June 1965, 50.

60. Casals, interview.

61. "Warning: Casals Dressed Down," *St. Petersburg Independent,* July 8, 1972, 5-C.

62. Bud Collins, "All Frocked-Up in Purple," *World Tennis,* September 1972, 23.

63. Ibid., 25.

64. Casals quoted in Thacher, *Raising a Racket,* 6.

65. Casals quoted in Collins and Hollander, eds., *Bud Collins' Tennis Encyclopedia,* 462.

66. Casals quoted in Bell, "Rosie Casals," 39

67. Dave Newhouse, "Mighty Martina," *Oakland Tribune,* February 22, 1988, D1.

68. Jim Bainbridge, "Martina Masters Sarchenko, Slims Jinx in 63 Minutes," *Oakland Tribune,* February 22, 1988, D1.

69. Susan Ware, *Game, Set, Match: Billie Jean King and the Revolution in Women's Sports* (Chapel Hill: University of North Carolina Press, 2011), 213.

70. Roberts, *A Necessary Spectacle,* 98.

71. Drucker, "Casals Far More Than King's Sidekick."

72. Casals, interview.

73. Lichtenstein, *A Long Way, Baby,* 52.

14. The Early Gay Games: The Bay Area Years

1. Pat Griffin, *Strong Women, Deep Closets: Lesbians and Homophobia in Sport* (Champaign, IL: Human Kinetics, 1998).

2. Federation of Gay Games (FGG) Official website. (2014), accessed September 17, 2014, http://www.gaygames.org.

3. George E. Haggerty, John Beynon, and Douglas Eisner, eds., *Gay Histories and Cultures: An Encyclopedia* (New York: Garland, 2000); Susan Stryker and Jim Van Buskirk, *Gay by the Bay: A History of Queer Culture in the San Francisco Bay Area* (San Francisco: Chronicle Books, 1996).

4. Roy M. Coe, *A Sense of Pride: The Story of Gay Games II* (San Francisco: Pride Publications, 1986); Tom Waddell and Dick Schaap, *Gay Olympian: The Life and Death of Dr. Tom Waddell* (New York: Alfred A. Knopf, 1996).

5. *Gay Athletic Games I* (1982). [Official Program]. San Francisco: San Francisco Arts & Athletics, Inc. (SFAA). San Francisco Public Library—History Centre and Archives. (SFPL), Gay and Lesbian Center Collection in the SFPL History Centre (GLC) 27, Box 1 -Gay Games II (GG II) Hal's Notebooks; Rick Peterson and Susan Kennedy, "Keeping the Flame Lit: The Federation of Gay Games," in *Unity: A Celebration of Gay Games IV and Stonewall,* ed. Lisa Labrecque (San Francisco: Labrecque, 1994), 12–13.

6. Waddell and Schaap, *Gay Olympian.*

7. Ibid.

8. "Gay Olympics Get Tax Status," *BAR,* January 21, 1982, 26.

9. Coe, *A Sense of Pride*; C. Duncan, "An Englishman's Perspective," *Gay Athletic Games I*, 1982, 40. [Official Program]. San Francisco: SFAA. SFPL, GLC 27, Box 1—GG II Hal's Notebooks.

10. P. Lorch, "Congress Gives Away Word: Gay Olympics Must Drop the Word 'Olympic,'" *Bay Area Reporter (BAR)*, January 21, 1982, 1. The *BAR* was the longest-running (but now-defunct) gay and lesbian newspaper in San Francisco/Bay Area.

11. "Gay Olympics Told to Drop Word 'Olympics,'" *Advocate*, March 18, 1982, 10; Lorch, "Congress Gives Away Word."

12. P. Lorch, "Word Monopoly: Gay Olympics Fights Back—Court Battle Looms Over Use of Word," *BAR*, January 28, 1982, 9.

13. R. Primavera, *Federal Court Order Provides Evidence of World Concern for Homosexuality*, August 10, 1982, [Press release]. San Francisco: Gay Olympic Games. SFPL, GLC 27, Box-GG I & II in acid free folders, File-GG I Press Kit; Lorch, "Word Monopoly."

14. Among others, see for example L. Barnett, "Fellow Americans?" (Letter to the editor), *San Francisco Sentinel*, September 16, 1982, 5; Satya, "Olympic Rites" (Letter to editor), *BAR*, February 25, 1982, 7; Tom Waddell, "Common Sense Is Not So Common," *BAR*, January 28, 1982, 25–26; E. Zoutte, "Letter to USOC," March 1982, SFPL, GLC 27, Box 1Series I-Folder: 1982 Gay Olympic Games.

15. W. April, "U.S. Court Decision: Gay Olympics Must Drop Word," *BAR*, August 12, 1982, 1.

16. W. April, "Gay Olympics Slapped with Permanent Injunction: Gay Games Files Emergency Motion to Nullify," *BAR*, August 26, 1982, 1; Coe, *A Sense of Pride*; Peterson and Kennedy, "Keeping the Flame Lit."

17. A. White, "Gay Games Torch Arrives Sunday," *BAR*, August 19, 1982, 2.

18. *Gay Athletic Games I*, 1982, 2.

19. Coe, *A Sense of Pride*; S. Salter, "Triumph in Long Race for Rights: 'Olympics' or Not, Many See Event as Symbolic of Gays' Gains," *San Francisco Chronicle*, August 29, 1982, B1.

20. April, "Gay Olympics Slapped with Permanent Injunction"; Salter, "Triumph in Long Race for Rights," B1; S. Treimel, "Gay Athletic Games Open to Cheers: 15,000 Watch Show in Kezar Stadium," *BAR*, September 2, 1982, 2, 4.

21. Treimel, "Gay Athletic Games Open to Cheers," 2, 4.

22. Coe, *A Sense of Pride*.

23. Kunkel as cited in Salter, "Triumph in Long Race for Rights," B1.

24. Waddell and Schaap, *Gay Olympian*, 1996..

25. Waddell as cited in B. McDell, "Waddell's Dream of an International Gay Games Is Fulfilled," *Celebration '90: Newsletter of Gay Games III and Cultural Festival*, June 1989, 4. SFPL, GLC 27, Box-Vancouver-Integrate into Series III, File: Celebration '90—Fundraising/Business Backer, 4.

26. Z. Artman, "Gay Games 'Olympics' Battle Continues" (Press release), February 28, 1984. SFPL, GLC 27, Box-GG I & II in acid free folders, File: Director of Communications Report, August 1986-Press Releases, 1.

27. S. Kulieke, "Deliberate Violation of Trademark Charged: Judge Orders Gay Games to Pay $96,000 in Lawyers' Fees to Olympics," *Advocate*, June 26, 1984, 24.

28. "Tom Waddell Dead at Age 49, Founder of S.F.'s Gay Games," *San Francisco Chronicle*, July 12, 1987, B1; A. White, "Hundreds Mourn Tom Waddell in City Hall Service," *BAR*, July 23, 1987, 13.

29. "Law Suit," *Gay Games II*, 1986, 55. [Official program]. San Francisco: SFAA. SFPL, GLC 27, Box 3-Games Clippings, File-Rosemary Mitchell-Manila Folder #3; "'Olympics' Suit Continues," *Triumph in '86, 3* (May 1986), 7. San Francisco: SFAA. SFPL, GLC 27, Box 3-Games Clippings, File-Rosemary Mitchell-Manila Folder #3.

30. T. Stroll, "Gays Protest Straight Olympics," *Gay Community News*, August 25, 1984, 1.

31. S. Kelly, *United States Olympic Committee vs. San Francisco Arts & Athletics and Thomas Waddell: Legal Issues*, May 28, 1985 [Press release], SFPL, GLC 27, Box #1-GG II-Hal's Notebooks, File: Departmental Communication; S. Kelly, *United States Olympic Committee vs. San Francisco Arts & Athletics and Thomas Waddell: History of the Suit*, June 1, 1985 [Press release]. SFPL, GLC 27, Box #1-GG II-Hal's Notebooks, File: Departmental Communication.

32. Brian Pronger, *The Arena of Masculinity: Sports, Homosexuality, and the Meaning of Sex* (Toronto: University of Toronto Press, 1990).

33. "Law Suit," 1986; J. Murphy, *Gay Games II*, July 9, 1986 [Press release]. SFPL, GLC 27, Box #3-Games Clippings, Folder #4.

34. Coe, *A Sense of Pride*.

35. SFAA Board of Directors. [Meeting minutes]. November 13, 1986. SFPL, GLC 27, Assorted Box Unprocessed-Box #3-Games Clippings from Rosemary Mitchell.

36. Paul Siegel, "On the Owning of Words: Reflections on San Francisco Arts and Athletics vs. United States Olympic Committee," in *Queer Words, Queer Images: Communication and the Construction of Homosexuality*, ed. R. Jeffrey Ringer (New York: New York University Press, 1994), 30–44.

37. Among others, see Vicky Krane and Jennifer Waldron, "The Gay Games: Creating Our Own Sports Culture," in *The Olympics at the Millenium: Power, Politics, and the Games*, ed. Kay Schaffer and Sidonie Smith (New Brunswick, NJ: Rutgers University Press, 2000), 147–64; Caroline Symons, *The Gay Games: A Cultural History* (New York: Routledge, 2010).

38. Judy Davidson, "Sporting Homonationalisms: Sexual Exceptionalism, Queer Privilege, and the 21st Century International Lesbian and Gay Sport Movement," *Sociology of Sport Journal* 30 (2013): 57–82; Judy Davidson, "Racism against the Abnormal? The 20th Century Gay Games, Biopolitics, and the Emergence of Homonational Sport," *Leisure Studies* 33 (2014): 357–78.

39. J. Karr and Richard Mandell, "Berlin Olympics, 1936 to Benefit Gay Olympics, 1982," *BAR*, March 4, 1982, 17.

40. Tom Waddell, "Update '82 Olympics: The Good News Is . . . ," *BAR*, February 11, 1982, 25.

41. Randy Shilts, "Gay Group Cancels a Classic Nazi Film," *San Francisco Chronicle*, March 10, 1982, 28.

42. A. White, "Pressure and Threats: Olympics Cancels Film," *BAR*, March 11, 1982, 1, 5; N. Offen, "Closing Down a Film" (Letter to the editor), *BAR*, March 11, 1982, 7.

43. T. Birch, "'Olympia' Cancellation" (Letter to the editor), *BAR*, March 18, 1982, 6; t. edwards, "Film Flam" (Letter to editor), *BAR*, March 25, 1982, 7.

44. Shilts, "Gay Group Cancels a Classic Nazi Film," 28.

45. Mary G. McDonald, "Mobilizing for a Cause: Historical Memory, Activisms, and the Sochi Olympics," Paper presented at the meeting of the North American Society for Sport History, Glenwood Springs, Colorado, June 2014; Pawas Bisht, "The Politics of Cosmopolitan Memory," *Media, Culture and Society* 35 (2013): 13–20.

46. Marusia Bociurkiw, "Disneyland in Sodom: Whose Borders? Whose Words?" *Fuse*, Winter 1991, 7.

47. Gordon Waitt, "Gay Games: Performing Community Out from the Closet of the Locker Room," *Social & Cultural Geography* 4 (2003): 167–84; Gordon Waitt, "The Sydney 2002 Gay Games and Querying Australian Nation Space," *Environment and Planning D* 23 (2005): 435–52; Gordon Waitt, "Boundaries of Desire: Becoming Sexual through the Spaces of Sydney's 2002 Gay Games," *Annals of the Association of American Geographers* 96 (2006): 773–87.

48. D. Montgomery, "Just to Let You Know" (Letter to editor), *BAR*, May 21, 1987, 7.

49. E. Glazier, "Visa 'Olympics'" (Letter to editor), *BAR*, August 13, 1987, 8; E. Glazier, "Exit Visa" (Letter to editor), *BAR*, August 20, 1987, 7.

50. Glazier, "Visa 'Olympics'" (Letter to editor), 8; P. Hastings, "Hey B of A . . . Withdraw!" (Letter to editor), *BAR*, August 27, 1987, 10.

51. R. Casetta, "Visa Support for Gay Games?" (Letter to editor), *BAR*, September 3, 1987, 7; R. Mollett, "Not with My Money, You Won't" (Letter to editor), *BAR*, August 20, 1987, 8; V. Nuanez Jr., "Use Mastercard" (Letter to editor), *BAR*, October 8, 1987, 8.

52. G. Johnson, "An Olympian Effort" (Letter to editor), *BAR*, August 20, 1987, 9; J. Newquist, "Cardholders Reject Olympic Promotion: Cutting Up Visa," *BAR*, September 24, 1987, 1.

53. A. Bennett, "Opinion: Close My Account," *BAR*, August 27, 1987, 8; J. Blankenship, "A Heavy Heart" (Letter to editor), *BAR*, November 5, 1987, 8; B. Ginns, "See You Next Year" (Letter to editor), *BAR*, November 26, 1987, 9; J. Kovach, "Abide by the Conditions" (Letter to editor), *BAR*, November 26, 1987, 9.

54. D. Montgomery, "Burning Plastic" (Letter to editor), *BAR*, September 24, 1987, 8.

55. Hastings, "Hey B of A . . . Withdraw!" (Letter to editor); Montgomery, "Burning Plastic" (Letter to editor); S. Nutting, "No to Visa" (Letter to editor), *BAR*, December 3, 1987, 8; D. Steward, "Close My Account" (Letter to editor), *BAR*, December 10, 1987, 9.

56. "Clipping Visa: A Protest Takes Shape," *BAR*, November 12, 1987, 16; Nuanez, "No to Visa" (Letter to editor).

57. S. Alyson, "Snip Your Plastic" (Letter to the editor), *BAR*, August 20, 1987, 9.

58. M. Dunlap, "Ta Dum!" (Letter to the editor), *BAR*, August 27, 1987, 7.

59. "Clipping Visa: A Protest Takes Shape," *BAR*, November 12, 1987, 16.

60. T. Sally, "Switch and Fight" (Letter to editor), *BAR*, December 31, 1987, 7.

61. "Money Fund Makes Visa Protest," *BAR*, February 11, 1988, 20.

62. R. O'Loughlin, "Chamber Apologizes for Olympic Promo," *BAR*, October 22, 1987, 14.

63. "Donation Scheme for USOC Rebuked," *BAR*, April 7, 1988, 10.

64. J. Newquist, "Donor Plan Snubs AIDS Charities," *BAR*, February 11, 1988, 20.

65. P. Duys, "Fundraising Letter from FGG Treasurer," January 31, 1993, SFPL, GLC 27, Box-FGG Business 82-94, Derek's Red Binder-FGG 1989 thru 1994.

66. Homonormativity is the idea that the culmination of a gay and lesbian politics is in equally accessing status quo institutions such as (same-sex) marriage, privileging white, middle-class, professional values, patriotic militarized citizenship, and full embracing consumption as a marker of success. It is often considered depoliticized and grounded in domesticity and private property (see Lisa Duggan, *The Twilight of Equality: Neoliberalism, Cultural Politics and the Attack on Democracy* (Boston: Beacon Press, 2003). Homonormativity fails to consider intersecting issues of privilege around white racialization, classism, sexism, misogyny, transphobia, and able-bodiedness.

67. Duggan, *The Twilight of Equality*.

68. "No Gay Olympics, No '96 Olympics, Says Britt," *BAR*, January 8, 1987, 1.

69. M. D'Angelo, "Call the Mayor" (Letter to editor), *BAR*, January 15, 1987, 7; J. De Young, "IOC Must Apologize" (Letter to editor), *BAR*, January 8, 1987, 8; J. Dibelka, "No to the USOC" (Letter to editor), *BAR*, January 8, 1987, 9.

70. J. Collins, "Bay Area Olympics" (Letter to editor), *BAR*, September 17, 1987, 7; "No Gay Olympics, No '96 Olympics, Says Britt," *BAR*, January 8, 1987, 1, 2; J. Dibelka, "No to the USOC" (Letter to editor), *BAR*, January 8, 1987, 9,

71. "Games People Play" (Editorial), *BAR*, January 15, 1987, 6.

72. Stephen Essex and Brian Chalkley, "Olympic Games: Catalyst of Urban Change," *Leisure Studies* 17 (1998): 187–206; Helen J. Lenskyj, *Inside the Olympic Industry: Power, Politics, and Activism* (Albany: SUNY Press, 2000); Helen J. Lenskyj, *Olympic Industry Resistance: Challenging Olympic Power and Propaganda* (Albany: SUNY Press, 2008); David Whitson and Donald Macintosh, "The Global Circus: International Sport, Tourism and the Marketing of Cities," *Journal of Sport and Social Issues* 20 (1996): 278–95.

73. "Olympic Ideals, Parochial Politics," *San Francisco Chronicle*, September 13, 1987, A18.

74. "A Bad Idea" (Editorial), *San Francisco Chronicle*, September 14, 1987, A18.

75. A. White, "GGBA Reps. Oppose Britt on Olympics," *BAR*, February 25, 1988, 3.

76. J. Gonzalez, "Gonzalez Says No to Olympics" (Letter to editor), *BAR*, January 22, 1987, 7.

77. "A Vote for the Olympics" (Editorial), *San Francisco Chronicle*, February 12, 1988, A28; A. White, "GGBA Reps. Oppose Britt on Olympics," *BAR*, February 25, 1988, 3.

78. Lenskyj, *Inside the Olympic Industry*.

79. Glenn Dickey, "Kopp Won't Give Up on S.F. Olympics," *San Francisco Chronicle*, March 9, 1988, C3.

80. White, "GGBA Reps. Oppose Britt on Olympics."

81. M. Kolbe, "Agnos Rebukes SF Olympics Bid," *BAR*, February 11, 1988, 1.

82. White, "GGBA Reps. Oppose Britt on Olympics."

83. L. McBride, R. Gross, M. Coles, A. Lazere, and J. Schmidt, "We Support Harry" (Letter to editor), *BAR*, March 3, 1988, 7.

84. R. Tobler, "Profits above Rights" (Letter to editor), *BAR*, March 10, 1988, 8.

85. W. Chambers, "Building Walls" (Letter to editor), *BAR*, March 10, 1988, 7; K. Frogge, "Us vs Them" (Letter to editor), *BAR*, February 11, 1988, 7; R. Palmer, "Olympics a Showcase," *BAR*, March 17, 1988, 6.

86. K. Wadsworth, "Eight Years from Now" (Letter to editor), *BAR*, March 3, 1988, 8; Palmer, "Olympics a Showcase," 6.

87. W. Snyder, "The Time for 'Compromising' Is Over," *BAR*, February 11, 1988, 52.

88. A. White, "Britt Demands USOC Retreat on Gay Games," *BAR*, March 3, 1988, 1, 2.

89. T. Keane, "Both Sides Give in Olympic Games," *San Francisco Chronicle*, February 27, 1988, A3; White, "Britt Demands USOC Retreat on Gay Games," 1, 2.

90. Art Agnos, Letter to USOC General Counsel, March 1, 1988, SFPL, GLC 27, Box 3-Games Clippings, File: Minutes from SFAA Board, GG II, #2, 5.

91. A. White, "S.F. Paper Attacks 'Faggots of Frisco' on Olympics Issue," *BAR*, April 28, 1988, 13.

92. R. O'Loughlin, "Kopp's Gay Advisors Threaten to Walk Out," *BAR*, April 15, 1988, 1, 2; A. White, "Charges Still Flying in Olympics Debate," *BAR*, April 21, 1988, 5.

93. D. Garcia and P. Stewart, "Too Late for 1996: S.F. to Put Olympics Bid on Ballot," *San*

Francisco Chronicle, March 10, 1988, A3; A. White, "Toklas Club Raps Kopp on Olympics," *BAR*, March 17, 1988, 1, 2.

94. A. White, "Kopp Charged with Scapegoating Gays," *BAR*, March 24, 1988, 4.

95. J. Goodsite, "In the Way" (Letter to editor), *BAR*, April 14, 1988, 9; T. Jasinski, "How Dare You?" (Letter to editor), *BAR*, March 24, 1988, 7; P. Martin, "Letter to Editor," *BAR*, March 24, 1988, 7; C. W. Nevius, "It's Their Own Fault," *San Francisco Chronicle*, March 16, 1988, D1; "Olympic Insult" (Editorial), *San Francisco Chronicle*, March 10, 1988, A20; White, "Kopp Charged with Scapegoating Gays," 4; White, "S.F. Paper Attacks."

96. Robert C. Bailey, *Gay Politics, Urban Politics: Identity and Economics in the Urban Setting* (New York: Columbia University Press, 1999).

97. For example, see "Good sports II." [Editorial]. *BAR*, March 17, 1988, 6.

98. Garcia and Stewart, "Too Late for 1996"; O'Loughlin, "Kopp's Gay Advisors Threaten to Walk Out"; White, "Toklas Club Raps Kopp on Olympics."

99. R. Tobler, "Kopp and the Olympics" (Letter to editor), *BAR*, February 25, 1988, 7.

100. White, "Toklas Club Raps Kopp on Olympics"; L. Whitney, "Remember in November" (Letter to editor), *BAR*, April 21, 1988, 7.

101. White, "Britt Demands USOC Retreat on Gay Games"; White, "Toklas Club Raps Kopp on Olympics."

102. Davidson, "Racism against the Abnormal?"

103. Davidson, "Sporting Homonationalisms."

15. The Larry Krueger Incident: Sports-Talk Radio and the Consequences of Imagery

1. It should be noted that the club was only 6.5 games behind San Diego by August 3, 2005.

2. Jorge L. Ortiz, "Alou Offended by Radio Host," *SFGate*, August 6, 2005, accessed March 1, 2012, http://www.sfgate.com/cgi-bin/article.cgi?f=/c/a/2005/08/06/SPG5CE459H1.DTL.

3. Ibid.

4. Scott Ostler, "Everybody Looks Bad in Kruegergate," *SFGate*, August 11, 2005, accessed March 10, 2012, http://www.sfgate.com/cgi-bin/article.cgi?f=/c/a/2005/08/11/SPG7DE66B31.DTL.

5. Charles Einstein, *Willie's Time* (New York: J. B. Lippincott Company, 1971), 111.

6. Samuel O. Regalado, *Viva Baseball!: Latin Major Leaguers and Their Special Hunger* (Urbana: University of Illinois Press, 1998), 124.

7. Felipe Alou with Herm Weiskopf, *Felipe Alou: My Life and Baseball* (Waco, TX: Word Books, 1967), 11.

8. Regalado, *Viva Baseball!*, 79.

9. Alou, *Felipe Alou*, 121.

10. Ibid., 119.

11. Ibid., 120–21.

12. Regalado, *Viva Baseball!*, 86.

13. Ibid., 85.

14. Ibid.

15. Ibid., 67.

16. Ibid., 123.

17. Ibid.

18. Ibid., 86.

19. Jay Sharbutt, "Jimmy the Greek Is Fired by CBS," *Los Angeles Times*, January 17, 1988, accessed March 17, 2012, http://articles.latimes.com/1988-01-17/sports/sp-36803_1_jimmy-snyder.

20. "Limbaugh's Comments Touch Off Controversy," *ESPN.com*, October 1, 2003, accessed February 22, 2012, http://sports.espn.go.com/nfl/news/story?id=1627887.

21. Neil Best, "First Time, Long Time for Bill Mazer," *Newsday*, June 16, 2011, accessed October, 1, 2015, http://www.newsday.com/sports/columnists/neil-best/first-time-long-time-for-bill-mazer-1.2962262; Paul F. Gullifor, "WFAN and the Birth of All-Sport Radio: Sporting a New Format," in *Sports-Talk Radio America: Its Context and Culture*, ed. Jack M. Dempsey, Frank Hoffman, and Martin J. Manning (London: Routledge, 2006), 53–63.

22. Joel Nathan Rosen, "All-Sports Radio: The Development of an Industry Niche," *Media History Monographs* 5, no. 1 (2001–2002): 6.

23. Ibid.

24. Ibid.

25. Ibid.

26. Eric C. Covil, "Radio and Its Impact on the Sports World," *American Sportscasters Online* (2005), accessed October 1, 2015, http://www.americansportscastersonline.com/radiohistory.html.

27. Ibid.

28. Joan Walsh, "A Loudmouth Hits Bottom" *Salon.com*, August 10, 2005, accessed February 22, 2012, http://www.salon.com/2005/08/10/krueger/.

29. Ibid.

30. Richard Sandomir, "Fox Fires Baseball Analyst over Ethnic Comments," *New York Times*, October 14, 2006, accessed September 29, 2015, http://www.nytimes.com/2006/10/14/sports/baseball/15lyonscnd.html?_r=0.

31. Ibid.

32. Robert Weintraub, "Color Commentators: Why Are Sports Broadcasters Always Making Racial Gaffes?" *Slate*, November 30, 2006, accessed September 29, 2015, http://www.slate.com/articles/sports/sports_nut/2006/11/color_commentators.html.

33. Ibid.

34. Ibid.

35. Allison McDonald, "Football Broadcaster Racism," *The Jeffrey S. Moorad Center for the Study of Sports Law*, December 1, 2012, accessed September 29, 2015, http://lawweb2009.law.villanova.edu/sportslaw/?p=1229.

36. Ibid.

37. Jorge L. Ortiz, "Alou Offended by Radio Host," *SFGate*, August 6, 2005, accessed March 1, 20112, http://www.sfgate.com/cgi-bin/article.cgi?f=/c/a/2005/08/06/SPG5CE459H1.DTL.

38. Ibid.

39. Ibid.

40. Ibid.

41. Ibid.

42. Henry Shulman, "Giants Report: Host's One-Week Suspension Not Enough for Alou," *SFGate*, August 7, 2005, accessed March 10, 2012, http://www.sfgate.com/cgi-bin/article.cgi?f=/c/a/2005/08/07/SPGRQE3DIN1.DTL.

43. Gwen Knapp "Alou Makes Right Moves," *SFGate*, August 9, 2005, accessed March 12, 2012, http://www.sfgate.com/cgi-bin/article.cgi?f=/c/a/2005/08/09/SPGBPE53TH1.DTL.

44. Scott Ostler, "Everybody Looks Bad in Kruegergate," *SFGate*, August 11, 2005, accessed March 10, 2012, http://www.sfgate.com/cgi-bin/article.cgi?f=/c/a/2005/08/11/SPG7DE66B31.DTL.

45. Steve Kroner, "Firings a Hot Topic," *SFGate*, August 11, 2005, accessed March 10, 2012, http://www.sfgate.com/cgi-bin/article.cgi?f=/c/a/2005/08/11/SPG7DE66B11.DTL.

46. Ibid.

47. Ibid.

48. Ibid.

49. Ibid.

50. Ostler, "Everybody Looks Bad in Kruegergate."

51. Bruce Jenkins, "There's a Human Side to Krueger Controversy," *SFGate*, August 20, 2005, accessed April 1, 2012, http://www.sfgate.com/cgi-bin/article.cgi?f=/c/a/2005/08/20/SPGBPEAG411.DTL&ao=all.

52. Ibid.

53. Michael Harrison, "Qualitative Aspects of Talk Show Audiences," *Talkers Magazine*, October 20, 2011, accessed October 4, 2015, http://www.talkers.com/2011/10/20/qualitative-aspects-of-the-talk-radio-audiences/.

Contributors

Rita Liberti is a professor in the Department of Kinesiology at California State University, East Bay, and director of the Center for Sport & Social Justice on the campus. Her work focuses on African American women's sport history in the twentieth century. She coauthored *(Re)Presenting Wilma Rudolph* (2015) with Maureen Smith. The monograph won the North American Society for Sport History Book Award in 2016. When not writing sport history, Liberti can be found hiking the many trails of the Bay Area.

Maureen M. Smith is a professor in the Department of Kinesiology and Health Science at California State University, Sacramento. She is the coauthor (with Rita Liberti) of *(Re)Presenting Wilma Rudolph* (2015), and the coeditor (with Joel Nathan Rosen) of the forthcoming *More Than Cricket and Football: International Sport and the Challenge of Celebrity*. Smith earned her PhD at The Ohio State University. She teaches courses in sport history and sport sociology at Sacramento State. Smith resides part-time in the beautiful coastal hamlet of Richmond, home of the Rosie the Riveter National Park, Point Isabel, and a short BART ride from Cal women's basketball games and other Bay Area sporting teams.

Beth Cavalier is an associate professor of sociology at Georgia Gwinnett College in Lawrenceville, Georgia. She primarily studies sport, with a focus on gender and sexuality. She has published work on the experiences of sexual minorities working in professional and collegiate sport, sexual consent laws, and Native American mascots in sport. Her current projects examine media representations of women's soccer, and the rebirth of modern roller derby. She is an active member of the Society for the Study of Social Problems (SSSP) and the North American Society for the Sociology of Sport (NASSS).

Judy Davidson is associate professor in the Faculty of Physical Education and Recreation at the University of Alberta in Edmonton, Alberta, Canada. She has written on the effects of homonormativity and homonationalism within the lesbigay sport movement. Her research interests include feminist and queer approaches to sport and leisure phenomena. She is currently finishing up a Social Sciences and Humanities Research Council of Canada funded project entitled "Coming to a Moving Body: Physical Movement at Mid-life," which articulates the movement experiences of people who would identify as being alienated from their kinaesthetic embodiments.

Chris Elzey teaches in the History/Art History Department at George Mason University. He also oversees the Sport and American Culture Minor and co-directs the Center for the Study of Sport and Leisure in Society at George Mason University. He is the coeditor of *DC Sports: The Nation's Capital at Play*.

Adam Fitch is a native to the Bay Area and a graduate of California State University, East Bay, with an MA in history. Inspired by a textbook and a teacher in a junior high history class he has developed a life-long love of studying the past. Currently, he plans to continue in the field of education and historical research. His interests include comparative history and the relationship between gender and power. He lives in the Bay Area.

Joel S. Franks teaches Asian Americans studies and American studies at San Jose State University. He has published several articles and books, including *Crossing Sidelines, Crossing Cultures: Sport and Asian Pacific American Cultural Citizenship* (2000), *Whose Baseball?: The National Pastime and Cultural Diversity in California, 1859–1941* (2001), *Hawaiian Sporting Experiences in the Twentieth Century* (2002), *Democracy in America: A History* (2008), *Asian Pacific Americans and Baseball* (2008), *The Barnstorming Hawaiian Travelers: A Multiethnic Baseball Team Tours the Mainland, 1912–1916* (2012), *Key Words and Key Concepts in Asian Pacific American History* (rev. ed. 2015). A proud father of two grown children, he lives with his wife of nearly twenty-eight years in Cupertino.

Matthew R. Hodler earned his Ph.D. in health and sport studies at the University of Iowa. His dissertation utilizes Michael Phelps and the sport of swimming as a point of entry to investigate the relationships between and among sport, nationalisms, and constructions of race. He has presented work at conferences for the North American Society for Sociology of Sport, the North American Society for Sport History, and the Southern Sociological Society. He has published work in *Communication & Sport*, *Journal of Sport History*, and *International Review for the Sociology of Sport*, is a contributor for the *Sport in American History* blog, and authored a piece about 1920s swimming star Sybil Bauer for the online swimming news site *Swimswam*.

Brian M. Ingrassia is assistant professor of history at West Texas A&M University in Canyon, Texas. He is author of *The Rise of Gridiron University: Higher Education's Uneasy Alliance with Big-Time Football* (2012), which won the 2013 NASSH monograph award. Ingrassia currently serves as series editor of the Sport and Popular Culture Series at the University of Tennessee Press. He earned a PhD at the University of Illinois at Urbana-Champaign in 2008 and resided briefly in the San Francisco Bay Area while conducting research on the history of Progressive Era football reform.

Linda L. Ivey is an associate professor of history at California State University, East Bay. Her work primarily focuses on environmental history and immigration in California, and has appeared in the journals *Agricultural History* and *Global Environments,* among others. She is currently at work on a chapter on the Filipino Race Riots in 1930, and an edited documents collection on the Japanese Internment. Dr. Ivey lives with her family in Alameda, California.

Deane Anderson Lamont received his doctoral degree from the University of California at Berkeley and has been at Saint Mary's College since 1995. His scholarly interests focus on the sociohistorical aspects of health, exercise, and sport. Dr. Lamont has published his research in various journals including the *Journal of Sport History*, the *Californian Journal of Health Promotion*, the *Journal of the West*, and the *Journal of Olympic History*. His book, *America's "Healthiest" City: A History of Early Oakland, California,* was published in 2010. He is currently at work on a book that has the provisional title: *Sport at U.S. Catholic Colleges: The Spiritual Meets the Secular.*

Jeffrey Montez de Oca is an associate professor of sociology at the University of Colorado, Colorado Springs, where he teaches courses on sport, media, sociological theory, gender/sexuality, and race. His past research focused on college football, media, and popular culture during the early Cold War. His current research primarily focuses on the National Football League's marketing strategies and doping in elite athletics. His monograph *Discipline and Indulgence: College Football, Media, and the American Way of Life during the Cold War* (2013) won the 2014 North American Society for the Sociology of Sport Outstanding Book Award. Montez de Oca grew up in the East Bay cheering for the Golden Bears of California, the Oakland Raiders, and the San Francisco Forty Niners.

Louis Moore is an associate professor of history at Grand Valley State University where he teaches African American history, civil rights, sports, and US history. His research and writing examine the interconnection of race, gender, and sports. He is finishing his manuscript *Beyond the Battle Royal*, a book about boxing, black manhood, and race in America from 1880 to 1915. He is also under contract to write a book about the black athlete and the civil rights movement.

Samuel O. Regalado is professor of history at California State University, Stanislaus, who authored *Viva Baseball! Latin Major Leaguers and Their Special*

Hunger (1998) and *Nikkei Baseball: Japanese American Players from Immigration and Internment to the Major Leagues* (2013). He is also coeditor of *Sport and the Law: Historical and Cultural Intersections* (2014) and was a Smithsonian Fellow in 1994.

Maria J. Veri is an associate professor in the Department of Kinesiology at San Francisco State University. She earned her doctorate in cultural studies from the University of Tennessee. Her research areas of interest include gender and race in sport, critical pedagogy, and the intersection of food, sport, and identity. A transplanted Upstate New Yorker, she is a proud resident of the East Bay.

Claire M. Williams is an associate professor in the Department of Kinesiology at Saint Mary's College of California. She teaches classes in sport and recreation management, sport law, sport marketing, and women in sport. Her primary research area of interest relates to women in sport.

Index

N

Y